# US WARSHIPS
## SINCE 1945
### PAUL H. SILVERSTONE

**Naval Institute Press**

First published 1987
Second printing 1987

Published and distributed in the United States
of America by the Naval Institute Press,
Annapolis, Maryland 21402

Library of Congress Catalog Card No. 86-63703

ISBN 0-87021-769-0

This edition is authorized for sale only in the
United States and its territories and possessions
and the Philippine Islands

© Paul H. Silverstone 1987

Manufactured in Great Britain

# CONTENTS

# PREFACE

At the end of World War 2 the United States Navy stood at the largest state in its mighty history with more ships in commission than at any time before or since. Many ships were then removed from service, the older ones first and the merchant conversions. In addition, hundreds of vessels which remained on the Navy List were laid up 'in mothballs'. New ships were also laid up, some without having seen any service.

Completion of a few ships under construction was delayed as they were modified to put new ideas into practice. In 1950 with the outbreak of the war in Korea, hundreds of laid-up vessels were quickly brought out of reserve and recommissioned. The Navy's size declined at the end of that war, and new construction did not make up in numbers for those decommissioned.

Ten years later, as fighting in Vietnam stepped up, a new wave of recommissionings took place. New construction followed apace but not evenly. The most noticeable area of growth occurred in the submarine force, now composed of ballistic missile submarines for strategic defence, and attack submarines for anti-submarine warfare. The 1980s saw a new increase in naval construction to make up for a slowdown in the late 1970s, both to replace ageing ships and to build up American naval power. The intention is to maintain a 600-ship Navy, increased from 450 in 1980.

During the period covered by this book, the Navy has conducted extensive naval operations in combat. On 25 June 1950 South Korea was invaded and two days later President Truman ordered American armed forces to support that country. During the next six months the Navy was engaged in that war including the major amphibious operation of the war, the landings at Inchon. The entry of China into the war after its troops crossed the Yalu River in October led to the important naval evacuation of Wonsan. The war continued for over two more years, principally a ground and air war on a fairly static line across the Korean peninsula. Until the ceasefire was signed on 23 July 1953, the Navy engaged in support of these land operations with gunfire and air attacks. During the war naval aircraft flew 275,912 sorties. Several ships were sunk and many more damaged, principally by enemy mines. Total casualties were 54,246 dead.

In October 1962 Soviet missile installations only 90 miles from US shores were discovered in Cuba. President Kennedy authorised a 'quarantine' of Cuba to prevent import of Soviet offensive weapons, which was enforced by the Navy for a month until the weapons were withdrawn.

Less than two years later, an incident in the Gulf of Tonkin led to direct American military involvement in the civil war in Vietnam. It appeared the destroyer *Maddox* had been attacked by North Vietnam torpedo boats, an incident later mired in controversy, and Congress authorised the President to take action to support South Vietnam. This seemingly innocuous action led to the long, gruelling, enervating war in Vietnam costing over 57,718 American lives. It was only in January 1973 that American forces ceased fighting in that country and all troops were evacuated. Only a year later North Vietnam completed the conquest of the South and the Navy assisted in the final evacuation of American personnel from Cam Ranh Bay, Da Nang and Saigon.

Since that time American naval forces have been active in the Mediterranean, Caribbean and Indian Ocean in confrontational situations. In 1986, operations were undertaken against Libya.

In September 1947 the Department of Defense was established, unifying the Army, Navy and Air Force under one agency. In 1950 the Navy took over operation of the Army's fleet of transports and other vessels, and the Military Sea Transportation Service (now the Military Sealift Command) was established. In the late 1970s plans for a Rapid Deployment Force involving all services were underway. After the seizure of the US embassy in Teheran, plans were realised and the RDF was created in late 1979. The concept provides for airlifting troops to the crisis area where they would receive weapons and supplies carried by already loaded supply ships. A number of ships have been acquired for this purpose including many merchant vessels chartered by the Navy. Prepositioning ships are currently anchored at Diego Garcia Island in the Indian Ocean.

Notable developments in technology have led to enormous changes in weapons and ships. Guided missiles and electronic detection and guidance systems have revolutionised naval warfare as much as did the introduction of the armoured warship, the submarine or the aircraft. On 1 May 1947 the submarine *Cusk* was the first to launch a guided missile (V-1/Loon). Shortly thereafter, on 6 September, the first ballistic missile, a V-2, was launched from the deck of an aircraft carrier, the *Midway*.

Nuclear propulsion was developed: in 1954 the submarine *Nautilus* was completed, the world's first nuclear-powered ship; in 1958 construction of the first ballistic missile submarines was begun. The nuclear submarines continue to be the most survivable of the strategic nuclear deterrent forces. The loss of the submarine *Thresher* did not deter continuation of the nuclear submarine programme, and nuclear-powered surface ships in the form of huge aircraft carriers and cruisers were built in the following years. Despite the fears of some, no major accidents involving nuclear propulsion have occurred in US vessels.

On 1 November 1978, for the first time in the history of the US Navy, women reported for regular sea duty in ships other than transports or hospital ships. This development will perhaps change the character of the Navy more than any other recent occurrence. On 15 March 1980 the aircraft carrier *Carl Vinson* was launched, the first time in modern history that a US naval vessel was named after a living person. Since that time two more ships have been so named, the submarine *Hyman G. Rickover* and the new destroyer *Arleigh Burke*.

The prospect for the future appears to lie in continued reliance on nuclear aircraft carriers and more nuclear submarines. Yet new types are appearing. Hydrofoil patrol vessels, glass fibre mine countermeasures ships, surface effects ships and other air-cushion vehicles are already in service.

# Acknowledgements

The writer wishes to extend his appreciation to Norman Polmar for all his assistance and to Martin E. Holbrook, Ernest Arroyo and Charles Haberlein for their assistance with photographs.

Acknowledgement is made of the use of the following works:

Morison & Rowe, *Warships of the US Navy* (1983).
*Dictionary of American Naval Fighting Ships*, vols 1-8 (1959-81).

ANNUALS (various editions):
*Combat Fleets of the World*
*Jane's Fighting Ships*
*The Ships & Aircraft of the US Fleet*

PUBLICATIONS:
*Marine News* (Journal of the World Ship Society)
*US Naval Institute Proceedings*
*Warship*
*Warship International* (Journal of the International Naval Research Organization)

*Paul H. Silverstone*

1986

*Below:*
**The guided missile cruiser *Chicago* (CG-11), with two twin Talos and two twin Tartar SAM launchers.**

# GUIDE TO THE BOOK

This book lists the ships of the United States Navy that were on the Navy List on 1 January 1946 and those which were added thereafter to the present date, 1986.

Each class is prefaced by the class name with the years in which the ships were originally ordered. This may differ from the fiscal years given in the table of Shipbuilding Programmes.

Details given are as follows:

**Displacement:** Navy light and full load displacement. For submarines surface/submerged displacement is given.

**Dimensions:** Length (overall/waterline)×beam× maximum draught, in feet and inches. For aircraft carriers maximum width of flight deck is also given.

**Machinery:** Number of propeller shafts, number of nuclear reactors (if nuclear-powered), type of propulsive machinery, designed shaft-horsepower and designed speed.

**Endurance:** Distance ship can steam at speed given.

**Armament:** Missile launchers refer to the type of missile (see table of missile types).

**Crew:** Total strength of crew including air personnel for carriers.

The columns in the tables give the following information:

**1** Navy number, as built. The prefix T-, used for ships assigned to the MSTS (later MSC), has been ignored in the listings in this volume (see accompanying list of *US Navy Type Designations* for classifications).

**2** Name, when launched. Former names if changed after 1946.

**3** Builder (see accompanying list of *Shipbuilders* for builders' full names).

**4** Launching date (day-month-year).

**5** Fate. Information in the last column includes the following data: dates the ship was in active service since 1948 including periods of non-commissioned service or naval reserve duty. '51-71', for instance, would indicate the ship was active during 1951 to 1971; during other periods, ship was out of commission and laid up in reserve. Where no dates are given in the last column, the ship remained out of commission after the war until disposed of. Where no second date is given, '60-', the ship was in service in 1986. Later Navy names or numbers as reclassified with year of change, and ultimate disposition (ie, stricken, broken up, etc), and in certain instances, first foreign or merchant name. Additional later names are not given here. 'Target' indicates the ship was sunk as a target.

Although exact dates of naval control are of interest to the specialist, US ships were often transferred from naval control to the Maritime Administration, for instance, for fiscal or similar reasons. Should the ship be required once again, it was a simple matter to transfer it on paper back to the Navy. In the interest of clarity, only the final disposition of ships is given, so that if the ship was stricken from the Navy list in 1960 but not scrapped until 1965, only the latter date is given. The reader is then aware that if the ship was decommissioned in 1955 and the next date is broken up in 1965, the vessel was laid up for 10 years under the control of a government department.

*Below:*
**The converted tank landing ship *Krishna* (ARL-38, ex-LST-1149), seen as a landing craft repair ship.**
*Official US Navy*

# Abbreviations

| | | | |
|---|---|---|---|
| ASROC | Anti-submarine rocket | MIRV | Multiple independent re-entry vehicle |
| ASW | Anti-submarine warfare | MRV | Multiple re-entry vehicle |
| BPDMS | Basic Point Defence Missile System | MSC | Military Sealift Command (from 1970) |
| BU | Broken up | MSTS | Military Sea Transportation Service (=MSC) |
| CIWS | Close-in Weapon System | na | not applicable |
| CODAG | Combination diesel and gas turbine | NOAA | National Oceanic & Atmospheric Administration |
| DASH | Drone anti-submarine helicopter | NRT | Naval Reserve Training |
| DSRV | Deep Submergence Rescue Vessel | OSP | Offshore Procurement Program |
| ECM | Electronic countermeasures | RDF | Rapid Deployment Force |
| ELINT | Electronic intelligence | SAM | Surface-to-air missile |
| F&WS | Fish & Wildlife Service | SES | Surface effects ship |
| FAST | Fast automatic shuttle transfer system | SLEP | Service Life Extension Program |
| FBM | Fleet Ballistic Missile | SSM | Surface-to-surface missile |
| FRAM | Fleet Rehabilitation & Modernization Program | str | Stricken from the Navy list |
| FY | Fiscal year | Subroc | Submarine rocket |
| GM | Guided missile | SURTASS | Surveillance Towed Array Sensor System |
| GUPPY | Greater Underwater Propulsion Power | USC&GS | US Coast & Geodetic Survey |
| IBM | Intercontinental ballistic missile | USCG | US Coast Guard |
| LAMPS | Light airborne multipurpose system | VDS | Variable depth sonar |
| MARAD | Maritime Administration | VLS | Vertical launch system |
| MCM | Mine countermeasures | VTE | Vertical triple expansion |

# US Navy and Coast Guard Type Designations

| | | | |
|---|---|---|---|
| ACM | Auxiliary Minelayer (=MMA) | AOG | Gasoline Tanker |
| ACS | Auxiliary Crane Ship | AOR | Replenishment Fleet Tanker |
| AD | Destroyer Tender | AOT | Transport Oiler |
| ADG | Degaussing Vessel | AP | Transport |
| AE | Ammunition Ship | APA | Attack Transport (=LPA) |
| AF | Storeship | APB | Barrack Ship, Self-Propelled |
| AFS | Combat Store Ship | APc | Coastal Transport |
| AG | Miscellaneous Auxiliary | APD | High Speed Transport (=LPR) |
| AGB | Ice Breaker | APSS | Transport Submarine |
| AGC | Amphibious Force Flagship (=LCC) | AR | Repair Ship |
| AGDE | Escort Research Ship (=AGFF) | ARB | Repair Ship, Battle Damage |
| AGDS | Deep Submergence Support Ship | ARC | Cable Repairing or Laying Ship |
| AGEH | Hydrofoil Research Ship | ARG | Repair Ship, Internal Combustion Engine |
| AGER | Environmental Research Ship | ARH | Heavy-hull Repair Ship |
| AGF | Miscellaneous Command Ship | ARL | Repair Ship, Landing Craft |
| AGFF | Frigate Research Ship (ex-AGDE) | ARS | Salvage Vessel/Ship |
| AGL | Lighthouse Tender | ARSD | Salvage Lifting Vessel |
| AGM | Missile Range Instrumentation Ship | ARST | Salvage Craft Tender |
| AGMR | Major Communications Relay Ship | ARVA | Aircraft Repair Ship (Airframe) |
| AGOR | Oceanographic Research Ship | ARVE | Aircraft Repair Ship (Engine) |
| AGOS | Ocean Surveillance Ship | ARVH | Helicopter Repair Ship |
| AGP | Patrol Craft Tender | AS | Submarine Tender |
| AGR | Ocean Radar Station Ship | ASR | Submarine Rescue Vessel/Ship |
| AGS | Surveying Ship | ASSA | Cargo Submarine |
| AGSC | Surveying Ship, Coastal | ASSP | Transport Submarine |
| AGSS | Auxiliary Research Submarine | ATA | Ocean Tug, Auxiliary |
| AGTR | Technical Research Ship | ATF | Ocean Tug, Fleet |
| AH | Hospital Ship | ATS | Salvage & Rescue Ship |
| AK | Cargo Ship | AV | Seaplane Tender |
| AKA | Attack Cargo Ship (=LKA) | AVB | Advance Aviation Base Ship |
| AKD | Cargo Ship, Dock | AVM | Guided Missile Ship |
| AKL | Light Cargo Ship | AVP | Small Seaplane Tender |
| AKN | Net Cargo Ship | AVS | Aviation Supply Ship |
| AKR | Vehicle Cargo Ship (ex-LSV) | AVT | Auxiliary Aircraft Transport |
| AKS | General Stores-Issue Ship | AVT | Training Carrier |
| AKV | Cargo Ship & Aircraft Ferry | AW | Distilling Ship |
| AM | Minesweeper (=MSF) | BB | Battleship |
| AMC | Minesweeper, Coastal | CA | Heavy Cruiser |
| AMCU | Minesweeper, Underwater Locator (=MHC) | CAG | Guided Missile Heavy Cruiser |
| AMS | Auxiliary Minesweeper (=MSC) | CB | Large Cruiser |
| AN | Net-Laying Ship (=ANL) | CBC | Large Tactical Command Ship |
| ANL | Net-Laying Ship (=AN) | CC | Command Ship |
| AO | Oiler | CG | Guided Missile Cruiser |
| AOE | Fast Combat Support Ship | CGN | Guided Missile Cruiser (Nuclear) |

| | | | |
|---|---|---|---|
| CL | Light Cruiser | MHC | Coastal Minehunter |
| CLAA | Anti-Aircraft Cruiser | MMA | Auxiliary Minelayer |
| CLC | Task Fleet Command Ship (=CC) | MMD | Fast Minelayer (ex-DM) |
| CLG | Guided Missile Light Cruiser | MMF | Fleet Minelayer |
| CLK | Hunter-Killer Ship (=DL) | MSC | Coastal Minesweeper |
| CM | Minelayer (=MMF) | MSCO | Coastal Minesweeper (Old) |
| CV | Aircraft Carrier | MSF | Fleet Minesweeper |
| CVA | Attack Aircraft Carrier | MSH | Mine Hunter |
| CVAN | Attack Aircraft Carrier (Nuclear) | MSI | Inshore Minesweeper |
| CVB | Large Aircraft Carrier | MSO | Ocean Minesweeper |
| CVE | Escort Aircraft Carrier | MSS | Special Minesweeper |
| CVHA | Assault Helicopter Aircraft Carrier | PB | Patrol Boat |
| CVHE | Escort Helicopter Aircraft Carrier | PC | Submarine Chaser (steel hull) |
| CVL | Light Aircraft Carrier | PCC | Submarine Chaser, Control |
| CVN | Aircraft Carrier (Nuclear) | PCE | Submarine Chaser, Escort |
| CVS | ASW Support Aircraft Carrier | PCEC | Submarine Chaser, Escort (Control) |
| CVT | Training Carrier | PCER | Submarine Chaser, Escort (Rescue) |
| CVU | Utility Aircraft Carrier | PCF | Fast Patrol Craft |
| DD | Destroyer | PCH | Patrol Craft, Hydrofoil |
| DDE | Escort Destroyer | PCS | Submarine Chaser, Sweeper |
| DDG | Guided Missile Destroyer | PF | Frigate |
| DDK | Hunter-Killer Destroyer | PG | Gunboat |
| DDR | Radar Picket Destroyer | PGH | Hydrofoil Gunboat |
| DE | Escort (=FF) | PHM | Motor Gunboat |
| DEC | Destroyer Escort, Control | PGM | Guided Missile Hydrofoil |
| DEG | Guided Missile Escort (=FFG) | PT | Motor Torpedo Boat |
| DER | Escort, Radar Picket | PTF | Fast Patrol Boat |
| DL | Frigate | SC | Submarine Chaser (wood hull) |
| DLG | Guided Missile Frigate (=CG) | SS | Submarine |
| DLGN | Guided Missile Frigate (Nuclear) (=CGN) | SSA | Cargo Submarine |
| DM | Light Minelayer (=MMD) | SSAG | Auxiliary Submarine |
| DMS | High Speed Minesweeper | SSBN | Ballistic Missile Submarine (Nuclear) |
| FF | Frigate | SSG | Guided Missile Submarine |
| FFG | Guided Missile Frigate | SSK | Anti-Submarine Submarine |
| IFS | Inshore Fire Support Ship (=LFR) | SSN | Submarine (Nuclear) |
| IX | Unclassified Auxiliary | SSO | Oiler Submarine |
| LCC | Amphibious Command Ship (ex-AGC) | SSP | Transport Submarine |
| LFR | Inshore Fire Support Ship (ex-LSMR) | SSR | Radar Picket Submarine |
| LHA | Amphibious Assault Ship | SST | Training Submarine |
| LHD | Amphibious Assault Ship | WAGO | Oceanographic Cutter |
| LKA | Amphibious Cargo Ship (ex-AKA) | WHEC | High Endurance Cutter |
| LPA | Amphibious Transport (ex-APA) | WLB | Seagoing Buoy Tender |
| LPD | Amphibious Transport Dock | WLI | Inland Buoy Tender |
| LPH | Amphibious Assault Ship (Helicopter) | WLM | Coastal Buoy Tender |
| LPR | Amphibious Transport, Small (ex-APD) | WLR | River Buoy Tender |
| LPSS | Amphibious Transport Submarine | WMEC | Medium Endurance Cutter |
| LSD | Landing Ship, Dock | WSES | Surface Effect Ship |
| LSFF | Landing Ship, Flotilla Flagship | WTR | Reserve Training Cutter |
| LSIL | Landing Ship, Infantry (Large) | YAG | Miscellaneous Auxiliary |
| LSIM | Landing Ship, Infantry (Mortar) | YFP | Floating Power Barge |
| LSM | Landing Ship, Medium | YFRT | Covered Lighter (Range Tender) |
| LSMR | Landing Ship, Medium (Rocket) (=LFR) | YMLC | Salvage Lift Craft (Medium) |
| LSSL | Landing Ship Support (Large) | YMS | Motor Minesweeper |
| LST | Landing Ship, Tank | YO | Fuel Oil Barge (self-propelled) |
| LSU | Landing Ship, Utility | YOG | Gasoline Barge (self-propelled) |
| LSV | Landing Ship, Vehicle | YP | Patrol Craft |
| LSV | Vehicle Cargo Ship (1963) | YRST | Salvage Craft Tender |
| MCM | Mine Countermeasures Ship | YTB | Large Harbour Tug |
| MCS | Mine Warfare Command & Support Ship | YV | Drone Aircraft Catapult/Control Craft |

# Shipbuilders

| | | |
|---|---|---|
| Alabama | Alabama DD & SB Co, Mobile, Ala | USA |
| Alameda | Bethlehem-Alameda Shipyard Inc, Alameda, Cal | USA |
| American | American SB Co, Toledo, Ohio | USA |
| American; Cleve | American SB Co, Cleveland, Ohio | USA |
| American; Lorain | American SB Co, Lorain, Ohio | USA |
| Associated | Associated Shipbuilders, Seattle, Wash | USA |
| Astoria | Astoria Marine Construction Co, Astoria, Ore | USA |
| Avondale | Avondale Shipyards, Westwego, La | USA |

| | | |
|---|---|---|
| Basalt | Basalt Rock Co Inc, Napa, Cal | USA |
| Bath | Bath Iron Works Corp, Bath, Me | USA |
| Bell Halter | Bell Halter, New Orleans, La | USA |
| Bellingham | Bellingham Iron Works, Bellingham, Wash | USA |
| Beth; S Fran | Bethlehem Steel Co, San Francisco, Cal | USA |
| Beth; S Pedro | Bethlehem Sbdg Corp, San Pedro, Cal | USA |
| Blohm & Voss | Blohm & Voss, Hamburg | Germany |
| Boeing | Boeing Marine Systems, Seattle, Wash | USA |
| Bollinger | Bollinger Machine Shop & Shipyard, Lockport, La | USA |
| Boston | Boston Naval Shipyard, Boston, Mass | USA |
| Brooke Marine | Brooke Marine Ltd, Lowestoft | UK |
| Broward | Broward Marine Shipbuilding Co Inc, Fort Lauderdale, Fla | USA |
| Brown | Brown SB Co, Houston, Tex | USA |
| Burger | Burger Boat Co, Manitowoc, Wis | USA |
| Bushey | Ira S. Bushey & Sons, Brooklyn, NY | USA |
| Butler; Sup | Walter Butler Shipbuilders, Superior, Wis | USA |
| Calship | California SB Co, Los Angeles, Cal | USA |
| Cargill | Cargill Inc, Savage, Minn | USA |
| Charleston | Charleston Naval Shipyard, Charleston, SC | USA |
| Charleston SB | Charleston SB & DD Co, Charleston, SC | USA |
| Christy | Christy Corp, Sturgeon Bay, Wis | USA |
| Colberg | Colberg Boat Works, Stockton, Cal | USA |
| Commercial | Commercial Ship Repair, Seattle, Wash | USA |
| Consol; NY | Consolidated Sbdg Co, New York, NY | USA |
| Consolidated | Consolidated Steel Corp, Orange, Tex | USA |
| Cramp | Cramp SB Co, Philadelphia, Pa | USA |
| Curtis Bay | US Coast Guard Yard, Curtis Bay, Md | USA |
| Defoe | Defoe SB Corp, Bay City, Mich | USA |
| Derecktor | Robert E. Derecktor, Middletown, RI | USA |
| Dravo | Dravo Corp, Wilmington, Del | USA |
| Dravo; Pitt | Dravo Corp Neville Island, Pittsburgh, Pa | USA |
| East Coast | East Coast Shipyard Inc, Bayonne, NJ | USA |
| Fairfield | Bethlehem-Fairfield Shipyard Inc, Baltimore, Md | USA |
| Federal | Federal SB & DD Co, Kearny, NJ | USA |
| Froemming | Froemming Bros Inc, Milwaukee, Wis | USA |
| Fulton | Fulton Shipyard, Antioch, Cal | USA |
| General | General Ship & Eng Works, East Boston Mass | USA |
| General Eng | General Engineering & DD Co, Alameda, Cal | USA |
| Gibbs | Gibbs Corp Jacksonville, Fla | USA |
| Globe; Duluth | Globe Shipbuilding Co, Duluth, Minn | USA |
| Groton | Electric Boat Co, Groton, Conn | USA |
| Grumman | Grumman Aircraft Corp, Stuart, Fla | USA |
| Gulf | Gulf SB Corp, Chickasaw, Ala | USA |
| Gulf, Madison | Gulf SB Co, Madisonville, La | USA |
| Gulfport | Gulfport Boiler & Welding Works, Port Arthur, Tex | USA |
| Halter | Halter Marine Services Inc, New Orleans, La | USA |
| Harbor | Harbor Boat Building Co, Terminal Island, Cal | USA |
| Hickinbotham | Hickinbotham Bros Constr Co, Stockton, Cal | USA |
| Higgins | Higgins Industries, New Orleans, La | USA |
| Hiltebrant | Hiltebrant DD Co, Kingston, NY | USA |
| Hingham | Bethlehem Steel Corp, Hingham, Mass | USA |
| Ingalls | Ingalls SB Div, Litton Systems, Pascagoula, Miss | USA |
| Jones | J. A. Jones Construction Co Inc, Panama City, Fla | USA |
| Kaiser; Richmond | Kaiser Cargo, Inc, Richmond, Cal | USA |
| Kaiser; Van | Kaiser Co Inc, Vancouver, Wash | USA |
| LD Smith | Leatham D. Smith SB Co, Sturgeon Bay, Wis | USA |
| Lake Washington | Lake Washington Shipyards, Houghton, Wash | USA |
| Levingston | Levingston SB Co, Orange, Tex | USA |
| Lockheed | Lockheed SB & Construction Co, Seattle, Wash | USA |
| Los Angeles | Los Angeles SB & DD Corp, San Pedro, Cal | USA |
| Luders | Luders Marine Construction Co, Stamford, Conn | USA |
| Manitowoc | Manitowoc SB Co, Manitowoc, Wis | USA |
| Mare Is | Mare Island Naval Shipyard, Vallejo, Cal | USA |
| Marietta | Marietta Manufacturing Co, Point Pleasant, WVa | USA |
| Marine Iron | Marine Iron & SB Co, Duluth, Minn | USA |

| | | |
|---|---|---|
| Marinette | Marinette Marine Co, Marinette, Wis | USA |
| Marinship | Marinship Corp, Sausalito, Cal | USA |
| Martinac | J. M. Martinac Boat Bldg Corp, Seattle, Wash | USA |
| Martinolich | Martinolich SB Co, San Diego, Cal | USA |
| Maryland | Maryland SB & DD Co, Baltimore, Md | USA |
| Mathis | John H. Mathis Co, Camden, NJ | USA |
| Moore | Moore Dry Dock Co, Oakland, Cal | USA |
| NY Sbdg | New York Shipbuilding Corp, Camden, NJ | USA |
| National | National Steel & SB Corp, San Diego, Cal | USA |
| New England | New England SB Corp, South Portland, Me | USA |
| New York | New York Naval Shipyard, New York, NY | USA |
| Newport News | Newport News SB & DD Co, Newport News, Va | USA |
| Norfolk | Norfolk Naval Shipyard, Norfolk, Va | USA |
| North Carolina | North Carolina SB Co, Wilmington, NC | USA |
| Northwest | Northwest Marine Iron Works, Portland, Ore | USA |
| Odense | Odense Staalskibvaerft, Odense | Denmark |
| Oregon | Oregon SB Corp, Portland, Ore | USA |
| PS Bridge | Puget Sound Bridge & DD Co, Seattle, Wash | USA |
| Penn | Pennsylvania Shipyards, Inc, Beaumont, Texas | USA |
| Permanente | Permanente Metals Corp, Richmond, Cal | USA |
| Peterson | Peterson Boat Works, Sturgeon Bay, Wis | USA |
| Philadelphia | Philadelphia Naval Shipyard, Philadelphia, Pa | USA |
| Portsmouth | Portsmouth Naval Shipyard, Kittery, Me | USA |
| Puget Sound | Puget Sound Naval Shipyard, Bremerton, Wash | USA |
| Pusey & Jones | Pusey & Jones Corp, Wilmington, Del | USA |
| Quincy | Bethlehem Steel Co, Quincy, Mass | USA |
| Quincy Adams | Quincy Adams Yacht Yard, Quincy, Mass | USA |
| Rheinstahl | Rheinstahl Nordseewerke, Emden | Germany |
| Rotterdam | Rotterdamsche Droogdok Mij, NV, Rotterdam | Netherland |
| Sample | Frank L. Sample Jr, Boothbay Harbor, Me | USA |
| San Francisco | San Francisco Naval Shipyard, San Francisco, Cal | USA |
| Savannah | Savannah Machine & Foundry Co, Savannah, Ga | USA |
| Schichau | F. Schichau GmbH, Danzig | Germany |
| Seattle | Seattle-Tacoma Shipbuilding Corp, Seattle, Wash | USA |
| Southeastern | Southeastern Shipbuilding Corp, Savannah, Ga | USA |
| Sparrows Pt | Bethlehem-Sparrows Point Shipyard Inc, Sparrows Point, Md | USA |
| Staten Is | Bethlehem Steel Corp, Staten Island, NY | USA |
| Sun | Sun SB & DD Co, Chester, Pa | USA |
| Swan Hunter | Swan, Hunter & Wigham Richardson Ltd, Wallsend-on-Tyne | UK |
| Tacoma Boat | Tacoma Boat Building Co, Tacoma, Wash | USA |
| Tampa | Tampa SB Co, Tampa, Fla | USA |
| Tampa Marine | Tampa Marine Co, Tampa, Fla | USA |
| Todd-Galveston | Todd-Galveston Dry Dock Inc, Galveston, Tex | USA |
| Todd-Houston | Todd Houston SB Corp, Houston, Tex | USA |
| Todd; LA | Todd Shipyards Co, Los Angeles, Cal | USA |
| Todd; S Pedro | Todd Shipyards Corp, San Pedro, Cal | USA |
| Todd; Seattle | Todd Shipyards Corp, Seattle, Wash | USA |
| Todd; Tacoma | Todd Shipyards Co, Tacoma, Wash | USA |
| Toledo | Toledo Sbdg Co, Toledo, Ohio | USA |
| United Eng | United Engineering Co Ltd, Alameda, Cal | USA |
| Upper Clyde | Upper Clyde SB Co, Glasgow | UK |
| Walsh-Kaiser | Walsh-Kaiser Co Inc, Providence, RI | USA |
| Weser | AG Weser, Bremen | Germany |
| Western Pipe | Western Pipe & Steel Corp, Los Angeles, Cal | USA |
| Willamette | Willamette Iron & Steel Co, Portland, Ore | USA |
| Wilmington | Wilmington Boat Works, Wilmington, Cal | USA |
| Zenith | Zenith Dredge Co, Duluth, Minn | USA |

# Guided Weapon Systems

| Official No | Name | Year | Length (ft) | Weight (lbs) | Range (miles) | Notes |
|---|---|---|---|---|---|---|
| **Surface-to-Air** | | | | | | |
| RIM-2 | Terrier | 1955 | 26'6 | 3,070 | 20-40 | *replaced by Standard-ER |
| RIM-8 | Talos | 1958 | 33 | 7,000 | 75 | * |
| RIM-24 | Tartar | 1960 | 15 | 1,425 | 10+ | replaced by Standard-MR |
| RIM-7 | Sea Sparrow | 1969 | 12 | 450 | 12 | BPDMS |
| RIM-67 | Standard-ER | 1981 | 26 | 2,900 | 65 | replaced Terrier/Talos |
| RIM-66 | Standard-MR SM-1 | 1970 | 14'8 | 1,100 | 15-20 | replaced Tartar |
| | Standard-MR SM-2 | 1981 | 14 | 1,400 | 40-90 | |
| RIM-116 | RAM | 1988 | 9'2 | 154 | 4+ | rapid reaction ship defence |
| **Surface-to-surface** | | | | | | |
| RGM-8 | Regulus I | 1953 | 33'9 | 12,000 | 500 | * |
| RGM-15 | Regulus II | 1959 | 57 | 22,000 | 1,000 | cancelled |
| RGM-84 | Harpoon | 1977 | 15'6 | 1,478 | 60+ | |
| BGM-109 | Tomahawk | 1983 | 18'6 | 3,200 | 250+ | *cruise missile |
| **Fleet Ballistic Missiles** | | | | | | |
| UGM-27 | Polaris A1 | 1957 | 28'6 | 28,000 | 1,500 | * |
| | Polaris A2 | 1961 | 31 | 30,000 | 1,725 | * |
| | Polaris A3 | 1964 | 32 | 36,000 | 2,880 | *MRV |
| UGM-73 | Poseidon C-3 | 1971 | 34 | 65,000 | 2,900+ | *MIRV |
| UGM-96 | Trident I C-4 | 1979 | 34 | 65,000 | 4,500+ | *MIRV |
| | Trident II D-5 | 1990 | 45 | 126,000 | 6,000 | * |
| **Anti-Submarine Warfare** | | | | | | |
| RUR-5 | Asroc | 1961 | 15 | 1,000 | 6 | anti-submarine rocket |
| RUR-4 | Weapon A | 1950 | 8'6 | 500 | 0.5 | |
| UUM-44 | Subroc | 1964 | 21 | 4,000 | c. 25 | *nuclear depth bomb |
| **Air-to-Ground** | | | | | | |
| AGM-12 | Bullpup-B | 1959 | 13'7 | 1,785 | 10 | |
| AGM-45 | Shrike | 1963 | 10 | 390 | 10 | replaced by HARM |
| AGM-62 | Walleye | 1967 | 11'4 | 1,100 | 16 | unpowered glider bomb |
| AGM-53 | Condor | | 13'10 | 2,100 | 60+ | |
| AGM-78 | Standard-ARM | 1968 | 15 | 1,350 | 35 | replaced by HARM |
| AGM-84 | Harpoon | 1979 | 12'7 | 1,100 | 35+ | |
| AGM-88 | HARM | 1985 | 13'7 | 796 | 80 | High Speed Anti Radiation Missile |

*nuclear capable
Joint Army-Navy nomenclature superseded by new system in 1963.
The official numbering system consists of serial numbers with a three-letter group:
1st letter, launch environment: A=air, B=multiple, R=ship, U=underwater
2nd letter, mission: G=surface attack, I=aerial intercept, U=underwater attack
3rd letter, type of vehicle: M=missile, R=rocket

# US Navy and Coast Guard Losses 1946-86

## Destroyers

*Bache* (DD-470) Wrecked in gale off Rhodes, 6 February 1968,

*Baldwin* (DD-624) Went aground off Montauk, Long Island, NY, 15 April 1961.

*Frank E. Evans* (DD-754) Cut in two in collision with Australian carrier *Melbourne*, 2 June 1969.

*Solar* (DE-221) Blew up at Earle, NJ, 30 April 1946.

*Warrington* (DD-843) Severely damaged by mine off Vietnam, 17 July 1972; later scrapped.

## Submarines

*Cochino* (SS-345) Sunk by battery explosion and fire north of Norway, 26 August 1949.

*Stickleback* (SS-415) Sunk in collision with escort *Silverstein* off Pearl Harbor, 29 May 1958.

*Scorpion* (SSN-589) Lost in North Atlantic near the Azores Islands, probably as result of explosion of torpedo, 27 May 1968.

*Thresher* (SSN-593) Lost during deep diving tests off Portsmouth, NH, 10 April 1963.

## Minesweepers

*Avenge* (MSO-423)   Damaged by fire in drydock at Baltimore, 1 February 1970; scrapped.

*Force* (MSO-445)   Burned and sank in Philippine Sea, west of Guam, 14 April 1973.

*Grouse* (MSCO-15)   Went aground off Rockport, Mass, 21 September 1963.

*Hobson* (DMS-26)   Sunk in collision with aircraft carrier *Wasp* west of Azores, 26 April 1952.

*Kingbird* (MSC-194)   Damaged in collision with merchant ship at Pensacola, Florida, 21 May 1971, not repaired.

*Magpie* (AMS-25)   Sunk by mine off east coast of Korea, 29 September 1950.

*Partridge* (AMS-31)   Sunk by mine off Kangnung, Korea, 2 February 1951.

*Pirate* (AM-275)   Sunk by mine off Wonsan, Korea, 12 October 1950.

*Pledge* (AM-277)   Sunk by mine off Wonsan, Korea, 12 October 1950.

*Prestige* (MSO-465)   Lost by grounding in Nasuto Strait, Japan, 23 August 1958.

*Stalwart* (MSO-493)   Sunk by fire and explosion in San Juan harbor, 25 June 1966; scrapped.

## Landing Ships

*Chittenden County* (LST-561)   Went aground off Kauai, Hawaii, 1 June 1958; constructive total loss.

LST-600 (T-LST-600)   Lost by grounding in storm off Okinawa, 23 December 1968.

*Mahnomen County* (LST-912)   Lost by grounding at Chulai, Vietnam, 31 December 1966.

## Oilers and Tankers

*Chehalis* (AOG-48)   Sunk by fire and explosion at Tutuila, Samoa, 7 October 1949.

*Cowanesque* (AO-79)   Went aground in Kin Bay, Okinawa, 23 April 1972.

*Mission San Francisco* (T-AO-123)   Sunk in collision with SS *Elna II* in Delaware River, 7 March 1957.

*Mission San Miguel* (T-AO-129)   Lost by grounding on Laysan Reef, 775 miles northwest of Hawaii, 8 October 1957.

*Ponaganset* (AO-86)   Broke in two at wharf at Boston, 9 December 1947.

*Potomac* (T-AO-150)   Sank after fire and explosion at Morehead City, NC, 16 September 1961 (later salved).

## Cargo Vessels

*Grommet Reefer* (T-AF-53)   Wrecked in gale off Leghorn, Italy, 15 December 1952.

*Pvt Joseph F. Merrell* (AK-275)   Damaged in collision off California coast, 19 December 1973, scrapped.

*Regulus* (AF-57)   Went aground in typhoon at Hong Kong, 16 August 1971.

*Sgt Jack J. Pendleton* (T-AK-276)   Went aground on Triton Island, Paracel Islands, 25 September 1973.

## Miscellaneous Auxiliaries

*Benevolence* (AH-13)   Sunk in collision with SS *Mary Luckenbach* at San Francisco, 15 August 1950.

*Pueblo* (AGER-2)   Seized at sea by North Korean MTBs off Korean coast, 13 January 1960.

*Sarsi* (ATF-111)   Sunk by mine of Hungnam, Korea, 27 August 1952.

*Simon Newcomb* (AGSc-14)   Went aground off Labrador, 9 August 1949; scrapped.

## Harbour Craft

*Iona* (YTB-220)   Sunk in collision in Philippines, May 1963.

*Lone Wolf* (YTB-179)   Sunk in collision with oiler *Caloosahatchee* at Newport, RI, 10 December 1946 (salved).

*Mahackeno* (YTB-223)   Foundered in tow off Cape Hatteras, 11 September 1948.

*Nanigo* (YTM-537)   Disappeared at sea en route to Bremerton in tow, 7 April 1973.

*Pokagon* (YTB-274)   Capsized and sank in tow en route to Green Cove, Fla, 27 September 1947.

*Poquim* (YTB-285)   Sank in tow at San Diego, 8 January 1949.

*Saguanash* (YTB-288)   Lost off coast of Washington, 7 November 1946.

*Secota* (YTM-415)   Sunk in collision with a Trident submarine off Midway Islands, 24 March 1986.

*Tamaroa* (YTB-136)   Sunk in collision with USS *Jupiter* in San Francisco Bay, 17 January 1946.

YO-132   Lost, 31 March 1947.

YO-163   Lost, February 1947.

YO-184   Lost in gale, 18 September 1946.

YO-188   Lost, September 1947.

YOG-74   Lost, 20 July 1946.

YP-280   Lost, 14 April 1946.

YTL-432   Lost while being transported on *General Meigs* (ex-AP-112) which broke her tow and ran aground off Cape Flattery, Washington, 9 January 1972.

## Coast Guard Cutters

*Blackthorn* (WLB-391)   Sunk in collision with tanker *Texas Capricorn* in Tampa Bay, 28 January 1980.

*Cuyahoga* (WIX-157)   Sunk in collision with SS *Santa Cruz II* off Smith Point, Va, 20 October 1978.

*White Alder* (WLM-541)   Sunk in collision with SS *Helena* at White Castle, La, 7 December 1968.

# US NAVY ANNUAL SHIPBUILDING PROGRAMMES

| FY | Carriers | Submarines | Cruisers | Destroyers | Frigates | Mine/Patrol | Amphibious | Auxiliaries |
|---|---|---|---|---|---|---|---|---|
| 1947 | — | SS-563-64 | — | — | — | — | — | — |
| 1948 | (CVA-58) | SS-565-66 | CLC-1 | — | — | PT-809-12 | — | — |
|  |  | SSK-1-2 | CLK-1 | — | — | — | — | — |
| 1949 | — | SS-567-68 | — | DL 2-5 | — | — | — | — |
|  |  | SSK-3 | — | — | — | — | — | — |

| FY | Carriers | Submarines | Cruisers | Destroyers | Frigates | Mine/Patrol | Amphibious | Auxiliaries |
|---|---|---|---|---|---|---|---|---|
| 1950 | — | AGSS-569 | — | — | — | — | — | — |
| 1951 | — | SST-1 | — | — | DE 1006 | MSO-421-49 | IFS-1 | AGB-4 |
| 1952 | CVA-59 | SSN-571, SSN-575 SS-572-74 SST-2 | CAG-1-2 | — | DE 1014-15 | MSO-455-74 | LSD-28-31 | AO-143-48 |
| 1953 | CVA-60 | — | — | DD-931-33 | — | MHC-1 MSO-488-96 | LST-1156-70 | AF-58-59 |
| 1954 | CVA-61 | SS-576 | — | DD-936-38 | DE-1021-22 | MSO-508-11 | LSD-32-33 LST-1173 | AE-21-22 |
| 1955 | CVA-62 | SS-577 SSN-578-79 | — | DD-940-44 | DE-1023-30 | MSO-519-21 | LSD-34-35 | AKD-1 AO-149-52 |
| 1956 | CVA-63 | SS-580-82 SSN-583-87 | — | DD-945-51 DLG-6-11 DLGN-25 | DE-1033-34 | MSI-1-2 | LST 1171 1174-78 | AE-23-24 |
| 1957 | CVA-64 | SSN-588-93 | CLG-3-8 CGN-9 | DDG-2-9 DLG-12-15 | DE-1035-36 | — | — | AE-25 |
| 1958 | CVAN-65 | SSN-594-97 SSBN-598-600 | CG-10 | DDG-10-14 | — | MSC-289-90 MSO-522 | LPH-2 | — |
| 1959 | — | SSBN 601-02 SSBN-608-11 SSN-603-07 | CG-11-12 | DDG-15-19 DLG-16-24 | — | — | LPH-3 LPD-1 | — |
| 1960 | — | SSN-612-15 | — | DDG-20-22 | DE-1037-38 | PCH-1 | LPD-2 LPH-7 | AGOR-3-5 AS-31 |
| 1961 | CVA-66 | AGSS-555 SSBN-616-26 SSN-261 | — | DDG-23-24 DLG-26-28 | DE-1040-41 | — | LPD-3 | AFS-1 AOE-1 AGDE 1 |
| 1962 | — | SSBN-627-36 SSN-637-39 | — | DLG-29-34 DLGN-35 | DEG-1-3 DE-1043-45 | | LPH-9 LPD-4-6 | AFS 2 AGEH-1 AGOR-6-7 AGS-25 |
| 1963 | CVA-67 | SSBN-640-45 SSN-646-53 | — | — | DEG-4-6 DE-1047-51 | PG-84-85 | LSV-9 LPH-10 LPD-7-10 | AGOR-9-10 AOE-2 AS-33 AGS 26 |
| 1964 | — | SSBN-654-59 SSN-660-64 SSN-671 | — | — | DE-1052-61 | PG-86-87 PTF-10-13 | LPD-11-13 | AD-37 AGS-27 AS-34 |
| 1965 | | SSN-665-70 | — | — | DE-1062-77 | PG-88-90 | LCC-19 LPD-14-15 LPH-11 LSD-36 LST-1179 | AD-38 AE-26-27 AFS-4-5 AGOR-12-13 AGS-29 AKA-113-16 AOE-3 (AO-166-67) (AS-35) |
| 1966 | — | SSN-672-77 | — | — | DE-1078-87 | PGH-1-2 PG-92-101 | LCC-20 LPH-12 LSD-37-39 LST-1180-88 (LPD-16) | AE-28-29 AFS-6 AGOR-14-15 AGS-32 AKA-117 AOE 4 AOR-3-4 AS-37 ATS-1 |
| 1967 | CVN-68 | SSN-678-82 | CGN-36 | — | DE-1088-97 | PTF-17-26 | LSD-40 LST-1189-98 | AE-32-33 AFS-7 AGOR-16 AGS-33-34 AOR-5-6 ASR-21 ATS-2-3 |
| 1968 | — | SSN-683-85 | CGN-37 | — | — | — | — | AE-34-35 ASR-22 (AOE-5) (AGOR-19-20) |

| FY | Carriers | Submarines | Cruisers | Destroyers | Frigates | Mine/Patrol | Amphibious | Auxiliaries |
|----|----------|------------|----------|------------|----------|-------------|------------|-------------|
| 1969 | — | SSN-686-87 | — | — | — | — | LHA-1 | (AD-39)<br>(AS-38) |
| 1970 | CVN-69 | SSN-688-90 | CGN-38 | DD-963-65 | — | — | LHA-1-3 | AO |
| 1971 | — | SSN-691-94 | CGN-39 | DD-966-71 | — | — | LHA-4-5 | AGOR-21-22 |
| 1972 | — | SSN-695-99 | CGN-40 | DD-972-78 | — | — | — | AOR-7<br>AS-39<br>(ATS-4) |
| 1973 | — | SSN-700-05 | — | — | FFG-7 | PHM-1-2 | — | AS-40<br>(ATS-5-6) |
| 1974 | CVN-70 | SSN-706-10<br>SSBN 726 | — | DD-979-85 | — | PHM-3-6 | — | — |
| 1975 | — | SSN-711-13<br>SSBN-727-28 | CGN-41 | DD-986-92 | FFG-8-10 | — | — | AD-41<br>ATF-166-69 |
| 1976 | — | SSN-714-15<br>SSBN-729 | — | — | FFG-11-16 | PHM-2 | — | AD-42<br>AO-177-78 |
| 1977 | — | SSN-716-18<br>SSBN-730 | — | — | FFG-19-26 | — | — | AD-43<br>AS-41<br>AO-179 |
| 1978 | — | SSN-719<br>SSBN-731-32 | CG-47 | DD-997 | FFG-27-34 | — | — | ATF-170-72<br>AO-186, |
| 1979 | — | SSN-720 | — | DDG-993-96 | FFG-36-43 | — | — | AD-44<br>AGOS-1-2<br>ARC-7 |
| 1980 | CVN-71 | SSN-721-22<br>SSBN-733 | CG-48 | — | FFG-45-49 | — | — | AGOS-3 |
| 1981 | — | SSN-723-24<br>SSBN-734 | CG-49-50 | — | FFG-50-55 | — | LSD-41 | AGOS-4-8<br>ARS-50 |
| 1982 | — | SSN-725, SSN-750 | CG-51-53 | — | FFG-56-58 | MCM-1 | LSD-42 | AGOS-9-12<br>AKR-287-90<br>AO-187<br>ARS-51-52 |
| 1983 | CVN-72-73 | SSN-751-52<br>SSBN-735-36 | CG-54-56 | — | FFG-59-60 | MCM-2 | LSD-43 | AH-19<br>AO-188<br>ARS-53 |
| 1984 | — | SSN-753-55<br>SSBN-737 | CG-57-59 | — | FFG-61 | MCM-3-5<br>MSH-1 | LSD-44<br>LHD-1 | AH-20<br>AKR-291-95<br>AO-189-90 |
| 1985 | — | SSN-756-59<br>SSBN-738 | CG-60-62 | DDG-51 | — | MCM-6-9 | LSD-45-46 | AO-191-193<br>AGOS-13-14<br>AGS-39-40 |
| 1986 | — | SSBN-739<br>SSN-760-763 | CG 63-65 | — | — | MSH-2-5<br>MCM-10-12 | LSD-47-48<br>LHD-2 | AO-194-195<br>AGOS-15-16 |
| 1987* | — | 1 SSBN<br>4 SSN-688 | 2 CG-47 | 3 DDG-51 | — | 4 MSH | — | 2 AGOS<br>2 AO-187<br>1 AGOR<br>1 AOE-6 |
| 1988* | — | 1 SSBN<br>3 SSN-688 | 2 CG-47 | 3 DDG-51 | — | 4 MSH<br>3 MCM | 1 LHD-1<br>1 LSD | 2 AO-187<br>1 AE-36<br>2 AGOS |
| 1989* | — | 1 SSBN<br>3 SSN-688<br>1 SSN-21 | 2 CG-47 | 3 DDG-51 | — | 4 MSH | 1 LHD<br>1 LSD | 2 AO-187<br>2 AGOS<br>1 AOE-6 |
| 1990* | — | 1 SSBN<br>4 SSN-688 | 2 CG-47 | 3 DDG-51 | — | — | 1 LSD | 2 AO-187<br>2 AE-36<br>1 AOE-6<br>2 AGOS<br>2 AGOR |
| 1991* | — | 1 SSBN<br>1 SSN-688<br>2 SSN-21 | | 5 DDG-51 | — | — | 1 LHD-1<br>1 LSD | 2 AO-187<br>2 AE-36<br>1 AOE-6<br>1 AR<br>3 AGOR |

*Proposed
*Note:* Those units in brackets were not built.

# AIRCRAFT CARRIERS

*Enterprise* (CV-6) remained on the list until 1958.

## 'Essex' Class (1940-43)

**Displacement:** 33,100 tons, 41,900f/l; CV-34: 33,250 tons, 42,625f/l; CV-36: 30,000 tons, 38,000f/l
**Dimensions:** 820 (wl) 899 (oa)×93×31; 9-13, 16-18, 20, 31: 872 oa (192 extreme width with angled flight deck; CV-36: 154)
**Machinery:** Four shafts, steam turbines,

SHP 150,000=32.7kt
**Endurance:** 16,900/15
**Aircraft:** 80+
**Armament:** 12×5in/38, 68×40mm, AA guns
**Complement:** 3,448

| CV-9 | Essex | Newport News | 31/07/42 | 51-69. CVS (60), BU75 |
|---|---|---|---|---|
| CV-10 | Yorktown | Newport News | 21/01/43 | 52-70. CVS (57), Str73 |
| CV-11 | Intrepid | Newport News | 26/04/43 | 54-74. CVS (61), Mus80 |
| CV-12 | Hornet | Newport News | 30/08/43 | 53-70. CVS (58) |
| CV-13 | Franklin | Newport News | 14/10/43 | CVS (53), AVT-8 (59), BU66 |
| CV-14 | Ticonderoga | Newport News | 07/02/44 | 52-73. CVS (69), BU74 |
| CV-15 | Randolph | Newport News | 29/06/44 | 44-48, 53-69. CVS (59), BU75 |
| CV 16 | Lexington | Quincy | 26/09/42 | 55- . CVS (62), CVT-16 (69) |
| CV-17 | Bunker Hill | Quincy | 07/12/42 | CVS (53), AVT-9 (59), BU73 |
| CV-18 | Wasp | Quincy | 17/08/43 | 51-72. CVS (56), BU73 |
| CV-19 | Hancock | Quincy | 24/01/44 | 54-75. Str76 |
| CV-20 | Bennington | New York | 26/02/44 | 52-70. CVS (59) |
| CV-21 | Boxer | Newport News | 14/12/44 | 45-69. CVS (55), LPH-4 (59), BU71 |
| CV-31 | Bon Homme Richard | New York | 29/04/44 | 51-71 |
| CV-32 | Leyte | Newport News | 23/08/45 | 46-59. CVS (53), AVT-10 (59), Str69 |
| CV-33 | Kearsarge | New York | 05/05/45 | 46-70. CVS (58), BU74 |
| CV-34 | Oriskany | New York | 13/10/45 | 50-76 |
| CV-36 | Antietam | Philadelphia | 20/08/44 | 51-63. CVS (53), BU73 |
| CV-37 | Princeton | Philadelphia | 08/07/45 | 45-70. CVS (54), LPH-5 (59), BU71 |
| CV-38 | Shangri-La | Norfolk | 24/02/44 | 51-71. CVS (69), Str82 |
| CV-39 | Lake Champlain | Norfolk | 02/11/44 | 52-66. CVS (57), BU72 |
| CV-40 | Tarawa | Norfolk | 12/05/45 | 45-49, 51-60. CVS (55), AVT-12 (61), BU68 |
| CV-45 | Valley Forge | Philadelphia | 18/11/45 | 46-70. CVS (53), LPH-8 (61), BU71 |
| CV-47 | Philippine Sea | Quincy | 05/09/45 | 46-58. AVT-11 (59), BU70 |

**Notes:** Various ships modified to angled deck (P125), hydraulic catapults (27A), two steam catapults (27C) as follows (with dates of refit):

| | 27A | 27C | P125 |
|---|---|---|---|
| Essex (CV-9) | 48-51 | — | 55-56 |
| Yorktown (CV-10) | 51-53 | — | 55 |
| Intrepid (CV-11) | — | 51-53 | 56-57 ASW |
| Hornet (CV-12) | — | 51-53 | 55-56 ASW |
| Ticonderoga (CV-14) | — | 51-54 | 55-57 |
| Randolph (CV-15) | 51-53 | — | 55-56 |
| Lexington (CV-16) | 51-55 (+P125) | — | — |
| Wasp (CV-18) | — | 48-51 | 55 ASW |
| Hancock (CV-19) | — | 51-54 | 55-56 |

Above:
**Hancock (CVA-19) refuelling the destroyers Maddox (DD-731) and Samuel N. Moore (DD-747) at sea, on 12 March 1957.** *Official US Navy*

Below:
**Bennington (CVS-20), as converted for anti-submarine warfare: note that the catapults have been removed.** *Official US Navy*

| | | | | |
|---|---|---|---|---|
| Bennington (CV-20) | 50-52 | — | — | 54-55 |
| Bon Homme Richard (CV-31) | — | 52-55 (+P125) | — | — |
| Kearsarge (CV-33) | 50-52 | — | — | 56-57 |
| Oriskany (CV-34) | — | 56-59 (+P125) | — | — |
| Antietam (CV-36) | — | — | — | 52 (experimental) |
| Shangri-La (CV-38) | — | 52-55 (+P125) | — | — |
| Lake Champlain (CV-39) | 50-52 | — | — | — |

Bon Homme Richard, Hancock, Lexington, Randolph and Shangri-La fitted to carry Regulus missiles 1956. These armed with 8×5in, 28×3in guns (also CV-14, 33, 11, 12, 9 and 34).

Oriskany completed to modified design. All reclassified CVA 1952. Franklin and Bunker Hill laid up after the war and not used again. Boxer, Princeton and Valley Forge never received angled flight deck and were converted to Amphibious Assault Ships, 1959-61. Leyte, Philippine Sea and Tarawa reclassified Aviation Transports 1959. Lexington assigned to pilot training from 1962.

Oriskany severely damaged by fire off Vietnam, 26 October 1966.

# 'Independence' Class (1942)

**Displacement:** 11,000 tons, 15,800f/l
**Dimensions:** 600 (wl) 622'6 (oa)×71'6×26; 115 extreme width
**Machinery:** Four shafts, steam turbines, SHP 100,000=31.5kt

**Endurance:** 10,100/15
**Aircraft:** 45
**Armament:** 1×5in/38, 26×40mm guns
**Complement:** 1,569

| | | | | |
|---|---|---|---|---|
| CVL-24 | Belleau Wood | NY Sbdg | 06/12/42 | French Bois Belleau (53) |
| CVL-25 | Cowpens | NY Sbdg | 17/01/43 | AVT-1, BU60 |
| CVL-26 | Monterey | NY Sbdg | 28/02/43 | 50-56. AVT-2, BU71 |
| CVL-27 | Langley | NY Sbdg | 22/05/43 | French La Fayette (51) |
| CVL-28 | Cabot | NY Sbdg | 04/04/43 | 48-55. AVT-3, Spanish Dedalo (67) |
| CVL-29 | Bataan | NY Sbdg | 01/08/43 | 50-54. AVT-4, BU61 |
| CVL-30 | San Jacinto | NY Sbdg | 26/09/43 | AVT-5, BU71 |

**Notes:** Laid down as 'Cleveland' class light cruisers and converted during construction. Cabot and Bataan refitted for ASW 1950-51, flight deck strengthened, port side catapult added, carried 26 aircraft. Cabot had only two funnels. Remainder reclassified Aircraft Transports 1959.

# 'Midway' Class (1942-43)

**Displacement:** 48,950 tons, 62,600f/l; 1970: 51,000 tons; 64,000f/l
**Dimensions:** 900 (wl) 968 (oa)×121×35'4; 1966: 979 (oa), extreme width 272
**Machinery:** Four shafts, steam turbines, SHP 212,000=33kt
**Endurance:** 11,520/15

**Aircraft:** 137, later 75
**Armament:** 18×5in/54, 84×40mm guns (by 1963, only 4-5in)
*1979* Two Sea Sparrow launchers (Midway)
*1980/85* Three Phalanx CIWS (Coral Sea and Midway)
**Complement:** 2,500+1,950 air crew

| | | | | |
|---|---|---|---|---|
| CVB-41 | Midway | Newport News | 20/03/45 | 45- |
| CVB-42 | Franklin D. Roosevelt | New York | 29/04/45 | 46-77. BU78 |
| CVB-43 | Coral Sea | Newport News | 02/04/46 | 47- |

**Notes:** Armoured flight deck strengthened for heavier aircraft 1947-48. Reclassified CVA 1952 and CV 1975. First guided missile fired from a carrier deck from Midway 6 September 1947.

Modernised 1954-56 (Roosevelt), 1955-57 (Midway), 1957-60 (Coral Sea): angled flight deck built and bow enclosed, three steam catapults added, larger elevators, new electronics, fuel increased, only 10-5in, 22-3in guns, new dimensions: 974 (oa)×210 (extreme beam). Roosevelt fitted with Regulus GM. Midway modernised 1966-70: new deck edge elevators installed, area of flight deck enlarged (996×258), three steam catapults replaced by two of new type. Conversion of Coral Sea cancelled. Midway had two Sea Sparrow launchers fitted 1979. Coral Sea scheduled to replace Lexington as training carrier 1991.

## 'Saipan' Class (1943)

**Displacement:** 14,500 tons, 20,000f/l
**Dimensions:** 664 (wl) 683'7 (oa)×76'9×28; 115
  extreme width
**Machinery:** Four shafts, steam turbines,
  SHP 120,000=33kt

**Endurance:** 8,000/15
**Aircraft:** 48
**Armament:** 40×40mm guns
**Complement:** 1,700

| | | | | |
|---|---|---|---|---|
| CVL-48 | Saipan | NY Sbdg | 08/07/45 | 46-57, 66-70. AVT-6, Arlington (AGMR-2) (64). Str75 |
| CVL-49 | Wright | NY Sbdg | 01/09/45 | 47-56, 63-70. AVT-7, CC-2 (62). Str77 |

**Notes:** *Saipan* had fore funnel removed 1950. Reclassified Aviation Transport 1959. *Wright* converted to NECPA Command Ship 1962-63 with flight deck forward supporting several tall antennas, hangar deck converted for command space. Conversion of *Saipan* to CC-3 cancelled when 64% complete 1964 and converted to Major Communication Relay Ship 1966.

## *United States* (1948)

**Displacement:** 66,850 tons, 78,500f/l
**Dimensions:** 1,030 (wl) 1,088 (oa)×130×34'6; 190
  extreme beam
**Machinery:** Four shafts, steam turbines,

SHP 280,000=33kt
**Endurance:** 12,000/20
**Armament:** 8×5in/54, 16×3in/70 AA guns
**Complement:** 4,127

| | | | | |
|---|---|---|---|---|
| CVA-58 | United States | Newport News | na | Cancelled 1949 |

**Notes:** Flush deck, no island. Keel laid 19 April 1949, cancelled 23 April 1949. Designed to carry long range bombers, but the USAF prevailed in maintaining its role as sole strategic nuclear attack force.

## 'Forrestal' Class (1951-54)

**Displacement:** 56,000 tons; 59: 54,600 tons, 78,000f/l
**Dimensions:** 990 (wl) 1,039 (oa)×129'6×37; 238
  extreme beam; 59-61: 1,046 oa
**Machinery:** Four shafts, steam turbines,
  SHP 280,000=34kt; 59: SHP 260,000=33kt
**Endurance:** 12,000/20

**Aircraft:** 90-100
**Armament:** 8×5in guns; 59: 36×3in guns
  *1983* Two Sea Sparrow Mk 25 launchers (59, 60); two
  NATO Sea Sparrow Mk 29 launchers (61, 62)
**Complement:** 2,833 to 3,306+2,500 air crew

| | | | | |
|---|---|---|---|---|
| CVA-59 | Forrestal | Newport News | 11/12/54 | 55- |
| CVA-60 | Saratoga | New York | 08/10/55 | 56- |
| CVA-61 | Ranger | Newport News | 29/09/56 | 57- |
| CVA-62 | Independence | New York | 06/06/58 | 59- |

**Notes:** *Forrestal* redesigned with angled deck. First two were planned to carry Regulus missiles, ordered as CVB, reclassified CVA October 1952. Guns removed as Sea Sparrow BPDMS became available. All to receive three Mk 29 launchers, three Phalanx CIWS.
  *Forrestal* severely damaged by fire and explosion in Gulf of Tonkin, 19 July 1967.
  SLEP, to add 10-15 years to the nominal 30-year life of each ship: *Saratoga* modernised at Philadelphia, 1980-83, *Forrestal* 1982-85, *Independence* from 1985. *Ranger* scheduled for 1992.

## 'Kitty Hawk' Class (1955-64)

**Displacement:** 56,300 tons, 80,800f/l
**Dimensions:** 990 (wl) 1,047'6 (oa)×129'4×37; 250
  extreme beam

**Machinery:** Four shafts, steam turbines,
  SHP 280,000=34kt
**Endurance:** 12,000/20

*Above:*
**Midway** (CVA-41), seen after her 1970
modernisation, with various aircraft parked on the
massive flight deck. The extensions on the bow
are part of the steam catapults.   *Official US Navy*

*Above:*
**Midway** (CVA-41), with greatly expanded deck
area following her 1970 conversion. There are two
starboard deck-edge elevators and one port one,
and two steam catapults forward.   *Official US Navy*

*Below:*
**Forrestal** (CVA-59), at Monaco on 7 June 1957: the
crew is manning the rail. Her 5in gun mounts fore
and aft were replaced in 1959.   *Official US Navy*

*Top:*
***Kitty Hawk* (CVA-63). Notice the multitude of aircraft parked on the flight deck, some in a seemingly precarious manner.**

*Above:*
***Enterprise* (CVN-65), the first nuclear powered aircraft carrier. The ship is seen in 1982 following an extensive refit; the distinctive superstructure housing the radar had been rebuilt.**
*Official US Navy*

*Right:*
**The nuclear-powered aircraft carrier *Nimitz* (CVN-68), operating off Guantanamo in July 1975, with the ammunition ship *Mount Baker* (AE-34) alongside. Two of the starboard deck-edge elevators are lowered.** *Official US Navy*

**Aircraft:** 85
**Armament:** Two twin Terrier Mk 10 launchers (63, 64, 66); three Sea Sparrow Mk 25 launchers (67).

*1980* Four NATO Sea Sparrow Mk 29 launchers, three Phalanx CIWS
**Complement:** 2,932+2,500 air crew

| | | | | |
|---|---|---|---|---|
| CVA-63 | *Kitty Hawk* | NY Sbdg | 21/05/60 | 61- |
| CVA-64 | *Constellation* | New York | 08/10/60 | 61- |
| CVA-66 | *America* | Newport News | 01/02/64 | 65- |
| CVA-67 | *John F. Kennedy* | Newport News | 27/05/67 | 68- |

**Notes:** Improved 'Forrestal' class. *John F. Kennedy*, delayed by controversy over whether propulsion should be nuclear, is officially a separate class, has stack angled to starboard. SLEP modernisation for *Kitty Hawk* scheduled for 1988, *Constellation* 1991. All modified from attack carriers (CVA) to multi-mission (CV) 1973-75.
*Constellation* damaged by fire while fitting out, 19 December 1960.

# *Enterprise* (1957)

**Displacement:** 75,700 tons, 89,600f/l
**Dimensions:** 1,040 (wl) 1,123 (oa)×133×35'9; 248'4 extreme beam
**Machinery:** Four shafts, eight reactors, steam turbines, SHP 280,000=35kt+
**Aircraft:** 90

**Armament:** None.
*1967* Two Sea Sparrow Mk 25 launchers
*1981* Three NATO Sea Sparrow Mk 29 launchers, three Phalanx CIWS
**Complement:** 3,158+2,625 air crew

| | | | | |
|---|---|---|---|---|
| CVAN-65 | *Enterprise* | Newport News | 24/09/60 | 61- |

**Notes:** World's second nuclear powered surface warship: cruising range of 200,000nm without refuelling. Reclassified CVN June 1975. Modified 'Kitty Hawk' class. Four steam catapults and four deck edge elevators. Built without defensive armament. Major overhaul at Puget Sound 1979-82.
First nuclear ship in combat (Vietnam) 1965. Severely damaged by fire and explosion off Hawaii 14 January 1969.

# 'Nimitz' Class (1967-84)

**Displacement:** 81,600 tons, 91,400f/l
**Dimensions:** 1,040 (wl) 1,089 (oa)×134×37; 250'9 extreme beam
**Machinery:** Four shafts, two reactors, steam turbines, SHP 280,000=30kt+

**Aircraft:** 90
**Armament:** Three Sea Sparrow Mk 25 launchers, three Phalanx CIWS (68, 69); Mk 29 and four Phalanx (others)
**Complement:** 3,047+2,625 air crew

| | | | | |
|---|---|---|---|---|
| CVN-68 | *Nimitz* | Newport News | 13/05/72 | 75- |
| CVN-69 | *Dwight D. Eisenhower* | Newport News | 11/10/75 | 77- |
| CVN-70 | *Carl Vinson* | Newport News | 15/03/80 | 82- |
| CVN-71 | *Theodore Roosevelt* | Newport News | 27/10/84 | na |
| CVN-72 | *Abraham Lincoln* | Newport News | Building | na |
| CVN-73 | *George Washington* | Newport News | Ordered | na |

**Notes:** Originally proposed as replacement for 'Midway' class; completion of first three delayed by labour problems. *Nimitz* took seven years from keel laying to completion. 68 and 69 ordered as CVAN. Similar to 'Kitty Hawk' class in hull arrangement, but no stacks. Four steam catapults and four deck edge elevators, three on starboard side. Maximum capacity includes 2.7 million gallons of aviation fuel.
*Carl Vinson* was first US warship named for a living person in over 120 years. *Abraham Lincoln* scheduled to commission in 1989 and *George Washington* in 1991.

# ESCORT AIRCRAFT CARRIERS

## 'Bogue' Class (1942)

**Displacement:** 7,800 tons, 14,000f/l
**Dimensions:** 465 (wl) 495'9 (oa)×69'6×26; 112 extreme width
**Machinery:** One shaft, steam turbines, SHP 8,500=18kt

**Aircraft:** 28
**Armament:** 2×5in/38, 20×40mm guns
**Complement:** 890

| | | | | |
|---|---|---|---|---|
| CVE-9 | Bogue | Seattle | 15/01/42 | BU60 |
| CVE-11 | Card | Seattle | 21/02/42 | 58-70. AKV-40, BU71 |
| CVE-12 | Copahee | Seattle | 21/10/41 | BU61 |
| CVE-13 | Core | Seattle | 15/05/42 | 58-69, AKV-41, BU71 |
| CVE-16 | Nassau | Seattle | 04/04/42 | BU61 |
| CVE-18 | Altamaha | Seattle | 25/05/42 | BU61 |
| CVE-20 | Barnes | Seattle | 22/05/42 | BU60 |
| CVE-23 | Breton | Seattle | 27/06/42 | 58-70. AKV-42, BU72 |
| CVE-25 | Croatan | Seattle | 01/08/42 | 58-70. AKV-43, BU71 |
| CVE-31 | Prince William | Seattle | 23/08/42 | BU61 |

**Notes:** All laid up at end of World War 2. Reclassified CVHE June 1955; 11, 13, 23 and 25 to CVU July 1958, to AKV 1959. *Card* sunk by mine at dock at Saigon 5 February 1964, raised and repaired.

## 'Casablanca' Class (1942)

**Displacement:** 7,800 tons, 10,200f/l
**Dimensions:** 490 (wl) 512'3 (oa)×65'3×19'9; 108 extreme width
**Machinery:** One shaft, VTE, SHP 11,200=19.2kt

**Aircraft:** 28
**Armament:** 1×5in/38, 16×40mm guns
**Complement:** 860

| | | | | |
|---|---|---|---|---|
| CVE-57 | Anzio | Kaiser | 01/05/43 | CVHE, BU60 |
| CVE-58 | Corregidor | Kaiser | 12/05/43 | 51-58. CVU, BU60 |
| CVE-59 | Mission Bay | Kaiser | 26/05/43 | CVU, BU60 |
| CVE-60 | Guadalcanal | Kaiser | 05/06/43 | CVU, BU60 |
| CVE-61 | Manila Bay | Kaiser | 10/07/43 | CVU, BU60 |
| CVE-62 | Natoma Bay | Kaiser | 20/07/43 | CVU, BU60 |
| CVE-64 | Tripoli | Kaiser | 02/09/43 | 52-58. CVU, BU60 |
| CVE-66 | White Plains | Kaiser | 27/09/43 | CVU, BU59 |
| CVE-69 | Kasaan Bay | Kaiser | 24/10/43 | CVHE, BU60 |
| CVE-70 | Fanshaw Bay | Kaiser | 01/11/43 | CVHE, BU59 |
| CVE-74 | Nehenta Bay | Kaiser | 28/11/43 | CVU, AKV-24, BU60 |
| CVE-75 | Hoggatt Bay | Kaiser | 04/12/43 | CVHE, AKV-25, BU60 |
| CVE-76 | Kadashan Bay | Kaiser | 11/12/43 | CVU, AKV-26, BU60 |
| CVE-77 | Marcus Island | Kaiser | 16/12/43 | CVHE, AKV-27, BU60 |
| CVE-78 | Savo Island | Kaiser | 22/12/43 | CVHE, AKV-28, BU60 |
| CVE-80 | Petrof Bay | Kaiser | 05/01/44 | CVU, BU59 |
| CVE-81 | Rudyerd Bay | Kaiser | 12/01/44 | CVU, AKV-29, BU60 |

| | | | | |
|---|---|---|---|---|
| CVE-82 | Saginaw Bay | Kaiser | 19/01/44 | CVHE, BU60 |
| CVE-83 | Sargent Bay | Kaiser | 31/01/44 | CVU, BU59 |
| CVE-84 | Shamrock Bay | Kaiser | 04/02/44 | CVU, BU59 |
| CVE-85 | Shipley Bay | Kaiser | 12/02/44 | CVHE, BU61 |
| CVE-86 | Sitkoh Bay | Kaiser | 19/02/44 | 50-54. CVU, AKV-30, BU60 |
| CVE-87 | Steamer Bay | Kaiser | 26/02/44 | CVHE, BU59 |
| CVE-88 | Cape Esperance | Kaiser | 03/03/44 | 50-59. CVU, BU61 |
| CVE-89 | Takanis Bay | Kaiser | 10/03/44 | CVU, AKV-31, BU60 |
| CVE-90 | Thetis Bay | Kaiser | 16/03/44 | 56-64. CVHA-1 (55), LPH-1 (59), BU66 |
| CVE-91 | Makassar Strait | Kaiser | 22/03/44 | CVU, target 58 |
| CVE-92 | Windham Bay | Kaiser | 29/03/44 | 51-59. CVU, BU61 |
| CVE-94 | Lunga Point | Kaiser | 11/04/44 | CVU, AKV-32, BU60 |
| CVE-97 | Hollandia | Kaiser | 28/04/44 | CVU, AKV-33, BU60 |
| CVE-98 | Kwajalein | Kaiser | 04/05/44 | CVU, AKV-34, BU61 |
| CVE-100 | Bougainville | Kaiser | 16/05/44 | CVU, AKV-35, BU |
| CVE-101 | Matanikau | Kaiser | 22/05/44 | CVHE, AKV-36, BU61 |
| CVE-104 | Munda | Kaiser | 02/06/44 | CVU, BU61 |

**Notes:** In 1955 all were reclassified CVHE (Escort Helicopter Carriers) or CVU (Utility Aircraft Carriers). Remainder reclassified AKV, 1959.

*Cape Esperance, Corregidon, Tripoli* and *Windham Bay* used as aircraft ferry ships by MSTS, 1952.

# 'Sangamon' Class (1942)

**Displacement:** 11,400 tons, 13,500f/l
**Dimensions:** 525 (wl) 553 (oa)×75×32, 114 extreme width
**Machinery:** Two shafts, steam turbines,

SHP 13,500=18.3kt
**Aircraft:** 34
**Armament:** 2×5in/38, 28×40mm guns
**Complement:** 1,100

| | | | Conversion completed | |
|---|---|---|---|---|
| CVE-27 | Suwannee | Federal | 24/09/42 | BU62 |
| CVE-28 | Chenango | Sun | 19/09/42 | BU62 |
| CVE-29 | Santee | Sun | 24/08/42 | BU60 |

**Notes:** Converted oilers, built 1939. Reclassified CVHE 1955, none in service after 1946.

# 'Commencement Bay' Class (1943-44)

**Displacement:** 11,373 tons, 23,875f/l
**Dimensions:** 525 (wl) 557 (oa)×75×30'7; 105 extreme width
**Machinery:** Two shafts, steam turbines,

SHP 16,000=19kt
**Aircraft:** 34
**Armament:** 2×5in/38, 36×40mm guns
**Complement:** 1,066

| | | | | |
|---|---|---|---|---|
| CVE-105 | Commencement Bay | Todd; Tacoma | 09/05/44 | AKV-37, BU71 |
| CVE-106 | Block Island | Todd; Tacoma | 10/06/44 | AKV-38, BU60 |
| CVE-107 | Gilbert Islands | Todd; Tacoma | 20/07/44 | 51-55, 64-69. AKV-39, *Annapolis* (AGMR-1) (63) |
| CVE-108 | Kula Gulf | Todd; Tacoma | 15/08/44 | 51-55, 65-70. AKV-8, BU71 |
| CVE-109 | Cape Gloucester | Todd; Tacoma | 12/09/44 | AKV-9, BU72 |
| CVE-110 | Salerno Bay | Todd; Tacoma | 26/09/44 | 51-54. AKV-10, BU62 |
| CVE-111 | Vella Gulf | Todd; Tacoma | 19/10/44 | AKV-11, BU71 |
| CVE-112 | Siboney | Todd; Tacoma | 09/11/44 | 48-49, 50-56. AKV-12, BU71 |
| CVE-113 | Puget Sound | Todd; Tacoma | 30/11/44 | AKV-13, BU62 |

| | | | | |
|---|---|---|---|---|
| CVE-114 | Rendova | Todd; Tacoma | 28/12/44 | 45-50, 51-55. AKV-14, BU72 |
| CVE-115 | Bairoko | Todd; Tacoma | 25/01/45 | 45-50, 50-55. AKV-15, BU61 |
| CVE-116 | Badoeng Strait | Todd; Tacoma | 15/02/45 | 47-57. AKV-16, BU72 |
| CVE-117 | Saidor | Todd; Tacoma | 17/03/45 | AKV-17, BU71 |
| CVE-118 | Sicily | Todd; Tacoma | 14/04/45 | 46-54. AKV-18, BU61 |
| CVE-119 | Point Cruz | Todd; Tacoma | 18/05/45 | 51-56, 65-70. AKV-19, BU71 |
| CVE-120 | Mindoro | Todd; Tacoma | 27/06/45 | 45-55. AKV-20, BU60 |
| CVE-121 | Rabaul | Todd; Tacoma | 14/07/45 | AKV-21, BU71 |
| CVE-122 | Palau | Todd; Tacoma | 06/08/45 | 46-54. AKV-22, BU60 |
| CVE-123 | Tinian | Todd; Tacoma | 05/09/45 | AKV-23, BU71 |

**Notes:** *Rabaul* and *Tinian* laid up on completion and never commissioned. CVE-105, 109, 111, 113, 117, 121 and 123 reclassified CVHE 1955. All reclassified AKV, 1959.

*Kula Gulf* and *Point Cruz* reconstructed 1965. *Gilbert Islands* converted to Major Communications Relay Ship 1962. Conversion of *Vella Gulf* cancelled.

*Below:*
**Sicily (CVE-118), an escort carrier of the 'Commencement Bay' class.**
*Official US Navy/Ernest Arroyo collection*

# BALLISTIC MISSILE SUBMARINES

## 'George Washington' Class (1957-58)

**Displacement:** 5,900/6,700 tons
**Dimensions:** 381'8 (oa)×33×29
**Machinery:** One shaft/reactor steam turbines,

SHP 15,000=20/25kt
**Armament:** 16 Polaris A-1 FBM; 6×21in TT
**Complement:** 139

| | | | | |
|---|---|---|---|---|
| SSBN-598 __ | George Washington __ | Groton _____ | 09/06/59 __ | 59-84. SSN (81) |
| SSBN-599 __ | Patrick Henry _____ | Groton _____ | 22/09/59 __ | 60-84. SSN (81) |
| SSBN-600 __ | Theodore Roosevelt __ | Mare Is _____ | 03/10/59 __ | 61-81. Str82 |
| SSBN-601 __ | Robert E. Lee _____ | Newport News __ | 18/12/59 __ | 60-83. SSN (82) |
| SSBN-602 __ | Abraham Lincoln _____ | Portsmouth _____ | 14/05/60 __ | 60-81. Str82 |

**Notes:** First Western ballistic missile submarines, adapted from 'Skipjack' class, lengthened 130ft. Refitted with Polaris A-3 1964-66. Withdrawn 1979-80. Modified to serve as attack submarines but not successful and withdrawn 1984.

## 'Ethan Allen' Class (1958-60)

**Displacement:** 6,955/7,900 tons
**Dimensions:** 410'5 (oa)×33×30
**Machinery:** One shaft/reactor, steam turbines,

SHP 15,000=20/25kt
**Armament:** 16 Polaris A-2 FBM; 4×21in TT
**Complement:** 144

| | | | | |
|---|---|---|---|---|
| SSBN-608 __ | Ethan Allen _____ | Groton _____ | 22/11/60 __ | 61-82. SSN (80), Str83 |
| SSBN-609 __ | Sam Houston _____ | Newport News __ | 02/02/61 __ | 62- . SSN (80) |
| SSBN-610 __ | Thomas A. Edison | Groton _____ | 16/06/61 __ | 62 03. SSN (00) |
| SSBN-611 __ | John Marshall _____ | Newport News __ | 15/07/61 __ | 62- . SSN (81 |
| SSBN-618 __ | Thomas Jefferson _____ | Newport News __ | 24/02/62 __ | 63-84. SSN (81) |

**Notes:** First US ballistic missile submarines built from keel up. Later refitted with Polaris A-3. Withdrawn 1981 and converted to attack submarines. Conversion not successful because of comparative slow speed, large size and limited torpedo reloads.

*Sam Houston* and *John Marshall* being converted for special missions to carry frogmen or commandos, 1984-86.

## 'Lafayette' Class (1960-63)

**Displacement:** 7,250/8,250 tons
**Dimensions:** 425 (oa)×33×31'6
**Machinery:** One shaft/reactor, steam turbines,

SHP 15,000=20/25kt
**Armament:** 16 Polaris A-3, 4×21in TT
**Complement:** 141

| | | | | |
|---|---|---|---|---|
| SSBN-616 __ | Lafayette _____ | Groton _____ | 08/05/62 __ | 63- |
| SSBN-617 __ | Alexander Hamilton __ | Groton _____ | 18/08/62 __ | 63- |
| SSBN-619 __ | Andrew Jackson _____ | Mare Is _____ | 15/09/62 __ | 63- |
| SSBN-620 __ | John Adams _____ | Portsmouth _____ | 12/01/63 __ | 64- |
| SSBN-622 __ | James Monroe _____ | Newport News __ | 04/08/62 __ | 63- |
| SSBN-623 __ | Nathan Hale _____ | Groton _____ | 12/01/63 __ | 63-86 |
| SSBN-624 __ | Woodrow Wilson _____ | Mare Is _____ | 22/02/63 __ | 63- |
| SSBN-625 __ | Henry Clay _____ | Newport News __ | 30/11/62 __ | 64- |
| SSBN-626 __ | Daniel Webster _____ | Groton _____ | 27/04/63 __ | 64- |

*Above:*
**Robert E. Lee** (SSBN-601), heading out to sea in
June 1966: notice the missile tube openings aft of
the sail. This class was converted during
construction, with hulls lengthened to
accommodate the missile tubes.   *Official US Navy*

*Below:*
**Mariano G. Vallejo** (SSBN-658) at sea in May 1968.
Notice the great length of the vessel, with the sail
mounted forward on the hull.   *US Navy*

| | | | |
|---|---|---|---|
| SSBN-627 — James Madison | Newport News | 15/03/63 | 64- |
| SSBN-628 — Tecumseh | Groton | 22/06/63 | 64- |
| SSBN-629 — Daniel Boone | Mare Is | 22/06/63 | 64- |
| SSBN-630 — John C. Calhoun | Newport News | 22/06/63 | 64- |
| SSBN-631 — Ulysses S. Grant | Groton | 02/11/63 | 64- |
| SSBN-632 — Von Steuben | Newport News | 18/10/63 | 64- |
| SSBN-633 — Casimir Pulaski | Groton | 01/02/64 | 64- |
| SSBN-634 — Stonewall Jackson | Mare Is | 30/11/63 | 64- |
| SSBN-635 — Sam Rayburn | Newport News | 20/12/63 | 64-86 |
| SSBN-636 — Nathanael Greene | Portsmouth | 12/05/64 | 64-86 |
| SSBN-640 — Benjamin Franklin | Groton | 05/12/64 | 65- |
| SSBN-641 — Simon Bolivar | Newport News | 22/08/64 | 65- |
| SSBN-642 — Kamehameha | Mare Is | 16/01/65 | 65- |
| SSBN-643 — George Bancroft | Groton | 20/03/65 | 66- |
| SSBN-644 — Lewis and Clark | Newport News | 21/11/04 | 65- |
| SSBN-645 — James K. Polk | Groton | 22/05/65 | 66- |
| SSBN-654 — George C. Marshall | Newport News | 21/05/65 | 66- |
| SSBN-655 — Henry L. Stimson | Groton | 13/11/65 | 66- |
| SSBN-656 — George Washington Carver | Newport News | 14/08/65 | 66- |
| SSBN-657 — Francis Scott Key | Groton | 23/04/66 | 66- |
| SSBN-658 — Mariano G. Vallejo | Mare Is | 23/10/65 | 66- |
| SSBN-659 — Will Rogers | Groton | 21/07/66 | 67- |

**Notes:** Originally built to carry Polaris; all were converted 1970-78 to carry Poseldon. Last 12 units have quieter machinery and are officially designated 'Benjamin Franklin' class. SSBN-627, 629, 630, 632-34, 640, 641, 643, 655, 657 and 658 converted to Tridont I 1978-83.

*Daniel Webster* has diving planes mounted on bow rather than on sail.

*Francis Scott Key* made the first operational Trident patrol October 1979.

*Below:*
**The strategic missile submarine *Ohio* (SSBN-726) during trials in September 1981.** *Official US Navy*

# 'Ohio' Class (1974-85)

**Displacement:** 16,760/18,700 tons
**Dimensions:** 560 (oa)×42×35'6
**Machinery:** One shaft, one GE reactor, steam turbines,

SHP 60,000=28/35kt+
**Armament:** 24 Trident C-4 FBM tubes, 4×21in TT
**Complement:** 160

| | | | | |
|---|---|---|---|---|
| SSBN-726 | *Ohio* | Groton | 07/04/79 | 81- |
| SSBN-727 | *Michigan* | Groton | 26/04/80 | 82- |
| SSBN-728 | *Florida* | Groton | 14/11/81 | 83- |
| SSBN-729 | *Georgia* | Groton | 06/11/82 | 84- |
| SSBN-730 | *Henry M. Jackson* | Groton | 15/10/83 | 84- |
| | *(ex-Rhode Island)* | | | |
| SSBN-731 | *Alabama* | Groton | 19/05/84 | 85- |
| SSBN-732 | *Alaska* | Groton | 12/01/85 | 86- |
| SSBN-733 | *Nevada* | Groton | 14/09/85 | 86- |
| SSBN-734 | *Tennessee* | Groton | Building | na |
| SSBN-735 | *Colorado* | Groton | Building | na |
| SSBN-736 | *na* | Groton | Ordered | na |
| SSBN-737 | *na* | Groton | Ordered | na |
| SSBN-738 | *na* | Groton | Ordered | na |
| SSBN-739 | *na* | Groton | Ordered | na |

**Notes:** Delivery of first ship was planned for April 1979, delayed by both Navy and shipyard problems and it commissioned November 1981, first deployed October 1982. Largest submarines built in the United States. 734 will be the first to carry Trident II. Total to be built not announced, will probably be at least 20 units.

Intended to operate 70-day patrols with alternating blue and gold crews. Overhaul and reactor refuelling planned for every 10 years.

# NUCLEAR ATTACK SUBMARINES

## *Nautilus* (1951)

**Displacement:** 3,530/4,092 tons
**Dimensions:** 319'5 (oa)×27'8×22
**Machinery:** Two shafts, one reactor, steam turbines,

SHP 15,000=18/20kt+
**Armament:** 6×21in TT
**Complement:** 109

SSN-571 ____ *Nautilus* _____ Groton _____ 21/01/54 ___ 54-80

**Notes:**  First nuclear powered submarine in the world.
Hull based on German Type XXI.

## *Seawolf* (1952)

**Displacement:** 3,720/4,280 tons
**Dimensions:** 337'6 (oa)×27'8×21'6
**Machinery:** Two shafts, one reactor, steam turbines,

SHP 13,000=20/20kt+
**Armament:** 6×21in TT
**Complement:** 132

SSN-575 ____ *Seawolf* _____ Groton _____ 21/07/55 ___ 57-

**Notes:**  Experimental sodium-cooled reactor replaced
1959 with type similar to that in *Nautilus*. Used for
research since 1969. Will decommission 1987

## 'Skate' Class (1955-56)

**Displacement:** 2,570/2,861 tons
**Dimensions:** 267'8 (oa)×25×20'3
**Machinery:** Two shafts, one reactor, steam turbines

SHP 6,600=15.5/20kt+
**Armament:** 8×21in TT
**Complement:** 111

SSN-578 ____ *Skate* _____ Groton _____ 16/05/57 ___ 57-86
SSN-579 ____ *Swordfish* _____ Portsmouth _____ 27/08/57 ___ 58-
SSN-583 ____ *Sargo* _____ Mare Is _____ 10/10/57 ___ 58-
SSN-584 ____ *Seadragon* _____ Portsmouth _____ 16/08/58 ___ 58-84

**Notes:**  First class of nuclear submarines. Nuclear plant
is a simplified version of that in *Nautilus*.

## *Triton* (1955)

**Displacement:** 5,940/6,770 tons
**Dimensions:** 447'5 (oa)×37×24
**Machinery:** Two shafts, two reactors, steam turbines,

SHP 34,000=27/20kt+
**Armament:** 6×21in TT
**Complement:** 159

SSRN-586 ___ *Triton* _____ Groton _____ 19/08/58 ___ 59-69. SSN (61)

**Notes:**  Largest submarine in the world when built.
Designed for high speed surface operations as a radar
picket with a task force. First submarine with multiple
nuclear power plant. Circumnavigated the world
submerged in 1960 (36,000 miles).

*Above:*
**Nautilus** (SSN-571), the first nuclear powered submarine, is seen at Portland, England, in 1958.

*Below:*
The 'Skipjack' class nuclear submarine **Shark** (SSN-591) arriving at Malta, with crew members standing on the sail-mounted diving planes.
*A. & J. Pavia*

# 'Skipjack' Class (1955-57)

**Displacement:** 3,075/3,500 tons
**Dimensions:** 251'9 (oa)×31'7×25
**Machinery:** One shaft, one reactor, steam turbines,

SHP 15,000=20/30kt+
**Armament:** 6×21in TT
**Complement:** 114

| | | | | |
|---|---|---|---|---|
| SSN-585 | Skipjack | Groton | 26/05/58 | 59- |
| SSN-588 | Scamp | Mare Is | 08/10/60 | 61- |
| SSN-589 | Scorpion | Groton | 19/12/59 | 62-68. Lost 17/05/68 |
| SSN-590 | Sculpin | Ingalls | 31/03/60 | 61- |
| SSN-591 | Shark | Newport News | 16/03/60 | 61- |
| SSN-592 | Snook | Ingalls | 31/10/60 | 61- |

**Notes:** First submarines with high speed teardrop shaped Albacore type hull. Performance on trials was impressive.

# Halibut (1956)

**Displacement:** 3,850/4,895 tons
**Dimensions:** 350 (oa)×29'7×21'6
**Machinery:** Two shafts, one reactor, steam turbines,

SHP 6,600=15.5/20kt+
**Armament:** 6×21in TT, Regulus GM
**Complement:** 123

| | | | | |
|---|---|---|---|---|
| SSGN-587 | Halibut | Mare Is | 09/01/59 | 60-76. SSN (65) |

**Notes:** Guided missile submarine, had to surface to fire missiles. Designed for Regulus II, armed with Regulus I. Used for research after 1965 when Regulus missile programme was ended.

# Tullibee (1957)

**Displacement:** 2,317/2,640 tons
**Dimensions:** 273 (oa)×23'4×21
**Machinery:** One shaft, one reactor, steam turbines and

turbo-electric drive, SHP 2,500=15/15kt+
**Armament:** 4×21in TT
**Complement:** 102

| | | | | |
|---|---|---|---|---|
| SSN-597 | Tullibee | Groton | 27/04/60 | 60- |

**Notes:** Designed as a small hunter-killer submarine to operate off enemy ports. First US submarine built with sonar mounted in the bow and torpedo tubes amidships.

# 'Thresher' ('Permit') Class (1958-60)

**Displacement:** 3,750/4,300 tons; 605, 613-615: 4,300/ 4,600 tons
**Dimensions:** 278'6 (oa)×31'8×20; 605: 296'9 (oa): 613-615: 292'3 (oa)

**Machinery:** One shaft, one reactor, steam turbines, SHP 15,000=20/30kt
**Armament:** 4×21in TT, Subroc
**Complement:** 125

| | | | | |
|---|---|---|---|---|
| SSN-593 | Thresher | Portsmouth | 09/07/60 | 61-63. Lost 10/04/63 |
| SSN-594 | Permit | Mare Is | 01/07/61 | 62- |
| SSN-595 | Plunger | Mare Is | 09/12/61 | 62- |
| SSN 596 | Barb | Ingalls | 12/02/62 | 63- |
| SSN-603 | Pollack | NY Sbdg | 17/03/62 | 64- |
| SSN-604 | Haddo | NY Sbdg | 18/08/62 | 64- |

*Above:*
**The *Tullibee* (SSN-597) was the smallest US nuclear-powered submarine, designed as a hunter-killer. Behind is the conventionally powered submarine *Tench* (SS-417).**

*Below :*
**The 'Permit' class submarine *Greenling* (SSN-614) alongside the dock landing ship *Pensacola* in 1982. Submarines in commission no longer wear numbers.** *Martin E. Holbrook collection*

| | | | | |
|---|---|---|---|---|
| SSN-605 | _Jack_ | Portsmouth | 24/04/63 | 67- |
| SSN-606 | _Tinosa_ | Portsmouth | 09/12/61 | 64- |
| SSN-607 | _Dace_ | Ingalls | 18/08/62 | 64- |
| SSN-612 | _Guardfish_ | NY Sbdg | 15/05/65 | 66- |
| SSN-613 | _Flasher_ | Quincy | 22/06/63 | 66- |
| SSN-614 | _Greenling_ | Groton* | 04/04/64 | 67- |
| SSN-615 | _Gato_ | Groton* | 14/05/64 | 68- |
| SSN-621 | _Haddock_ | Ingalls | 21/05/66 | 67- |

* Completed at Quincy.

**Notes:** Established the standard for later nuclear submarines with deep-diving capacity, sonar mounted in the bow and torpedo tubes amidships. 594-596 and 607 originally ordered as SSGN to carry Regulus II, re-ordered 1958. Completion of later units delayed after loss of _Thresher_, and class renamed. This class is being fitted with Harpoon missiles.

# 'Sturgeon' Class (1961-69)

**Displacement:** 3,640/4,650 tons
**Dimensions:** 292'3 (oa)×31'8×29'6
**Machinery:** One shaft, one reactor, steam turbines,

SHP 15,000=20/30kt
**Armament:** 4×21in TT, Harpoon (some units), Subroc
**Complement:** 134

| | | | | |
|---|---|---|---|---|
| SSN-637 | _Sturgeon_ | Groton | 26/02/66 | 67- |
| SSN-638 | _Whale_ | Quincy | 14/10/66 | 68- |
| SSN-639 | _Tautog_ | Ingalls | 15/04/67 | 68- |
| SSN-646 | _Grayling_ | Portsmouth | 22/06/67 | 69- |
| SSN-647 | _Pogy_ | NY Sbdg* | 03/06/67 | 71- |
| SSN-648 | _Aspro_ | Ingalls | 29/11/67 | 69- |
| SSN-649 | _Sunfish_ | Quincy | 14/10/66 | 69- |
| SSN-650 | _Pargo_ | Groton | 17/09/66 | 68- |
| SSN-651 | _Queenfish_ | Newport News | 25/02/66 | 66- |
| SSN-652 | _Puffer_ | Ingalls | 30/03/68 | 69- |
| SSN-653 | _Ray_ | Newport News | 21/06/66 | 67- |
| SSN-660 | _Sand Lance_ | Portsmouth | 11/11/69 | 71- |
| SSN-661 | _Lapon_ | Newport News | 16/12/66 | 67- |
| SSN-662 | _Gurnard_ | Mare Is | 20/05/67 | 68- |
| SSN-663 | _Hammerhead_ | Newport News | 14/04/67 | 68- |
| SSN-664 | _Sea Devil_ | Newport News | 05/10/67 | 69- |
| SSN-665 | _Guitarro_ | Mare Is | 27/07/68 | 72- |
| SSN-666 | _Hawkbill_ | Mare Is | 12/04/69 | 71- |
| SSN-667 | _Bergall_ | Groton | 17/02/68 | 69- |
| SSN-668 | _Spadefish_ | Newport News | 15/05/68 | 69- |
| SSN-669 | _Seahorse_ | Groton | 15/06/68 | 69- |
| SSN-670 | _Finback_ | Newport News | 07/12/68 | 70- |
| SSN-672 | _Pintado_ | Mare Is | 16/08/69 | 71- |
| SSN-673 | _Flying Fish_ | Groton | 17/05/69 | 70- |
| SSN-674 | _Trepang_ | Groton | 27/09/69 | 70- |
| SSN-675 | _Bluefish_ | Groton | 10/01/70 | 71- |
| SSN-676 | _Billfish_ | Groton | 01/05/70 | 71- |
| SSN-677 | _Drum_ | Mare Is | 23/05/70 | 72- |
| SSN-678 | _Archerfish_ | Groton | 16/01/71 | 71- |
| SSN-679 | _Silversides_ | Groton | 04/06/71 | 72- |
| SSN-680 | _William H. Bates_ (ex-_Redfish_) | Ingalls | 11/12/71 | 73- |

| | | | | |
|---|---|---|---|---|
| SSN-681 | Batfish | Groton | 09/10/71 | 72- |
| SSN-682 | Tunny | Ingalls | 10/06/72 | 74- |
| SSN-683 | Parche | Ingalls | 13/01/73 | 74- |
| SSN-684 | Cavalla | Groton | 19/02/72 | 73- |
| SSN-686 | L. Mendel Rivers | Newport News | 02/06/73 | 75- |
| SSN-687 | Richard B. Russell | Newport News | 12/01/74 | 75- |

\* Completed by Ingalls.

**Notes:** Improved 'Permit' class with greater under-ice operational capability. Able to carry Harpoon and Tomahawk missiles.

*Guitarro* sank at pier while fitting out 16 May 1969, delaying completion.

# Narwhal (1964)

**Displacement:** 4,450/5,350 tons
**Dimensions:** 314'1 (oa)×38×26
**Machinery:** One shaft, one reactor, steam turbines,

SHP 17,000=25/30kt
**Armament:** 4×21in TT, Harpoon
**Complement:** 120

| | | | | |
|---|---|---|---|---|
| SSN-671 | Narwhal | Groton | 09/09/67 | 69- |

**Notes:** Built to evaluate quieter circulation S5G reactor, otherwise similar to 'Sturgeon' class. To be fitted with Tomahawk.

# Glenard P. Lipscomb (1968)

**Displacement:** 5,800/6,480 tons
**Dimensions:** 365 (oa)×31'9×31
**Machinery:** One shaft, one reactor, turbo-electric drive,

SHP 12,000=18/25kt
**Armament:** 4×21in TT, Subroc, Harpoon
**Complement:** 120

| | | | | |
|---|---|---|---|---|
| SSN-685 | Glenard P. Lipscomb | Groton | 04/08/73 | 74- |

**Notes:** Built to evaluate turbine-electric drive propulsion with speed sacrificed to reduce noise. Decision was made for faster ships as in 'Los Angeles' class. To be fitted with Tomahawk.

# 'Los Angeles' Class (1970-)

**Displacement:** 5,723/6,927 tons
**Dimensions:** 360 (oa)×33×32'3
**Machinery:** One shaft, one reactor, steam turbines,

SHP 35,000=20/32kt
**Armament:** 4×21in TT, Subroc, Harpoon, Tomahawk
**Complement:** 129

| | | | | |
|---|---|---|---|---|
| SSN-688 | Los Angeles | Newport News | 06/04/74 | 76- |
| SSN-689 | Baton Rouge | Newport News | 26/04/75 | 77- |
| SSN-690 | Philadelphia | Groton | 19/20/74 | 77- |
| SSN-691 | Memphis | Newport News | 03/04/76 | 77- |
| SSN-692 | Omaha | Groton | 21/02/76 | 78- |
| SSN-693 | Cincinnati | Newport News | 19/02/77 | 78- |
| SSN-694 | Groton | Groton | 09/10/76 | 78- |
| SSN-695 | Birmingham | Newport News | 29/10/77 | 78- |
| SSN-696 | New York City | Groton | 18/06/77 | 78- |
| SSN-697 | Indianapolis | Groton | 30/07/77 | 80- |
| SSN-698 | Bremerton | Groton | 22/07/78 | 81- |
| SSN-699 | Jacksonville | Groton | 18/11/78 | 81- |

*Above:*
**The *L. Mendel Rivers* (SSN-686), a 'Sturgeon' class submarine, looking aft. This vessel was named after a congressman active in military affairs.**

| SN-700 | Dallas | Groton | 28/04/79 | 81- |
| SN 701 | La Jolla | Groton | 11/08/79 | 81- |
| SSN-702 | Phoenix | Groton | 08/12/79 | 81- |
| SSN-703 | Boston | Groton | 19/04/80 | 82- |
| SSN-704 | Baltimore | Groton | 13/12/80 | 82- |
| SSN-705 | City of Corpus Christie (ex-Corpus Christie) | Groton | 25/04/81 | 83- |
| SSN-706 | Albuquerque | Groton | 13/03/82 | 83- |
| SSN-707 | Portsmouth | Groton | 18/09/82 | 83- |
| SSN-708 | Minneapolis-Saint Paul | Groton | 17/03/83 | 84- |
| SSN-709 | Hyman G. Rickover | Groton | 27/08/83 | 84- |
| SSN-710 | Augusta | Groton | 21/01/84 | 85- |

*Below:*
**San Francisco (SSN-711), a nuclear-powered attack submarine of the 'Los Angeles' class, on the surface during sea trials in March 1981. The ridge along the hull houses the towed array passive sonar.**
*Official US Navy*

| | | | | |
|---|---|---|---|---|
| SSN-711 | San Francisco | Newport News | 27/10/79 | 81- |
| SSN-712 | Atlanta | Newport News | 16/08/80 | 82- |
| SSN-713 | Houston | Newport News | 21/03/81 | 82- |
| SSN-714 | Norfolk | Newport News | 31/10/81 | 83- |
| SSN-715 | Buffalo | Newport News | 08/05/82 | 83- |
| SSN-716 | Salt Lake City | Newport News | 16/10/82 | 84- |
| SSN-717 | Olympia | Newport News | 30/04/83 | 84- |
| SSN-718 | Honolulu | Newport News | 24/09/83 | 85- |
| SSN-719 | Providence | Groton | 04/08/84 | 85- |
| SSN-720 | Pittsburgh | Groton | 08/12/84 | 85- |
| SSN-721 | Chicago | Newport News | 13/10/84 | 86- |
| SSN-722 | Key West | Newport News | 20/07/85 | na |
| SSN-723 | Oklahoma City | Newport News | 02/11/85 | na |
| SSN-724 | Louisville | Groton | 14/12/85 | na |
| SSN-725 | Helena | Groton | Building | na |
| SSN-750 | Newport News | Newport News | 15/03/86 | na |
| SSN-751 | San Juan | Groton | Building | na |
| SSN-752 | Pasadena | Groton | Building | na |
| SSN-753 | na | Newport News | Building | na |
| SSN-754 | na | Groton | Ordered | na |
| SSN-755 | na | Groton | Ordered | an |
| SSN-756 | na | Newport News | Ordered | na |
| SSN-757 | na | Groton | Ordered | na |
| SSN-758 | na | Newport News | Ordered | na |
| SSN-759 | na | Newport News | Ordered | na |
| SSN-760 | na | na | Ordered | na |
| SSN-761 | na | na | Ordered | na |
| SSN-762 | na | na | Ordered | na |
| SSN-763 | na | na | Ordered | na |

**Notes:** Sixty-four ships planned through 1989. Large attack submarines designed as response to Soviet 'Victor' class. Have larger reactor than previous classes to obtain extra 5kt speed. Fastest and quietest US submarines built. Earlier units to be retrofitted with vertical launch tubes for Tomahawk.

## Seawolf (1989?)

**Displacement:** —/10,000 tons
**Dimensions:** 350 (oa)
**Machinery:** One propulsor, steam turbines, one reactor, 30kt+
**Armament:** Harpoon and Tomahawk SSM, 8×30in TT
**Complement:** 130

| | | | |
|---|---|---|---|
| na | Seawolf | na | na na |

**Notes:** Temporarily designated SSN-21. Will be shorter but with greater diameter than 'Los Angeles' class and slightly faster; TT amidships; diving planes on bow. No missile tubes. Order for first ship expected to be FY89 and in service about 1995. Thirty ships planned.

# NON-NUCLEAR SUBMARINES

## 'Gato' Class (1940-42)

**Displacement:** 1,526/2,424 tons
**Dimensions:** 307 (wl), 311'9 (oa)×27'3×15'3
**Machinery:** Two shafts, diesel/electric, HP 5,400/

2,740=20.2/8.7kt
**Armament:** 10×21in TT, 1×5in/25 gun
**Complement:** 85

| | | | | |
|---|---|---|---|---|
| SS-212 | Gato | Groton | 21/08/41 | 46-60. BU61 |
| SS-213 | Greenling | Groton | 20/09/41 | 46-60. BU61 |
| SS-214 | Grouper | Groton | 27/10/41 | 42-68. SSK (51), BU70 |
| SS-217 | Guardfish | Groton | 20/01/42 | 48-60. Target 61 |
| SS-220 | Barb | Groton | 02/04/42 | 51-54. Italian *Enrico Tazzoli* (55) |
| SS-221 | Blackfish | Groton | 18/04/42 | 49-60. Str58 |
| SS-222 | Bluefish | Groton | 21/02/43 | 52-53. Str58 |
| SS-224 | Cod | Groton | 21/03/43 | Str71 |
| SS-225 | Cero | Groton | 04/04/43 | 52-53. Str67 |
| SS-228 | Drum | Portsmouth | 12/05/41 | 47-62. Str |
| SS-229 | Flying Fish | Portsmouth | 09/07/41 | 41-54. BU59 |
| SS-230 | Finback | Portsmouth | 25/08/41 | 46-50. Sold 59 |
| SS-231 | Haddock | Portsmouth | 20/10/41 | 48-60. BU60 |
| SS-234 | Kingfish | Portsmouth | 02/03/42 | BU60 |
| SS-235 | Shad | Portsmouth | 15/04/42 | 47-60. BU61 |
| SS-236 | Silversides | Mare Is | 26/08/41 | -69. Str69 |
| SS-239 | Whale | Mare Is | 14/03/42 | 56-57. Str60 |
| SS-240 | Angler | Groton | 04/07/43 | 51-69. SSK (51), BU74 |
| SS-241 | Bashaw | Groton | 25/07/43 | 51-68. SSK (51), Target 69 |
| SS-242 | Bluegill | Groton | 08/08/43 | 51-69. Str69 |
| SS-243 | Bream | Groton | 17/10/43 | 51-69. SSK (51), Target 69 |
| SS-244 | Cavalla | Groton | 14/11/43 | 51-69. SSK (51), Str69 |
| SS-245 | Cobia | Groton | 28/11/43 | 51-54. Str70 |
| SS-246 | Croaker | Groton | 19/12/43 | 51-68. SSK (51), BU72 |
| SS-247 | Dace | Groton | 25/04/43 | 51-53. Italian *Leonardo Da Vinci* (54) |
| SS-249 | Flasher | Groton | 20/06/43 | BU63 |
| SS-251 | Flounder | Groton | 22/08/43 | Str59 |
| SS-252 | Gabilan | Groton | 19/09/43 | BU60 |
| SS-253 | Gunnel | Groton | 17/05/42 | BU59 |
| SS-254 | Gurnard | Groton | 01/06/42 | 49-60. BU61 |
| SS-255 | Haddo | Groton | 21/06/42 | BU59 |
| SS-256 | Hake | Groton | 17/07/42 | 56-67. BU73 |
| SS-258 | Hoe | Groton | 17/09/42 | 56-60. BU60 |
| SS-259 | Jack | Groton | 16/10/42 | Greek *Amfitriti* (58) |
| SS-260 | Lapon | Groton | 27/10/42 | Greek *Poseidon* (57) |
| SS-261 | Mingo | Groton | 30/11/42 | Japanese *Kuroshio* (55) |
| SS-262 | Muskallunge | Groton | 13/12/42 | Brazilian *Humaita* (57) |
| SS-263 | Paddle | Groton | 30/12/42 | Brazilian *Riachuelo* (57) |
| SS-264 | Pargo | Groton | 24/01/43 | 46-60. BU61 |
| SS-265 | Peto | Manitowoc | 30/04/42 | 56-60. BU61 |
| SS-266 | Pogy | Manitowoc | 23/06/42 | BU59 |

| | | | | |
|---|---|---|---|---|
| SS-267 | Pompon | Manitowoc | 15/08/42 | 53-59. SSR (51), BU60 |
| SS-268 | Puffer | Manitowoc | 22/11/42 | 46-60. BU61 |
| SS-269 | Rasher | Manitowoc | 20/12/42 | 51-67. SSR (51), AGSS (60), BU74 |
| SS-270 | Raton | Manitowoc | 24/01/43 | 43-48, 53-69. SSR (51), Target 69 |
| SS-271 | Ray | Manitowoc | 28/02/43 | 52-58. SSR (51), BU60 |
| SS-272 | Redfin | Manitowoc | 04/04/43 | 53-70. SSR (51), AGSS (63), BU71 |
| SS-274 | Rock | Manitowoc | 20/06/43 | 53-69. Target 69 |
| SS-276 | Sawfish | Portsmouth | 23/06/42 | 47-60. BU61 |
| SS-280 | Steelhead | Portsmouth | 11/09/42 | Str60 |
| SS-281 | Sunfish | Mare Is | 02/05/42 | Str60 |
| SS-282 | Tunny | Mare Is | 30/06/42 | 53-69. SSG (53-65), APSS (66), LPSS (68), BU73 |
| SS-283 | Tinosa | Mare Is | 11/11/42 | 52-53. Str58 |

**Notes:** Seven converted to ASW submarines (SSK) 1951. *Tunny* converted to carry Regulus I SSM 1953. Six converted to radar pickets (SSR) 1951, length increased to 343 (oa), displacement 2,500 tons; reclassified AGSS 1960.

*Below:*
**The *Tunny* (SSG-282), a 'Gato' class vessel, was rebuilt for experimental guided missile tests, with a missile hangar aft.** *Official US Navy*

# 'Balao' Class (1941-42)

**Displacement:** 1,525/2,424 tons
**Dimensions:** 307 (wl) 311'9 (oa)×27'3×15'3
**Machinery:** Two shafts, diesel/electric, HP 5,400/

2,740=20.2/8.7kt
**Armament:** 10×21in TT, 1 or 2×5in/25 gun
**Complement:** 85

| | | | | |
|---|---|---|---|---|
| SS-285 | Balao | Portsmouth | 27/10/42 | 52-63. Target 64 |
| SS-286 | Billfish | Portsmouth | 12/11/42 | Str68 |
| SS-287 | Bowfin | Portsmouth | 07/12/42 | 51-54. Str71 |
| SS-288 | Cabrilla | Portsmouth | 24/12/42 | Str68 |
| SS-291 | Crevalle | Portsmouth | 22/02/43 | 51-68. Str68 |
| SS-292 | Devilfish | Cramp | 30/05/43 | Target 68 |
| SS-293 | Dragonet | Cramp | 18/04/43 | Target 62 |
| SS-295 | Hackleback | Cramp | 30/05/43 | BU68 |
| SS-297 | Ling | Cramp | 15/08/43 | Str71 |
| SS-298 | Lionfish | Cramp | 07/11/43 | 51-53. Str71 |
| SS-299 | Manta | Cramp | 07/11/43 | Target 69 |
| SS-300 | Moray | Cramp | 14/05/44 | Target 70 |

| SS-301 | Roncador | Cramp | 14/05/44 | Str71 |
|---|---|---|---|---|
| SS-302 | Sabalo | Cramp | 04/06/44 | 51-71, Target 73 |
| SS-303 | Sablefish | Cramp | 04/06/44 | 45-69. BU71 |
| SS-304 | Seahorse | Mare Is | 09/01/43 | BU68 |
| SS-307 | Tilefish | Mare Is | 25/10/43 | 43-59. Venezuelan *Carite* (60) |
| SS-309 | Aspro | Portsmouth | 07/04/43 | 51-62. Target 63 |
| SS-310 | Batfish | Portsmouth | 05/05/43 | 51-65. Str69 |
| SS-311 | Archerfish | Porstmouth | 28/05/43 | 52-55, 57-68. Target 68 |
| SS-312 | Burrfish | Portsmouth | 18/06/43 | 48-56. SSR (48), Canadian *Grilse* (61) |
| SS-313 | Perch | Groton | 12/09/43 | 48-60, 61-67. SSP (48), ASSP (50), APSS (56), LPSS (69), BU72 |
| SS-315 | Sealion | Groton | 31/10/43 | 48-70. SSP (48), ASSP (50), APSS (56), LPSS (69), Target 78 |
| SS-317 | Barbero | Groton | 12/12/43 | 48-50, 55-64. SSA (48), SSG (55), Target 65 |
| SS-318 | Baya | Groton | 02/01/44 | 48-72. AGSS (49), BU73 |
| SS-319 | Becuna | Groton | 30/01/44 | 44-69. Str73 |
| SS-320 | Bergall | Groton | 16/02/44 | 44-58. Turkish *Turgut Reis* (58) |
| SS-321 | Besugo | Groton | 27/02/44 | 44-57. Italian *Francesco Morosini* (66) |
| SS-322 | Blackfin | Groton | 12/03/44 | 44-72. Target 73 |
| SS-323 | Caiman | Groton | 30/03/44 | 44-72. Turkish *Dumlupinar* (72) |
| SS-324 | Blenny | Groton | 09/04/44 | 44-69. Target 73 |
| SS-325 | Blower | Groton | 23/04/44 | 44-50. Turkish *Dumlupinar* (50); lost 03/04/53 |
| SS-326 | Blueback | Groton | 07/05/44 | Turkish *Ikinci Inonu* (48) |
| SS-327 | Boarfish | Groton | 21/05/44 | Turkish *Sakarya* (48) |
| SS-328 | Charr | Groton | 28/05/44 | 44-71. BU72 |
| SS-329 | Chub | Groton | 18/06/44 | Turkish *Gur* (48) |
| SS-330 | Brill | Groton | 25/06/44 | Turkish *Birinci Inonu* (48) |
| SS-331 | Bugara | Groton | 02/07/44 | 44-70. Str70 |
| SS-333 | Bumper | Groton | 06/08/44 | 44-50. Turkish *Canakkale* (50) |
| SS-334 | Cabezon | Groton | 27/08/44 | 44-53. Str70 |
| SS-335 | Dentuda | Groton | 10/09/44 | BU69 |
| SS-336 | Capitaine | Groton | 01/10/44 | 45-50, 57-65. Italian *Alfredo Cappellini* (66) |
| SS-337 | Carbonero | Groton | 19/10/44 | 45-70. Target 71 |
| SS-338 | Carp | Groton | 12/11/44 | 45-71. BU73 |
| SS-339 | Catfish | Groton | 19/11/44 | 45-71. Argentine *Santa Fe* (71), lost 25/04/82 |
| SS-340 | Entemedor | Groton | 17/12/44 | 45-48, 50-72. Turkish *Preveze* (72) |
| SS-341 | Chivo | Groton | 14/01/45 | 45-71. Argentine *Santiago Del Estero* (71) |
| SS-342 | Chopper | Groton | 04/02/45 | 45-71. Str71 |
| SS-343 | Clamagore | Groton | 25/02/45 | 45-75. Str75 |
| SS-344 | Cobbler | Groton | 01/04/45 | 45-73. Turkish *Canakkale* (73) |
| SS-345 | Cochino | Groton | 20/04/45 | 45-49. Lost 26/08/49 |
| SS-346 | Corporal | Groton | 10/06/45 | 45-73. Turkish *Ikinci Inonu* (73) |
| SS-347 | Cubera | Groton | 17/06/45 | 45-72. Venezuelan *Tiburon* (72) |
| SS-348 | Cusk | Groton | 28/07/45 | 46-69. SSG (48-54), BU72 |
| SS-349 | Diodon | Groton | 10/09/45 | 46-71. BU72 |
| SS-350 | Dogfish | Groton | 27/10/45 | 46-72. Brazilian *Guanabara* (72) |
| SS-351 | Greenfish | Groton | 21/12/45 | 46-73. Brazilian *Amazonas* (73) |
| SS-352 | Halfbeak | Groton | 19/02/46 | 46-71. BU72 |
| SS-362 | Guavina | Manitowoc | 29/08/43 | 50-67. SSO (49), AGSS (52), AOSS (57), Target 67 |
| SS-363 | Guitarro | Manitowoc | 26/09/43 | 52-54. Turkish *Preveze* (54) |
| SS-364 | Hammerhead | Manitowoc | 24/10/43 | 52-54. Turkish *Cerbe* (54) |

| SS-365 | Hardhead | Manitowoc | 12/12/43 | 53-72. Greek *Papanikolis* (72) |
| SS-366 | Hawkbill | Manitowoc | 09/01/44 | Dutch *Zeeleeuw* (53) |
| SS-367 | Icefish | Manitowoc | 20/02/44 | 52-53. Dutch *Walrus* (53) |
| SS-368 | Jallao | Manitowoc | 12/03/44 | 53-74. Spanish *Narciso Monturiol* (74) |
| SS-370 | Kraken | Manitowoc | 30/04/44 | Spanish *Almirante Garcia De Los Reyes* (59) |
| SS-372 | Lamprey | Manitowoc | 18/06/44 | Argentine *Santa Fe* (60) Lost |
| SS-373 | Lizardfish | Manitowoc | 16/07/44 | Italian *Evangelista Torricelli* (60) |
| SS-374 | Loggerhead | Manitowoc | 13/08/44 | BU69 |
| SS-375 | Macabi | Manitowoc | 19/09/44 | Argentine *Santiago Del Estero* (60) |
| SS-376 | Mapiro | Manitowoc | 09/11/44 | Turkish *Piri Reis* (60) |
| SS-377 | Menhaden | Manitowoc | 20/12/44 | 51-71. Target 77 |
| SS-378 | Mero | Manitowoc | 17/01/45 | Turkish *Hizir Reis* (60) |
| SS-381 | Sand Lance | Portsmouth | 25/06/43 | Brazilian *Rio Grande Do Sul* (63) |
| SS-382 | Picuda | Portsmouth | 12/07/43 | 53-72. Spanish *Narciso Monturiol* (72) |
| SS-383 | Pampanito | Portsmouth | 12/07/43 | Str71 |
| SS-384 | Parche | Portsmouth | 24/07/43 | BU70 |
| SS-385 | Bang | Portsmouth | 30/08/43 | 52-73. Spanish *Cosme Garcia* (73) |
| SS-387 | Pintado | Portsmouth | 15/09/43 | BU69 |
| SS-388 | Pipefish | Portsmouth | 12/10/43 | BU69 |
| SS-389 | Piranha | Portsmouth | 27/10/43 | BU70 |
| SS-390 | Plaice | Portsmouth | 15/11/43 | Briazilian *Bahia* (63) |
| SS-391 | Pomfret | Portsmouth | 27/10/43 | 44-71. Turkish *Oruc Reis* (71) |
| SS-392 | Sterlet | Portsmouth | 27/10/43 | 44-48, 50-68. Target 69 |
| SS-393 | Queenfish | Portsmouth | 30/11/43 | 44-63. Target 64 |
| SS-394 | Razorback | Portsmouth | 27/01/44 | 44-70. Turkish *Murat Reis* (70) |
| SS-395 | Redfish | Portsmouth | 27/01/44 | 44-68. Target 69 |
| SS-396 | Ronquil | Portsmouth | 27/01/44 | 44-71. Spanish *Isaac Peral* (71) |
| SS-397 | Scabbardfish | Portsmouth | 27/01/44 | 44-48. Greek *Triana* (65) |
| SS-398 | Segundo | Portsmouth | 05/02/44 | 44-70. Target 70 |
| SS-399 | Sea Cat | Portsmouth | 21/02/44 | 44-68. Target 69 |
| SS-400 | Sea Devil | Portsmouth | 28/02/44 | 44-48, 51-54, 57-64. Target 64 |
| SS-401 | Sea Dog | Portsmouth | 28/03/44 | 44-56. Str68 |
| SS-402 | Sea Fox | Portsmouth | 28/03/44 | 44-70. Turkish *Burak Reis* (70) |
| SS-403 | Atule | Portsmouth | 06/03/44 | 51-69. Peruvian *Pacocha* (74) |
| SS-404 | Spikefish | Portsmouth | 26/04/44 | 44-63. Target 63 |
| SS-405 | Sea Owl | Portsmouth | 07/05/44 | 44-69. Str69 |
| SS-406 | Sea Poacher | Portsmouth | 20/05/44 | 44-69. Peruvian *La Pedrera* (74) |
| SS-407 | Sea Robin | Portsmouth | 25/05/44 | 44-70. BU71 |
| SS-408 | Sennet | Portsmouth | 06/06/44 | 44-68. Target 69 |
| SS-409 | Piper | Portsmouth | 26/06/44 | 44-67. Str70 |
| SS-410 | Threadfin | Portsmouth | 26/06/44 | 44-72. Turkish *Birinci Inonu* (72) |
| SS-411 | Spadefish | Mare Is | 08/01/44 | BU68 |
| SS-412 | Trepang | Mare Is | 23/03/44 | Target 69 |
| SS-413 | Spot | Mare Is | 19/05/44 | Chilean *Simpson* (62) |
| SS-414 | Springer | Mare Is | 03/08/44 | Chilean *Thompson* (61) |
| SS-415 | Stickleback | Mare Is | 01/01/45 | 45-58. Lost 29/05/58 |
| SS-416 | Tiru | Mare Is | 16/09/47 | 48-75. Str75 |

**Notes:** The standard submarine of World War 2, repeat 'Gato' class with 100ft greater diving depth capability. Between 1946 and 1952 most of this class were converted to streamlined hull with snorkel (GUPPY). GUPPY IA conversions: 319, 322-324, 341-342, 366-367, 403, 406-407. GUPPY II: 339, 343-347, 349-352, 416. GUPPY IIA (one main engine removed, HP 3,450): 340, 365, 368, 377, 382, 385, 391, 394, 396, 402, 410, 415. In 1960-62, 343-344, 346, 351 and 416 were converted to GUPPY III. Converted to snorkel with no streamlining:

Top:
*Sea Fox* (SS-402), a later Guppy IIA conversion of the 'Balao' class, with a greater streamlined sail.

Above:
*Tirante* (SS-420), a 'Tench' class submarine in February 1957. It is seen after a Guppy IIA conversion, with streamlined hull and sail.
Wright & Logan

Below:
The 'Tench' class submarine *Requin* (SSR-481) was adapted as a radar picket. It was photographed in Malta harbour in May 1949. Notice the cut-down conning tower and multiple radars.   A. & J. Pavia

302-303, 320 328, 331, 337-338, 348, 392, 398-399, 405, 408-409.

*Barbero* converted to cargo submarine 1948 and to missile submarine 1954. *Cusk* converted to missile submarine 1948; was first submarine to launch a guided missile. *Carbonero* also tested missiles 1949-51. *Guavina* converted to submarine oiler 1948 with exterior tanks for bulk liquids, beam 37ft. *Sealion* and *Perch* converted to transports with cylindrical chamber abaft conning tower for amphibious craft, forward engines and TT removed. *Burrfish* converted to radar picket. *Manta* converted to target ship. *Baya* used for electronic experiments and *Sea Cat* for snorkel experiments.


# 'Tench' Class (1943)

**Displacement:** 1,570/2,416 tons
**Dimensions:** 307 (wl) 311'8 (oa)×27'2×15'3
**Machinery:** Two shafts, diesel/electric,

SHP 5,400/2,740=20.2/8.7kt
**Armament:** 10×21in TT, 1×5in/25 gun
**Complement:** 66

| | | | | |
|---|---|---|---|---|
| SS-417 | Tench | Portsmouth | 07/07/44 | 50-70. Str73 |
| SS-418 | Thornback | Portsmouth | 07/07/44 | 53-71. Turkish *Uluc Ali Reis* (71) |
| SS-419 | Tigrone | Portsmouth | 20/07/44 | 48-57, 62-75. SSR (48-61), AGSS (63), Str75 |
| SS-420 | Tirante | Portsmouth | 09/08/44 | 52-73. BU74 |
| SS-421 | Trutta | Portsmouth | 18/08/44 | 51-72. Turkish *Cerbe* (72) |
| SS-422 | Toro | Portsmouth | 23/08/44 | 47-63. BU56 |
| SS-423 | Torsk | Portsmouth | 06/09/44 | 44-71. Str71 |
| SS-424 | Quillback | Portsmouth | 01/10/44 | 44-73. BU74 |
| SS-425 | Trumpetfish | Cramp | 13/05/45 | 46-73. Brazilian *Goias* (73) |
| SS-426 | Tusk | Cramp | 08/07/45 | 46-73. Taiwan *Hai Pao* (73) |
| SS-435 | Corsair | Groton | 03/05/46 | 46-63. BU64 |
| SS-475 | Argonaut | Portsmouth | 01/10/44 | 45-68. Canadian *Rainbow* (68) |
| SS-476 | Runner | Portsmouth | 17/10/44 | 45-71. Str71 |
| SS-477 | Conger | Portsmouth | 17/10/44 | 45-63. BU64 |
| SS-478 | Cutlass | Portsmouth | 05/11/44 | 45-73. Taiwan *Hai Shih* (73) |
| SS-479 | Diablo | Portsmouth | 01/12/44 | 45-63. Pakistani *Ghazi* (64); lost 5/12/71 |
| SS-480 | Medregal | Portsmouth | 15/12/44 | 45-70. Target 70 |
| SS-481 | Requin | Portsmouth | 01/01/45 | 45-71. SSR (48-59), Str71 |
| SS-482 | Irex | Portsmouth | 26/01/45 | 45-69. Str69 |
| SS-483 | Sea Leopard | Portsmouth | 02/03/45 | 45-73. Brazilian *Bahia* (73) |
| SS-484 | Odax | Portsmouth | 10/04/45 | 45-72. Brazilian *Rio De Janeiro* (72) |
| SS-485 | Sirago | Portsmouth | 11/05/45 | 45-72. BU73 |
| SS-486 | Pomodon | Portsmouth | 12/06/45 | 45-70. Str70 |
| SS-487 | Remora | Portsmouth | 12/07/45 | 46-73. Greek *Katsonis* (73) |
| SS-488 | Sarda | Portsmouth | 24/08/45 | 46-64. BU65 |
| SS-489 | Spinax | Portsmouth | 20/11/45 | 46-69. SSR (48-59), Str69 |
| SS-490 | Volador | Portsmouth | 17/01/46 | 48-72. Italian *Gianfranco Priaroggia Gazzano* (72) |
| SS-522 | Amberjack | Boston | 15/12/44 | 76-73. Brazilian *Ceara* (73) |
| SS-523 | Grampus | Boston | 15/12/44 | 49-72. Brazilian *Rio Grande Do Sul* (72) |
| SS-524 | Pickerel | Boston | 15/12/44 | 49-72. Italian *Piero Longobardo* (72) |
| SS-525 | Grenadier | Boston | 15/12/44 | 51-73. Venezuelan *Picua* (73) |

**Notes:** Improved 'Balao' class. *Requin* and *Spinax* converted to radar pickets 1946, *Tigrone* 1948. GUPPY conversions (1946-52): Type I: 484-86. Type IA: 417. Type II: 425-26, 478, 483-87, 490, 522-25. IIA: 418, 420-21, 424. Type III: 425, 487, 490, 524 (1960-62). *Odax* and *Pomodon* were first GUPPY conversions. 1950-52 snorkel conversions (no streamlining): 423, 475-76, 480, 482.

## 'Tang' Class (1947-48)

**Displacement:** 1,560/2,260 tons; 1957: 2,100/2,700 tons
**Dimensions:** 269'2 (oa)×27'3×17; 1957: 287 (oa)
**Machinery:** Two shafts, diesel/electric,

BHP 4,200/3,200 = 20/27kt
**Armament:** 8×21in TT
**Complement:** 83

| SS-563 | Tang | Portsmouth | 19/06/51 | 51-80. Turkish Piri Reis (80) |
|---|---|---|---|---|
| SS-564 | Trigger | Groton | 14/06/51 | 52-73. Italian Divio Piomarta (73) |
| SS-565 | Wahoo | Portsmouth | 16/10/51 | 52-80. BU85 |
| SS-566 | Trout | Groton | 21/08/51 | 53-78. Str78 |
| SS-567 | Gudgeon | Portsmouth | 11/06/52 | 52-83. Turkish Hizir Reis (83) |
| SS-568 | Harder | Groton | 03/12/51 | 52-74. Italian Romeo Romei (74) |

**Notes:** Fast attack submarines, with features of German Type XXI vessels. First four had radial diesel engines which were unsatisfactory and were replaced by similar machinery as in last two 1957. Lengthened 1957-58. All FRAM II refit.

Tang, Wahoo and Trout were to be transferred to Iran. Trout was formally transferred 12/78 but was abandoned by its Iranian crew 3/79 at New London. New names were to be Dolfin, Nahang and Kusseh.

## 'K' Class (1948-49)

**Displacement:** 890/1,160 tons
**Dimensions:** 196'1 (oa)×24'7×16
**Machinery:** Two shafts; diesel/electric,

BHP 1,050/1,050 = 13/10kt
**Armament:** 4×21in TT
**Complement:** 47

| SSK-1 | K-1 | Groton | 02/03/51 | 51-73. Barracuda (55), SST-3 (59), BU74 |
|---|---|---|---|---|
| SSK-2 | K-2 | Mare Is | 02/05/51 | 52-58. Bass (55), SS-551 (59), Str65 |
| SSK-3 | K-3 | Mare Is | 21/06/51 | 52-58. Bonita (55), SS-552 (59), Str65 |

**Notes:** Submarine killers. Named 1955. K-3 originally ordered from NY Sbdg. Large sonar dome in bow. Very successful in detecting submerged submarines, but too small and slow.

Below:
**The attack submarine Wahoo (SS-565) in February 1961, after lengthening. The 'Tang' class was the first postwar US submarine design.**
Official US Navy

*Above:*
**The *K-3* (SSK-3), seen in April 1953, was later renamed *Bonita*. 'K' class submarines were designed to sink enemy submarines.**
*Official US Navy*

*Below:*
**Albacore (AGSS-569) was an experimental submarine with the new teardrop hull shape.**
*Official US Navy*

# 'T' Class (1951-52)

**Displacement:** 303/347 tons
**Dimensions:** 131'3 (oa)×13'7×11
**Machinery:** One shaft, diesel/electric,

BHP 250/250=10/20kt
**Armament:** 1×21in TT
**Complement:** 14

| | | | | | |
|---|---|---|---|---|---|
| SST-1 | T-1 | Groton | 17/07/53 | 53-73. *Mackerel* (56), Str73 |
| SST-2 | T-2 | Groton | 14/10/53 | 53-73. *Marlin* (56), Str73, memorial |

**Notes:** Training submarines and ASW targets, named 1956. *T-1* ordered as AGSS-570.

# *Albacore* (1950)

**Displacement:** 1,517/1,847 tons
**Dimensions:** 203'9 (oa)×27'4×22
**Machinery:** One shaft, diesel/electric,

BHP 1,500/15,000=25/33kt
**Armament:** None
**Complement:** 52

| | | | | |
|---|---|---|---|---|
| AGSS-569 | *Albacore* | Portsmouth | 01/08/53 | 53-72. Target 81 |

**Notes:** Experimental vessel, no combat capability. First teardrop hull design. Rebuilt several times to test new equipment.

# *Sailfish* Class (1952)

**Displacement:** 2,485/3,170 tons
**Dimensions:** 350'6 (oa)×30×18
**Machinery:** Two shafts, diesel/electric, BHP 6,000/

?=20.5/15kt; electric, BHP?=15kt
**Armament:** 2×21in TT
**Complement:** 95

| | | | | |
|---|---|---|---|---|
| SSR-572 | *Sailfish* | Portsmouth | 07/09/55 | 56-77. Str78 |
| SSR-573 | *Salmon* | Portsmouth | 25/02/56 | 56-77. Str77. Target |

**Notes:** Radar picket submarines with one antenna on sail and another aft. Converted to attack submarines SS 1961. FRAM refit 1964.

# *Grayback* (1952)

**Displacement:** 2,671/3,652 tons
**Dimensions:** 322'4 (oa)×30×19; 1969: 334 (oa)
**Machinery:** Two shafts, diesel/electric,

BHP 4,500/5,600=20/12kt
**Armament:** Regulus II (removed 67), 6×21in TT (68)
**Complement:** 84

| | | | | |
|---|---|---|---|---|
| SSG-574 | *Grayback* | Mare Is | 02/07/57 | 58-64, 68-84. LPSS (68), SS (75), Str84 |

**Notes:** Ordered as 'Darter' class unit, built as guided missile submarine with Regulus II SSM. Decommissioned 1964 when Polaris replaced Regulus missile programme. Converted to transport at Mare Is 1967-69, lengthened, sail raised.

# *Darter* (1954)

**Displacement:** 1,870/2,388 tons
**Dimensions:** 268'7 (oa)×27'2×19
**Machinery:** Two shafts, diesel/electric,

BHP 4,500/4,500=19.4/14kt
**Armament:** 8×21in TT
**Complement:** 85

| | | | | |
|---|---|---|---|---|
| SS-576 | *Darter* | Groton | 28/05/56 | 56- |

**Notes:** Improved 'Tang' class

# *Growler* (1954)

**Displacement:** 2,540/3,515 tons
**Dimensions:** 317'7 (oa)×27'2×19
**Machinery:** Two shafts, diesel/electric,

BHP 4,000/5,600=20/12kt
**Armament:** Regulus II GM, 6×21in TT
**Complement:** 95

SSG-577 ——— *Growler* ——————— Portsmouth ———— 05/04/57 —— 58-64. Str80

**Notes:** Originally ordered as 'Darter' class vessel, converted to missile submarine, improved *Grayback*. Conversion to transport cancelled.


# 'Barbel' Class (1955-56)

**Displacement:** 2,155/2,895 tons
**Dimensions:** 219'6 (oa)×29×28
**Machinery:** One shaft,

diesel/electric, BHP 4,800/3,150=15.5/25kt
**Armament:** 6×21in TT
**Complement:** 78

SS-580 ——— *Barbel* ——————— Portsmouth ———— 19/07/58 —— 59
SS-581 ——— *Blueback* ——————— Ingalls ——————— 16/05/59 —— 59-
SS-582 ——— *Bonefish* ——————— NY Sbdg ————— 22/11/58 —— 59-

**Notes:** Attack submarines, last diesel/electric combat submarines built for US Navy. High speed, with teardrop hull shape. Diving planes were originally mounted on bow, later moved to sail.


# *Dolphin* (1960)

**Displacement:** 800/930 tons
**Dimensions:** 152 (oa)×19'4×18
**Machinery:** One shaft, diesel, BHP ?; electric,

BHP 1,650=12kt
**Armament:** 1×21in TT (removed 70)
**Complement:** 29

AGSS-555 —— *Dolphin* ——————— Portsmouth ———— 08/06/68 —— 68-

**Notes:** Experimental deep-diving submarine, with constant-diameter pressure hull. Reported to have reached the greatest depth of any operational US submarine. Being modified to test new steel for deep diving.

# BATTLESHIPS

## 'Iowa' Class (1939-40)

**Displacement:** 48,425 tons, 57,500f/l
**Dimensions:** 861'3 (wl) 887'3 (oa)×108'2×38
**Machinery:** Four shafts, steam turbines,
  SHP 212,000=33kt
**Endurance:** 15,000/15

**Armament:** 9×16in/50, 20×5in/38, 80×40mm guns
  *1982* Four quad Harpoon and 4 quad Tomahawk
  launchers, four Phalanx CIWS; 8×5in guns removed
**Complement:** 2,700

| | | | | |
|---|---|---|---|---|
| BB-61 | *Iowa* | New York | 27/08/42 | 43-49, 51-58, 84- |
| BB-62 | *New Jersey* | Philadelphia | 07/12/42 | 43-48, 50-57, 68-69, 82- |
| BB-63 | *Missouri* | New York | 29/01/44 | 45-55, 86- |
| BB-64 | *Wisconsin* | Philadelphia | 07/12/43 | 44-48, 51-58 |
| BB-66 | *Kentucky* | Norfolk | 20/01/50 | BU incomplete 58 |

**Notes:** *Kentucky* launched to clear slipway. Various
plans to complete it as a missile ship were proposed
(BBG). Stern catapults removed 1949-50. All fitted with
mast stepped against after funnel in 1950s.
  *Missouri* ran aground in Chesapeake Bay 7 January
1950 and not refloated until 1 February. *New Jersey*
recommissioned without 40mm guns, electronic
warfare equipment added to fore tower. *Wisconsin*
scheduled to recommission 1988.

The following battleships remained on the navy list in
reserve: *Tennessee* (43), *California* (44), *Maryland* (45),

*Colorado* (46) and *West Virginia* (48), all stricken 1959;
and *North Carolina* (55), *Washington* (56), *South Dakota*
(57), *Massachusetts* (58), *Indiana* (59) and *Alabama* (60).
Stricken 1960-62.

*Below:*
**This is *Iowa* (BB-61) as she appeared during the
1950s. Many of her World War 2 anti-aircraft guns
had been removed by this time.** *Ted Stone*

# LARGE CRUISERS

## 'Alaska' Class (1940)

**Displacement:** 27,500 tons; 32,500f/l
**Dimensions:** 791'6 (w/l) 808'6 (oa)×90'10×31'6
**Machinery:** Four shafts, steam turbines,

SHP 150,000=33kt
**Armament:** 9×12in/50, 12×5in/38, 56×40mm guns
**Complement:** 1,517

| | | | | |
|---|---|---|---|---|
| CB-1 | Alaska | NY Sbdg | 15/08/43 | BU61 |
| CB-2 | Guam | NY Sbdg | 21/11/43 | BU61 |
| CB-3 | Hawaii | NY Sbdg | 03/11/45 | CBC-1 (52), BU60 incomplete |

**Notes:** Various plans to complete *Hawaii* as large command ship or missile ship were proposed, but no conversion work was started, and the project was cancelled 1954. 1-2 decommissioned 1946.

# CRUISERS

Heavy cruisers *New Orleans* (CA-32), *Minneapolis* (36), *Tuscaloosa* (37), *San Francisco* (38) and *Wichita* (45), and light cruisers *Brooklyn* (CL-40), *Philadelphia* (41), *Savannah* (42) and *Honolulu* (48) remained on the list in reserve until stricken 1959.

## 'Atlanta' Class (1939-43)

**Displacement:** 6,200 tons; 8,600f/l
**Dimensions:** 530 (wl) 541'6 (oa)×53'2×25
**Machinery:** Two shafts, steam turbines, SHP 75,000=32kt
**Endurance:** 7,500/12

**Armament:** 12×5in/38 guns, 16×40mm AA guns; 119: 14×3in/50 replaced 40mm; 53-54: 16×5in. TT removed
**Complement:** 623

| | | | | |
|---|---|---|---|---|
| CL-53 | San Diego | Quincy | 26/07/41 | BU60 |
| CL-54 | San Juan | Quincy | 06/09/41 | BU62 |
| CL-95 | Oakland | Beth S Fran | 23/10/42 | 43-49. BU62 |
| CL-96 | Reno | Beth S Fran | 23/12/42 | BU62 |
| CL-97 | Flint | Beth S Fran | 25/01/44 | BU66 |
| CL-98 | Tucson | Beth S Fran | 03/09/44 | 45-49. BU71 |
| CL-119 | Juneau | Federal | 15/07/45 | 46-56. BU61 |
| CL-120 | Spokane | Federal | 22/09/45 | 46-50. AG-191 (66); BU73 |
| CL-121 | Fresno | Federal | 05/03/46 | 46-49. BU66 |

**Notes:** Anti-Aircraft Cruisers (CLAA). *Spokane* used as sonar test ship 1966-72.

# 'Cleveland' Class (1940-42)

**Displacement:** 10,000 tons, 13,750f/l; 106-107:
  10,500 tons, 14,000f/l
**Dimensions:** 600 (w/l) 610'1 (oa)×66'6×25
**Machinery:** Four shafts, steam turbines,

SHP 100,000=33kt
**Endurance:** 7,500/15
**Armament:** 12×6in/47, 12×5in/38, 24×40mm AA guns
**Complement:** 992

| | | | | |
|---|---|---|---|---|
| CL-55 | Cleveland | NY Sbdg | 01/11/41 | BU60 |
| CL-56 | Columbia | NY Sbdg | 17/12/41 | BU60 |
| CL-57 | Montpelier | NY Sbdg | 12/2/42 | BU60 |
| CL-58 | Denver | NY Sbdg | 04/04/42 | BU60 |
| CL-60 | Santa Fe | NY Sbdg | 10/06/42 | BU60 |
| CL-62 | Birmingham | Newport News | 20/03/42 | BU59 |
| CL-63 | Mobile | Newport News | 15/05/42 | BU60 |
| CL-64 | Vincennes | Quincy | 17/07/43 | Target 69 |
| CL-65 | Pasadena | Quincy | 28/12/43 | 44-50. BU72 |
| CL-66 | Springfield | Quincy | 09/03/44 | 44-49. CLG-7 (57). Str74 |
| CL-67 | Topeka | Quincy | 19/08/44 | 44-49. CLG-8 (57), BU75 |
| CL-80 | Biloxi | Newport News | 23/02/43 | BU62 |
| CL-81 | Houston | Newport News | 19/06/43 | BU61 |
| CL-82 | Providence | Quincy | 28/12/44 | 45-49. CLG-6 (57). Str73 |
| CL-83 | Manchester | Quincy | 05/03/46 | 46-56. BU61 |
| CL-86 | Vicksburg | Newport News | 14/12/43 | BU64 |
| CL-87 | Duluth | Newport News | 13/01/44 | 44-49. BU61 |
| CL-89 | Miami | Cramp | 08/12/42 | BU62 |
| CL-90 | Astoria | Cramp | 06/03/43 | 44-49. BU71 |
| CL-91 | Oklahoma City | Cramp | 20/02/44 | CLG-5 (57). Str79 |
| CL-92 | Little Rock | Cramp | 27/08/44 | 45-49. CLG-4 (57), BU76 |
| CL-93 | Galveston | Cramp | 22/04/45 | CLG3 (57), BU75 |
| CL-101 | Amsterdam | Newport News | 25/04/44 | Str71 |
| CL-102 | Portsmouth | Newport News | 20/09/44 | 45-49. BU74 |
| CL-103 | Wilkes-Barre | NY Sbdg | 24/12/43 | Expended 72 |
| CL-104 | Atlanta | NY Sbdg | 06/02/44 | 44-49. IX-304 (64). Target 70 |
| CL-105 | Dayton | NY Sbdg | 19/03/44 | 45-49. BU63 |
| CL-106 | Fargo | NY Sbdg | 25/02/45 | 45-50. BU71 |
| CL-107 | Huntington | NY Sbdg | 08/04/45 | 46-49. BU62 |

**Notes:** *Fargo* and *Huntingon* were of a modified type
with single funnel. *Galveston* not completed until after
conversion to missile cruiser. *Atlanta* used as explosives
test vessel.


# 'Baltimore' Class (1940-42)

**Displacement:** 13,600 tons, 17,200f/l; 122-124:
  13,700 tons, 17,500f/l
**Dimensions:** 664 (wl) 675 (oa)×70'10×26; 68-71,
  122-124: 673'5 oa
**Machinery:** Four shafts, steam turbines,
  SHP 120,000=33kt

**Endurance:** 9,000/15
**Armament:** 9×8in/55. 12×5in/38, 52×40mm. AA guns
  *1956* 20×3in replaced 40mm (73-75, 123, 124, 130, 132,
  133, 135)
**Complement:** 1,142

| | | | | |
|---|---|---|---|---|
| CA-68 | Baltimore | Quincy | 28/07/42 | 51-56. BU72 |
| CA-69 | Boston | Quincy | 26/08/42 | CAG-1 (52), BU75 |
| CA-70 | Canberra | Quincy | 19/04/43 | CAG-2 (52). Str78 |
| CA-71 | Quincy | Quincy | 23/06/43 | 52-54. BU74 |

*Above:*
**Providence** (CL-82), the 'Cleveland' class light cruiser, in 1948. Here little changed from the World War 2 appearance of this class, she was converted to a guided missile cruiser in 1957.
*Marius Bar*

*Below:*
The 'Baltimore' class cruiser *Los Angeles* (CA-135), as she appeared in the 1950s, with new radars and electronics gear. Notice the 3in mount forward of the main turrets.

| | | | | |
|---|---|---|---|---|
| CA-72 | Pittsburgh | Quincy | 22/02/44 | 51-56. BU74 |
| CA-73 | Saint Paul | Quincy | 16/09/44 | 45-71. Str78 |
| CA-74 | Columbus | Quincy | 30/11/44 | 45-59. CG12 (59), BU77 |
| CA-75 | Helena | Quincy | 28/04/45 | 45-63. BU74 |
| CA-122 | Oregon City | Quincy | 09/06/45 | BU73 |
| CA-123 | Albany | Quincy | 30/06/45 | 46-58. CG-10 (58) |
| CA-124 | Rochester | Quincy | 28/08/45 | 46-61. BU74 |
| CA-130 | Bremerton | NY Sbdg | 02/07/44 | 51-60. BU74 |
| CA-131 | Fall River | NY Sbdg | 13/08/44 | BU72 |
| CA-132 | Macon | NY Sbdg | 15/10/44 | 45-61. BU73 |
| CA-133 | Toledo | NY Sbdg | 06/05/45 | 46-60. BU74 |
| CA-135 | Los Angeles | Philadelphia | 20/08/44 | 45-48, 51-63. BU75 |
| CA-136 | Chicago | Philadelphia | 20/08/44 | 45-47. CG-11 (58). Str84 |

**Notes:** *Oregon City, Albany* and *Rochester* were of a modified type with single funnel and simpler superstructure. *Northampton* of this class completed as Tactical Command Ship (CLC-1). *Helena, Macon, Toledo* ˉnd *Los Angeles* fitted with Regulus SSM, 1956. *Boston* and *Canberra* converted to first guided missile cruisers 1952. *Chicago, Fall River* and *Oregon City* were to convert to guided missile cruisers in 1958, but last two were cancelled and replaced by *Columbus* and *Albany* in 1959.

## 'Worcester' Class (1943)

**Displacement:** 14,700 tons, 18,300f/l
**Dimensions:** 664 (w/l) 679'6 (oa)×70'8×26
**Machinery:** Four shafts, steam turbines, SHP 120,000=32kt

**Endurance:** 12,000/15
**Armament:** 12×6in/47, 24×in/50
**Complement:** 1,401

| | | | | |
|---|---|---|---|---|
| CL-144 | *Worcester* | NY Sbdg | 04/02/47 | 48-58. BU72 |
| CL-145 | *Roanoke* | NY Sbdg | 16/06/47 | 49-58. BU72 |

**Notes:** Final development of the AA cruiser concept, built around new 6in gun. The 6in guns proved unreliable. 12×40mm AA guns planned but not installed.

*Above:*
**The *Worcester* (CL-144) was a development of the anti-aircraft cruiser concept; there was a similarity in the layout of her turrets to the 'Atlanta' class ships.** *INRO*

*Below:*
**This 1960 picture shows the *Newport News* (CA-148) of the 'Des Moines' class, the ultimate American cruiser design.** *Official US Navy*

## 'Des Moines' Class (1943-44)

**Displacement:** 17,000 tons, 21,500f/l
**Dimensions:** 700 (wl) 716'6 (oa)×76'6×26
**Machinery:** Four shafts, steam turbines,
SHP 120,000=33kt

**Endurance:** 10,500/15
**Armament:** 9×8in/55, 12×5in/38, 24×3in/50 guns
**Complement:** 1,790

| | | | | |
|---|---|---|---|---|
| CA-134 | *Des Moines* | Quincy | 27/09/46 | 48-75 |
| CA-139 | *Salem* | Quincy | 25/03/47 | 49-59 |
| CA-148 | *Newport News* | Newport News | 06/03/47 | 49-75. Str78 |

**Notes:** Modified 'Oregon City' class. Carried improved
8in guns requiring larger hulls. *Newport News* had
explosion in centre gun of B turret, 1 October 1972; it
was not replaced.

## Tactical Command Ship

**Displacement:** 13,000 tons, 17,200f/l
**Dimensions:** 676 (oa)×71×29
**Machinery:** Four shafts, steam turbines,

SHP 120,000=32kt
**Armament:** 4×5in/54, 8×3in/70 guns, two helicopters
**Complement:** 1,675

| | | | | |
|---|---|---|---|---|
| CLC-1 | *Northampton* | Quincy | 17/01/51 | 53-70. CC-1 (61). Str77 |

**Notes:** Laid down as CA-125 of 'Oregon City' class,
re-ordered 1948 as a successor to AGC. Completed one
deck higher than a normal cruiser. Converted 1961 to
serve as National Emergency Command Post Afloat
(NECPA), superstructure extended forward, large radar
placed on foremast and armament reduced ultimately to
1×5in.

*Below:*
**The *Northampton* (CLC-1) was a command ship
built from the hull of a 'Oregon City' class cruiser.
The single 5in mounts forward are off centre to
clear the 125ft foremast. Notice the higher deck
level, 3in mounts amidships and large array of
electronics gear.** *Official US Navy*

# GUIDED MISSILE CRUISERS

## 'Boston' Class (1952)

**Armament:** Two twin Terrier SAM, 6×8in, 10×5in,
12×3in guns

| | | | *Completed* | |
|---|---|---|---|---|
| CAG-1 _____ | *Boston* _____ | see CA-69 _____ | 01/11/55 __ | 55-70. CA69 (68). BU75 |
| CAG-2 _____ | *Canberra* _____ | see CA-70 _____ | 15/06/56 __ | 56-70. CA70 (68). Str78 |

**Notes:** Converted from 'Baltimore' class cruisers, with missile launcher replacing aft turret, superstructure remodelled and single funnel replacing previous two.

*Below:*
**Canberra (CAG-2) in 1956, as rebuilt as a guided missile cruiser with two twin Talos launchers, visible aft. The two forward triple turrets have been retained.** *Real Photographs (N623)*

## 'Galveston' Class (1956-57)

**Armament:** 3: One twin Talos SAM, 6×6in, 6×5in guns
4-5: One twin Talos SAM, 3×6in, 2×5in guns
6-7: One twin Terrier SAM, 3×6in, 2×5in guns
8: One twin Terrier SAM, 6×6in, 6×5in guns

| | | | | |
|---|---|---|---|---|
| CLG-3 _____ | *Galveston* _____ | see CL-93 _____ | 25/05/58 __ | 58-70. BU75 |
| CLG-4 _____ | *Little Rock* _____ | see CL-92 _____ | 03/06/60 __ | 60-76. BU76 |
| CLG-5 _____ | *Oklahoma City* _____ | see CL-91 _____ | 07/09/60 __ | 60-79. Str79 |
| CLG-6 _____ | *Providence* _____ | see CL-82 _____ | 17/09/59 __ | 59-73. Str73 |

| CLG-7 | Springfield | see CL-66 | 02/07/60 | 60-74. Str74 |
| CLG-8 | Topeka | see CL-67 | 26/03/60 | 60-69. BU75 |

**Notes:** Single-ended conversion to missile cruisers, converted from 'Cleveland' class cruisers. *Galveston* was not commissioned after completion and held in reserve until conversion in 1958. *Little Rock, Oklahoma City, Providence* and *Springfield* fitted as fleet flagships.

# 'Albany' Class (1957-58)

**Armament:** Two twin Talos SAM launchers, two 2 twin Tartar SAM launchers, 2×5in/38 guns, ASROC, 2 Mk 32 triple TT.

| CG-10 | Albany | see CA-123 | 04/11/62 | 62-80. Str85 |
| CG-11 | Chicago | see CA-136 | 02/05/64 | 64-80. Str84 |
| CG-12 | Columbus | see CA-74 | 01/12/62 | 62-75. BU77 |

**Notes:** Double-ended full conversion to missile cruisers, converted from 'Baltimore' class cruisers. New superstructure with two tall combination 'macks' (combination mast and stack).

# *Long Beach* (1957)

**Displacement:** 14,200 tons, 17,350f/l
**Dimensions:** 721'4 (oa)×73'4×29
**Machinery:** Two shafts, two nuclear reactors, steam turbines; SHP 80,000=30.5kt+
**Endurance:** 360,000/20
**Armament:** Two twin Terrier launchers, one twin Talos launcher (removed 79), 2×5in/38 guns. 6×21in TT
*1981* Two twin Terrier/Standard-ER Mk 10 SAM launchers, Two quad Harpoon SSM, 2×5in/38 guns, ASROC, 6×12.75in TT. Two Phalanx CIWS added
**Complement:** 1,080

| CGN-9 | Long Beach | Quincy | 14/07/59 | 61- |

**Notes:** First nuclear-powered surface warship and first warship with guided missiles as main battery. Ordered as CLGN-160, then CG(N)-160. Originally planned with two Terrier launchers forward, Regulus amidships and twin Talos aft.

*Below:*
**Little Rock (CLG-4), a 'Cleveland' class vessel rebuilt as a missile cruiser with a twin Talos mount aft. A single main turret was retained forward with a superfiring twin 5in mount. Notice the massive superstructure and tall radar masts.**
*Official US Navy*

*Above:*
**The guided missile cruiser *Topeka* (CLG-8) was less extensively rebuilt than *Little Rock*, with a twin Terrier launcher aft. She retained both forward 6in turrets.** *Official US Navy*

*Below:*
**The *Chicago* (CG-11) in 1964, as a full double-ended conversion to a missile cruiser, with Talos SAM launchers forward and aft. Notice the Tartar launcher alongside the forward tower bridge and the 5in guns on either side of the second funnel. An ASROC launcher is between the funnels.** *Official US Navy*

# 'Leahy' Class (1958-59)

**Displacement:** 5,670 tons, 37,800f/l
**Dimensions:** 510 (wl), 533 (oa)×54'10×24'6
**Machinery:** Two shafts, steam turbines, SHP 85,000=32kt
**Endurance:** 8,000/20
**Armament:** Two Twin Terrier SAM, ASROC, DASH,

4×3in/50 guns, 6×12.75in TT
*1980* 4×3in replaced by Harpoon; two twin Mk 10 Terrier/Standard-ER launchers, two quad Harpoon launchers
*1985* Two Phalanx CIWS added
**Complement:** 423

| | | | | | |
|---|---|---|---|---|---|
| DLG-16 | *Leahy* | Bath | 01/07/61 | 62- |
| DLG-17 | *Harry E. Yarnell* | Bath | 09/12/61 | 63- |

**Long Beach (CGN-9)**, the first nuclear-powered surface warship and the first built-for-the-purpose missile cruiser, on her sea trials in 1961. Two twin Terrier launchers are forward, with a Talos mount aft; the 5in guns have not yet been mounted. The Terrier launchers were replaced with standard launchers in 1981. *Official US Navy*

**Harry E. Yarnell (DLG-17)** as completed in 1964: the vessel's classification was changed to cruiser (CG-17) in 1975. Terrier SAM and ASROC launchers are forward, with reload chambers behind them. The 'Leahy' class vessels received new armaments in the 1980s. *Official US Navy*

| | | | | |
|---|---|---|---|---|
| DLG-18 | *Worden* | Bath | 02/06/62 | 63- |
| DLG-19 | *Dale* | NY Sbdg | 28/07/62 | 62- |
| DLG-20 | *Richmond K. Turner* | NY Sbdg | 06/04/63 | 64- |
| DLG-21 | *Gridley* | PS Bridge | 31/07/61 | 63- |
| DLG-22 | *England* | Todd; S Pedro | 06/03/62 | 62- |
| DLG-23 | *Halsey* | San Francisco | 15/01/62 | 63- |
| DLG-24 | *Reeves* | Puget Sound | 12/05/62 | 64- |

**Notes:** Originally classified Frigates, reclassified CG in 1975. Introduced 'mack' superstructure, combination mast and smokestack. Carry 80 missiles for reloads. All had AAW refit in late 1960s. Harpoon replaced 3in guns in 1980s refit.

## Bainbridge (1959)

**Displacement:** 7,850 tons, 8,580f/l
**Dimensions:** 550 (wl), 565 (oa)×57'10×29
**Machinery:** Two shafts, two reactors, steam turbines;
  SHP 60,000=32kt+
**Endurance:** 90,000/20
**Armament:** Two twin Terrier SAM, ASROC, 4×3in/50

guns, 6×12.75in TT
*1982* Two twin Mk 10 Terrier/Standard-ER launchers,
two quad Harpoon launchers, guns removed
*1985* Two Phalanx CIWS added
**Complement:** 497

| | | | | |
|---|---|---|---|---|
| DLGN-25 | *Bainbridge* | Quincy | 15/04/61 | 62- |

**Notes:** Originally classified Frigate, reclassified CGN in 1975. Nuclear version of 'Leahy' class. Modernised 1975. Quad Harpoon launcher replaced 3in guns 1979.


## 'Belknap' Class (1961-62)

**Displacement:** 5,340 tons, 7,930f/l
**Dimensions:** 524 (wl), 547 (oa)×54'10×29
**Machinery:** Two shafts, steam turbines,
  SHP 85,000=34kt
**Endurance:** 7,100/20
**Armament:** One twin Terrier SAM, ASROC, DASH,

1×5in/54, 2×3in/50 guns, 6×12.75in TT
*1982* One twin Mk 10 Terrier/Standard-ER launcher,
two quad Harpoon launchers replacing 3in guns, two
Phalanx CIWS, DASH removed
**Complement:** 428

| | | | | |
|---|---|---|---|---|
| DLG-26 | *Belknap* | Bath | 20/07/63 | 64-75, 80- |
| DLG-27 | *Josephus Daniels* | Bath | 02/12/63 | 65- |
| DLG-28 | *Wainwright* | Bath | 25/04/64 | 66- |
| DLG-29 | *Jouett* | Puget Sound | 30/06/64 | 66- |
| DLG-30 | *Horne* | San Francisco | 30/10/64 | 67- |
| DLG-31 | *Sterett* | Puget Sound | 30/06/64 | 67- |
| DLG-32 | *William H. Standley* | Bath | 19/12/64 | 66- |
| DLG-33 | *Fox* | Todd; S Pedro | 21/11/64 | 66- |
| DLG-34 | *Biddle* | Bath | 02/07/65 | 67 |

**Notes:** Originally classified Frigates, reclassified CG in 1975.
  *Belknap* severely damaged in collision with carrier *John E. Kennedy* on 22 November 1975, rebuilt at Philadelphia and recommissioned 1980. First class armed with Standard SM-2ER missiles. Two quad Harpoon launchers replaced 3in guns 1980s.


## Truxtun (1962)

**Displacement:** 8,250 tons, 9,200f/l
**Dimensions:** 540 (wl), 564 (oa)×58×31
**Machinery:** Two shafts, two reactors, steam turbines;
  SHP 60,000=30kt+

**Armament:** One twin Terrier, ASROC, DASH, 1×5in/54,
  2×3in/50 guns, 2×21in TT, 4×12.75in TT
**Complement:** 538

| | | | | |
|---|---|---|---|---|
| DLGN-35 | *Truxtun* | NY Sbdg | 19/12/64 | 67- |

**Notes:** Originally classified Frigate, reclassified CGN in 1975. Modified 'Belknap' class with arrangement of armament reversed. 3in guns replaced by Harpoon SSM and 21in TT in stern, and DASH removed.


## 'California' Class (1967-68)

**Displacement:** 9,561 tons, 10,150f/l
**Dimensions:** 570 (wl), 596 (oa)×61×31'6
**Machinery:** Two shafts, two reactors, steam turbines,
  SHP 60,000=30kt+

**Armament:** Two single Tartar/Standard-MR launchers,
  2×5in/54 guns, ASROC, 4×12.75in TT. Two quad
  Harpoon launchers added
**Complement:** 540

*Above:*
**Bainbridge (DLGN-25)**, a nuclear-powered version of the 'Leahy' class, with similar armament.
*Official US Navy*

*Left:*
**Jouett (CG-29)**, a 'Belknap' class cruiser originally classified as a frigate. The raised portion behind the Terrier launcher forward is for reloading, and the white radome next to the aft funnel indicates a **Phalanx CIWS.** *Official US Navy*

*Below:*
**Truxtun (DLGN-35)**, at sea in June 1970. Notice the single 5in gun mount forward and single torpedo tubes below the bridge. **ASROC** is fired from the Terrier launcher aft. *Official US Navy*

| | | | | |
|---|---|---|---|---|
| DLGN-36 | *California* | Newport News | 22/09/71 | 74- |
| DLGN-37 | *South Carolina* | Newport News | 01/07/72 | 75- |

**Notes:** Escorts for nuclear carrier forces. A third unit authorised in 1968 not built. Helicopter landing area but no helicopters carried. Reclassified CGN in 1975.

## 'Virginia' Class (1970-75)

**Displacement:** 8,625 tons, 11,000f/l
**Dimensions:** 560 (wl), 585 (oa)×63×29'6
**Machinery:** Two shafts, two reactors, steam turbines,
  SHP 60,000=30kt+
**Armament:** Two twin Tartar/Standard-MR/Harpoon

Mk 26 launchers, 2×5in/54 guns, ASROC, 6×12.75in TT
*1985* Two Phalanx CIWS added
**Complement:** 519

| | | | | |
|---|---|---|---|---|
| CGN-38 | *Virginia* | Newport News | 14/12/74 | 76- |
| CGN-39 | *Texas* | Newport News | 09/08/75 | 77- |
| CGN-40 | *Mississippi* | Newport News | 31/07/76 | 78- |
| CGN-41 | *Arkansas* | Newport News | 21/10/78 | 80- |

**Notes:** Improved 'California' class. Construction of additional units halted in favour of 'Ticonderoga' class. Originally ordered as DLGN. Helicopter hangar in stern replaced with Tomahawk launchers 1984-88. First class to carry Mk 26 launcher to handle three different missile types.

## 'Ticonderoga' Class (1979-    )

**Displacement:** 6,560 tons, 9,200f/l
**Dimensions:** 529 (wl), 568'4 (oa)×55×31
**Machinery:** Two shafts, gas turbines,
  SHP 80,000=30kt+
**Endurance:** 6,000/20

**Armament:** Two twin Standard-MR Mk 26 or Mk 41 launchers, two quad Harpoon launchers, two Phalanx CIWS, 2×5in/54 guns, 6×12.75in TT
**Complement:** 346

| | | | | |
|---|---|---|---|---|
| CG-47 | *Ticonderoga* | Ingalls | 25/04/81 | 83- |
| CG-48 | *Yorktown* | Ingalls | 17/01/83 | 84- |
| CG-49 | *Vincennes* | Ingalls | 14/01/84 | 85- |
| CG-50 | *Valley Forge* | Ingalls | 23/06/84 | 86- |
| CG-51 | *Thomas S. Gates* | Bath | 14/12/85 | na |
| CG-52 | *Bunker Hill* | Ingalls | 11/03/85 | 86- |
| CG 53 | *Mobile Bay* | Ingalls | 24/08/85 | na |
| CG-54 | *Antietam* | Ingalls | Building | na |
| CG-55 | *Leyte Gulf* | Ingalls | Building | na |
| CG-56 | *San Jacinto* | Ingalls | Building | na |
| CG-57 | *Lake Champlain* | Ingalls | Building | na |
| CG-58 | na | Bath | Ordered | na |
| CG-59 | na | Ingalls | Ordered | na |
| CG-60 | na | Bath | Ordered | na |
| CG-61 | na | Bath | Ordered | na |
| CG-62 | na | Ingalls | Ordered | na |
| CG-63 | na | Bath | Ordered | na |
| CG-64 | na *Gettysburg* | Bath | Ordered | na |
| CG-65 | na | Ingalls | Ordered | na |

**Notes:** Originally ordered as DDG, a modification of 'Spruance' design with same hull and propulsion but enlarged superstructure and heavier armament. Intended to provide AA defence for carrier battle groups with AEGIS system, designed to automatically detect, track and attack multiple targets.
  *Bunker Hill* is first unit built with vertical launching tubes for Tomahawk. 27 ships of class planned.

*Left:*
***South Carolina* (CGN-37), with the single Tartar/ Standard launcher and 5in mount aft duplicated forward. Notice the helicopter landing pad for DASH.** *Official US Navy*

*Below:*
***Virginia* (CGN-38), whose twin launcher forward can fire Tartar, Standard and Harpoon missiles. The ship is designed to carry the AEGIS system, which can be fitted during a major overhaul.** *Official US Navy*

*Left:*
***Ticonderoga* (CG-47), a guided missile cruiser, in 1982. The panels on the forward superstructure mark the position of the AEGIS long-range multi-function radar.** *Official US Navy*

1982

## HULLS BY DYE

| CLASS | CODES: BUSHIPS 441 & 443 NAVSEC 6433, 3132 & 6128 NAVSEA 3231 | NUMBER OF HULLS | FULL LOAD DISPLACEMENT (TONS) | TOTAL DISPLACEMENT (TONS) |
|-------|------|------|------|------|
| DEG 7 | DESIGN | 8 | 4,100 | 32,800 |
| DD 445 | MODIFICATION | 12 | 2,830 | 33,960 |
| DD 692 | MODIFICATION (FRAM) | 21 | 3,320 | 69,720 |
| DD 710 | MODIFICATION (FRAM I) | 14 | 3,500 | 49,000 |
| DD 931 | DESIGN/MODIFICATION | 23 | 3,960 | 91,080 |
| DDG 2 | DESIGN/MODIFICATION | 28 | 4,500 | 126,000 |
| DDG 37 | DESIGN DLG 6/9 | 10 | 5,370 | 53,700 |
| CLC 3 | MODIFICATION | 6 | 14,670 | 88,020 |
| CG 10 | MODIFICATION | 9 | 19,000 | 171,000 |
| CG 16 | DESIGN/MODIFICATION | 9 | 7,000 | 63,000 |
| CG 26 | DESIGN/MODIFICATION | 1 | 7,900 | 7,900 |
| CGN 9 | DESIGN/MODIFICATION | 1 | 17,100 | 17,100 |
| CGN 35 | DESIGN | 1 | 9,130 | 9,130 |
| CGN 36 | DESIGN | 2 | 9,560 | 19,120 |
| CGN 38 | DESIGN | 4 | 9,470 | 37,880 |
| DD 963 | DESIGN | 31 | 8,000 | 248,000 |
| DDG 993 | DESIGN | 4 | 8,500 | 34,000 |
| FF 1037 | DESIGN/MODIFICATION | 2 | 2,650 | 5,300 |
| FF 1040 | DESIGN/MODIFICATION | 10 | 3,400 | 34,000 |
| FF 1052 | DESIGN/MODIFICATION | 46 | 3,880 | 178,480 |
| FFG 1 | DESIGN/MODIFICATION | 6 | 3,590 | 21,540 |
| FFG 7 | DESIGN | 52 | 3,900 | 202,800 |
| CG 47 | DESIGN | 5 | 10,400 | 52,000 |
| PG 84 | DESIGN | 7 | 240 | 1,680 |
| PCG 612 | DESIGN | 4 | 380 | 1,520 |
| PGG 511 | DESIGN | 9 | 500 | 4,500 |
| BB 61 | MODIFICATION | 4 | 59,000 | 236,000 |
| DDG 51 | DESIGN | ? | | |

DESIGNS - 21 CLASSES
MODIFICATION - 15 CLASSES    329 HULLS    1,889,230 (TONS)

# Retirement Luncheon

for

# *Lloyd Dye*

## Thursday, April 1, 1982

# Howard Johnson's

GUEST _____

# DESTROYERS

## 'Benson-Livermore' Class (1938-41)

**Displacement:** 1,620 tons, 2,580f/l
**Dimensions:** 341 (wl), 348'3 (oa)×36'1×18
**Machinery:** Two shafts, steam turbines,
  SHP 50,000=33kt

**Endurance:** 6,500/12
**Armament:** 4×5in/38 guns, 10×21in TT
**Complement:** 208

| | | | | |
|---|---|---|---|---|
| DD-421 | Benson | Quincy | 15/11/39 | Taiwan *Lo Yang* (54) |
| DD-422 | Mayo | Quincy | 26/03/40 | BU72 |
| DD-423 | Gleaves | Bath | 09/12/39 | BU72 |
| DD-424 | Niblack | Bath | 18/05/40 | BU73 |
| DD-425 | Madison | Boston | 20/10/39 | Str68 |
| DD-427 | Hilary P. Jones | Charleston | 14/12/39 | Taiwan *Han Yang* (54) |
| DD-428 | Charles F. Hughes | Puget Sound | 16/05/40 | Str68 |
| DD-429 | Livermore | Bath | 03/08/40 | 40-50. BU61 |
| DD-430 | Eberle | Bath | 14/09/40 | 40-51. Greek *Niki* (51) |
| DD-431 | Plunkett | Federal | 09/03/40 | Taiwan *Nan Yang* (69) |
| DD-432 | Kearny | Federal | 09/03/40 | BU72 |
| DD-435 | Grayson | Charleston | 07/08/40 | BU72 |
| DD-437 | Woolsey | Bath | 12/02/41 | BU74 |
| DD-438 | Ludlow | Bath | 11/11/40 | 41-51. Greek *Doxa* (51) |
| DD-439 | Edison | Federal | 23/11/40 | Str66 |
| DD-440 | Ericsson | Federal | 23/11/40 | BU71 |
| DD-441 | Wilkes | Boston | 31/05/40 | BU72 |
| DD-442 | Nicholson | Boston | 31/05/40 | 41-51. Italian *Aviere* (51) |
| DD-443 | Swanson | Charleston | 02/11/40 | BU72 |
| DD-460 | Woodworth | Beth: S Fran | 29/11/41 | 42-51. Italian *Artigliere* (51) |
| DD-484 | Buchanan | Federal | 22/11/41 | Turkish *Gelibolu* (49) |
| DD-486 | Landsdowne | Federal | 20/02/42 | Turkish *Gaziantep* (49) |
| DD-487 | Lardner | Federal | 20/03/42 | Turkish *Gemlik* (49) |
| DD-488 | McCalla | Federal | 20/03/42 | Turkish *Giresun* (49) |
| DD-491 | Farenholt | Staten Is | 19/11/41 | Str71 |
| DD-492 | Bailey | Staten Is | 19/12/41 | Str68 |
| DD-497 | Frankford | Staten Is | 17/05/42 | Str71 |
| DD-598 | Bancroft | Quincy | 31/12/41 | BU73 |
| DD-600 | Boyle | Quincy | 15/06/42 | Str71 |
| DD-601 | Champlin | Quincy | 25/07/42 | BU72 |
| DD-602 | Meade | Staten Is | 15/02/42 | Str71 |
| DD-603 | Murphy | Staten Is | 29/04/42 | BU71 |
| DD-604 | Parker | Staten Is | 12/05/42 | BU71 |
| DD-605 | Caldwell | Beth; S Fran | 15/01/42 | BU66 |
| DD-606 | Coghlan | Beth; S Fran | 12/02/42 | BU74 |
| DD-607 | Frazier | Beth; S Fran | 17/03/42 | BU72 |
| DD-608 | Gansevoort | Beth; S Fran | 11/04/42 | Target 72 |
| DD-609 | Gillespie | Beth; S Fran | 08/05/42 | Target 72 |
| DD-610 | Hobby | Beth; S Fran | 04/06/42 | Target 72 |
| DD-611 | Kalk | Beth; S Fran | 18/07/42 | Str68 |

| | | | | | |
|---|---|---|---|---|---|
| DD-612 | Kendrick | Beth; S Pedro | 02/04/42 | Target 66 |
| DD-613 | Laub | Beth; S Pedro | 28/04/42 | BU75 |
| DD-614 | Mackenzie | Beth; S Pedro | 27/06/42 | Target 74 |
| DD-615 | McLanahan | Beth; S Pedro | 07/09/42 | BU74 |
| DD-616 | Nields | Quincy | 01/10/42 | BU72 |
| DD-617 | Ordronaux | Quincy | 09/11/42 | BU73 |
| DD-619 | Edwards | Quincy | 19/07/42 | BU72 |
| DD-623 | Nelson | Quincy | 15/09/42 | BU69 |
| DD-624 | Baldwin | Seattle | 14/06/42 | Lost 15/04/61 |
| DD-626 | Satterlee | Seattle | 17/07/42 | BU72 |
| DD-628 | Welles | Seattle | 07/09/42 | BU69 |
| DD-638 | Herndon | Norfolk | 05/02/42 | Target 74 |
| DD-641 | Tillman | Charleston | 20/12/41 | BU72 |
| DD-645 | Stevenson | Federal | 11/11/42 | Str68 |
| DD-646 | Stockton | Federal | 11/11/42 | Str71 |
| DD-647 | Thorn | Federal | 28/02/43 | Target 74 |

**Notes:** All laid up after 1946. For units of this class converted to minesweepers (DMS), see page 122.

# 'Fletcher' Class (1940-42)

**Displacement:** 2,050 tons, 3,040f/l
**Dimensions:** 369'3 (wl), 376'6 (oa)×39'8×17'9
**Machinery:** Two shafts, steam turbines, SHP 60,000=37kt

**Endurance:** 6,500/15
**Armament:** 5×5in/38, 10×40mm AA guns, 10×21in TT
Units marked*: 4×5in/38, 6×3in/50 guns
**Complement:** 273

| | | | | |
|---|---|---|---|---|
| DD-445 | Fletcher | Federal | 03/05/42 | 49-69. DDE; Str69 |
| DD-446 | Radford | Federal | 03/05/42 | 49-69. DDE; Str69 |
| DD-447 | Jenkins | Federal | 21/06/42 | 51-69. DDE; Str69 |
| DD-448 | La Vallette | Federal | 21/06/42 | Sold 74 |
| DD-449 | Nicholas | Bath | 19/02/42 | 51-70. DDE; Str70 |
| DD-450 | O'Bannon | Bath | 14/03/42 | 51-70. DDE; Str70 |
| DD-465 | Saufley | Federal | 19/07/42 | 49-64. DDE; Target 68 |
| DD-466 | Waller | Federal | 15/08/42 | 50-69. DDE; Target 70 |
| DD-468 | Taylor | Bath | 07/06/42 | 51-69. DDE; Italian Lanciere (69) |
| DD-470 | Bache | Staten Is | 07/07/42 | 51-68. Lost 06/02/68 |
| DD-471 | Beale | Staten Is | 24/08/42 | 51-68. DDE; Target 69 |
| DD-472 | Guest | Boston | 20/02/42 | Brazilian Para (59) |
| DD-473 | Bennett | Boston | 16/04/42 | Brazilian Paraiba (59) |
| DD-474 | Fullam | Boston | 16/04/42 | Target 62 |
| DD-475 | Hudson | Boston | 03/06/42 | BU73 |
| DD-478 | Stanly | Charleston | 02/05/42 | BU72 |
| DD-479 | Stevens | Charleston | 24/06/42 | BU73 |
| DD-480 | Halford | Puget Sound | 29/10/42 | Str68 |
| DD-498 | Philip | Federal | 13/10/42 | 50-68. DDE; Sold 71 |
| DD-499 | Renshaw | Federal | 13/10/42 | 50-69. DDE; BU70 |
| DD-500 | Ringgold | Federal | 11/11/42 | W German Z-2 (59) |
| DD-501 | Schroeder | Federal | 11/11/42 | BU73 |
| DD-502 | Sigsbee | Federal | 07/12/42 | BU75 |
| DD-507 | Conway | Bath | 16/08/42 | 50-69. DDE; Target 70 |
| DD-508 | Cony | Bath | 30/08/42 | 49-69. DDE; Target 69 |
| DD-509 | Converse | Bath | 30/08/42 | Spanish Almirante Valdes (59) |
| DD-510 | Eaton | Bath | 20/09/42 | 51-69. DDE; Target 69 |

*Above:*
**Waller** (DDE-466), a 'Fletcher' class conversion to an escort destroyer. Notice the bank of ASW torpedo tubes between the funnels, and the Weapon A mount in 'B' position.

*Below:*
**The Sullivans** (DD-537), a typical four-gun 'Fletcher' class unit, during the 1950s. Notice the hedgehog alongside 'B' turret and the small ASW torpedo tubes just to the right of the second funnel. This vessel was named after five brothers who died in 1942 when the cruiser *Juneau* was sunk, and is now preserved as a memorial at **Buffalo, NY.** *Our Navy*

| | | | | |
|---|---|---|---|---|
| DD-511 | Foote | Bath | 11/10/42 | BU73 |
| DD-513 | Terry | Bath | 22/11/42 | Sold 74 |
| DD-515 | Anthony | Bath | 20/12/42 | W German *Z-1* (58) |
| DD-516 | Wadsworth | Bath | 10/01/43 | W German *Z-3* (59; Greek *Nearchos* (80) |
| DD-517 | Walker | Bath | 31/01/43 | 51-69. DDE; Italian *Fante* (69) |
| DD-519 | Daly* | Staten Is | 24/10/42 | 51-60. BU76 |
| DD-520 | Isherwood* | Staten Is | 24/11/42 | 51-61. Peruvian *Guise* (61) |
| DD-521 | Kimberly | Staten Is | 04/02/43 | 51-66. Taiwan *An Yang* (67) |
| DD-527 | Ammen* | Beth; S Fran | 17/09/42 | 51-60. Damaged 19/07/60, not repaired |
| DD-528 | Mullany* | Beth; S Fran | 10/10/42 | 51-71. Taiwan *Chiang Yang* (71) |

| | | | | |
|---|---|---|---|---|
| DD-530 | Trathen* | Beth; S Fran | 22/10/42 | 50-65. Target 72 |
| DD-531 | Hazelwood | Beth; S Fran | 20/11/42 | 51-65. BU76 |
| DD-532 | Heermann* | Beth; S Fran | 05/12/42 | 51-57. Argentine Brown (61) |
| DD-534 | McCord | Beth; S Fran | 10/01/43 | 51-54. BU73 |
| DD-535 | Miller* | Beth; S Fran | 07/03/43 | 51-64. James Miller (71); BU75 |
| DD-536 | Owen | Beth; S Fran | 21/03/43 | 51-58. BU73 |
| DD-537 | The Sullivans* | Beth; S Fran | 04/04/43 | 51-65. Memorial 77 |
| DD-538 | Stephen Potter* | Beth; S Fran | 28/04/43 | 51-58. BU73 |
| DD-539 | Tingey | Beth; S Fran | 28/05/43 | 51-63. Target 66 |
| DD-540 | Twining | Beth; S Fran | 11/07/43 | 50-71. Taiwan Kwei Yang (71) |
| DD-541 | Yarnall* | Beth; S Fran | 25/07/43 | 51-58. Taiwan Kuen Yang (68) |
| DD-544 | Boyd* | Beth; S Pedro | 29/10/42 | 50-69. Turkish Iskenderun (69) |
| DD-545 | Bradford | Beth; S Pedro | 12/12/42 | 50-61. Greek Thyella (62) |
| DD-546 | Brown | Beth; S Pedro | 21/02/43 | 50-62. Greek Navarinon (62) |
| DD-547 | Cowell* | Beth; S Pedro | 18/03/43 | 51-71. Argentine Almirante Storni (71) |
| DD-550 | Capps | Gulf | 31/05/42 | Spanish Lepanto (57) |
| DD-551 | David W. Taylor | Gulf | 04/07/42 | Spanish Almirante Ferrandiz (57) |
| DD-553 | John D. Henley | Gulf | 15/11/42 | Str68 |
| DD-554 | Franks | Seattle | 07/12/42 | BU74 |
| DD-556 | Hailey* | Seattle | 09/03/43 | 51-60. Brazilian Pernambuco (61) |
| DD-558 | Laws | Seattle | 22/04/43 | 51-64. BU73 |
| DD-561 | Prichett* | Seattle | 31/07/43 | 51-68. Italian Geniere (70) |
| DD-562 | Robinson | Seattle | 28/08/43 | 51-64. Str74 |
| DD-563 | Ross* | Seattle | 10/09/43 | 51-59. Str74 |
| DD-564 | Rowe* | Seattle | 30/09/43 | 51-59. Str74 |
| DD-565 | Smalley | Seattle | 27/10/43 | 51-57. BU65 |
| DD-566 | Stoddard* | Seattle | 19/11/42 | 50-69. Str75 |
| DD-567 | Watts | Seattle | 31/12/43 | 51-64. BU74 |
| DD-568 | Wren | Seattle | 29/01/44 | 51-63. BU75 |
| DD-569 | Aulick | Consolidated | 02/03/42 | Greek Sfendoni (59) |
| DD-570 | Charles Ausburne | Consolidated | 16/03/42 | W German Z-6 (60) |
| DD-571 | Claxton | Consolidated | 01/04/42 | W German Z-4 (59) |
| DD-572 | Dyson | Consolidated | 15/04/42 | W German Z-5 (60) |
| DD-573 | Harrison | Consolidated | 07/05/42 | Mexican Cuauhtemoc (71) |
| DD-574 | John Rodgers | Consolidated | 07/05/42 | Mexican Cuitlahuac (71) |
| DD-575 | McKee | Consolidated | 02/08/42 | BU73 |
| DD-576 | Murray | Consolidated | 16/08/42 | 51-65. DDE; BU66 |
| DD-577 | Sproston | Consolidated | 31/08/42 | 50-68. DDE; BU71 |
| DD-578 | Wickes | Consolidated | 13/09/42 | Target 72 |
| DD-580 | Young | Consolidated | 11/10/42 | Str68 |
| DD-581 | Charrette | Boston | 03/06/42 | Greek Velos (59) |
| DD-582 | Conner | Boston | 18/07/42 | Greek Aspis (59) |
| DD-583 | Hall | Boston | 18/07/42 | Greek Lonkhi (60) |
| DD-585 | Haraden | Boston | 19/03/43 | BU73 |
| DD-587 | Bell | Charleston | 24/06/42 | Target 75 |
| DD-588 | Burns | Charleston | 08/08/42 | Target 74 |
| DD-589 | Izard | Charleston | 08/08/42 | Str68 |
| DD-590 | Paul Hamilton | Charleston | 07/04/43 | Str68 |
| DD-592 | Howorth | Puget Sound | 10/01/43 | Target 62 |
| DD-593 | Killen | Puget Sound | 10/01/43 | Used as target 64-75 |
| DD-594 | Hart | Puget Sound | 25/09/44 | BU73 |
| DD-595 | Metcalf | Puget Sound | 25/09/44 | BU72 |
| DD-596 | Shields | Puget Sound | 25/09/44 | 50-72. Brazilian Maranhao (72) |

| | | | | |
|---|---|---|---|---|
| DD-597 | _Wiley_ | Puget Sound | 25/09/44 | Str68 |
| DD-629 | _Abbot*_ | Bath | 17/02/43 | 51-65. BU75 |
| DD-630 | _Braine*_ | Bath | 07/03/43 | 51-71. Argentine _Almirante Domecq Garcia_ (71) |
| DD-631 | _Erben_ | Bath | 21/03/43 | 51-58. Korean _Chung Mu_ (63) |
| DD-642 | _Hale*_ | Bath | 04/04/43 | 51-60. Colombian _Antioquia_ (61) |
| DD-643 | _Sigourney_ | Bath | 24/04/43 | 51-60. BU75 |
| DD-644 | _Stembel*_ | Bath | 08/05/43 | 51-58. Argentine _Rosales_ (61) |
| DD-649 | _Albert W. Grant_ | Charleston | 29/05/43 | BU72 |
| DD-650 | _Caperton*_ | Bath | 22/05/43 | 51-60. BU75 |
| DD-651 | _Cogswell*_ | Bath | 05/06/43 | 51-69. Turkish _Izmit_ (69) |
| DD-652 | _Ingersoll*_ | Bath | 28/06/43 | 51-70. Target 74 |
| DD-653 | _Knapp_ | Bath | 10/07/43 | 51-57. BU73 |
| DD-654 | _Bearss*_ | Gulf | 25/07/43 | 51-63. BU76 |
| DD-655 | _John Hood_ | Gulf | 25/10/43 | 51-64. BU76 |
| DD-656 | _Van Valkenburgh_ | Gulf | 19/12/43 | 51-54. Turkish _Izmir_ (67) |
| DD-657 | _Charles J. Badger_ | Staten Is | 03/04/43 | 51-59. Sold 73 |
| DD-658 | _Colahan_ | Staten Is | 03/05/43 | 50/66. Target 67 |
| DD-659 | _Dashiell ˣ_ | Federal | 06/02/43 | 51-60. BU75 |
| DD-660 | _Bullard_ | Federal | 28/02/43 | BU73 |
| DD-661 | _Kidd_ | Federal | 28/02/43 | 51-64. Str74 |
| DD-662 | _Bennion_ | Boston | 04/07/43 | Str71 |
| DD-663 | _Heywood L. Edwards_ | Boston | 06/10/43 | Japanese _Ariake_ (59) |
| DD-664 | _Richard P. Leary_ | Boston | 06/10/43 | Japanese _Yugure_ (59) |
| DD-665 | _Bryant_ | Charleston | 29/05/43 | Target 69 |
| DD-666 | _Black*_ | Federal | 28/03/43 | 51-69. Str69 |
| DD-667 | _Chauncey_ | Federal | 28/03/43 | 50-54. BU73 |
| DD-668 | _Clarence K. Bronson_ | Federal | 18/04/43 | 51-60. Turkish _Istanbul_ (67) |
| DD-669 | _Cotten*_ | Federal | 12/06/43 | 51-60. BU75 |
| DD-670 | _Dortch*_ | Federal | 20/06/43 | 51-57. Argentine _Espora_ (61) |
| DD-671 | _Gatling_ | Federal | 20/06/43 | 51-60. Str74 |
| DD-672 | _Healy_ | Federal | 04/07/43 | 51-58. BU76 |
| DD-673 | _Hickox_ | Federal | 04/07/43 | 51-57. Korean _Pusan_ (68) |
| DD-674 | _Hunt*_ | Federal | 01/08/43 | 51-63. BU75 |
| DD-675 | _Lewis Hancock_ | Federal | 01/08/43 | 51-57. Brazilian _Piaui_ (67) |
| DD-676 | _Marshall_ | Federal | 29/08/43 | 51-69. BU70 |
| DD-677 | _McDermut*_ | Federal | 17/10/43 | 50-63. BU66 |
| DD-678 | _McGowan*_ | Federal | 14/11/43 | 51-60. Spanish _Jorge Juan_ (60) |
| DD-679 | _McNair*_ | Federal | 14/11/43 | 51-63. BU75 |
| DD-680 | _Melvin_ | Federal | 17/10/43 | 51-54. BU75 |
| DD-681 | _Hopewell*_ | Beth; S Pedro | 02/05/43 | 51-70. Str70 |
| DD-682 | _Porterfield_ | Beth; S Pedro | 13/06/43 | 51-69. Str75 |
| DD-683 | _Stockham_ | Beth; S Fran | 25/06/43 | 51-57. Str74 |
| DD-684 | _Wedderburn_ | Beth; S Fran | 01/08/43 | 50-69. Str69 |
| DD-685 | _Picking*_ | Staten Is | 01/06/43 | 51-69. Str75 |
| DD-686 | _Halsey Powell_ | Staten Is | 30/06/43 | 51-68. Korean _Seoul_ (68) |
| DD-687 | _Uhlmann*_ | Staten Is | 30/07/43 | 43-72. BU74 |
| DD-688 | _Remey_ | Bath | 25/07/43 | 51-63. BU75 |
| DD-689 | _Wadleigh*_ | Bath | 07/08/43 | 51-62. Chilean _Blanco Encalada_ (62) |
| DD-690 | _Norman Scott_ | Bath | 28/08/43 | BU73 |
| DD-691 | _Mertz_ | Bath | 11/09/43 | Str70 |
| DD-793 | _Cassin Young_ | Beth; S Pedro | 12/09/43 | 51-60. Str74 |
| DD-794 | _Irwin_ | Beth; S Pedro | 31/10/43 | 51-58. Brazilian _Santa Catarina_ (68) |

DD-795 _____ Preston* _____ Beth; S Pedro _____ 12/12/43 __ 51-69. Turkish *Icel* (69)
DD-796 _____ Benham* _____ Staten Is _____ 30/08/43 __ 51-60. Peruvian *Villar* (60)
DD-797 _____ Cushing _____ Staten Is _____ 30/09/43 __ 51-60. Brazilian *Parana* (61)
DD-798 _____ Monssen _____ Staten Is _____ 30/10/43 __ 51-57. BU63
DD-799 _____ Jarvis* _____ Todd; Seattle _____ 14/01/44 __ 51-60. Spanish *Alcala Galiano* (60)
DD-800 _____ Porter _____ Todd; Seattle _____ 13/03/44 __ 51-53. BU74
DD-802 _____ Gregory _____ Todd; Seattle _____ 08/05/44 __ 50-66. Str66
DD-804 _____ Rooks* _____ Todd; Seattle _____ 06/06/44 __ 51-62. Chilean *Cochrane* (62)

**Notes:** Seventeen units converted to escort destroyers (DDE) with 2×5in, 4×3in guns, 4×21in fixed TT and Hedgehog, 1950-52. All were to be given FRAM II refit but only *Radford*, *Jenkins* and *Nicholas* were refitted retaining Weapon A, Hedgehog, DASH and funnel caps; FRAM refit for others cancelled. All DDE reclassified DD 1962. As DASH test ship, *Hazelwood* was fitted with experimental helicopter pad replacing Nos 3 and 4 5in guns, 1959. *Tingey* damaged in collision with escort *Vammen* 1963, not repaired.

# 'Allen M. Sumner' Class (1942-43)

**Displacement:** 2,290 tons, 3,320f/l
**Dimensions:** 369 (wl), 376'6 (oa)×40'10×19
**Machinery:** Two shafts, steam turbines, SHP 60,000=34kt

**Endurance:** 6,500/15
**Armament:** 6×5in/38, 12×40mm AA guns, 10×21in TT (many 5)
**Complement:** 336

DD-692 _____ Allen M. Sumner* _____ Federal _____ 15/12/43 __ 44-73. BU74
DD-693 _____ Moale* _____ Federal _____ 16/01/44 __ 44-73. BU74
DD-694 _____ Ingraham* _____ Federal _____ 16/01/44 __ 44-71. Greek *Miaoulis* (71)
DD-696 _____ English _____ Federal _____ 27/02/44 __ 44-70. Taiwan *Hueiyang* (70)
DD-697 _____ Charles S. Sperry* _____ Federal _____ 13/03/44 __ 44-73. Chilean *Ministro Zenteno* (74)
DD-698 _____ Ault* _____ Federal _____ 26/03/44 __ 44-73. BU74
DD-699 _____ Waldron* _____ Federal _____ 26/03/44 __ 44-73. Colombian *Santander* (75)
DD-700 _____ Haynsworth _____ Federal _____ 15/04/44 __ 47-70. Taiwan *Yuen Yang* (70)
DD-701 _____ John W. Weeks _____ Federal _____ 21/05/44 __ 47-70. Target 70
DD-702 _____ Hank _____ Federal _____ 21/05/44 __ 44-72. Argentine *Segui* (72)
DD-703 _____ Wallace L. Lind* _____ Federal _____ 14/06/44 __ 44-73. Korean *Daegu* (73)
DD-704 _____ Borie* _____ Federal _____ 04/07/44 __ 44-69. Argentine *Hipolito Bouchard* (72)
DD-705 _____ Compton _____ Federal _____ 17/09/44 __ 44-72. Brazilian *Mato Grosso* (72)
DD-706 _____ Gainard _____ Federal _____ 17/09/44 __ 44-71. BU74
DD-707 _____ Soley _____ Federal _____ 08/09/44 __ 44-47, 49-70. Target 70
DD-708 _____ Harlan R. Dickson _____ Federal _____ 17/12/44 __ 45-73. BU73
DD-709 _____ Hugh Purvis* _____ Federal _____ 17/12/44 __ 45-72. Turkish *Zafer* (72)
DD-722 _____ Barton _____ Bath _____ 10/10/43 __ 49-68. Str68
DD-723 _____ Walke* _____ Bath _____ 27/10/43 __ 50-70. BU75
DD-724 _____ Laffey* _____ Bath _____ 21/11/43 __ 51-75. Target 75
DD-725 _____ O'Brien* _____ Bath _____ 08/12/43 __ 50-72. Target 72
DD-727 _____ De Haven* _____ Bath _____ 09/01/44 __ 44-71. Korean *In Cheon* (73)
DD-728 _____ Mansfield* _____ Bath _____ 29/01/44 __ 44-71. Str75
DD-729 _____ Lyman K. Swenson* ___ Bath _____ 12/02/44 __ 44-71. BU74
DD-730 _____ Collett* _____ Bath _____ 05/03/44 __ 44-70. Argentine *Piedrabuena* (74)
DD-731 _____ Maddox _____ Bath _____ 19/03/44 __ 44-69. Taiwan *Po Yang* (72)
DD-732 _____ Hyman _____ Bath _____ 08/04/44 __ 44-69. BU70
DD-734 _____ Purdy _____ Bath _____ 07/05/44 __ 44-73. BU74
DD-744 _____ Blue* _____ Staten Is _____ 28/11/43 __ 50-71. Target 74
DD-745 _____ Brush _____ Staten Is _____ 28/12/43 __ 44-69. Taiwan *Hsiang Yang* (60)
DD-746 _____ Taussig* _____ Staten Is _____ 25/01/44 __ 44-70. Taiwan *Lo Yang* (74)
DD-747 _____ Samuel N. Moore _____ Staten Is _____ 23/02/44 __ 44-69. Taiwan *Heng Yang* (69)

*Above:*
**The 'Sumner' class destroyer *Waldron* (DD-699) after FRAM conversion, with a DASH hangar aft.**
*Official US Navy*

*Below:*
**The *Willard Keith* (DD-775) entering Pearl Harbor in March 1954. This 'Sumner' class unit is in original configuration, with 21 in torpedo tubes between the funnels.** *Official US Navy*

| | | | | |
|---|---|---|---|---|
| DD-748 | *Harry E. Hubbard* | Staten Is | 24/03/44 | 50-69. BU70 |
| DD-752 | *Alfred A. Cunningham\** | Staten Is | 03/08/44 | 50-71. Target 1974 |
| DD-753 | *John R. Pierce* | Staten Is | 01/09/44 | 44-73. BU74 |
| DD-754 | *Frank E. Evans\** | Staten Is | 03/10/44 | 45-69. Lost 02/06/69 |
| DD-755 | *John A. Bole\** | Staten Is | 01/11/44 | 45-70. BU74 |

| DD-756 | Beatty | Staten Is | 30/11/44 | 45-65. Venezuelan *Carabobo* (72) |
| DD-757 | Putnam* | Beth; S Fran | 26/03/44 | 44-73. BU74 |
| DD-758 | Strong* | Beth; S Fran | 23/04/44 | 49-73. Brazilian *Rio Grande Do Norte* (73) |
| DD-759 | Lofberg* | Beth; S Fran | 12/08/44 | 45-71. BU74 |
| DD-760 | John W. Thomason | Beth; S Fran | 30/09/44 | 45-70. Taiwan *Nan Yang* (74) |
| DD-761 | Buck* | Beth; S Fran | 11/03/45 | 46-72. Brazilian *Alagoas* (73) |
| DD-762 | Henley | Beth; S Fran | 08/04/45 | 46-73. BU74 |
| DD-770 | Lowry* | Beth; S Pedro | 06/02/44 | 50-72. Brazilian *Espirito Santo* (73) |
| DD-775 | Willard Keith | Beth; S Pedro | 29/08/44 | 50-72. Colombian *Caldas* (72) |
| DD-776 | James C. Owens* | Beth; S Pedro | 01/10/44 | 45-73. Brazilian *Sergipe* (73) |
| DD-777 | Zellars* | Todd; Seattle | 19/07/44 | 44-71. Iranian *Babr* (73) |
| DD-778 | Massey* | Todd; Seattle | 19/08/44 | 44-69. BU74 |
| DD-779 | Douglas H. Fox | Todd; Seattle | 30/09/44 | 44-73. Chilean *Ministro Portales* (74) |
| DD-780 | Stormes* | Todd; Seattle | 04/11/44 | 45-70. Iranian *Palang* (73) |
| DD-781 | Robert K. Huntington* | Todd; Seattle | 05/12/44 | 45-73. Venezuelan *Falcon* (73) |
| DD-857 | Bristol | Beth: S Pedro | 29/10/44 | 45-69. Taiwan *Hwa Yang* (69) |

**Notes:** Twelve units completed as minelayers (DM) (see page 121). FRAM II refits given units marked*, 1959-62: DASH hangar and deck, VDS, two Mk 25 and three triple Mk 32 TT, new radar added. FRAM II refit gave a lifetime extension of five years.

*Mansfield*, *Brush* and *Barton* damaged by mines off Korea, 1950-52. *English* lost bow in collision with *Wallace L. Lind* 1953. *Collett* lost bow in collision with *Ammen* 1960, repaired with bow of incomplete *Seaman*. *Beatty* damaged in collision with carrier *Intrepid* 1958.

# 'Gearing' Class (1942-43)

**Displacement:** 2,425 tons, 3,500f/l
**Dimensions:** 383 (wl) 390'6 (oa)×41'1×19
**Machinery:** Two shafts, steam turbines, SHP 60,000=35kt

**Endurance:** 6,370/12 (trials)
**Armament:** 6×5in/38, 12×40mm AA guns (DDE and 837, 848: 4×5in) 5×21in TT
**Complement:** 336

| DD-710 | Gearing | Federal | 18/02/45 | 45-73. BU74 |
| DD-711 | Eugene A. Greene | Federal | 18/03/45 | 45-72. DDR; Spanish *Churruca* (72) |
| DD-712 | Gyatt | Federal | 15/04/45 | 45-69. DDG (55), DDG-1 (57-62); Target 70 |
| DD-713 | Kenneth D. Bailey | Federal | 17/06/45 | 45-70. DDR; BU75 |
| DD-714 | William R. Rush | Federal | 08/07/45 | 45-78. DDR; Korean *Kang Won* (78) |
| DD-715 | William M. Wood | Federal | 29/07/45 | 45-76. DDR; Target 83 |
| DD-716 | Wiltsie | Federal | 31/08/45 | 46-76. Pakistani *Tariq* (77) |
| DD-717 | Theodore E. Chandler | Federal | 20/10/45 | 46-75. BU75 |
| DD-718 | Hamner | Federal | 24/11/45 | 46-79. Taiwan *Chao Yang* (80) |
| DD-719 | Epperson | Federal | 22/12/45 | 49-75. DDE; Pakistani *Taimur* (77) |
| DD-742 | Frank Knox | Bath | 17/09/44 | 44-70. DDR: Greek *Themistocles* (71) |
| DD-743 | Southerland | Bath | 05/10/44 | 44-81. DDR; str |
| DD-763 | William C. Lawe | Beth; S Fran | 21/05/45 | 44-83. Str83 |
| DD-764 | Lloyd Thomas | Beth; S Fran | 05/10/45 | 47-72. DDE; Taiwan *Dang Yang* (72) |
| DD-765 | Keppler | Beth; S Fran | 24/6/46 | 47-72. DDE; Turkish *Tinaztepe* (72) |
| DD-782 | Rowan | Todd; Seattle | 29/12/44 | 45-75. Taiwan *Chao Yang* (77), lost 22/08/77 |
| DD-783 | Gurke | Todd; Seattle | 15/02/45 | 45-76. Greek *Tompazis* (77) |
| DD-784 | McKean | Todd; Seattle | 31/03/45 | 45-81. DDR; str82 |
| DD-785 | Henderson | Todd; Seattle | 28/05/45 | 45-81. Pakistani *Tughril* (80) |
| DD-786 | Richard B. Anderson | Todd; Seattle | 07/07/45 | 45-75. Taiwan *Kai Yang* (75) |
| DD-787 | James B. Kyes | Todd; Seattle | 04/08/45 | 46-73. Taiwan *Chien Yang* (73) |
| DD-788 | Hollister | Todd; Seattle | 09/10/45 | 46-79. Taiwan (83). |
| DD-789 | Eversole | Todd; Seattle | 08/01/46 | 46-73. Turkish *Gayret* (73) |
| DD-790 | Shelton | Todd; Seattle | 08/03/46 | 46-73. Taiwan *Laoyang* (73) |

Above:
**Shelton** (DD-790) after FRAM refit, with DASH hangar and landing pad aft. Notice the ASROC launcher between the funnels. *Official US Navy*

Below:
**Basilone** (DD-824), the former escort destroyer, after FRAM refit. Her 5in turrets were retained fore and aft, and ASROC is carried amidships. *Official US Navy*

DD-805 ____ *Chevalier* _____ Bath _____ 29/10/44 ___ 45-72. DDR; Korean *Chung Buk* (72)

DD-806 ____ *Higbee* _____ Bath _____ 12/11/44 ___ 45-79. DDR; Target

DD-807 ____ *Benner* _____ Bath _____ 30/11/44 ___ 45-70. DDR; BU75

DD-808 ____ *Dennis J. Buckley* ____ Bath _____ 20/12/44 ___ 45-73. DDR; BU74

DD-817 ____ *Corry* _____ Consolidated ____ 28/07/45 ___ 46-81. DDR; Greek *Kriezis* (81)

DD-818 ____ *New* _____ Consolidated ____ 18/08/45 ___ 46-76. DDE; Korean *Taejon* (77)

DD-819 ____ *Holder* _____ Consolidated ____ 25/08/45 ___ 46-76. DDE; Ecuadorean
                                                              *Presidente Eloy Alfaro* (78)

DD-820 ____ *Rich* _____ Consolidated ____ 05/10/45 ___ 46-73. DDE; Str77

DD-821 ____ *Johnston* _____ Consolidated ____ 19/10/45 ___ 46-81. Taiwan (81)

DD-822 ____ *Robert H. McCard* ____ Consolidated ____ 09/11/45 ___ 46-80. Turkish *Kilic Ali Pasa* (80)

DD-823 ____ *Samuel B. Roberts* ____ Consolidated ____ 30/11/45 ___ 46-70. Target 71

DD-824 ____ *Basilone* _____ Consolidated ____ 21/12/45 ___ 49-77. DDE; Str77

DD-825 ____ *Carpenter* _____ Consolidated ____ 28/12/45 ___ 49-81. DDK (48), DDE (50), Turkish
                                                              *Anittepe* (81)

DD-826 ____ *Agerholm* _____ Bath _____ 30/03/46 ___ 46-78. Target 82

DD-827 ____ *Robert A. Owens* ____ Bath _____ 15/07/46 ___ 49-81. DDE

DD-828 ____ *Timmerman* _____ Bath _____ 19/05/51 ___ 52-56. EAG-152 (54), BU59

DD-829 ____ *Myles C. Fox* ____ Bath _____ 13/01/45 ___ 45-79. DDR; Greek *Apostolis* (80)

DD-830 ____ *Everett F. Larson* ____ Bath _____ 28/01/45 ___ 45-72. DDR; Korean *Jeongbuk* (72)

| | | | | | |
|---|---|---|---|---|---|
| DD-831 | Goodrich | Bath | 25/02/45 | 45-69. DDR; BU77 |
| DD-832 | Hanson | Bath | 11/03/45 | 45-73. DDR; Taiwan *Liao Yang* (73) |
| DD-833 | Herbert J. Thomas | Bath | 25/03/45 | 45-70. DDR; Taiwan *Han Yang* (74) |
| DD-834 | Turner | Bath | 08/04/45 | 45-69. DDR; BU70 |
| DD-835 | Charles P. Cecil | Bath | 22/04/45 | 45-79. DDR; BU80 |
| DD-836 | George K. Mackenzie | Bath | 13/05/45 | 34-76. Target 76 |
| DD-837 | Sarsfield | Bath | 27/05/45 | 45-77. Taiwan *Te Yang* (77) |
| DD-838 | Ernest G. Small | Bath | 14/06/45 | 45-70. DDR; Taiwan *Fu Yang* (71) |
| DD-839 | Power | Bath | 30/6/45 | 45-77. Taiwan *Shen Yang* (77) |
| DD-840 | Glennon | Bath | 14/07/45 | 45-76. Target 81 |
| DD-841 | Noa | Bath | 30/07/45 | 45-73. Spanish *Blas De Lezo* (73) |
| DD-842 | Fiske | Bath | 08/09/45 | 45-81. DDR; Turkish *Piyale Pasa* (80) |
| DD-843 | Warrington | Bath | 27/09/45 | 45-72. BU74 |
| DD-844 | Perry | Bath | 25/10/45 | 46-73. BU74 |
| DD-845 | Bausell | Bath | 19/11/45 | 46-78. Target 79 |
| DD-846 | Ozbourn | Bath | 22/12/45 | 46-75. BU75 |
| DD-847 | Robert L. Wilson | Bath | 05/01/46 | 46-74. DDE; Str74 |
| DD 848 | Witck | Bath | 02/02/46 | 46-68. EDD (46), str68 |
| DD-849 | Richard E. Kraus | Bath | 02/03/46 | 46-76. AG-151 (47-51), |
| | | | | Korean *Kwang Ju* (77) |
| DD-850 | Joseph P. Kennedy Jr | Quincy | 26/7/45 | 45-73. Str73 |
| DD-851 | Rupertus | Quincy | 21/09/45 | 46-73. Greek *Koundouriotis* (73) |
| DD-852 | Leonard F. Mason | Quincy | 04/01/46 | 46-76. Taiwan *Lai Yang* (78) |
| DD-853 | Charles H. Roan | Quincy | 15/03/46 | 46-73. Turkish *M. Fevzi Cakmak* (73) |
| DD-858 | Fred T. Berry | Beth; S Pedro | 28/01/45 | 45-70. DDE; Target 72 |
| DD-859 | Norris | Beth; S Pedro | 25/02/45 | 45-70. DDE; Turkish *Kocatepe* (75) |
| DD-860 | McCaffery | Beth; S Pedro | 12/04/45 | 45-70. DDE; BU74 |
| DD-861 | Harwood | Beth; S Pedro | 22/05/45 | 45-71. DDE; Turkish *Kocatepe* (71); |
| | | | | lost 21/07/74 |
| DD-862 | Vogelgesang | Staten Is | 15/01/45 | 45-82. Mexican *Quetzalcoatl* (82) |
| DD-863 | Steinaker | Staten Is | 13/02/45 | 45-82. DDR; Mexican *Netzahuacoyotl* (82) |
| DD-864 | Harold J. Ellison | Staten Is | 14/03/45 | 45-83. Pakistani *Shah Jehan* (83) |
| DD-865 | Charles R. Ware | Staten Is | 12/04/45 | 45-74. Str74 |
| DD-866 | Cone | Staten Is | 10/05/45 | 45-82. Pakistani *Alamgir* (82) |
| DD-867 | Stribling | Staten Is | 08/06/45 | 45-76. Target 80 |
| DD-868 | Brownson | Staten Is | 07/07/45 | 45-76. BU77 |
| DD-869 | Arnold J. Isbell | Staten Is | 06/08/45 | 46-73. Greek *Sakhtouris* (73) |
| DD-870 | Fechteler | Staten Is | 19/09/45 | 46-70. DDR; BU70 |
| DD-871 | Damato | Staten Is | 21/11/45 | 46-81. DDE; Pakistani *Tippu Sultan* (80) |
| DD-872 | Forrest Royal | Staten Is | 17/01/46 | 46-71. Turkish *Adatepe* (71) |
| DD-873 | Hawkins | Consolidated | 07/10/44 | 45-79. DDR; BU83 |
| DD-874 | Duncan | Consolidated | 27/10/44 | 45-71. DDR; Str73 |
| DD-875 | Henry W. Tucker | Consolidated | 08/11/44 | 45-73. DDR; Brazilian *Marcilio Dias* (73) |
| DD-876 | Rogers | Consolidated | 20/11/44 | 45-81. DDR; Korean *Jeongju* (81) |
| DD-877 | Perkins | Consolidated | 07/12/44 | 45-73. DDR; Argentine *Comodoro Py* (73) |
| DD-878 | Vesole | Consolidated | 29/12/44 | 45-76. DDR; Target 83 |
| DD-879 | Leary | Consolidated | 20/01/45 | 45-73. DDR; Spanish *Langara* (73) |
| DD-880 | Dyess | Consolidated | 26/01/45 | 45-81. DDR; Greece (81) |
| DD-881 | Bordelon | Consolidated | 03/03/45 | 45-77. DDR; Str77 |
| DD-882 | Furse | Consolidated | 09/03/45 | 45-72. DDR; Spanish *Gravina* (72) |
| DD-883 | Newman K. Perry | Consolidated | 17/03/45 | 45-81. DDR; Korean *Kyong Kai* (81) |
| DD-884 | Floyd B. Parks | Consolidated | 31/03/45 | 45-73. BU74 |
| DD-885 | John R. Craig | Consolidated | 14/04/45 | 45-79. Str79 |

Top:
**Robert A. Owens** (DDE-827) of the 'Gearing' class
in 1958. The vessel was completed as a hunter-
killer in 1949. Notice the new twin 3in and
Weapon A mounts fore and aft, and the different
bridge.

Above:
**Warrington** (DD-843), a 'Gearing' class destroyer
in July 1958, appearing little altered from her
original condition.  *Wright & Logan*

Below:
The 'Gearing' class radar picket destroyer **Vesole**
(DDR-878) in July 1956, showing her additional
radar aft.  *Official US Navy*

| DD-886 | Orleck | Consolidated | 12/05/45 | 45-82. Turkish *Yucetepe* (82) |
| DD-887 | *Brinkley Bass* | Consolidated | 26/05/45 | 45-73. Brazilian *Mariz e Barros* (73) |
| DD-888 | *Stickell* | Consolidated | 26/05/45 | 45-72. DDR; Greek *Kanaris* (72) |
| DD-889 | *O'Hare* | Consolidated | 22/06/45 | 45-73. DDR; Spanish *Mendez Nunez* (73) |
| DD-890 | *Meredith* | Consolidated | 28/06/45 | 45-79. Turkish *Savas Tepe* (79) |

**Notes:** Three incomplete units (766, 767, 791) scrapped 1958. *Epperson* and *Basilone* converted to DDE 1949 with four×5in guns, 4 fixed TT, Weapon A and Hedgehog. *Carpenter* and *Robert A. Owens* completed at Newport News as prototype ASW hunter-killers (DDK); *Lloyd Thomas, Keppler, Fred T. Berry, Norris, McCaffery* and *Harwood* converted to DDK with 4×3in/50 guns, two Hedgehogs. DDK changed to DDE 1950. 3in/50 replaced by 70 calibre guns 1957, but immediately reverted to 50 calibre. *New, Holder, Rich, Robert L. Wilson* and *Damato* converted to DDE with B mount replaced by Hedgehog.

24 converted to radar pickets (DDR) 1945, TT removed, 6×3in replaced 40mm guns in some; small tripod mast between funnels. 12 more (711-714, 784, 817, 838, 842, 863, 870, 888, 889) converted to DDR 1952. The heavier radar installation could not be mounted on a mast and arrangement of 3in guns was changed. *Gyatt* converted to guided missile destroyer with twin Terrier launcher 1955, removed 1962. *Richard E. Kraus* used as sonar training ship until 1953. *Timmerman* had experimental light-weight machinery with 100,000hp designed for cancelled *Percival* (DD-452), modified bow and different fire control system. *Agerholm* made the only test firing

of a nuclear depth charge 11 May 1962.

All units (except as noted) given FRAM I refit in 1960s for improved ASW. FRAM I included new superstructure and stacks, hangar for two DASH drones, ASROC launcher amidships, no VDS. One twin 5in mount, TT and secondary battery removed. DASH included in FRAM design before it was fully tested. System was a failure with over half the helicopter drones crashing within five years. The landing pad was too lightly constructed for heavier manned helicopters.

All DDE and DDR reverted to DD except 6 DDR. FRAM II refits given to former DDR-805, 807, 830 and 877 and former DDE-764-765, 858-861; similar to FRAM I but no ASROC. DDR-713, 742, 831, 834, 838 and 874 received VDS, no DASH.

*Frank Knox* ran aground in South China Sea 18 July 1965, not refloated until 25 August. *Ernest G. Small* mined and lost bow off Korea October 1951, repaired with bow of incomplete *Seymour D. Owens*. *Ozbourn* lost bow in collision with *Theodore E. Chandler* 1948. *Charles H. Roan* lost bow in collision with *Brownson* 1950. *Floyd B. Parks* lost bow in collision with cruiser *Columbus* 1956, repaired with bow of incomplete *Lansdale*.

# 'Forrest Sherman' Class (1952-56)

**Displacement:** 2,850 tons, 4,050f/l
**Dimensions:** 407' (wl) 418'6 (oa)×45'2×20
**Machinery:** Two shafts, steam turbines, SHP 70,000=33kt

**Endurance:** 4,500/20
**Armament:** 3×5in/54, 4×3in/50 guns 4×21in TT, six fixed TT
**Complement:** 337

| DD-931 | *Forrest Sherman* | Bath | 05/02/55 | 55-82. |
| DD-932 | *John Paul Jones* | Bath | 07/05/55 | 56-82. DDG-32 (67) |
| DD-933 | *Barry* | Bath | 01/10/55 | 55-82. Str83 |
| DD-936 | *Decatur* | Quincy | 15/12/55 | 56-83. DDG-31 (66) |
| DD-937 | *Davis* | Quincy | 28/03/56 | 57-82 |
| DD-938 | *Jonas Ingram* | Quincy | 08/07/56 | 57-83. Str83 |
| DD-940 | *Manley* | Bath | 12/04/56 | 57-83 |
| DD-941 | *Dupont* | Bath | 08/09/56 | 57-83 |
| DD-942 | *Bigelow* | Bath | 02/02/57 | 57-82 |
| DD-943 | *Blandy* | Quincy | 19/12/56 | 57-82 |
| DD-944 | *Mullinnix* | Quincy | 18/03/57 | 58-83 |
| DD-945 | *Hull* | Bath | 10/08/57 | 58-83. Str83. Target |
| DD-946 | *Edson* | Bath | 01/01/58 | 58- |
| DD-947 | *Somers* | Bath | 30/05/58 | 59-82. DDG-34 (67) |
| DD-948 | *Morton* | Ingalls | 23/05/58 | 59-82 |
| DD-949 | *Parsons* | Ingalls | 19/08/58 | 59-82. DDG-33 (67) |
| DD-950 | *Richard S. Edwards* | PS Bridge | 24/09/57 | 59-82 |
| DD-951 | *Turner Joy* | PS Bridge | 05/05/58 | 59-82 |

**Notes:** First destroyers designed and built after World War 2. Units after 936 had higher freeboard. Only 931 and 932 completed with TT. Eight units (933, 937, 938, 940, 941, 943, 948, 950) modified for ASW with 1×5in

*Above:*
**The *Jonas Ingram* (DD-938) during trials in 1970 after her refit, which included an ASROC launcher replacing the 5in mount amidships. 'Forrest Sherman' class units were all decommissioned in 1983.** *Official US Navy*

*Right:*
***Parsons* (DDG-33), a 'Forrest Sherman' class destroyer, was converted to a missile destroyer with ASROC amidships and Tartar launcher aft. Two tall trellis masts were added for electronics apparatus.** *Official US Navy*

*Below:*
***Caron* (DD-970) of the 'Spruance' class, in May 1980, showing the 5in mount and ASROC forward.** *Mike Lennon*

gun replaced by 8-tube ASROC launcher. 3in guns removed in 1960s. Four units converted to DDG with ASROC between funnels; conversion programme cancelled because of high cost and limited value of Tartar SAM. *Hull* was test ship for 8in Mk 71 gun 1975-79. Decommissioned 1982-83.

**Notes:** DD-927-930 became DL-2-5, 1951. DD-934 was the former Japanese *Hanazuki*, DD-935 the former German *T-35* and DD-939 the former German *Z-39*. DD-952-959 became DDG-2-9, 1957. DD-960-962 were OSP for Japan and Pakistan.

## 'Spruance' Class (1970-78)

**Displacement:** 5,830 tons, 7,800f/l
**Dimensions:** 529 (wl) 563'3 (oa)×55'2×29
**Machinery:** Two shafts, gas turbines, SHP 80,000=33kt
**Endurance:** 6,000/20

**Armament:** 2×5in/54 guns, 1×8 tube ASROC launcher, one Sea Sparrow launcher, two quad Harpoon launchers, 6×12.75in, two Mk 32 ASW launchers; two Phalanx CIWS added
**Complement:** 324

| | | | | |
|---|---|---|---|---|
| DD-963 | Spruance | Ingalls | 10/11/73 | 75- |
| DD-964 | Paul F. Foster | Ingalls | 23/02/74 | 76- |
| DD-965 | Kinkaid | Ingalls | 25/05/74 | 76- |
| DD-966 | Hewitt | Ingalls | 24/08/74 | 76- |
| DD-967 | Elliott | Ingalls | 19/12/74 | 77- |
| DD-968 | Arthur W. Radford | Ingalls | 01/03/75 | 77- |
| DD-969 | Peterson | Ingalls | 21/06/75 | 77- |
| DD-970 | Caron | Ingalls | 24/06/75 | 77- |
| DD-971 | David R. Ray | Ingalls | 23/08/75 | 77- |
| DD-972 | Oldendorf | Ingalls | 21/10/75 | 78- |
| DD-973 | John Young | Ingalls | 07/02/76 | 78- |
| DD-974 | Comte de Grasse | Ingalls | 26/03/76 | 78- |
| DD-975 | O'Brien | Ingalls | 08/07/76 | 77- |
| DD-976 | Merrill | Ingalls | 01/09/76 | 78- |
| DD-977 | Briscoe | Ingalls | 15/12/76 | 78- |
| DD-978 | Stump | Ingalls | 29/01/77 | 78- |
| DD-979 | Conolly | Ingalls | 19/02/77 | 78- |
| DD-980 | Moosbrugger | Ingalls | 23/07/77 | 78- |
| DD-981 | John Hancock | Ingalls | 29/10/77 | 79- |
| DD-982 | Nicholson | Ingalls | 11/11/77 | 79- |
| DD-983 | John Rodgers | Ingalls | 25/02/78 | 79- |
| DD-984 | Leftwich | Ingalls | 08/04/78 | 79- |
| DD-985 | Cushing | Ingalls | 17/06/78 | 79- |
| DD-986 | Harry W. Hill | Ingalls | 10/08/78 | 79- |
| DD-987 | O'Bannon | Ingalls | 25/09/78 | 79- |
| DD-988 | Thorn | Ingalls | 14/11/78 | 80- |
| DD-989 | Deyo | Ingalls | 20/01/79 | 80- |
| DD-990 | Ingersoll | Ingalls | 10/03/79 | 80- |
| DD-991 | Fife | Ingalls | 01/05/79 | 80- |
| DD-992 | Fletcher | Ingalls | 16/06/79 | 80- |
| DD-997 | Hayler | Ingalls | 02/03/82 | 83 |

**Notes:** Replacements for 'Sumner' and 'Gearing' classes for ASW. Technical problems delayed construction. Built by single shipyard for ease of design and mass production; new yard established at Pascagoula by Ingalls. First major Navy surface combatant vessels built with gas turbines. Funnels off centre to port and starboard. To be fitted with vertical launch system for Tomahawk and ASROC.

# FRIGATES
## (Old Designation)

## *Norfolk* (1948)

**Displacement:** 5,600 tons, 7,300f/l
**Dimensions:** 520 (wl), 540'2 (oa)×53'6×26
**Machinery:** Two shafts, steam turbines,
SHP 80,000=32kt

**Endurance:** 6,000/20
**Armament:** 8×3in/50, 8×21in TT, Weapon A
**Complement:** 546

| | | | | |
|---|---|---|---|---|
| DL-1 | *Norfolk* | NY Sbdg | 29/12/51 | 53-70. BU74 |
| CLK-2 | *New Haven* | Philadelphia | na | Cancelled 1951 |

**Notes:** Originally ordered as Hunter-Killer Cruiser
(CLK), later Destroyer Leader. Used mostly as a test ship.
Conversion to Terrier DLG cancelled. Too expensive for
ASW unit.

*Below:*
***Norfolk*** **(DL-1) as an ASROC test ship c1963.**
**Notice the ASROC launcher forward of the aft gun**
**mounts, and also the two Weapon A mounts**
**forward.** *Our Navy*

## 'Mitscher' Class (1948)

**Displacement:** 3,675 tons, 4,770f/l
**Dimensions:** 450 (wl), 493 (oa)×50×21
**Machinery:** Two shafts, steam turbines,
SHP 80,000=35kt

**Endurance:** 4,500/20
**Armament:** 2×5in/54, 4×3in/70 guns, 4×21in TT,
Weapon A
**Complement:** 440

| | | | | |
|---|---|---|---|---|
| DL-2 | *Mitscher* | Bath | 26/01/52 | 53-78. DDG-35 (67), Str78 |
| DL-3 | *John S. McCain* | Bath | 12/07/52 | 53-78. DDG-36 (67), Str78 |
| DL-4 | *Willis A. Lee* | Quincy | 26/01/52 | 54-69. BU73 |
| DL-5 | *Wilkinson* | Quincy | 23/04/52 | 54-69. BU75 |

**Notes:** Originally ordered as DD-927-930, reclassified
1951. Designed as fast ocean escorts; machinery
unreliable. Conversion to DDG included 3in guns
replaced by ASROC forward and Tartar launcher aft;
quadruped trellis masts for radars added. Conversion of
others to DDG-37-38 cancelled 1969.

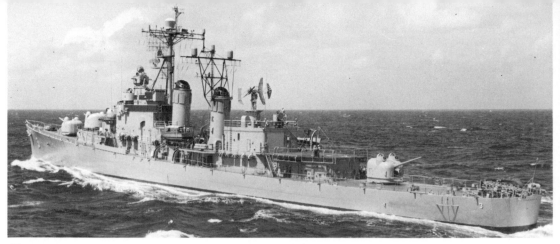

*Above:*
**John S. McCain (DL-3)**, a 'Mitscher' class frigate,
in March 1965. One 3in mount aft has been
replaced by a DASH hangar and pad.
*Official US Navy*

*Below:*
**Preble (DLG-15)** in June 1970. This 'Farragut' class
missile frigate is carrying a twin Terrier launcher
aft and an ASROC launcher forward. The ship's
classification changed to missile destroyer
(DDG-46) in 1975. *Official US Navy*

# 'Farragut' Class (1956-57)

**Displacement:** 4,150 tons; increased to 4,700 tons,
5,800f/l
**Dimensions:** 490 (wl), 512'6 (oa)×52'6×25
**Machinery:** Two shafts, steam turbines,
SHP 85,000=34kt; 6-8, 14-15: SHP 80,000

**Endurance:** 5,000/20
**Armament:** 1×5in/54, 4×3in/50 guns, one twin Terrier,
ASROC, 6×21in TT
**Complement:** 392

| | | | | | |
|---|---|---|---|---|---|
| DLG-6 | Farragut | Quincy | 18/07/58 | 61- | DDG-37 (75) |
| DLG-7 | Luce | Quincy | 11/12/58 | 61- | DDG-38 (75) |
| DLG-8 | MacDonough | Quincy | 09/07/59 | 61- | DDG-39 (75) |
| DLG-9 | Coontz | Puget Sound | 06/12/58 | 60- | DDG-40 (75) |
| DLG-10 | King | Puget Sound | 06/12/58 | 60- | DDG-41 (75) |
| DLG-11 | Mahan | San Francisco | 07/10/59 | 60- | DDG-42 (75) |
| DLG-12 | Dahlgren | Philadelphia | 16/03/60 | 61- | DDG-43 (75) |
| DLG-13 | William V. Pratt | Philadelphia | 16/03/60 | 61- | DDG-44 (75) |
| DLG-14 | Dewey | Bath | 30/11/58 | 59- | DDG-45 (75) |
| DLG-15 | Preble | Bath | 23/05/59 | 60- | DDG-46 (75) |

**Notes:** First missile ships built from the keel up;
reclassified Guided Missile Destroyers 1975.

# GUIDED MISSILE DESTROYERS

## 'Charles F. Adams' Class (1957-61)

**Displacement:** 3,370 tons, 4,500f/l
**Dimensions:** 420 (wl), 437 (oa)×47×22
**Machinery:** Two shafts, steam turbines,
  SHP 70,000=31.5kt

**Endurance:** 4,500/20
**Armament:** 2×5in/54 guns, twin Tartar, ASROC,
  6×12.75in TT
**Complement:** 354

| | | | | | |
|---|---|---|---|---|---|
| DDG-2 | Charles F. Adams | Bath | 08/09/59 | 60- | |
| DDG-3 | John King | Bath | 30/01/60 | 61- | |
| DDG-4 | Lawrence | NY Sbdg | 27/02/60 | 62- | |
| DDG-5 | Biddle | NY Sbdg | 04/06/60 | 62- | . Claude V. Ricketts (64) |
| DDG-6 | Barney | NY Sbdg | 10/12/60 | 62- | |
| DDG-7 | Henry B. Wilson | Defoe | 23/04/59 | 60- | |
| DDG-8 | Lynde McCormick | Defoe | 28/07/59 | 61- | |
| DDG-9 | Towers | Todd; Seattle | 23/04/59 | 61- | |
| DDG-10 | Sampson | Bath | 21/05/60 | 61- | |
| DDG-11 | Sellers | Bath | 09/09/60 | 61- | |
| DDG 12 | Robison | Defoe | 27/04/60 | 61- | |
| DDG-13 | Hoel | Defoe | 04/08/60 | 62- | |
| DDG-14 | Buchanan | Todd; Seattle | 11/05/60 | 62- | |
| DDG-15 | Berkeley | NY Sbdg | 29/07/61 | 62- | |
| DDG-16 | Joseph Strauss | NY Sbdg | 09/12/61 | 63- | |
| DDG-17 | Conyngham | NY Sbdg | 19/05/62 | 63- | |
| DDG-18 | Semmes | Avondale | 20/05/61 | 62- | |
| DDG-19 | Tattnall | Avondale | 26/08/61 | 63- | |
| DDG-20 | Goldsborough | PS Bridge | 16/12/61 | 63 | |
| DDG-21 | Cochrane | PS Bridge | 18/07/62 | 64- | |
| DDG-22 | Benjamin Stoddert | PS Bridge | 08/01/63 | 64- | |
| DDG-23 | Richard E. Byrd | Todd; Seattle | 06/02/62 | 64- | |
| DDG-24 | Waddell | Todd; Seattle | 26/02/63 | 64 | |

**Notes:** Intended as missile version of 'Forrest Sherman' class. Final units had sonar mounted in bow. DDG-25-27 of this class were built for Australia and DDG-28-30 for West Germany. DDG-1 was *Gyatt* of 'Gearing' class. Only DDG-19, 20 and 22 will be modernised for extension of service life. Class was well regarded when built but hulls do not allow for installation of Harpoon launchers or Phalanx.

**Notes:** DDG-31-46 were reclassified units of 'Forrest Sherman', 'Mitscher' and 'Farragut' classes.

## 'Kidd' Class (1979)

**Displacement:** 6,210 tons, 8,140f/l
**Dimensions:** 529 (wl), 563'3 (oa)×55×30
**Machinery:** Two shafts, gas turbines,
  SHP 80,000=30kt+
**Endurance:** 6,000/20

**Armament:** Two twin Standard-ER launchers, two
  quad Harpoon launchers, 2×5in/54 guns, ASROC,
  6×12.75in TT
**Complement:** 338

| | | | | | |
|---|---|---|---|---|---|
| DDG-993 | Kidd | Ingalls | 13/10/79 | 81- | |
| DDG-994 | Callaghan | Ingalls | 19/01/80 | 81- | |

| DDG-995 | Scott | Ingalls | 29/03/80 | 81- |
| DDG-996 | Chandler | Ingalls | 24/05/80 | 82- |

**Notes:** Originally six units were ordered for Iran; two cancelled and remaining four purchased by USN 1979. Iranian names were to be *Kouroush, Daryush, Nader* and *Andudshirvan*. Missile versions of 'Spruance' class. Harpoon and Phalanx added after completion.

# 'Arleigh Burke' Class (1985)

**Displacement:** 8,200 tons f/l
**Dimensions:** 466 (oa)×59×27
**Machinery:** Two shafts, gas turbines, SHP 100,000=30kt+
**Endurance:** 5,000/20

**Armament:** 90 cell VLS Standard-SM two Tomahawk (ASROC) launchers, two quad Harpoon launchers, 1×5in/54 gun, two Phalanx CIWS, 6×12.75in TT
**Complement:** 325

| DDG-51 | Arleigh Burke | Bath | Ordered | na |

**Notes:** Twenty-nine units proposed. Steel superstructure. To be smaller and less expensive than 'Ticonderoga' class with same propulsion plant and Aegis. Vertical missile launchers for Tomahawk, Standard and ASROC missiles. Planned to enter service 1991, to replace 'Charles F. Adams' and 'Farragut' classes.

*Above:*
**Richard F. Byrd (DDG-23) of the highly satisfactory 'Charles F. Adams' class, with ASROC amidships and Tartar launcher aft. The type is considered too small for upgrading with new Harpoon or Phalanx weapons.**

*Left:*
**The 'Kidd' class guided missile destroyer, Chandler (DDG-996) underway in March 1982.**
*Official US Navy*

# FRIGATES
## (Formerly Destroyer Escorts)

## 'Buckley' Class (1942-43)

**Displacement:** 1,400 tons, 2,000f/l
**Dimensions:** 300 (wl), 306 (oa)×37×14
**Machinery:** Two shafts, turbine electric,
  SHP 12,000=23.5kt
**Endurance:** 6,000/12

**Armament:** 3×3in/50, 6×40mm AA guns, 3×21in TT;
  2×5in/38 (DE-217-219, 678-680, 696-698, 700-701,
  DER)
**Complement:** 186

| | | | | |
|---|---|---|---|---|
| DE-51 | Buckley | Hingham | 09/01/43 | DER (49-54), sold 69 |
| DE-57 | Fogg | Hingham | 20/03/43 | DER (49-54), BU66 |
| DE-59 | Foss | Hingham | 10/04/43 | 43-57. Str65 |
| DE-153 | Reuben James | Norfolk | 06/02/43 | DER (49-54), Target 71 |
| DE-198 | Lovelace | Norfolk | 04/07/43 | Target 69 |
| DE-199 | Manning | Charleston | 01/06/43 | Sold 69 |
| DE-200 | Neuendorf | Charleston | 01/06/43 | Target 68 |
| DE-201 | James E. Craig | Charleston | 22/07/43 | Str68 |
| DE-202 | Eichenberger | Charleston | 22/07/43 | BU73 |
| DE-203 | Thomason | Charleston | 23/08/43 | Sold 69 |
| DE-210 | Otter | Charleston | 23/10/43 | Str69 |
| DE-213 | William T. Powell | Charleston | 27/11/43 | 44-49, 50-57. DER (49-54) BU66 |
| DE-214 | Scott | Philadelphia | 03/04/43 | BU67 |
| DE-217 | Coolbaugh | Philadelphia | 29/05/43 | 43-60. BU73 |
| DE-218 | Darby | Philadelphia | 29/05/43 | 50-62. Str68 |
| DE-219 | J. Douglas Blackwood | Philadelphia | 29/05/43 | 51-70. Target 71 |
| DE-220 | Francis M. Robinson | Philadelphia | 29/05/43 | 44-60. BU73 |
| DE-221 | Solar | Philadelphia | 29/05/43 | Lost 30/04/46 |
| DE-222 | Fowler | Philadelphia | 03/07/43 | Sold 66 |
| DE-223 | Spangenberg | Philadelphia | 03/07/43 | DER (49-54). BU66 |
| DE-575 | Ahrens | Hingham | 21/12/43 | BU67 |
| DE-577 | Alexander J. Luke | Hingham | 28/12/43 | DER (49-54), Str70 |
| DE-578 | Robert I. Paine | Hingham | 30/12/43 | DER (49-54), BU69 |
| DE-633 | Foreman | Beth; S Fran | 01/08/43 | Str65 |
| DE-634 | Whitehurst | Beth; S Fran | 05/09/43 | 50-69. Target 71 |
| DE-638 | Willmarth | Beth; S Fran | 21/11/43 | BU68 |
| DE-639 | Gendreau | Beth; S Fran | 12/12/43 | BU73 |
| DE-640 | Fieberling | Beth; S Fran | 02/04/44 | Sold 72 |
| DE-641 | William C. Cole | Beth; S Fran | 02/04/44 | Sold 72 |
| DE-642 | Paul G. Baker | Beth; S Fran | 12/03/44 | BU70 |
| DE-643 | Damon M. Cummings | Beth; S Fran | 18/04/44 | BU73 |
| DE-644 | Vammen | Beth; S Fran | 21/05/44 | 52-69. Target 71 |
| DE-665 | Jenks | Dravo | 11/09/43 | BU68 |
| DE-666 | Durik | Dravo | 09/10/43 | BU67 |
| DE-667 | Wiseman | Dravo | 06/11/43 | 50-73. BU74 |
| DE-678 | Harmon | Quincy | 25/07/43 | BU67 |
| DE-679 | Greenwood | Quincy | 21/08/43 | 51-67. BU67 |
| DE-680 | Loeser | Quincy | 11/09/43 | 51-68. Str68 |
| DE-681 | Gillette | Quincy | 25/09/43 | BU73 |

*Above:*
**Vammen (DE-644), seen as an experimental ASW ship. Notice the large hedgehog abaft the forward gun.** *Official US Navy*

| | | | | |
|---|---|---|---|---|
| DE-683 | Henry R. Kenyon | Quincy | 30/10/43 | BU70 |
| DE-696 | Spangler | Defoe | 15/07/43 | 43-58. BU72 |
| DE-697 | George | Defoe | 14/08/43 | 43-58. BU70 |
| DE-698 | Raby | Defoe | 04/09/43 | 43-53. DEC (49-57). BU69 |
| DE-699 | Marsh | Defoe | 25/09/43 | 44-69. BU74 |
| DE-700 | Currier | Defoe | 14/10/43 | 44-60. Target 67 |
| DE-701 | Osmus | Defoe | 04/11/43 | BU73 |
| DE-702 | Earl V. Johnson | Defoe | 24/11/43 | BU68 |
| DE-703 | Holton | Defoe | 15/12/43 | BU74 |
| DE-704 | Cronin | Defoe | 05/01/44 | 51-53. DEC (50-57). Str70 |
| DE-705 | Frybarger | Defoe | 25/01/44 | 50-54. DEC (50-57). BU73 |
| DE-790 | Borum | Consolidated | 14/08/43 | BU76 |
| DE-791 | Maloy | Consolidated | 18/08/43 | 43-65. EDE (46). BU66 |
| DE-795 | Gunason | Consolidated | 16/10/43 | Target 74 |
| DE-796 | Major | Consolidated | 23/10/43 | BU73 |
| DE-797 | Weeden | Consolidated | 27/10/43 | 44-58. BU69 |
| DE-798 | Varian | Consolidated | 06/11/43 | BU73 |
| DE-799 | Scroggins | Consolidated | 06/11/43 | BU67 |
| DE-800 | Jack W. Wilke | Consolidated | 18/12/43 | 44-60. BU74 |

**Notes:** Type TE. *Buckley, Fogg, Reuben James, William T. Powell, Spangenberg, Alexander J. Luke* and *Robert I. Paine* converted to radar pickets (DER) 1945 had only 2×5in guns, no TT, reverted to DE 1954.

*Vammen* converted to experimental ASW 1951. *Maloy* fitted with experimental VDS 1960. *Cronin, Frybarger* and *Raby* converted to Control Escort Ships.

# 'Cannon' Class (1942)

**Displacement:** 1,240 tons, 1,900f/l
**Dimensions:** 306 (oa)×36'8×14
**Machinery:** Two shafts, diesel-electric, SHP 6,000=21kt

**Endurance:** 6,000/12
**Armament:** 3×3in/50, 2×40mm guns, 3×21in TT
**Complement:** 186

| | | | | |
|---|---|---|---|---|
| DE-102 | Thomas | Dravo | 31/07/43 | Chinese *Tai Ho* (48) |
| DE-103 | Bostwick | Dravo | 30/08/43 | Chinese *Tai Tsang* (48) |
| DE-104 | Breeman | Dravo | 04/09/43 | Chinese *Tai Hu* (48) |
| DE-105 | Burrows | Dravo | 02/10/43 | Dutch *Van Amstel* (50) |
| DE-112 | Carter | Dravo | 29/02/44 | Chinese *Tai Chao* (48) |
| DE-113 | Clarence L. Evans | Dravo | 22/03/44 | French *Berbere* (52) |
| DE-162 | Levy | Federal | 28/03/43 | BU74 |

| | | | | |
|---|---|---|---|---|
| DE-163 | McConnell | Federal | 28/03/43 | BU74 |
| DE-164 | Osterhaus | Federal | 18/04/43 | BU74 |
| DE-165 | Parks | Federal | 18/04/43 | BU73 |
| DE-166 | Baron | Federal | 09/05/43 | Uruguayan *Uruguay* (52) |
| DE-167 | Acree | Federal | 09/05/43 | BU73 |
| DE-168 | Amick | Federal | 27/05/43 | Japanese *Asahi* (55); Philippine *Datu Sikatuna* (76) |
| DE-169 | Atherton | Federal | 27/05/43 | Japanese *Hatsuhi* (55); Philippine *Rajah Humabon* (76) |
| DE-170 | Booth | Federal | 21/06/43 | Philippine *Datu Kaliantaw*, lost 21/09/81 |
| DE-171 | Carroll | Federal | 21/06/43 | Str65 |
| DE-172 | Cooner | Federal | 25/07/43 | BU73 |
| DE-173 | Eldridge | Federal | 25/07/43 | Greek *Leon* (51) |
| DE-176 | Micka | Federal | 22/08/43 | BU67 |
| DE-180 | Trumpeter | Federal | 19/09/43 | BU74 |
| DE-181 | Straub | Federal | 19/09/43 | BU74 |
| DE-182 | Gustafson | Federal | 03/10/43 | Dutch *Van Ewijk* (50) |
| DE-183 | Samuel S. Miles | Federal | 03/10/43 | French *Arabe* (50) |
| DE-184 | Wesson | Federal | 17/10/43 | Italian *Andromeda* (51) |
| DE-185 | Riddle | Federal | 17/10/43 | French *Kabyle* (50) |
| DE-186 | Swearer | Federal | 31/10/43 | French *Bambara* (50) |
| DE-187 | Stern | Federal | 31/10/43 | Dutch *Van Zijll* (51) |
| DE-188 | O'Neill | Federal | 14/11/43 | Dutch *Dubois* (50) |
| DE-189 | Bronstein | Federal | 14/11/43 | Uruguayan *Artigas* (52) |
| DE-190 | Baker | Federal | 28/11/43 | French *Malgache* (52) |
| DE-191 | Coffman | Federal | 28/11/43 | BU73 |
| DE-192 | Eisner | Federal | 12/12/43 | Dutch *De Zeeuw* (51) |
| DE-193 | Garfield Thomas | Federal | 12/12/43 | Greek *Panthir* (51) |
| DE-194 | Wingfield | Federal | 30/12/43 | French *Sakalave* (50) |
| DE-195 | Thornhill | Federal | 30/12/43 | Italian *Aldebaran* (51) |
| DE-196 | Rinehart | Federal | 09/01/44 | Dutch *De Bitter* (50) |
| DE-739 | Bangust | Western Pipe | 06/06/43 | Peruvian *Castilla* (52) |
| DE-740 | Waterman | Western Pipe | 20/06/43 | Peruvian *Aguirre* (51) |
| DE-741 | Weaver | Western Pipe | 04/07/43 | Peruvian *Rodriguez* (51) |
| DE-742 | Hilbert | Western Pipe | 18/07/43 | BU73 |
| DE-743 | Lamons | Western Pipe | 01/08/43 | BU73 |
| DE-744 | Kyne | Western Pipe | 15/08/43 | 44-60. BU73 |
| DE-745 | Snyder | Western Pipe | 29/08/43 | 44-60. BU73 |
| DE-746 | Hemminger | Western Pipe | 12/09/43 | 44-57. Thai *Pin Klao* (59) |
| DE-747 | Bright | Western Pipe | 26/09/43 | French *Touareg* (50) |
| DE-748 | Tills | Western Pipe | 03/10/43 | 47-68. Target 69 |
| DE-749 | Roberts | Western Pipe | 14/11/43 | 44-68. Str68 |
| DE-750 | McClelland | Western Pipe | 28/11/43 | 44-59. BU73 |
| DE-763 | Cates | Tampa | 10/10/43 | French *Soudanais* (50) |
| DE-764 | Gandy | Tampa | 12/12/43 | Italian *Altair* (51) |
| DE-765 | Earl K. Olsen | Tampa | 13/02/44 | 44-58. BU73 |
| DE-766 | Slater | Tampa | 13/02/44 | Greek *Aetos* (51) |
| DE-767 | Oswald | Tampa | 25/04/44 | BU73. |
| DE-768 | Ebert | Tampa | 11/05/44 | Greek *Ierax* (51) |
| DE-769 | Neal A. Scott | Tampa | 04/06/44 | BU69 |
| DE-770 | Muir | Tampa | 04/06/44 | Korean *Kyong Ki* (56) |
| DE-771 | Sutton | Tampa | 06/08/44 | Korean *Kang Won* (56) |

**Notes:** Type DET.

# 'Edsall' Class (1942)

**Displacement:** 1,200 tons, 1,710f/l  
**Dimensions:** 300 (wl) 306 (oa)×36'7×14  
**Machinery:** Two shafts, diesel, BHP 6,000=21kt  

**Endurance:** 6,000/12  
**Armament:** 3×3in/50, 8×40mm guns, 3×21in TT  
**Complement:** 186  

DE-129 _____ Edsall _____ Consolidated _____ 01/11/42 _____ BU69  
DE-130 _____ Jacob Jones _____ Consolidated _____ 29/11/42 _____ BU73  
DE-131 _____ Hammann _____ Consolidated _____ 13/12/42 _____ BU73  
DE-132 _____ Robert E. Peary _____ Consolidated _____ 03/01/43 _____ BU67  
DE-133 _____ Pillsbury _____ Consolidated _____ 10/01/43 _____ 55-60. DER (54), BU66  
DE-134 _____ Pope _____ Consolidated _____ 12/01/43 _____ BU73  
DE-135 _____ Flaherty _____ Consolidated _____ 17/01/43 _____ BU66  
DE-137 _____ Herbert C. Jones _____ Consolidated _____ 19/01/43 _____ BU73  
DE-138 _____ Douglas L. Howard _____ Consolidated _____ 24/01/43 _____ BU74  
DE-139 _____ Farquhar _____ Consolidated _____ 13/02/43 _____ BU74  
DE-140 _____ J. R. Y. Blakely _____ Consolidated _____ 07/03/43 _____ BU73  
DE-141 _____ Hill _____ Consolidated _____ 28/02/43 _____ BU73  
DE-142 _____ Fessenden _____ Consolidated _____ 09/03/43 _____ 52-60. DER (51), Str66  
DE-144 _____ Frost _____ Consolidated _____ 21/03/43 _____ BU66  
DE-145 _____ Huse _____ Consolidated _____ 23/03/43 _____ 51-65. BU74  
DE-146 _____ Inch _____ Consolidated _____ 04/04/43 _____ BU74  
DE-147 _____ Blair _____ Consolidated _____ 06/04/43 _____ 51-71. DER (56), BU74  
DE-148 _____ Brough _____ Consolidated _____ 10/04/43 _____ 51-65. BU66  
DE-149 _____ Chatelain _____ Consolidated _____ 21/04/43 _____ BU74  
DE-150 _____ Neunzer _____ Consolidated _____ 27/04/43 _____ BU73  
DE-151 _____ Poole _____ Consolidated _____ 08/05/43 _____ BU74  
DE-152 _____ Peterson _____ Consolidated _____ 15/05/43 _____ 52-65. BU74  
DE-238 _____ Stewart _____ Brown _____ 22/11/42 _____ Str72  
DE-239 _____ Sturtevant _____ Brown _____ 03/12/42 _____ 51-60. DER (57), BU73  
DE-240 _____ Moore _____ Brown _____ 21/12/42 _____ Target 74  
DE-241 _____ Keith _____ Brown _____ 21/12/42 _____ BU73  
DE-242 _____ Tomich _____ Brown _____ 28/12/42 _____ BU73  
DE-243 _____ J. Richard Ward _____ Brown _____ 06/01/43 _____ BU72  
DE-244 _____ Otterstetter _____ Brown _____ 19/01/43 _____ 52-60. DER (51). Target 74  
DE-245 _____ Sloat _____ Brown _____ 21/01/43 _____ BU72  
DE-246 _____ Snowden _____ Brown _____ 19/02/43 _____ 51-68. Target 69  
DE-247 _____ Stanton _____ Brown _____ 21/02/43 _____ Target 71  
DE-248 _____ Swasey _____ Brown _____ 18/03/43 _____ BU74  
DE-249 _____ Marchand _____ Brown _____ 20/03/43 _____ BU74  
DE-250 _____ Hurst _____ Brown _____ 14/04/43 _____ Mexican *Com Manuel Azueta* (73)  
DE-251 _____ Camp _____ Brown _____ 16/04/43 _____ 56-70. DER (55), Vietnam *Tran Hung Dao* (71); Philippine *Rajah Lakandula* (76)  
DE-252 _____ Howard D. Crow _____ Brown _____ 26/04/43 _____ 51-68. BU70  
DE-253 _____ Pettit _____ Brown _____ 28/04/43 _____ Target 74  
DE-254 _____ Ricketts _____ Brown _____ 10/05/43 _____ BU74  
DE-255 _____ Sellstrom _____ Brown _____ 12/05/43 _____ 55-60. DER (46), BU67  
DE-316 _____ Harveson _____ Consolidated _____ 22/05/43 _____ 51-60. DER (51). Target 67  
DE-317 _____ Joyce _____ Consolidated _____ 26/05/43 _____ 51-60. DER (50), BU73  
DE-318 _____ Kirkpatrick _____ Consolidated _____ 05/06/43 _____ 51-60. DER (51), BU75  
DE-320 _____ Menges _____ Consolidated _____ 15/06/43 _____ BU72  
DE-321 _____ Mosley _____ Consolidated _____ 26/06/43 _____ BU73  
DE-322 _____ Newell _____ Consolidated _____ 29/06/43 _____ 57-68. USCG (51-54), DER (57), BU72  
DE-323 _____ Pride _____ Consolidated _____ 03/07/43 _____ BU74

| | | | | |
|---|---|---|---|---|
| DE-324 | Falgout | Consolidated | 24/07/43 | 55-71. USCG (51-54), DER (54), Target 76 |
| DE-325 | Lowe | Consolidated | 28/07/43 | 51-68. USCG (51-54), DER (55), sold 69 |
| DE-326 | Thomas J. Gary | Consolidated | 21/08/43 | 57-73. DER (56), Tunisian |
| | | | | Pres Habib Bourguiba (73) |
| DE-327 | Brister | Consolidated | 24/08/43 | 56-71. DER (55), BU72 |
| DE-328 | Finch | Consolidated | 28/08/43 | 56-73. USCG (51-54), DER (56), BU74 |
| DE-329 | Kretchmer | Consolidated | 31/08/43 | 56-73. DER (56), BU74 |
| DE-330 | O'Reilly | Consolidated | 02/10/43 | BU72 |
| DE-331 | Koiner | Consolidated | 05/10/43 | 55-68. USCG (51-54), DER (54), sold 69 |
| DE-332 | Price | Consolidated | 30/10/43 | 56-60. DER (55), BU75 |
| DE-333 | Strickland | Consolidated | 02/11/43 | 52-58. DER (51), BU74 |
| DE-334 | Forster | Consolidated | 13/11/43 | 56-71. USCG (51-54), DER (55), Vietnam |
| | | | | Tran Khanh Du (71), lost 75 |
| DE-335 | Daniel | Consolidated | 16/11/43 | BU74 |
| DE-336 | Roy O. Hale | Consolidated | 20/11/43 | 57-63. DER (55), BU75 |
| DE-337 | Dale W. Peterson | Consolidated | 22/12/43 | BU72 |
| DE-338 | Martin H. Ray | Consolidated | 29/12/43 | BU67 |
| DE-382 | Ramsden | Brown | 24/05/43 | 57-60. USCG (52-54), DER (56), Target 75 |
| DE-383 | Mills | Brown | 26/05/43 | 57-70. DER (57), BU75 |
| DE-384 | Rhodes | Brown | 29/06/43 | 55-63. DER (54), BU75 |
| DE-385 | Richey | Brown | 30/06/43 | 43-50. USCG (52-54). Target 68 |
| DE-386 | Savage | Brown | 15/07/43 | 55-69. DER (54). Target 76 |
| DE-387 | Vance | Brown | 16/07/43 | 55-68. USCG (52-54), DER (56), Target 76 |
| DE-388 | Lansing | Brown | 02/08/43 | 56-65. USCG (52-54), DER (55), BU74 |
| DE-389 | Durant | Brown | 03/08/43 | 56-71. USCG (52-54), DER (55), BU74 |
| DE-390 | Calcaterra | Brown | 16/08/43 | 55-73. DER (54), BU74 |
| DE-391 | Chambers | Brown | 17/08/43 | 55-60. USCG (52-54), DER (54), BU75 |
| DE-392 | Merrill | Brown | 29/08/43 | BU74 |
| DE-393 | Haverfield | Brown | 30/08/43 | 55-69. DER (54), BU71 |
| DE-394 | Swenning | Brown | 13/09/43 | BU74 |
| DE-395 | Willis | Brown | 14/09/43 | BU73 |
| DE-396 | Janssen | Brown | 04/10/43 | BU73 |
| DE-397 | Wilhoite | Brown | 05/10/43 | 55-69. DER (54), BU72 |
| DE-398 | Cockrill | Brown | 29/10/43 | Target 74 |
| DE-399 | Stockdale | Brown | 30/10/43 | Target 74 |
| DE-400 | Hissem | Brown | 26/12/43 | 56-70. DER (56). Target 76 |

**Notes:** Type FMR. 34 units converted to radar pickets (DER) 1950-56, to provide early-warning for land-based interceptors *Peterson* converted to ASW 1951. Torpedo tubes removed.

# 'Rudderow' Class (1942-43)

**Displacement:** 1,450 tons, 2,000f/l
**Dimensions:** 300 (wl) 306 (oa)×36'10×14
**Machinery:** Two shafts, turbine/electric, SHP 12,000=24kt

**Endurance:** 6,000/12
**Armament:** 2×5in/38, 4×40mm guns, 3×21in TT
**Complement:** 186

| | | | | |
|---|---|---|---|---|
| DE-224 | Rudderow | Philadelphia | 14/10/43 | BU70 |
| DE-225 | Day | Philadelphia | 14/10/43 | Target 69 |
| DE-231 | Hodges | Charleston | 09/12/43 | BU73 |
| DE-579 | Riley | Hingham | 29/12/43 | Taiwan Tai Yuan (68) |
| DE-580 | Leslie L. B. Knox | Hingham | 08/01/44 | BU73 |

*Above:*
**The *Camp* (DER-251) was an 'Edsall' class vessel rebuilt as a radar picket. Transferred to South Vietnam, this ship was one of many which escaped after the collapse of that country and was later given to the Philippines.**

*Below:*
**De Long (DE-684), a 'Rudderow' class escort with 5in guns in mounts. 'John C. Butler' class vessels were similar in appearance.**

| DE-581 | McNulty | Hingham | 08/01/44 | Target 72 |
|---|---|---|---|---|
| DE-582 | Metivier | Hingham | 12/01/44 | BU69 |
| DE-583 | George A. Johnson | Hingham | 12/01/44 | 44-57. BU66 |
| DE-584 | Charles J. Kimmel | Hingham | 15/01/44 | Str68 |
| DE-585 | Daniel A. Joy | Hingham | 15/01/44 | 50-65. BU66 |
| DE-586 | Lough | Hingham | 22/01/44 | BU70 |
| DE-587 | Thomas F. Nickel | Hingham | 22/01/44 | 48-58. BU73 |
| DE-588 | Peiffer | Hingham | 26/01/44 | Target 67 |
| DE-589 | Tinsman | Hingham | 29/01/44 | BU73 |
| DE-684 | De Long | Quincy | 23/11/43 | 51-69. Target 70 |
| DE-685 | Coates | Quincy | 12/12/43 | 51-62. Target 71 |
| DE-686 | Eugene E. Elmore | Quincy | 23/12/43 | BU69 |
| DE-706 | Holt | Defoe | 15/02/44 | Korean *Chung Nam* (63) |
| DE-707 | Jobb | Defoe | 04/03/44 | BU70 |
| DE-708 | Parle | Defoe | 25/03/44 | 51-70. Target 71 |

**Notes:** Type TEV. Torpedo tubes removed.

# 'John C. Butler' Class (1942-43)

**Displacement:** 1,350 tons 2,000f/l
**Dimensions:** 300 (wl) 306 (oa)×36'8×14
**Machinery:** Two shafts, steam turbines,
  SHP 12,000=24kt

**Endurance:** 6,000/12
**Armament:** 2×5in/38, 4×40mm guns, 3×21in TT
**Complement:** 186

| | | | | |
|---|---|---|---|---|
| DE-339 | John C. Butler | Consolidated | 11/12/43 | 50-57. Str70) |
| DE-340 | O'Flaherty | Consolidated | 14/12/43 | BU73 |
| DE-341 | Raymond | Consolidated | 08/01/44 | 51-60. Target 71 |
| DE-342 | Richard W. Suesens | Consolidated | 11/01/44 | BU73 |
| DE-343 | Abercrombie | Consolidated | 14/01/44 | Target 68 |
| DE-345 | Robert Brazier | Consolidated | 22/01/44 | Target 68 |
| DE-346 | Edwin A. Howard | Consolidated | 25/01/44 | BU73 |
| DE-347 | Jesse Rutherford | Consolidated | 29/01/44 | Target 68 |
| DE-348 | Key | Consolidated | 12/02/44 | BU72 |
| DE-349 | Gentry | Consolidated | 15/02/44 | BU72 |
| DE-350 | Traw | Consolidated | 12/02/44 | Target 68 |
| DE-351 | Maurice J. Manuel | Consolidated | 19/02/44 | 51-57. Target 66 |
| DE-352 | Naifeh | Consolidated | 29/02/44 | 51-60. Target 66 |
| DE-353 | Doyle C. Barnes | Consolidated | 04/03/44 | BU73 |
| DE-354 | Kenneth M. Willett | Consolidated | 07/03/44 | 51-59. Target 74 |
| DE-355 | Jaccard | Consolidated | 18/03/44 | Str67 |
| DE-356 | Lloyd E. Acree | Consolidated | 21/03/44 | BU73 |
| DE-357 | George E. Davis | Consolidated | 08/04/44 | 51-54. BU73 |
| DE-358 | Mack | Consolidated | 11/04/44 | BU73 |
| DE-359 | Woodson | Consolidated | 20/04/44 | 51-62. BU66 |
| DE-360 | Johnnie Hutchins | Consolidated | 02/05/44 | 44-58. BU74 |
| DE-361 | Walton | Consolidated | 20/05/44 | 51-68. Target 69 |
| DE-362 | Rolf | Consolidated | 23/05/44 | BU73 |
| DE-363 | Pratt | Consolidated | 01/06/44 | BU72 |
| DE-364 | Rombach | Consolidated | 06/06/44 | 44-68. BU72 |
| DE-365 | McGinty | Consolidated | 05/08/44 | 51-68. BU69 |
| DE-366 | Alvin C. Cockrell | Consolidated | 08/08/44 | 51-68. Target 69 |
| DE-367 | French | Consolidated | 17/06/44 | BU73 |
| DE-368 | Cecil J. Doyle | Consolidated | 01/07/44 | Target 68 |
| DE-369 | Thaddeus Parker | Consolidated | 26/08/44 | 51-67. BU68 |
| DE-370 | John L. Williamson | Consolidated | 29/08/44 | BU73 |
| DE-371 | Presley | Consolidated | 19/08/44 | Str68 |
| DE-372 | Williams | Consolidated | 22/08/44 | Target 68 |
| DE-402 | Richard S. Bull | Brown | 16/11/43 | Target 69 |
| DE-403 | Richard M. Rowell | Brown | 17/11/43 | BU69 |
| DE-405 | Dennis | Brown | 04/12/43 | BU73 |
| DE-406 | Edmonds | Brown | 17/12/43 | 51-71. BU73 |
| DE-408 | Straus | Brown | 30/12/43 | Target 73 |
| DE-409 | La Prade | Brown | 31/12/43 | BU72 |
| DE-410 | Jack Miller | Brown | 10/01/44 | Sold 69 |
| DE-411 | Stafford | Brown | 11/01/44 | BU73 |
| DE-412 | Walter C. Wann | Brown | 19/01/44 | Sold 69 |
| DE-414 | Le Ray Wilson | Brown | 28/01/44 | 51-59. BU73 |
| DE-415 | Lawrence C. Taylor | Brown | 29/01/44 | BU73 |
| DE-416 | Melvin R. Nawman | Brown | 07/02/44 | 51-60. BU73 |
| DE-417 | Oliver Mitchell | Brown | 08/02/44 | Sold 72 |
| DE-418 | Tabberer | Brown | 18/02/44 | 51-59. BU73 |

| | | | | |
|---|---|---|---|---|
| DE-419 | Robert F. Keller | Brown | 19/02/44 | 44-65. BU74 |
| DE-420 | Leland E. Thomas | Brown | 28/02/44 | BU73 |
| DE-421 | Chester T. O'Brien | Brown | 29/02/44 | 51-60. BU74 |
| DE-422 | Douglas A. Munro | Brown | 08/03/44 | 51-60. Target 66 |
| DE-423 | Dufilho | Brown | 09/03/44 | BU73 |
| DE-424 | Haas | Brown | 20/03/44 | BU67 |
| DE-438 | Corbesier | Federal | 13/02/44 | BU73 |
| DE-439 | Conklin | Federal | 13/02/44 | Str70 |
| DE-440 | McCoy Reynolds | Federal | 22/02/44 | 51-57. Portuguese *Corte Real* (57) |
| DE-441 | William Seiverling | Federal | 07/03/44 | 50-57. BU73 |
| DE-442 | Ulvert M. Moore | Federal | 07/03/44 | 51-58. Target 66 |
| DE-443 | Kendall C. Campbell | Federal | 19/03/44 | Sold 72 |
| DE-444 | Goss | Federal | 19/03/44 | 50-58. Sold 72 |
| DE-445 | Grady | Federal | 02/04/44 | 44-57. Sold 69 |
| DE-446 | Charles E. Brannon | Federal | 23/04/44 | 44-68. Sold 69 |
| DE-447 | Albert T. Harris | Federal | 16/04/44 | 51-68. Target 69 |
| DE-448 | Cross | Federal | 04/07/44 | 51-58. BU68 |
| DE-449 | Hanna | Federal | 04/07/44 | 50-59. BU73 |
| DE-450 | Joseph E. Connolly | Federal | 06/08/44 | Str70 |
| DE-508 | Gilligan | Federal | 22/02/44 | 50-59. Sold 72 |
| DE-509 | Formoe | Federal | 02/04/44 | 51-57. Portuguese *Diego Cao* (57) |
| DE-510 | Heyliger | Federal | 06/08/44 | 51-58. Target 67 |
| DE-531 | Edward H. Allen | Boston | 07/10/43 | 51-58. BU74 |
| DE-532 | Tweedy | Boston | 07/10/43 | 52-69. Target 69 |
| DE-533 | Howard F. Clark | Boston | 08/11/43 | BU73 |
| DE-534 | Silverstein | Boston | 08/11/43 | 51-59. BU73 |
| DE-535 | Lewis | Boston | 07/12/43 | Target 66 |
| DE-536 | Bivin | Boston | 07/12/43 | Str68 |
| DE-537 | Rizzi | Boston | 07/12/43 | 51-58. BU74 |
| DE-538 | Osberg | Boston | 07/12/43 | BU74 |
| DE-539 | Wagner | Boston | 27/12/43 | 55-60. DER (54), BU77 |
| DE-540 | Vandivier | Boston | 27/12/43 | 55-60. DER (54). Target 74 |

**Notes:** Type WGT. *Wagner* and *Vandivier* suspended 1945 and completed 1954 as radar pickets. *Tweedy* converted to ASW 1951 with four fixed Hedgehogs atop bridge; *Lewis* had two Hedgehogs in No 2 gun position.

# 'Dealey' Class (1951-55)

**Displacement:** 1,280 tons, 1,877f/l
**Dimensions:** 308 (wl) 314'6 (oa)×36'9×18
**Machinery:** One shaft, steam turbines, SHP 20,000=27kt

**Endurance:** 6,000/12
**Armament:** 4×3in/50 guns, 6 ASW TT, Weapon A (except 1006)
**Complement:** 170

| | | | | |
|---|---|---|---|---|
| DE-1006 | Dealey | Bath | 08/11/53 | 54-72. Uruguayan *18 de Julio* (72) |
| DE-1014 | Cromwell | Bath | 04/06/54 | 54-72. BU73 |
| DE-1015 | Hammerberg | Bath | 20/08/54 | 55-73. BU74 |
| DE-1021 | Courtney | Defoe | 02/11/55 | 56-73. BU74 |
| DE-1022 | Lester | Defoe | 05/01/56 | 57-73. BU74 |
| DE-1023 | Evans | PS Bridge | 14/09/55 | 57-73. BU74 |
| DE-1024 | Bridget | PS Bridge | 25/04/56 | 57-73. BU74 |
| DE-1025 | Bauer | Beth; S Fran | 04/06/57 | 57-73. BU74 |
| DE-1026 | Hooper | Beth; S Fran | 01/08/57 | 58-73. BU74 |
| DE-1027 | John Willis | NY Sbdg | 04/02/56 | 57-72. BU73 |
| DE-1028 | Van Voorhis | NY Sbdg | 28/07/56 | 57-72. BU73 |

| DE-1029 | Hartley | NY Sbdg | 24/11/56 | 57-72. Colombian Boyaca (72) |
| DE-1030 | Joseph K. Taussig | NY Sbdg | 03/01/57 | 57-72. BU73 |

**Notes:** Successor to 173ft submarine chasers, built with aluminium superstructure. Modified units built for Norway and Portugal. Refitted 1961-63: After 3in mount replaced with DASH (except 1006, 1014, 1021), Weapon A removed.

**Note:** DE-1007-13, 1016-20, 1031-32, 1039, 1042, 1046, OSP for France, Italy and Portugal.

*Below:*
**Van Voorhis (DE-1028), with Weapon A visible abaft the forward twin 3in gun mount; a DASH hangar has replaced the aft 3in mount. The 'Dealey' class was the first postwar class of escort vessels.**

*Bottom:*
**McMorris (DE-1036) in May 1962, with its aft 3in mount not in a shield. Notice the ASW torpedo tubes in the well amidships and hedgehog forward of the bridge.** *Official US Navy*

# 'Claud Jones' Class (1956-57)

**Displacement:** 1,284 tons, 1,916f/l
**Dimensions:** 301 (wl) 312 (oa)×38×17'2
**Machinery:** One shaft, diesels, SHP 20,000=23kt

**Endurance:** 7,000/12
**Armament:** 2×3in/50 guns, six ASW TT, Hedgehog
**Complement:** 175

| DE-1033 | Claud Jones | Avondale | 27/05/58 | 59-74. Indonesian Mongindisi (74) |
| DE-1034 | John R. Perry | Avondale | 29/07/58 | 59-73. Indonesian Samadikun (73) |
| DE-1035 | Charles Berry | American | 17/03/59 | 59-73. Indonesian Martadinata (74) |
| DE-1036 | McMorris | American | 26/05/59 | 60-74. Indonesian Ngurah Rai (74) |

**Notes:** These ships had good stability but were too lightly armed, considered a failure. Used as ELINT ships.

Norwegian Terne III ASW missile tested on 1035 and 1036, 1961-64.

## 'Bronstein' Class (1960)

**Displacement:** 2,360 tons, 2,650f/l
**Dimensions:** 350 (wl), 371'6 (oa)×40'5×23
**Machinery:** Two shafts, steam turbines,
  SHP 23,000=25kt

**Endurance:** 3,200/20
**Armament:** 3×3in/50 guns, 6×12.75in ASW TT, DASH,
  ASROC
**Complement:** 190

| | | | | |
|---|---|---|---|---|
| DE-1037 | Bronstein | Avondale | 31/03/62 | 63- |
| DE-1038 | McCloy | Avondale | 09/06/62 | 63- |

**Notes:** Reclassified FF 1975. Lead ships for new ASW escorts with sonar mounted in bow and ASROC. 1×3in gun removed.


## 'Garcia' Class (1961-63)

**Displacement:** 2,620 tons, 3,400f/l
**Dimensions:** 390 (wl), 414'6 (oa)×44'3×24
**Machinery:** One shaft, steam turbines,
  SHP 35,000=27kt

**Endurance:** 4,000/20
**Armament:** 2×5in/38 guns, ASROC, DASH, 6×12.75in
  ASW TT
**Complement:** 258

| | | | | |
|---|---|---|---|---|
| DE-1040 | Garcia | Beth; S Fran | 31/10/63 | 64- |
| DE-1041 | Bradley | Beth; S Fran | 26/03/64 | 65- |
| DE-1043 | Edward McDonnell | Avondale | 15/02/64 | 65- |
| DE-1044 | Brumby | Avondale | 06/06/64 | 65- |
| DE-1045 | Davidson | Avondale | 02/10/64 | 65- |
| DE-1047 | Voge | Defoe | 04/02/65 | 66- |
| DE-1048 | Sample | Lockheed | 28/04/64 | 68- |
| DE-1049 | Koelsch | Defoe | 08/06/65 | 67- |
| DE-1050 | Albert David | Lockheed | 19/12/64 | 68- |
| DE-1051 | O'Callahan | Defoe | 20/10/65 | 68- |

**Notes:** Reclassified FF 1975. Similar to 'Brooke' class with additional 5in gun.


## Glover (1961)

**Displacement:** 2,643 tons, 3,426f/l
**Dimensions:** 390 (wl), 414'6 (oa)×44'3×24
**Machinery:** One shaft, steam turbines,
  SHP 35,000=27kt

**Endurance:** 4,000/20
**Armament:** 1×5in/38 gun, one ASROC, two ASW TT
  (removed), 6×12.75in ASW TT
**Complement:** 281

| | | | | |
|---|---|---|---|---|
| AGDE-1 | Glover | Bath | 17/04/65 | AGFF-1 (75), FF-1098 (79) |

**Notes:** Ordered as AG-163. Built as experimental frigate, similar to 'Knox' class with 'shrouded' propeller.


## 'Knox' Class (1964-67)

**Displacement:** 3,011 tons, 4,100f/l
**Dimensions:** 415 (wl), 438 (oa)×46'9×24'9
**Machinery:** One shaft, steam turbines,
  SHP 35,000=27kt

**Endurance:** 4,500/20
**Armament:** 1×5in/54 gun, 1×8-tube ASROC,
  4×12.75in ASW TT. Phalanx CIWS being installed.
**Complement:** 257

| | | | | |
|---|---|---|---|---|
| DD-1052 | Knox | Todd; Seattle | 19/11/66 | 69- |
| DE-1053 | Roark | Todd; Seattle | 24/04/67 | 69- |

*Above:*
**Voge** (DE-1047) of the 'Garcia' class. The type's
second 5in gun mount can be seen amidships, and
the ASROC launcher is forward of the bridge with
the ship's number painted up. Notice the anchor in
the bow which indicates a bow-mounted sonar.
*Official US Navy*

*Below:*
The 'Knox' class frigate **Paul** (FF-1080) as
completed. One tube of the ASROC launcher is
raised. *Official US Navy*

| | | | | |
|---|---|---|---|---|
| DE-1054 | Gray | Todd; Seattle | 03/11/67 | 70- |
| DE-1055 | Hepburn | Todd; Seattle | 25/03/67 | 69- |
| DE-1056 | Connole | Avondale | 20/07/68 | 69- |
| DE-1057 | Rathburne | Lockheed | 02/05/69 | 70- |
| DE-1058 | Meyerkord | Todd; S Pedro | 15/07/67 | 69- |
| DE-1059 | W. S. Sims | Avondale | 04/01/69 | 70- |
| DE-1060 | Lang | Todd; S Pedro | 17/02/68 | 70- |
| DE-1061 | Patterson | Avondale | 03/05/69 | 70- |

| | | | | |
|---|---|---|---|---|
| DE-1062 | Whipple | Todd; S Pedro | 12/04/68 | 70- |
| DE-1063 | Reasoner | Lockheed | 01/08/70 | 71- |
| DE-1064 | Lockwood | Todd; Seattle | 05/09/68 | 70- |
| DE-1065 | Stein | Lockheed | 19/12/70 | 72- |
| DE-1066 | Marvin Shields | Todd; Seattle | 23/10/69 | 71- |
| DE-1067 | Francis Hammond | Todd; S Pedro | 11/05/68 | 70- |
| DE-1068 | Vreeland | Avondale | 14/06/69 | 70- |
| DE-1069 | Bagley | Lockheed | 24/04/71 | 72- |
| DE-1070 | Downes | Todd; Seattle | 13/12/69 | 71- |
| DE-1071 | Badger | Todd; S Pedro | 07/12/68 | 70- |
| DE-1072 | Blakely | Avondale | 23/08/69 | 70- |
| DE-1073 | Robert E. Peary ex-Conolly | Lockheed | 23/06/71 | 72 |
| DE-1074 | Harold E. Holt | Todd; S Pedro | 03/05/69 | 71- |
| DE-1075 | Trippe | Avondale | 01/11/69 | 70- |
| DE-1076 | Fanning | Todd; S Pedro | 24/01/70 | 71- |
| DE-1077 | Ouellet | Avondale | 17/01/70 | 70- |
| DE-1078 | Joseph Hewes | Avondale | 07/03/70 | 71- |
| DE-1079 | Bowen | Avondale | 02/05/70 | 71- |
| DE-1080 | Paul | Avondale | 20/06/70 | 71- |
| DE-1081 | Aylwin | Avondale | 29/08/70 | 71- |
| DE-1082 | Elmer Montgomery | Avondale | 21/11/70 | 71- |
| DE-1083 | Cook | Avondale | 23/01/71 | 71- |
| DE-1084 | McCandless | Avondale | 20/03/71 | 72- |
| DE-1085 | Donald B. Beary | Avondale | 22/05/71 | 72- |
| DE-1086 | Brewton | Avondale | 24/07/71 | 72- |
| DE-1087 | Kirk | Avondale | 25/09/71 | 72- |
| DE-1088 | Barbey | Avondale | 04/12/71 | 72- |
| DE-1089 | Jesse L. Brown | Avondale | 18/03/72 | 73- |
| DE-1090 | Ainsworth | Avondale | 15/04/72 | 73- |
| DE-1091 | Miller | Avondale | 03/06/72 | 73- |
| DE-1092 | Thomas C. Hart | Avondale | 12/08/72 | 73- |
| DE-1093 | Capodanno | Avondale | 21/10/72 | 73- |
| DE-1094 | Pharris | Avondale | 16/12/72 | 74- |
| DE-1095 | Truett | Avondale | 03/02/73 | 74- |
| DE-1096 | Valdez | Avondale | 24/03/73 | 74- |
| DE-1097 | Moinester | Avondale | 12/05/73 | 74- |

**Notes:** Reclassified FF 1975. DE-1098 to DE-1107 cancelled. Distinctive cylindrical mack combines mast and stack. Hangar for DASH enlarged to accommodate LAMPS. Forecastle raised to improve seakeeping after 1979. Sea Sparrow BPDMS launcher added 1971-75 in 31 ships (1052-1069).

Criticised for single screw and inferior armament as lacking redundancy required in a warship, a defect partially rectified by adding Harpoon to be fired from ASROC launcher.

Five of guided missile version with Tartar aft (DEG-7-11) built in Spain.

# GUIDED MISSILE FRIGATES

## 'Brooke' Class (1962-63)

**Displacement:** 2,640 tons, 3,245f/l
**Dimensions:** 390 (wl), 414'6 (oa)×44'3×24
**Machinery:** One shaft, steam turbines,
   SHP 35,000=27kt
**Endurance:** 4,000/20

**Armament:** One Tartar/Standard SAM, 1×5in/38 gun,
   two ASW TT (removed), 6×12.75in ASW TT, DASH,
   ASROC
**Complement:** 248

| | | | | |
|---|---|---|---|---|
| DEG-1 | Brooke | Lockheed | 19/07/63 | 66- |
| DEG-2 | Ramsey | Lockheed | 15/10/63 | 67- |
| DEG-3 | Schofield | Lockheed | 07/12/63 | 68- |
| DEG-4 | Talbot | Bath | 06/01/66 | 67- |
| DEG-5 | Richard L. Page | Bath | 04/04/66 | 67- |
| DEG-6 | Julius A. Furer | Bath | 22/07/66 | 67- |

**Notes:** Reclassified FFG 1975. As 'Garcia' class with SAM missile launcher aft. Ten additional ships not built. Carry one LAMPS helicopter. *Talbot* used for test of weapons for 'Perry' class 1974-75.

*Below:*
**The *Julius A. Furer* (DEG-6), a 'Brooke' class missile frigate. The type is similar to the 'Garcia' class, with a SAM launcher aft of the stack.**

## 'Oliver Hazard Perry' Class (1973-81)

**Displacement:** 2,750 tons, 3,710f/l
**Dimensions:** 408 (wl), 445 (oa)×47'5×24'6
**Machinery:** One shaft, gas turbines, SHP 40,000=29kt
**Endurance:** 4,500/20+

**Armament:** One Standard SAM-Harpoon Mk 13
   launcher, 1×76mm/62 gun, 6×12.75in TT; One
   Phalanx CIWS being installed
**Complement:** 193

| | | | | |
|---|---|---|---|---|
| FFG-7 | Oliver Hazard Perry | Bath | 25/09/76 | 77- |
| FFG-8 | McInerney | Bath | 04/11/76 | 79- |
| FFG-9 | Wadsworth | Todd; S Pedro | 29/07/78 | 80- |
| FFG-10 | Duncan | Todd; Seattle | 01/03/78 | 80- |
| FFG-11 | Clark | Bath | 24/03/79 | 80- |
| FFG-12 | George Philip | Todd; S Pedro | 16/12/78 | 80- |

*Above:*
**The *Mahlon S. Tisdale* (FFG-27), a 'Perry' class missile frigate, on sea trials in September 1982. A Standard/Harpoon launcher is forward and a 76mm gun can be seen amidships. Phalanx CIWS is visible on top of the hangar aft.** *John Graham*

| | | | | | |
|---|---|---|---|---|---|
| FFG-13 | Samuel Eliot Morison | Bath | 14/07/79 | 80- | |
| FFG-14 | John H. Sides | Todd; S Pedro | 19/05/79 | 81- | |
| FFG-15 | Estocin | Bath | 03/11/79 | 81- | |
| FFG-16 | Clifton Sprague | Bath | 16/02/80 | 81- | |
| FFG-19 | John A. Moore | Todd; S Pedro | 20/10/79 | 81- | |
| FFG-20 | Antrim | Todd; Seattle | 27/03/79 | 81- | |
| FFG-21 | Flatley | Bath | 15/05/80 | 81- | |
| FFG-22 | Fahrion | Todd; Seattle | 24/08/79 | 82- | |
| FFG-23 | Lewis B. Puller | Todd; S Pedro | 15/03/80 | 82- | |
| FFG-24 | Jack Williams | Bath | 30/08/80 | 81 | |
| FFG-25 | Copeland | Todd; S Pedro | 26/07/80 | 82 | |
| FFG-26 | Gallery | Bath | 20/12/80 | 81- | |
| FFG-27 | Mahlon S. Tisdale | Todd; S Pedro | 07/02/81 | 82- | |
| FFG-28 | Boone | Todd; Seattle | 16/01/80 | 82 | |
| FFG-29 | Stephen W. Groves | Bath | 04/04/81 | 82 | |
| FFG-30 | Reid | Todd; S Pedro | 27/06/81 | 83- | |
| FFG-31 | Stark | Todd; Seattle | 30/05/80 | 82- | |
| FFG-32 | John L. Hall | Bath | 24/07/81 | 82- | |
| FFG-33 | Jarrett | Todd; S Pedro | 17/10/81 | 83- | |
| FFG-34 | Aubrey Fitch | Bath | 17/10/81 | 82- | |
| FFG-36 | Underwood | Bath | 06/02/82 | 83- | |

| | | | | |
|---|---|---|---|---|
| FFG-37 | Crommelin | Todd; Seattle | 01/07/81 | 83- |
| FFG-38 | Curts | Todd; S Pedro | 06/03/82 | 83- |
| FFG-39 | Doyle | Bath | 23/05/82 | 83- |
| FFG-40 | Halyburton | Todd; Seattle | 15/10/81 | 84- |
| FFG-41 | McClusky | Todd; S Pedro | 18/09/82 | 83- |
| FFG-42 | Klakring | Bath | 18/09/82 | 83- |
| FFG-43 | Thach | Todd; S Pedro | 18/12/82 | 84- |
| FFG-45 | DeWert | Bath | 18/12/82 | 83- |
| FFG-46 | Rentz | Todd; S Pedro | 16/07/83 | 84- |
| FFG-47 | Nicholas | Bath | 23/04/83 | 84- |
| FFG-48 | Vandegrift | Todd; Seattle | 15/10/82 | 84- |
| FFG-49 | Robert G. Bradley | Bath | 13/08/83 | 84- |
| FFG-50 | Taylor | Bath | 05/11/83 | 84- |
| FFG-51 | Gary | Todd; S Pedro | 19/11/83 | 84- |
| FFG-52 | Carr | Todd; Seattle | 26/02/83 | 85- |
| FFG-53 | Hawes | Bath | 18/02/84 | 85- |
| FFG-54 | Ford | Todd; S Pedro | 23/06/84 | 85- |
| FFG-55 | Elrod | Bath | 12/05/84 | 85- |
| FFG-56 | Simpson | Bath | 21/08/84 | 85- |
| FFG-57 | Reuben James | Todd; S Pedro | 08/02/85 | 86- |
| FFG-58 | Samuel B. Roberts | Bath | 08/12/84 | 86- |
| FFG-59 | Kauffman | Bath | 08/04/85 | 86- |
| FFG-60 | Rodney M. Davis | Todd; S Pedro | 11/01/86 | na |
| FFG-61 | Ingraham | Todd; S Pedro | Ordered | na |

**Notes:** Ocean escorts for merchant convoys, undersea replenishment groups and amphibious forces. No ASROC, better AA capacity. Stern extended for hangar and deck for LAMPS III helicopter. Four additional units (17, 18, 35 and 44) built for Australia.

*Above:*
**Estocin (FFG-15), a guided missile frigate of the 'Oliver Hazard Perry' class.** *Official US Navy*

# AMPHIBIOUS VESSELS

## AMPHIBIOUS ASSAULT SHIPS

### 'Iwo Jima' Class (1958-66)

**Displacement:** 10,722 tons, 18,300f/l
**Dimensions:** 556 (wl), 598 (oa)×84×26; extreme beam
112; LPH-2: 602'4 (oa); LPH-10 and LPH-11: 592 (oa)
**Machinery:** One shaft, steam turbine, SHP 22,000=23kt

**Endurance:** 10,000/20
**Armament:** Two Sea Sparrow BPDMS launchers,
8×3in/50 guns
**Complement:** 609

| | | | | |
|---|---|---|---|---|
| LPH-2 | Iwo Jima | Puget Sound | 17/09/60 | 61- |
| LPH-3 | Okinawa | Philadelphia | 14/08/61 | 62- |
| LPH-7 | Guadalcanal | Philadelphia | 16/03/63 | 63- |
| LPH-9 | Guam | Philadelphia | 22/08/64 | 65- |
| LPH-10 | Tripoli | Ingalls | 31/07/65 | 66- |
| LPH-11 | New Orleans | Philadelphia | 03/02/68 | 68- |
| LPH-12 | Inchon | Ingalls | 24/05/69 | 70- |

**Notes:** Can carry a full Marine battalion and up to 20
helicopters. 4×3in guns replaced by Sea Sparrow
1970-74. Phalanx to replace Sea Sparrow 1982.

#### Conversions

| | | ex- | Converted | |
|---|---|---|---|---|
| LPH-4 | Boxer | CV-21 | 1959 | 59-69 |
| LPH-5 | Princeton | CV-37 | 1959 | 59-70 |
| LPH-6 | Thetis Bay | CVE-90 | 1956 | 56-64 |
| LPH-8 | Valley Forge | CV-45 | 1961 | 61-70 |

**Notes:** LPH-1 *Block Island*, conversion cancelled.
LPH-4, -5 and -8 former 'Essex' class aircraft carriers,
displacement 25,800 tons, 38,000f/l.

### 'Tarawa' Class (1969-71)

**Displacement:** 25,330 tons, 39,300f/l
**Dimensions:** 778 (wl), 820 (oa)×106'8×26
**Machinery:** Two shafts, steam turbines,
SHP 70,000=24kt

**Endurance:** 10,000/20
**Armament:** Two Sea Sparrow BPDMS launchers,
3×5in/54, 6×20mm guns
**Complement:** 902

| | | | | |
|---|---|---|---|---|
| LHA-1 | Tarawa | Ingalls | 01/12/73 | 76- |
| LHA-2 | Saipan | Ingalls | 18/07/74 | 77- |
| LHA-3 | Belleau Wood | Ingalls | 11/04/77 | 78- |
| LHA-4 | Nassau | Ingalls | 21/01/78 | 79- |
| LHA-5 | Peleliu | Ingalls | 25/11/78 | 80- |
| | ex-Da Nang (15/02/78) | | | |

**Notes:** Intended to combine the capabilities of several
types of amphibious vessels in a single hull. Stern
docking well can hold four LCU. Completion long
delayed, nine planned but LHA-6 to LHA-9 not built,
1971.

Top:
**The 'Iwo Jima' class assault ship _Guadalcanal_ (LPH-7).** _Official US Navy_

Above:
**_Boxer_ (LPH-4), a former aircraft carrier of the 'Essex' class, as converted to an amphibious assault ship. Notice the battalion of Marines** paraded on the flight deck with helicopters and equipment. _Official US Navy_

Below:
**The amphibious assault ship _Thetis Bay_ (CVHA-1), a former escort carrier of the 'Casablanca' class, seen in 1956. Its classification was later changed to LPH-6.** _Real Photographs_

## 'Wasp' Class (1985)

**Displacement:** 40,500 tons f/l
**Dimensions:** 844 (oa)×106×26'1
**Machinery:** two shafts, steam turbine SHP
140,000=22kt+

**Armament:** Two NATO Sea Sparrow launchers, three
Phalanx CIWS
**Complement:** 1,080

LHD-1 _____ *Wasp* _____ Ingalls _____ Building
LHD-2 _____ *Essex* _____ Ingalls _____ Ordered

**Notes:** A class of five units planned, as tentative
replacements for 'Iwo Jima' class. Similar to 'Tarawa'
class with larger well-deck. Will carry 1,300 troops.

# AMPHIBIOUS TRANSPORTS DOCK

## 'Raleigh' Class (1959-60)

**Displacement:** 8,040 tons, 13,900f/l
**Dimensions:** 500 (wl) 521'9 (ao)×84×22
**Machinery:** two shafts, steam turbines, SHP
24,000=21kt

**Endurance:** 9,600/16
**Armament:** 6×3in/50 guns
**Complement:** 490

LPD-1 _____ *Raleigh* _____ New York _____ 17/03/62 ___ 62-
LPD-2 _____ *Vancouver* _____ New York _____ 15/09/62 ___ 63-
LPD-3 _____ *La Salle* _____ New York _____ 03/08/63 ___ 63-. AGF-3 (72)

**Notes:** A development of the LSD, with fixed
helicopter deck over the docking well. Carry 930 troops.
*La Salle* converted to command ship 1972 to serve as
Middle East flagship.

## 'Austin' Class (1962-65)

**Displacement:** 9,700 tons, 16,900f/l
**Dimensions:** 569'9 (oa)×84×23
**Machinery:** two shafts, steam turbines, SHP
24,000=21kt

**Endurance:** 7,700/20
**Armament:** 8×3in/50 guns
**Complement:** 447

LPD-4 _____ *Austin* _____ New York _____ 27/06/64 ___ 65-
LPD-5 _____ *Ogden* _____ New York _____ 27/06/64 ___ 65-
LPD-6 _____ *Duluth* _____ New York* _____ 14/08/65 ___ 65-
LPD-7 _____ *Cleveland* _____ Ingalls _____ 07/05/66 ___ 67-
LPD-8 _____ *Dubuque* _____ Ingalls _____ 06/08/66 ___ 67-
LPD-9 _____ *Denver* _____ Lockheed _____ 23/01/65 ___ 68-
LPD-10 _____ *Juneau* _____ Lockheed _____ 12/02/66 ___ 69-
LPD-11 _____ *Coronado* _____ Lockheed _____ 30/07/66 ___ 70-. AGF-11 (80)
LPD-12 _____ *Shreveport* _____ Lockheed _____ 22/10/66 ___ 70-
LPD-13 _____ *Nashville* _____ Lockheed _____ 07/10/67 ___ 70-
LPD-14 _____ *Trenton* _____ Lockheed _____ 03/08/68 ___ 71-
LPD-15 _____ *Ponce* _____ Lockheed _____ 20/05/70 ___ 71-

\* completed at Philadelphia

**Note:** Enlarged 'Raleigh' class, similar to LSDs with
docking well and flight deck. LPD-16 cancelled 1969.
4×3in guns removed 1970s. Carry 900 troops. *Coronado*
modified for use as flagship. SLEP modernisation to
begin in 1989.

Above:
**John Young** (DD-973) with **Belleau Wood** (LHA-3) —
a 'Spruance' class destroyer escorting a 'Tarawa'
class assault ship. **Compare the relative size of the
vessels.** *Official US Navy*

Below:
**Duluth** (LPD-6), an 'Austin' class amphibious
transport dock, with a hangar between the funnels.
**The docking well is covered by the helicopter flight
deck.** *Official US Navy*

# LANDING SHIPS, VEHICLE

**Displacement:** 5,875 tons, 9,040f/l (1-2), 5,625 tons,
8,160f/l (3-6)
**Dimensions:** 440 (wl) 455'5 (oa)×60'2×20; 3-6:
451'4(oa)

**Machinery:** two shafts, steam turbines, SHP
11,000=20.3kt
**Armament:** 2×5in/38, 8×40mm guns
**Complement:** 564

| | | | | |
|---|---|---|---|---|
| LSV-1 | *Catskill* | Willamette | 19/05/42 | 67-70. BU73 |
| LSV-2 | *Ozark* | Willamette | 15/06/42 | 66-70. Str71 |

| | | | | |
|---|---|---|---|---|
| LSV-3 | _Osage_ | Ingalls | 30/06/43 | BU74 |
| LSV-4 | _Saugus_ | Ingalls | 04/09/43 | BU76 |
| LSV-5 | _Monitor_ | Ingalls | 29/01/43 | Str |
| LSV-6 | _Montauk_ | Ingalls | 14/04/43 | _Galilea_ (AKN-6)(46), BU73 |

**Notes:** _Terror_ (CM-5) was same class as LSV-1-2. Stern ramp. 1 and 2 had two stacks, 3-6 only one. Reclassified Mine Warfare Command & Support Ships, MCS, 1956.

_Catskill_ and _Ozark_ re-acquired 1963-64 and converted to carry 20 minesweeping boats and two helicopters.
LSV-7-9 became AK-269, AK-273 and AKR-9, 1968 (qv).

# DOCK LANDING SHIPS

## 'Ashland' Class

**Displacement:** 4,790 tons, 8,700f/l
**Dimensions:** 454 (wl) 457'9 (oa)×72'2×18
**Machinery:** two shafts, steam turbines, SHP

7,000=15.4kt, 1-8: reciprocating, SHP 7,400−17kt
**Armament:** 1×5in/38, 12×40mm guns
**Complement:** 240

| | | | | |
|---|---|---|---|---|
| LSD-1 | _Ashland_ | Moore | 21/12/42 | 50 69. BU71 |
| LSD-2 | _Belle Grove_ | Moore | 17/02/43 | 50-53. BU70 |
| LSD-3 | _Carter Hall_ | Moore | 04/03/43 | 51-69. BU70 |
| LSD-4 | _Epping Forest_ | Moore | 02/04/43 | 50-68. MCS-7 (62), sold (69) |
| LSD-5 | _Gunston Hall_ | Moore | 01/05/43 | 49-70. Argentine _Candido De Lasala_ (70) |
| LSD-6 | _Lindenwald_ | Moore | 11/06/43 | 49-67. BU68 |
| LSD-7 | _Oak Hill_ | Moore | 25/06/43 | 51-69. Str69 |
| LSD-8 | _White Marsh_ | Moore | 19/07/43 | 50-56. Taiwan _Tung Hai_ (60) |
| LSD-13 | _Casa Grande_ | Newport News | 11/04/44 | 50-69 |
| LSD-14 | _Rushmore_ | Newport News | 10/05/44 | 50-70 |
| LSD-15 | _Shadwell_ | Newport News | 24/05/44 | 50-70. Str85 |
| LSD-16 | _Cabildo_ | Newport News | 22/12/44 | 50-70 |
| LSD-17 | _Catamount_ | Newport News | 27/01/45 | 46-70. Str74 |
| LSD-18 | _Colonial_ | Newport News | 28/02/45 | 45-70 |
| LSD-19 | _Comstock_ | Newport News | 28/04/45 | 45-70 |
| LSD-20 | _Donner_ | Boston | 06/04/45 | 45-49, 50-70 |
| LSD-21 | _Fort Mandan_ | Boston | 02/06/45 | 50-71. Greek _Nafkratoussa_ (71) |
| LSD-22 | _Fort Marion_ | Gulf | 22/05/45 | 46-70. Taiwan _Chen Hai_ (77) |
| LSD-25 | _San Marcos_ | Philadelphia | 10/01/45 | 51-71. Spanish _Galicia_ (71) |
| LSD-26 | _Tortuga_ | Boston | 21/01/45 | 50-70. Str77 |
| LSD-27 | _Whetstone_ | Boston | 18/07/45 | 45-48, 50-70. Str71 |

**Notes:** _Gunston Hall_ and _Lindenwald_ 'winterised', bows strengthened for ice breaking 1949. Conversion of _Ashland_ to seaplane tender (AV-21) for jet-powered

Seamaster seaplane cancelled with cancellation of Seamaster.

## 'Thomaston' Class (1952-55)

**Displacement:** 6,880 tons, 11,270f/l
**Dimensions:** 510 (oa)×84×19
**Machinery:** two shafts, steam turbines, SHP 24,000=22.5kt

**Endurance:** 13,000/10
**Armament:** 16×3in/50 guns
**Complement:** 341

| | | | | |
|---|---|---|---|---|
| LSD-28 | _Thomaston_ | Ingalls | 09/02/54 | 54-84 |
| LSD-29 | _Plymouth Rock_ | Ingalls | 07/05/54 | 54-83 |
| LSD-30 | _Fort Snelling_ | Ingalls | 16/07/54 | 55-84 |
| LSD-31 | _Point Defiance_ | Ingalls | 28/09/54 | 55-83 |

| | | | | |
|---|---|---|---|---|
| LSD-32 | *Spiegel Grove* | Ingalls | 10/11/55 | 56- |
| LSD-33 | *Alamo* | Ingalls | 20/01/56 | 56- |
| LSD-34 | *Hermitage* | Ingalls | 12/06/56 | 56- |
| LSD-35 | *Monticello* | Ingalls | 10/08/56 | 57-85 |

**Notes:** 4×3in guns removed in 1960s, six additional in 1970s.

*Above:*
**The landing ship dock Plymouth Rock (LSD-29), seen in 1963.** *Official US Navy*

*Right:*
**Portland (LSD-37), a landing ship dock of the 'Anchorage class', on trials.** *General Dynamics*

# 'Anchorage' Class (1965-67)

**Displacement:** 8,600 tons, 13,700f/l
**Dimensions:** 561 (oa)×84×20; 36: 562 (oa); 37: 553'4 (oa)
**Machinery:** two shafts, steam turbines, SHP 24,000=22kt
**Armament:** 8×3in/50 guns
**Complement:** 397

| | | | | |
|---|---|---|---|---|
| LSD-36 | *Anchorage* | Ingalls | 05/05/68 | 69- |
| LSD-37 | *Portland* | Quincy | 20/12/69 | 70- |
| LSD-38 | *Pensacola* | Quincy | 11/07/70 | 71- |
| LSD-39 | *Mount Vernon* | Quincy | 17/04/71 | 72- |
| LSD-40 | *Fort Fisher* | Quincy | 22/04/72 | 72- |

**Notes:** Tripod masts. 2×3in guns removed in 1970s.

## 'Whidbey Island' Class (1981-84)

**Displacement:** 11,125 tons, 15,726 f/l
**Dimensions:** 580 (wl) 609'7 (oa)×84×19'9
**Machinery:** Two shafts, diesels, BHP 34,000=23kt

**Armament:** Two Phalanx CIWS
**Complement:** 356

| | | | | |
|---|---|---|---|---|
| LSD-41 | _Whidbey Island_ | Lockheed | 10/06/83 | 85- |
| LSD-42 | _Germantown_ | Lockheed | 29/06/84 | 86- |
| LSD-43 | _Fort McHenry_ | Lockheed | 01/02/86 | na |
| LSD-44 | na | Avondale | Building | na |
| LSD-45 | na | Avondale | Ordered | na |
| LSD-46 | na | Avondale | Ordered | na |
| LSD-47 | na | Avondale | Ordered | na |
| LSD-48 | na | Avondale | Ordered | na |

**Notes:** Replacements for 'Thomaston' class. Funnel arrangement asymmetrical.


# TANK LANDING SHIPS

**Details:** 1,653 tons; 4,080f/l; 328 (oa)×50×14'4; two shafts, diesels, SHP 1,700=10.8kt

| | | |
|---|---|---|
| LST-17 | na | Target 56 |
| LST-31 | _Addison County_ | Target 56 |
| LST-32 | _Alameda County_ | 51-62. AVB-1 (57), Italian _Anteo_ (62) |
| LST-47 | na | 52-76. Philippine _Tarlac_ (76) |
| LST-50 | na | ARB-13 (52), Norwegian _Ellida_ (52), Greek _Sakipis_ (60) |
| LST-53 | na | 43-55. APL-59 (54), Korean _Chang Su_ (55) |
| LST-57 | _Armstrong County_ | Str55 |
| LST-60 | _Atchison County_ | Sold 58 |
| LST-117 | na | 52-73. Str73 |
| LST-176 | na | 52-73. Str73 |
| LST-209 | _Bamberg County_ | 52-58. Sold 61 |
| LST-218 | na | Korean _Bi Bong_ (55) |
| LST-222 | na | 52-72. Philippine _Mindoro Occidental_ (72) |
| LST-227 | na | Korean _Duk Bong_ (55) |

_Below:_
**LST-117 (T-LST-117), a landing ship tank operated by the Military Sea Transportation Service with a civilian crew: notice the lack of armament and radar.**

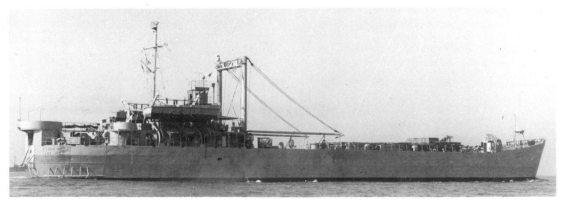

| | | |
|---|---|---|
| LST-230 ___ na ___ | 52-76. Philippine *Laguna* (76) | |
| LST-263 ___ Benton County ___ | Sold 60 | |
| LST-266 ___ Benzie County ___ | Str59 | |
| LST-276 ___ na ___ | 52-73. Str73 | |
| LST-277 ___ na ___ | 52-73. Chilean *Comandante Toro* (73) | |
| LST-279 ___ Berkeley County ___ | Taiwan *Chung Chih* (55) | |
| LST-281 ___ na ___ | Str54 | |
| LST-287 ___ na ___ | Philippine *Samar Oriental* (76) | |
| LST-288 ___ Berkshire County ___ | Korean *Kae Bong* (56) | |
| LST-306 ___ Bernalillo County ___ | Korean (55) | |
| LST-325 ___ na ___ | Greek *Syros* (64) | |
| LST-344 ___ Blanco County ___ | 43-69. Sold 75 | |
| LST-356 ___ Bledsoe County ___ | Sold 60 | |
| LST-389 ___ Boone County ___ | Greek *Lesvos* (60) | |
| LST-391 ___ Bowman County ___ | 42-60. Greek *Rodos* (60) | |
| LST-399 ___ na ___ | 52-73. Str73. IX-511 (80) | |
| LST-400 ___ Bradley County ___ | 43-55. Taiwan *Chung Suo* (55) | |
| LST-456 ___ na ___ | 43-73. Sold 73 | |
| LST-482 ___ Branch County ___ | Target 56 | |
| LST-483 ___ Brewster County ___ | Str55 | |
| LST-491 ___ na ___ | 52-75. Philippine *Lanao Del Sur* (76) | |
| LST-503 ___ na ___ | Taiwan *Chung Kuang* (55) | |
| LST-504 ___ Buchanan County ___ | Str55 | |
| LST-509 ___ Bulloch County ___ | 44-70. Vietnam *Qui Nhon* (70) | |
| LST-510 ___ Buncombe County ___ | Sold 59 | |
| LST-512 ___ Burnett County ___ | Peruvian *Paita* (57) | |
| LST-515 ___ Caddo Parish ___ | 44-55, 63-69. Philippine *Maquindanao* (69) | |
| LST-516 ___ Calaveras County ___ | 44-55. BU60 | |
| LST-519 ___ Calhoun County ___ | 44-62. Str62 | |
| LST-520 ___ na ___ | Taiwan *Chung Shu* (58) | |
| LST-521 ___ Cape May County ___ | Sold 1961 | |
| LST-525 ___ Caroline County ___ | 50-54, 65-74. Sold 75 | |
| LST-527 ___ Cassia County ___ | 50-56. Target 58 | |
| LST-528 ___ Catahoula Parish ___ | 44-54. Sold 61 | |
| LST-529 ___ Cayuga County ___ | 50-63. Vietnam *Thi Nai* (63), Philippine *Cotabato Del Sur* (75) | |
| LST-530 ___ na ___ | 52-73. Sold 73 | |
| LST-532 ___ Chase County ___ | 44-55, 67-73. Singapore (74) | |
| LST-533 ___ Cheboygan County ___ | 44-55, 61-69. Sold 75 | |
| LST-535 ___ na ___ | 52-58. Taiwan *Chung Wan* (58) | |
| LST-542 ___ Chelan County ___ | 44-56. Sold 61 | |
| LST-546 ___ na ___ | 44-72. Philippine *Surigao Del Sur* (72) | |
| LST-548 ___ na ___ | 52-60. BU60 | |
| LST-550 ___ na ___ | 52-73. BU74 | |
| LST-551 ___ Chesterfield County ___ | 44-55, 65-70. Str70 | |
| LST-561 ___ Chittenden County ___ | 50-58. Target 58 | |
| LST-566 ___ na ___ | 52-73. Philippine *Lanao Del Norte* (76) | |
| LST-572 ___ na ___ | 52-73. Sold 73 | |
| LST-574 ___ na ___ | Taiwan *Chung Yung* (59) | |
| LST-578 ___ na ___ | 52-58. Taiwan *Chung Pang* (58) | |
| LST-579 ___ na ___ | 52-75. Singapore *Intrepid* (76) | |
| LST-581 ___ na ___ | 52-72. Sold 73 | |
| LST-583 ___ Churchill County ___ | 60-68. Sold 75 | |
| LST-587 ___ na ___ | 52-72. Sold 73 | |

LST-590 _____ na _____ 52-73. Sold 73
LST-600 _____ na _____ 44-68. Lost 23/12/68
LST-601 _____ Clarke County _____ 44-55, 66-70. Indonesian *Teluk Saleh* (70)
LST-602 _____ Clearwater County _____ 50-69. Mexican *Rio Manzanillo* (72)
LST-603 _____ Coconino County _____ 44-55, 66-69. Vietnam *Vung Tau* (69)
LST-607 _____ na _____ 52-76. Philippine *Leyte Del Sur* (76)
LST-611 _____ Crook County _____ 44-56. Str59
LST-613 _____ na _____ 52-75. Singapore *Persistence* (76)
LST-616 _____ na _____ 52-61. Indonesian *Teluk Bayur* (61)
LST-623 _____ na _____ 44-75. Singapore *Perseverance* (76)
LST-625 _____ na _____ 52-54. Str54
LST-626 _____ na _____ 52-72. Sold 73
LST-629 _____ na _____ 52-75. Singapore *Excellence* (76)
LST-630 _____ na _____ 52-73. Sold 73
LST-643 _____ na _____ 44-73. Sold 73
LST-649 _____ na _____ 52-75. Singapore *Resolution* (76)
LST-652 _____ na _____ 52-61. Indonesian *Teluk Kau* (61)
LST-657 _____ na _____ 52-61. Indonesian *Teluk Menado* (61)
LST-664 _____ na _____ 44-73. Sold 73
LST-685 _____ Curry County _____ 47-50. Sold 60
LST-689 _____ Daggett County _____ Japanese *Oosumi* (61), Philippine *Davao Oriental* (78)
LST-692 _____ Daviess County _____ 51-76. Philippine *Benguet* (76)
LST-694 _____ na _____ 50-58. Sold 59
LST-715 _____ De Kalb County _____ 50-73. Str73
LST-722 _____ Dodge County _____ 51-56. Thai *Prathong* (75)
LST-731 _____ Douglas County _____ 44-50. Str59
LST-735 _____ Dukes County _____ 50-57. Taiwan *Chung Hsi* (57)
LST-742 _____ Dunn County _____ 50-61. Sold 63
LST-758 _____ Duval County _____ 50-69. Stricken
LST-759 _____ Eddy County _____ Str59
LST-761 _____ Esmeraldo County _____ Str59
LST-762 _____ Floyd County _____ 50-69. Sold 76
LST-772 _____ Ford County _____ 50-57. Str57
LST-784 _____ Garfield County _____ Target 60
LST-786 _____ Garrett County _____ 66-71. AGP-786 (70), Vietnam *Can Tho* (71), Philippine *Apayao* (76)
LST-794 _____ Gibson County _____ Target 59
LST-799 _____ Greer County _____ 50-60. W.German *Bamberg* (61)
LST-802 _____ Hamilton County _____ 50-60. Japanese *Hayatomo* (60)
LST-803 _____ Hampden County _____ 50-58. Target 58
LST-819 _____ Hampshire County _____ 50-55, 66-70. Sold 75
LST-821 _____ Harnett County _____ 66-70. AGP-821 (70), Vietnam *My Tho* (70) Philippine *Dumagat* (76)
LST-822 _____ Harris County _____ 50-76. Philippine *Aurora* (76)
LST-824 _____ Henry County _____ 59-76. Malaysian *Sri Benggi* (76)
LST-825 _____ Hickman County _____ 50-56, 63-69. Philippine *Cagayan* (69)
LST-827 _____ Hillsborough County ____ 44-49, 50-58. Target 58
LST-835 _____ Hillsdale County _____ Japanese *Shimokita* (61), Philippine *Cavite* (78)
LST-836 _____ Holmes County _____ 50-71. Singapore *Endurance* (71)
LST-838 _____ Hunterdon County _____ 66-71. AGP-838 (70), Malaysian *Sri Langkawi* (71)
LST-839 _____ Iredell County _____ 66-70. Indonesian *Teluk Bome* (70)
LST-840 _____ Iron County _____ 50-57. Taiwan *Chung Fu* (58)
LST-845 _____ Jefferson County _____ 45-61. Sold 61
LST-846 _____ Jennings County _____ 45-49, 50-55, 66-70. Sold 71
LST-848 _____ Jerome County _____ 59-70, Vietnam *Nha Trang* (70), Philippine *Agusan Del Sur* (75)

Above:
The *Greer County* (LST-799), a landing ship tank, with a trellis mast.

LST-849 _____ *Johnson County* _____ Korean *Wee Bong* (59)
LST-850 _____ *Juniata County* _____ Target 59
LST-853 _____ *Kane County* _____ Korean *Su Yong* (58)
LST-854 _____ *Kemper County* _____ 44-49, 50-69. Barbados (76)
LST-855 _____ *Kent County* _____ 44-50, 50-58. Target 58
LST-857 _____ *King County* _____ 44-60. EAG 157 (58), BU61
LST-859 _____ *Lafayette County* _____ 45-58. Taiwan *Chung Cheng* (58)
LST-880 _____ *Lake County* _____ 51-58. Target 60
LST-883 _____ *La Moure County* _____ 50-69. BU60
LST-887 _____ *Lawrence County* _____ 50-60. Indonesian *Tandjung Nusanive* (60)
LST-888 _____ *Lee County* _____ Sold 61
LST-898 _____ *Lincoln County* _____ 50-61. Thai *Chang* (62)
LST-900 _____ *Linn County* _____ Korean *Buk Han* (58)
LST-901 _____ *Litchfield County* _____ 51-69. Str75
LST-902 _____ *Luzerne County* _____ 52-55, 63-70. Str 70
LST-903 _____ *Lyman County* _____ Target 59
LST-904 _____ *Lyon County* _____ Target 59
LST-905 _____ *Madera County* _____ 63-69. Philippine *Ilicos Norte* (69)
LST-912 _____ *Mahnomen County* _____ 44-55, 63-66. Lost 30/12/66
LST-914 _____ *Mahoning County* _____ 50-59. Sold 60
LST-938 _____ *Maricopa County* _____ 44-49. 51-56. Vietnam *Danang* (62)
LST-953 _____ *Marinette County* _____ Sold 59
LST-975 _____ *Marion County* _____ 50-62. Vietnam *Camranh* (62)
LST-980 _____ *Meeker County* _____ 44-55, 66-71. Sold 76
LST-983 _____ *Middlesex County* _____ 44-56, 61-69. Indonesian *Teluk Tomani* (75)

LST-987 _____ *Millard County* _____ 44-50. Str60

LST-988 _____ *Mineral County* _____ 44-50, 51-57. Target 57

LST-1032 _____ *Monmouth County* _____ 44-55, 63-70. Sold 71

LST-1038 _____ *Monroe County* _____ 45-49. Sold 59

LST-1041 _____ *Montgomery County* _____ 45-56. Str60

LST-1048 _____ *Morgan County* _____ 50-59. Sold 60

LST-1064 _____ *Nansemond County* _____ Japanese *Shiretoko* (61), Philippine *Samar Del Norte* (76)

LST-1066 _____ *New London County* _____ 65-73. Chilean *Cdte. Hemmerdinger* (73)

LST-1067 _____ *Nye County* _____ 65-73. Chilean *Cdte Araya* (73)

LST-1068 _____ *Orange County* _____ 50-57. Target 58

LST-1069 _____ *Orleans Parish* _____ 52-76. MCS-6 (59-66), Philippine *Cotabato Del Norte* (75)

LST-1071 _____ *Ouachita County* _____ 51-56. Sold 60

LST-1072 _____ *na* _____ 45-76. Philippine *Tawi Tawi* (76)

LST-1073 _____ *Outagamie County* _____ 50-71. Brazilian *Garcia D'Avila* (71)

LST-1074 _____ *Overton County* _____ Sold 59

LST-1076 _____ *Page County* _____ 60-71. Greek *Kriti* (71)

LST-1077 _____ *Park County* _____ 50-55, 66-71. Mexican *Rio Panuco* (71)

LST-1079 _____ *Payette County* _____ 50-59. Sold 60

LST-1080 _____ *Pender County* _____ 50-58. Korean *Hwa San* (58)

LST-1081 _____ *Pima County* _____ 51-56. Sold 59

LST-1082 _____ *Pitkin County* _____ 50-55, 66-71. Sold 76

LST-1083 _____ *Plumas County* _____ 50-65. Sold 73

LST-1084 _____ *Polk County* _____ 50-69. Str74

LST-1086 _____ *Potter County* _____ Greek *Ikaria* (60)

LST-1088 _____ *Pulaski County* _____ 63-74. Sold 75

LST-1089 _____ *Rice County* _____ 50-60. W German *Bochum* (60), Turkish *Sancaktar* (72)

LST-1090 _____ *Russell County* _____ 50-60. Indonesian *Tandjung Radja* (60)

LST-1091 _____ *Sagadahoc County* _____ Taiwan *Chung Chih* (58)

LST-1096 _____ *St Clair County* _____ 50-69. Sold 76

LST-1101 _____ *Saline County* _____ 50-60. W German *Bottrop* (60), Turkish *Bayraktar* (72)

LST-1110 _____ *San Bernardino County* 45-58. Taiwan *Chung Chiang* (58)

LST-1122 _____ *San Joaquin County* _____ 45-49, 50-69. Sold 74

LST-1123 _____ *Sedgwick County* _____ 45-55, 66-75. Malaysian *Rajah Jarom* (76)

LST-1126 _____ *Snohomish County* _____ 45-70. BU71

LST-1128 _____ *Solano County* _____ Indonesian *Teluk Langsa* (60)

LST-1129 _____ *Somervell County* _____ Str58

LST-1134 _____ *Stark County* _____ 45-66. Thai *Pangan* (66)

LST-1138 _____ *Steuben County* _____ 45-61. BU62

LST-1141 _____ *Stone County* _____ 45-49, 50-70. Thai *Lanta* (70)

LST-1142 _____ *Strafford County* _____ Sold 59

LST-1144 _____ *Sublette County* _____ 45-60. Taiwan *Chung Yeh* (61)

LST-1146 _____ *Summit County* _____ 45-69. Ecuadorian *Hualcopo* (77)

LST-1148 _____ *Sumner County* _____ 50-69. Sold 75

LST-1150 _____ *Sutter County* _____ 66-70. Sold 75

LST-1152 _____ *Sweetwater County* _____ Taiwan *Chung Ming* (58)

**Notes:** Named 1955. *Garrett County, Harnett County, Hunterdon County* converted to coastal craft tender. *King County,* converted to missile test ship. *Orleans Parish* converted to mine countermeasures support ship.

---

**Details:** 2,324 tons, 6,000f/l; 382 (oa)×54×14'5; two shafts, steam turbines, SHP 6,000=14kt; 2×5in/38, 4×40mm guns; 190 crew

*Above:*
**The landing ship tank *Talbot County* (LST-1153) in
1959. Single 5in guns are carried at bow and
stern.** *Official US Navy*

LST-1153 —— *Talbot County* ———— Boston ———————— 24/04/47 —— 47-70. Sold 74
LST-1154 —— *Tallahatchie County* —— Boston ———————— 19/07/46 —— 49-70. AVB-2 (61), Str70

**Notes:** LST-1155 not built. LST-1154 converted to
aviation base ship. Named 1955.

**Details:** 2,590 tons, 5,800f/l; 384 (oa)×56×17; two
shafts, diesel, SHP 6,000=14kt; 6×3in/50 guns; 116
crew

LST-1156 —— *Terrebonne Parish* ——— Bath ——————— 09/08/52 —— 52-71. Spanish *Velasco* (71)
LST-1157 —— *Terrell County* ———————— Bath ——————— 06/12/52 —— 53-71. Greek *Oinoussa* (77)
LST-1158 —— *Tioga County* ——————————— Bath ——————— 11/04/53 —— 53-73. Str73
LST-1159 —— *Tom Green County* ——— Bath ——————— 02/07/53 —— 53-71. Spanish *Conde Del Venadito* (71)
LST-1160 —— *Traverse County* ————— Bath ——————— 03/10/53 —— 53-70. Peruvian *Eten* (84)
LST-1161 —— *Vernon County* ——————— Ingalls ——————— 25/11/52 —— 53-73. Venezuelan *Amazonas* (73)
LST-1162 —— *Wahkiakum County* —— Ingalls ——————— 23/01/53 —— 53-73. Str73
LST-1163 —— *Waldo County* ——————— Ingalls ——————— 17/03/53 —— 53-73. Peruvian *Pisco* (84)
LST-1164 —— *Walworth County* ——— Ingalls ——————— 18/05/53 —— 53-73. Peruvian *Piata* (84)
LST-1165 —— *Washoe County* ——————— Ingalls ——————— 14/07/53 —— 53-73. Peruvian *Callao* (84)
LST-1166 —— *Washtenaw County* —— Christy ——————— 22/11/52 —— 53-73. MSS-2 (73), Str73
LST-1167 —— *Westchester County* — Christy ——————— 18/04/53 —— 53-73. Turkish *Serdar* (74)
LST-1168 —— *Wexford County* ——————— Christy ——————— 28/11/53 —— 54-71. Spanish *Martin Alvarez* (71)
LST-1169 —— *Whitfield County* ——— Christy ——————— 22/08/53 —— 54-73. Greek *Kos* (77)
LST-1170 —— *Windham County* ————— Christy ——————— 22/05/54 —— 54-73. Turkish *Ertogrul* (73)

**Notes:** Named 1955. 1166 converted to station ship for
minesweepers in Vietnam.

Above:
**The landing ship tank *Wahkiakum County* (LST-1162).**
*Below:*
***Wood County* (LST-1178). This class of landing ship tank was significantly larger than its World War 2 predecessors.**

Bottom:
***Cayuga* (LST-1186), a landing ship tank of the 'Newport class', with 'horns' over the bow to lower the tank ramp which replaced the bow doors of previous classes. Lashed aft are pontoon causeways for unloading on to shallow beaches.**
*Michael D. J. Lennon*

**Details:** 4,164 tons, 7,100f/l; 445 (oa)×62×16'5; two shafts, diesels, SHP 14,400=17.5kt; 6×3in/50 guns; 184 crew

| | | | | |
|---|---|---|---|---|
| LST-1171 | De Soto County | Avondale | 28/01/57 | 58-72. Italian Grado (72) |
| LST-1173 | Suffolk County | Boston | 5/09/56 | 57-72 |
| LST-1174 | Grant County | Avondale | 12/10/56 | 57-73. Brazilian Duque De Caxias (73) |
| LST-1175 | York County | Newport News | 05/03/57 | 57-72. Italian Caorle (72) |
| LST-1176 | Graham County | Newport News | 19/09/57 | 58-77. AGP-1176 (72) Str77 |
| LST-1177 | Lorain County | American | 22/06/57 | 58-72 |
| LST-1178 | Wood County | American | 14/12/57 | 59-72 |

**Notes:** 1172 cancelled. 1176 converted to coastal craft tender.

**Details:** 4,750 tons, 8,342 f/l; 522'3 (oa)×69'5×17'6; two shafts, diesels, SHP 16,000=20kt; 4×3in/50 guns; 218 crew

| | | | | |
|---|---|---|---|---|
| LST-1179 | Newport | Philadelphia | 03/02/68 | 69- |
| LST-1180 | Manitowoc | Philadelphia | 04/01/69 | 70- |
| LST-1181 | Sumter | Philadelphia | 13/12/69 | 70- |
| LST-1182 | Fresno | National | 28/09/68 | 69- |
| LST-1183 | Peoria | National | 23/11/68 | 70- |
| LST-1184 | Frederick | National | 08/03/69 | 70- |
| LST-1185 | Schenectady | National | 24/05/69 | 70- |
| LST-1186 | Cayuga | National | 12/07/69 | 70- |
| LST-1187 | Tuscaloosa | National | 6/09/69 | 70- |
| LST-1188 | Saginaw | National | 07/02/70 | 71- |
| LST-1189 | San Bernardino | National | 28/03/70 | 71- |
| LST-1190 | Boulder | National | 22/06/70 | 71 |

*Left:*
**The landing ship tank Boulder (LST-1190) when 60% complete at its shipyard in San Diego in 1970. Note the asymmetrical funnels and lowered stern ramp.**
*Official US Navy*

LST-1191 —— *Racine* ———————— National ————— 15/08/70 —— 71-
LST-1192 —— *Spartanburg County* —— National ————— 07/11/70 —— 71-
LST-1193 —— *Fairfax County* ————— National ————— 18/12/70 —— 71-
LST-1194 —— *La Moure County* ——— National ————— 13/02/71 —— 71-
LST-1195 —— *Barbour County* ———— National ————— 15/05/71 —— 72-
LST-1196 —— *Harlan County* ————— National ————— 24/07/71 —— 72-
LST-1197 —— *Barnstable County* —— National ————— 02/10/71 —— 72-
LST-1198 —— *Bristol County* ———— National ————— 04/12/71 —— 72-

**Notes:** Departure from traditional LST design without bow doors, with ramp lowered from bow by an overhanging crane. Pointed bow allows higher speed. Asymmetrical funnels.

# MEDIUM LANDING SHIPS

**Details:** 520 tons, 1,095f/l; 196′6 (wl), 203′6 (oa)×34′6×8′4; two shafts, diesels, SHP 2,800=13kt; 2×40mm AA guns; 50 crew.

**Notes:** 161 were on the list 1949, 12 in 1958. Carry five tanks.

**Names:** *Kodiak* (161), *Oceanside* (175), *Lakeland* (373), *Raritan* (540). 445-446 converted to drone catapult control craft, renamed *Catapult* (YV 1) and *Launcher* (YV-2).

# INSHORE FIRE SUPPORT SHIP

**Displacement:** 1,040 tons; 1,500 f/l
**Dimensions:** 237 (wl), 245 (oa)×38′6×11
**Machinery:** Two shafts, diesel, SHP 3,100=15kt

**Endurance:** 5,000/12
**Armament:** 1×5in/38 gun, eight twin rocket launchers
**Complement:** 156

IFS-1 ———————— *Carronade* —————————— PS Bridge ————— 26/05/53 —— 55-60. 65-70. BU74

**Note:** Prototype, improved LSMR. Reclassified LFR 1969.

*Below:*
**The *Carronade* (IFS-1) was an inshore fire support ship for rocket support of amphibious landings: it was a one-of-a-kind ship that was not repeated. The rocket launchers are positioned forward of a single 5in gun.** *Martin E. Holbrook collection*

# ROCKET LANDING SHIPS

**Details:** 790 tons; 204'6 (wl), 206'3 (oa)×34'6×7'3; Two
shafts, diesels, SHP 2,800=13kt; 1×5in/38, 4×40mm
AA guns, 4×4.2in mortars, 20 automatic rocket
launchers; 75 crew.

LSMR-401 ___ *Big Black River* _____ 50-53. Sold 74

LSMR-402 ___ *Big Horn River* _____ Sold 60

LSMR-403 ___ *Blackstone River* _____ Sold 60

LSMR-404 ___ *Black Warrior River* _____ Sold 60

LSMR-405 ___ *Broadkill River* _____ 65 . Sold 74

LSMR-406 ___ *Canadian River* _____ Str60

LSMR-407 ___ *Chariton River* _____ Sold 60

LSMR-408 ___ *Charles River* _____ Sold 60

LSMR-409 ___ *Clarion River* _____ 50-53, 65-70. Sold 70

LSMR-410 ___ *Clark Fork River* _____ Str60

LSMR-411 ___ *Cumberland River* _____ Str60

LSMR-412 ___ *Des Plaines River* _____ 50-53. Sold 73

LSMR-501 ___ *Elk River* _____ 45- . IX-501 (67)

LSMR-502 ___ *Escalante River* _____ Sold 60

LSMR-503 ___ *Flambeau River* _____ Sold 60

LSMR-504 ___ *Gila River* _____ Sold 60

LSMR-505 ___ *Grand River* _____ Sold 59

LSMR-506 ___ *Green River* _____ Sold 59

LSMR-507 ___ *Greenbrier River* _____ Sold 59

LSMR-508 ___ *Gunnison River* _____ *Targeteer* (YV-3) (60). Sold 69

LSMR-509 ___ *Holston River* _____ Sold 59

LSMR-510 ___ *James River* _____ Sold 61

LSMR-511 ___ *John Day River* _____ Sold 60

LSMR-512 ___ *Lamoille River* _____ 45-55. Sold 74

LSMR-513 ___ *Laramie River* _____ BU74

LSMR-514 ___ *Maurice River* _____ 45-54. Sold 61

LSMR-515 ___ *Owyhee River* _____ 45-55. Sold 74

LSMR-516 ___ *Pearl River* _____ Sold 59

LSMR-517 ___ *Pee Dee River* _____ 54-55. Sold 61

LSMR-518 ___ *Pit River* _____ Sold 59

LSMR-519 ___ *Powder River* _____ Sold 59

LSMR-520 ___ *Raccoon River* _____ 52-55. Sold 61

LSMR-521 ___ *Rainy River* _____ Sold 59

LSMR-522 ___ *Red River* _____ 51-55. Sold 74

LSMR-523 ___ *Republican River* _____ Str60

LSMR-524 ___ *St Croix River* _____ Str58

LSMR-525 ___ *St Francis River* _____ 50-55, 65-70. BU70

LSMR-526 ___ *St Johns River* _____ Sold 59

*Right:*
**The *St Francis River* (LMSR-525), seen in 1965. This
rocket landing ship was converted from the hull of
a landing ship medium.** *Official US Navy*

LSMR-527 __ *St Joseph River* _____ 50-55. Korean *Si Hung* (60)

LSMR-528 __ *St Mary's River* _____ Sold 59

LSMR-529 __ *St Regis River* _____ Sold 60

LSMR-530 __ *Salmon Falls River* _____ Sold 59

LSMR-531 __ *Smoky Hill River* _____ Panamanian *Tiburon* (75)

LSMR-532 __ *Smyrna River* _____ W German *Otter* (58)

LSMR-533 __ *Snake River* _____ Sold 59

LSMR-534 __ *Thames River* _____ W German *Natter* (58)

LSMR-535 __ *Trinity River* _____ Str59

LSMR-536 __ *White River* _____ 50-56, 65-70. Sold 70

**Notes:** Modified LSM. Rocket launchers can fire 30×5in rounds per minute. Reclassified LFR 1955. *Elk River* lengthened and converted to deep sea diving and salvage training ship 1968.

# INFANTRY LANDING SHIPS

**Details:** 209 tons, 387f/l; 159 (oa)×23′8×5′8; two shafts, diesel, SHP 1,600=14.4kt; carry 205 troops.

**Notes:** Built as LCI(L), reclassified LSIL. 74 LSIL, 6 LSIM and 25 LSFF of this type were on the list in 1950.

# SUPPORT LANDING SHIPS

**Details:** 227 tons, 383f/l; 158′5 (oa)×23′3×5′10; machinery as LSIL. 1×3in/50, 4×40mm guns; 73 crew.

**Notes:** Built as LCS(L), reclassified LSSL. 106 were on the list in 1950.

*Below:*
**The support landing ship LSSL-24 in 1959.**
*Official US Navy/Ernest Arroyo collection*

# AMPHIBIOUS COMMAND SHIPS

**Details:** 7,430 tons, 12,800f/l; 435 (wl), 459'3
(oa)×63×24; one shaft, steam turbines,
SHP 6,000=16.4kt; 2×5in/38, 8×40mm AA guns

AGC-1 _____ *Appalachian* _____ Federal _____ 29/01/43 ___ BU60
AGC-2 _____ *Blue Ridge* _____ Federal _____ 07/03/43 ___ BU61
AGC-3 _____ *Rocky Mount* _____ Federal _____ 07/03/43 ___ Str60
AGC-5 _____ *Catoctin* _____ Moore _____ 23/01/43 ___ Str59

**Details:** 7,234 tons (13: 7,201; 15-17: 6,884), 15,295f/l;
435 (wl), 459'2 (oa)×63×24; one shaft, steam
turbines, SHP 6,000=16kt; 2×5in/38, 8×40mm AA
guns

AGC-7 _____ *Mount McKinley* _____ North Carolina _____ 27/09/43 ___ 44-70. LCC, Str76
AGC-8 _____ *Mount Olympus* _____ North Carolina _____ 03/10/43 ___ 44-56. Str61
AGC-9 _____ *Wasatch* _____ North Carolina _____ 08/10/43 ___ Str60
AGC-10 _____ *Auburn* _____ North Carolina _____ 19/10/43 ___ Str60
AGC-11 _____ *Eldorado* _____ North Carolina _____ 26/10/43 ___ 44-72, LCC, Str72
AGC-12 _____ *Estes* _____ North Carolina _____ 01/11/43 ___ 51-70, LCC, Str76
AGC-13 _____ *Panamint* _____ North Carolina _____ 09/11/43 ___ Str60
AGC-14 _____ *Teton* _____ North Carolina _____ 05/02/44 ___ Str61
AGC-15 _____ *Adirondack* _____ North Carolina _____ 13/01/45 ___ 45-50, 51-55. Str61
AGC-16 _____ *Pocono* _____ North Carolina _____ 25/01/45 ___ 45-49, 51-71. LCC. Str76
AGC-17 _____ *Taconic* _____ North Carolina _____ 10/02/45 ___ 45-69. LCC, Str76

**Notes:** Reclassified LCC 1969. Active units received
helicopter decks in 1950. *Williamsburg*, formerly PG-56,
Presidential Yacht, was classified AGC-369.

**Details:** 11,500 tons, 19.290f/l; 620 (oa)×82×25'5; 108'
extreme width; one shaft, steam turbines,
SHP 22,000=20kt; 4×3in/50 guns, two Sea Sparrow
BPDMS (added 1974); 1,000 crew.

*Above:*
**The amphibious command ship *Pocono* (AGC-16),
showing its postwar modifications which included
a helicopter deck aft and a large radar mast.**

| LCC-19 | Blue Ridge | Philadelphia | 04/01/69 | 70- |
| LCC-20 | Mount Whitney | Newport News | 08/01/71 | 70- |

**Notes:** Ordered as AGC; LCC-21 cancelled. Hull and propulsion similar to 'Iwo Jima' class LPH. Used as fleet flagships.

*Right:*
**The amphibious command ship *Mount Whitney* (LCC-20) has large open decks which allow space for antennae. Accommodation is provided for a navy amphibious task force commander and a Marine assault force commander and their staffs.**
*Official US Navy*

# AMPHIBIOUS CARGO SHIPS

**Details:** 6,194 tons, 10,432f/l; 435 (wl), 459'1
(oa)×63×25'10; one shaft, diesels, SHP 6,000=15.5kt.

| AKA-3 | Bellatrix | Tampa | 15/08/41 | 52-55. Peruvian *Independencia* (64) |
| AKA-4 | Electra | Tampa | 18/11/41 | 51-55. Str61 |

**Notes:** Re-acquired 1951.

**Details:** 5,185 tons, 14,440f/l; 435 (wl), 459'2
(oa)×63×25'10; one shaft, steam turbines,
SHP 6,000=16.5kt; 1×5in/38m 8×40mm AA guns; 250
crew.

| AKA-12 | Libra | Federal | 12/11/41 | 42-48, 50-55. Str60 |
| AKA-13 | Titania | Federal | 28/02/42 | 42-55. Str61 |
| AKA-14 | Oberon | Federal | 18/03/42 | 42-55. Str60 |

**Details:** 6,556 tons, 11,000f-l; 435 (wl), 459'2
(oa)×63×25'9; one shaft, steam turbines,
SHP 6,000=16.4kt; 1×5in/38, 8×40mm AA guns; 247
crew.

| AKA-15 | Andromeda | Federal | 22/12/42 | 43-56. Str60 |
| AKA-19 | Thuban | Federal | 26/04/43 | 43-68. LKA; Str77 |
| AKA-20 | Virgo | Federal | 04/06/43 | 43-58, 66-71. AE-30 (65), Str71 |
| AKA-53 | Achernar | Federal | 03/12/43 | 44-56. Spanish *Castilla* (65) |
| AKA-54 | Algol | Moore | 17/02/43 | 44-58, 65-70. LKA; Str77 |
| AKA-55 | Alshain | Federal | 26/01/44 | 44-55. Str60 |
| AKA-56 | Arneb | Moore | 06/07/43 | 44-71. LKA; BU73 |
| AKA-57 | Capricornus | Moore | 14/08/43 | 50-70. LKA; Str77 |
| AKA-58 | Chara | Federal | 15/03/44 | 44-59, 65-72. AE-31 (65), Str72 |

112

Above:
**The amphibious cargo ship *Libra* (AKA-12) in 1954.** *Marius Bar*

Below:
**Capricornus (AKA-57), an amphibious cargo ship.**

| AKA-59 | Diphda | Federal | 11/05/44 | 44-56. Str61 |
|---|---|---|---|---|
| AKA-60 | Leo | Federal | 29/06/44 | 44-55. BU76 |
| AKA-61 | Muliphen | Federal | 26/08/44 | 44-70. LKA; Str77 |
| AKA-88 | Uvalde | Moore | 20/05/44 | 44-68. BU69 |
| AKA-89 | Warrick | Moore | 29/05/44 | 44-57. Target 71 |
| AKA 90 | Whiteside | Moore | 12/06/44 | 44-58. Target 71 |
| AKA-91 | Whitley | Moore | 22/06/44 | 44-55. Italian *Etna* (62) |
| AKA-92 | Wyandot | Moore | 28/06/44 | 44-59, 61-75. AK-283 (69) |
| AKA-93 | Yancey | Moore | 08/07/44 | 44-57, 61-70. LKA; Str77 |
| AKA-94 | Winston | Federal | 30/11/44 | 45-69. LKA; Str76 |
| AKA-95 | Marquette | Federal | 29/04/45 | 45-55. BU72 |
| AKA-96 | Mathews | Federal | 22/12/44 | 51-68. BU69 |
| AKA-97 | Merrick | Federal | 28/01/45 | 52-69. LKA |
| AKA-98 | Montague | Federal | 11/02/45 | 45-55. BU71 |
| AKA-99 | Rolette | Federal | 11/03/45 | 51-56. Str60 |
| AKA-100 | Oglethorpe | Federal | 15/04/45 | 45-67. BU69 |

**Notes:** *Arneb* modified for polar navigation 1948.
*Virgo* and *Chara* converted to ammunition ships.
*Mathews*, *Merrick* and *Rolette* re-acquired 1951.
*Wyandot* stricken 1960 and re-acquired 1961.
Reclassified LKA 1969.

**Details:** 6,318 tons, 10,440f/l; 435 (wl), 459'2
(oa)×63×26'4; one shaft, steam turbines,
SHP 6,000=16.5kt; 1×5in/38, 8×40mm AA guns; 247
crew

| | | | | |
|---|---|---|---|---|
| AKA-103 | *Rankin* | North Carolina | 22/12/44 | 52-71. LKA, Str77 |
| AKA-104 | *Seminole* | North Carolina | 28/12/44 | 45-70. LKA |
| AKA-105 | *Skagit* | North Carolina | 18/11/44 | 45-49, 50-69. LKA; Str69 |
| AKA-106 | *Union* | North Carolina | 23/11/44 | 45-70. LKA; Str76 |
| AKA-107 | *Vermilion* | North Carolina | 12/12/44 | 45-49, 50-71. LKA; Str77 |
| AKA-108 | *Washburn* | North Carolina | 18/12/44 | 45-70. LKA; Str76 |

**Notes:** *Rankin* re-acquired 1951. Reclassified LKA
1969.

**Details:** 9,050 tons, 16,800f/l; 528'6 (wl), 564
(oa)×76×28; one shaft, steam turbines,
SHP 22,000=22kt; 12×3in/50 guns; 325 crew

| | | | | |
|---|---|---|---|---|
| AKA-112 | *Tulare* | Beth; S Fran | 22/12/53 | 56-80. LKA; Str81 |
| | ex-*Evergreen Mariner* | | | |

**Notes:** Acquired 1956. 6×3in guns removed 1975.

*Above:*
**The amphibious cargo ship *Tulare* (AKA-112) was
converted from a 'Mariner' class freighter'.**

**Details:** 13,727 tons, 20,700f/l; 575'6 (oa)×82×25'6;
one shaft, steam turbines, SHP 22,000=22kt; 8×3in/50
guns; 334 crew

| | | | | |
|---|---|---|---|---|
| LKA-113 | *Charleston* | Newport News | 02/12/67 | 68- |

| | | | | | |
|---|---|---|---|---|---|
| LKA-114 | Durham | Newport News | 29/03/68 | 69- |
| LKA-115 | Mobile | Newport News | 19/10/68 | 69- |
| LKA-116 | St Louis | Newport News | 04/01/69 | 69- |
| LKA-117 | El Paso | Newport News | 17/05/69 | 70- |

**Notes:** FY65. Ordered as AKA, reclassified 1968. 2×3in removed.

# AMPHIBIOUS TRANSPORTS

**Details:** 10,210 tons, 14,400f/l; 465 (wl) 491'10
   (oa)×69'6×26'6; one shaft, steam turbines, SHP
   8,500=18.4kt; 4×3in/50, 6×40mm guns; 512 crew

| | | | | |
|---|---|---|---|---|
| APA-18 | President Jackson | Newport News | 07/06/40 | 42-55. Str58 |
| APA-19 | President Adams | Newport News | 31/01/41 | 41-50. Str58 |
| APA-20 | President Hayes | Newport News | 04/10/40 | 41-49. Str58 |
| APA-30 | Thomas Jefferson | Newport News | 20/11/40 | 42-55. Str58 |

**Notes:** Acquired 1941-42. Carried 1,500 troops.

**Details:** 8,429 tons, 13,100f/l; 465 (wl) 491
   (oa)×65'6×25'8; one shaft, steam turbines, SHP
   8,600=17kt; 1×5in/38, 4×3in/50, 4×40mm guns

| | | | | |
|---|---|---|---|---|
| APA-21 | Crescent City | Sparrows Pt | 17/02/40 | Str58 |
| APA-28 | Charles Carroll | Sparrows Pt | 24/03/42 | Str58 |
| APA-31 | Monrovia | Sparrows Pt | 19/09/42 | 50-68. Str68 |
| APA-32 | Calvert | Sparrows Pt | 22/06/42 | 50-66. Str66 |

**Notes:** Acquired 1941-42.

**Details:** 10,812 tons, 15,500f/l; 465 (wl) 489
   (oa)×69'9×27'4; one shaft, steam turbines, SHP
   8,400=18.4kt; 4×3in/50, 4×40mm AA guns

| | | | | |
|---|---|---|---|---|
| APA-25 | Arthur Middleton | Ingalls | 28/06/41 | Str58 |
| APA-26 | Samuel Chase | Ingalls | 25/08/41 | Str58 |
| APA-27 | George Clymer | Ingalls | 27/09/41 | 42-66. Str67 |

**Notes:** Acquired 1942. Carried 1,600 troops.

**Details:** 8,920 tons, 12,900f/l; 465 (wl) 492
   (oa)×69'6×26'6; one shaft, steam turbines, SHP
   8,500=18.4kt; 2×5in/38, 8×40mm guns

| | | | | |
|---|---|---|---|---|
| APA-33 | Bayfield | Western Pipe | 15/02/43 | 43-68. BU69 |
| APA-36 | Cambria | Western Pipe | 10/11/42 | 50-70. LPA; Sold 71 |
| APA-37 | Cavalier | Western Pipe | 15/03/43 | 44-68. BU69 |
| APA-38 | Chilton | Western Pipe | 29/12/42 | 43-73. LPA; Str72 |
| APA-44 | Fremont | Ingalls | 31/03/43 | 43-69. LPA; Str73 |
| APA-45 | Henrico | Ingalls | 31/03/43 | 43-68. LPA; Str73 |

**Notes:** Carried 1,900 troops.

Above:
***Bayfield* (APA-33), an attack transport, in 1955.**
*Official US Navy*

**Details:** 4,100 tons; 400 (wl) 426 (oa)×58×15′6; two
shafts, turbine-electric, SHP 6,600=16.5kt; 1×5in/38,
8×40mm guns

| APA-63 | Bladen | Consolidated | 31/05/44 | Str53 |
| APA-67 | Burleson | Consolidated | 11/07/44 | IX-67 (56) |
| APA-87 | Niagara | Consolidated | 10/02/45 | BU50 |

**Details:** 6,873 tons, 10,680f/l; 436′6 (wl) 455
(oa)×62×24; one shaft, steam turbines; SHP
8,500=17.7kt; 1×5in/38, 12×40mm guns; 536 crew

| APA-128 | Arenac | Calship | 14/09/44 | Str58 |
| APA-132 | Barnwell | Calship | 30/09/44 | Str58 |
| APA-136 | Botetourt | Calship | 19/10/44 | 50-56. Str61 |
| APA-140 | Brookings | Calship | 20/11/44 | Str58 |
| APA-144 | Clinton | Calship | 29/11/44 | Str58 |
| APA-148 | Crockett | Kaiser | 28/11/44 | Str58 |
| APA-152 | Latimer | Oregon | 04/07/44 | 50-56. Str60 |
| APA-156 | Mellette | Oregon | 04/08/44 | 50-55. Str60 |
| APA-160 | Deuel | Oregon | 04/09/44 | 50-56. Str58 |
| APA-164 | Edgecombe | Oregon | 24/09/44 | Str58 |
| APA-168 | Gage | Oregon | 14/10/44 | Str58 |
| APA-172 | Grimes | Oregon | 27/10/44 | Str58 |
| APA-176 | Kershaw | Oregon | 12/11/44 | Str58 |
| APA-180 | Lavaca | Oregon | 27/11/44 | Str58 |
| APA-188 | Olmsted | Kaiser | 04/07/44 | 52-59. Str60 |
| APA-192 | Rutland | Kaiser | 10/08/44 | Str58 |
| APA-193 | Sanborn | Kaiser | 19/08/44 | 51-56. Str60 |
| APA-194 | Sandoval | Kaiser | 02/09/44 | 51-55, 61-70. LPA; Str71 |
| APA-195 | Lenawee | Kaiser | 11/09/44 | 50-67. Str68 |
| APA-196 | Logan | Kaiser | 19/09/44 | 51-55. Str60 |
| APA-197 | Lubbock | Kaiser | 25/09/44 | Str58 |
| APA-198 | McCracken | Kaiser | 29/09/44 | Str58 |

| | | | | |
|---|---|---|---|---|
| APA-199 | Magoffin | Kaiser | 04/10/44 | 50-68. LPA; Str68 |
| APA-201 | Menard | Kaiser | 11/10/44 | 44-48, 50-55. Str61 |
| APA-202 | Menifee | Kaiser | 15/10/44 | 50-55. Str58 |
| APA-203 | Meriwether | Kaiser | 18/10/44 | Str58 |
| APA-204 | Sarasota | Permanente | 14/06/44 | 51-55. Str60 |
| APA-205 | Sherburne | Permanente | 10/07/44 | Str58; *Range Sentinel* (AGM-22)(69) |
| APA-206 | Sibley | Permanente | 19/07/44 | Str58 |
| APA-207 | Mifflin | Permanente | 07/08/44 | Str58 |
| APA-208 | Talladega | Permanente | 17/08/44 | 51-69. LPA; Str71 |
| APA-209 | Tazewell | Permanente | 22/08/44 | Str58 |
| APA-210 | Telfair | Permanente | 30/08/44 | 50-58, 61-68. Str68 |
| APA-211 | Missoula | Permanente | 06/09/44 | Str58 |
| APA-212 | Montrose | Permanente | 13/09/44 | 50-69. LPA; Str69 |
| APA-213 | Mountrail | Permanente | 20/09/44 | 50-69. LPA; Str71 |
| APA-214 | Natrona | Permanente | 27/09/44 | Str58 |
| APA-215 | Navarro | Permanente | 03/10/44 | 50-69. LPA; Str70 |
| APA-216 | Neshoba | Permanente | 07/10/44 | Str58 |
| APA-217 | New Kent | Permanente | 12/10/44 | 44-49, 51-54. Str58 |
| APA-218 | Noble | Permanenté | 18/10/44 | 44-64, Spanish *Aragon* (64) |
| APA-219 | Okaloosa | Permanente | 22/10/44 | 44-49. Str58 |
| APA-220 | Okanogan | Permanente | 26/10/44 | 44-70. LPA; Str73 |
| APA-221 | Oneida | Permanente | 31/10/44 | Str58 |
| APA-222 | Pickaway | Permanente | 05/11/44 | 44-70. LPA; Str71 |
| APA-224 | Randall | Permanente | 15/11/44 | 44-56. Str60 |
| APA-226 | Rawlins | Kaiser | 21/10/44 | Str58 |

*Below:*
**The amphibious transport *Deuel* (APA-160), one of a large class of which many remained in service for decades after World War 2.**

U.S.S. DEUEL (APA-160)

| APA-227 | Renville | Kaiser | 25/10/44 | 45-49, 52-68. Str58 |
| APA-228 | Rockbridge | Kaiser | 28/10/44 | 50-68. Str68 |
| APA-229 | Rockingham | Kaiser | 01/11/44 | Str58 |
| APA-230 | Rockwall | Kaiser | 05/11/44 | 51-55. Str68 |
| APA-232 | San Saba | Kaiser | 12/11/44 | Str58 |
| APA-235 | Bottineau | Kaiser | 22/11/44 | 51-55. Str61 |
| APA-236 | Bronx | Oregon | 14/07/45 | 45-49. Str58 |
| APA-237 | Bexar | Oregon | 25/07/45 | 45-69. LPA; Str70 |
| APA-238 | Dane | Oregon | 09/08/45 | Str58 |
| APA-239 | Glynn | Oregon | 25/08/45 | 51-55. Str60 |

**Notes:** Victory ship hulls built as transports.
*Sherburne* re-acquired for conversion to missile range
instrumentation ship.

**Details:** 10,709 tons, 16,838f/l; 528 (wl) 563'6
(oa)×76×28; one shaft, steam turbines, SHP
19,250=22kt; 4×3in/50 guns; complement 414

| APA-248 | Paul Revere | NY Sbdg | 11/04/53 | 58-79. LPA; Spanish *Castilla* (80) |
| | ex-*Diamond Mariner* | | | |
| APA-249 | Francis Marion | NY Sbdg | 13/02/54 | 61-79. LPA; Spanish *Aragon* (80) |
| | ex-*Prairie Mariner* | | | |

**Notes:** 'Mariner' class hulls acquired 1959. Carried
1,657 troops. Helicopter deck aft.

# HIGH SPEED TRANSPORTS

**Details:** 1,400 tons, 2,130f/l; 306 (oa)×37×12'7; two
shafts, turbo-electric drive; SHP 12,000=23.6kt;
1×5in/38 guns; 214 crew

| APD-37 | Charles Lawrence | Hingham | 16/02/43 | BU66 |
| APD-38 | Daniel T. Griffin | Hingham | 25/02/43 | Chilean *Virgilio Uribe* (67) |
| APD-39 | Barr | Hingham | 28/12/43 | Str60 |
| APD-40 | Bowers | Beth: S Fran | 31/10/43 | 51-58. Philippine *Rajah Soliman* (61), lost 06/64 |
| APD-42 | Gantner | Hingham | 17/04/43 | 43-49. Taiwan *Wen Shan* (66) |
| APD-43 | George W. Ingram | Hingham | 08/05/43 | Taiwan *Kang Shan* (67) |
| APD-44 | Ira Jeffery | Hingham | 15/05/43 | Sunk as target 62 |
| APD-45 | Lee Fox | Hingham | 29/05/43 | BU66 |
| APD-46 | Amesbury | Hingham | 06/06/43 | Sold 62 |
| APD-48 | Blessman | Hingham | 19/06/43 | Taiwan *Chung Shan* (67) |
| APD-49 | Joseph E. Campbell | Hingham | 26/06/43 | Chilean *Riquelme* (66) |
| APD-50 | Sims | Norfolk | 06/02/43 | BU61 |
| APD-51 | Hopping | Norfolk | 10/03/43 | BU66 |
| APD-52 | Reeves | Norfolk | 22/04/43 | Sold 1961 |
| APD-53 | Joseph L. Hubbard | Charleston | 11/11/43 | BU68 |
| APD-55 | Laning | Norfolk | 04/07/43 | 51-57. LPR; sold 75 |
| APD-56 | Loy | Norfolk | 04/07/43 | BU66 |
| APD-57 | Barber | Norfolk | 20/05/43 | Mexican *Coahuila* (69) |
| APD-59 | Newman | Charleston | 09/08/43 | BU66 |
| APD-60 | Liddle | Charleston | 09/08/43 | 50-59, 61-67. BU68 |

| | | | | | |
|---|---|---|---|---|---|
| APD-61 | Kephart | Charleston | 06/09/43 | Korean *Kyong Buk* (67) |
| APD-62 | Cofer | Charleston | 06/09/43 | BU68 |
| APD-63 | Lloyd | Charleston | 23/10/43 | 51-58. BU68 |
| APD-65 | Burke | Philadelphia | 03/04/43 | 43-49. Colombian *Almirante Brion* (68) |
| APD-66 | Enright | Philadelphia | 29/05/43 | Ecuadorian *25 de Julio* (67) |
| APD-69 | Yokes | Dravo; Pitt | 27/11/43 | BU65 |
| APD-70 | Pavlic | Dravo; Pitt | 18/12/43 | BU68 |
| APD-71 | Odum | Dravo; Pitt | 19/01/44 | Chilean *Serrano* (66) |
| APD-72 | Jack C. Robinson | Dravo; Pitt | 08/01/44 | Chilean *Orella* (66) |
| APD-73 | Bassett | Dravo; Pitt | 15/01/44 | 50-53, Colombian *Almirante Tono* (68) |
| APD-74 | John P. Gray | Dravo; Pitt | 18/03/44 | Sold 68 |
| APD-75 | Weber | Quincy | 01/05/43 | Str60 |
| APD-76 | Schmitt | Quincy | 29/05/43 | 44-49. Taiwan *Lung Shan* (69) |
| APD-77 | Frament | Quincy | 28/06/43 | Sold 61 |
| APD-78 | Bull | Defoe | 25/03/43 | Taiwan *Lu Shan* (66) |
| APD-79 | Bunch | Defoe | 29/05/43 | Sold 65 |
| APD-80 | Hayter | Charleston | 11/11/43 | Korean *Chun Nam* (67) |
| APD-81 | Tatum | Consolidated | 07/08/43 | BU61 |
| APD-84 | Haines | Consolidated | 26/08/43 | BU61 |
| APD-85 | Runels | Consolidated | 04/09/43 | BU61 |
| APD-86 | Hollis | Consolidated | 11/09/43 | 51-56. LPR; sold 75 |
| APD-87 | Crosley | Philadelphia | 12/02/44 | Sold 61 |
| APD-88 | Cread | Philadelphia | 12/02/44 | Str60 |
| APD-89 | Ruchamkin | Philadelphia | 14/06/44 | 51-69. LPR; Colombian *Cordoba* (69) |
| APD-90 | Kirwin | Philadelphia | 15/06/44 | 65-68. LPR; sold 75 |
| APD-91 | Kinzer | Charleston | 09/12/43 | Taiwan *Yu Shan* (65) |
| APD-92 | Register | Charleston | 20/01/44 | Taiwan *Tai Shan* (66) |
| APD-93 | Brock | Charleston | 20/01/44 | Sold 61 |
| APD-94 | John Q. Roberts | Charleston | 11/02/44 | BU62 |
| APD-95 | William M. Hobby | Charleston | 11/02/44 | Korean *Chi Ju* (67) |
| APD-96 | Ray K. Edwards | Charleston | 19/02/44 | Sold 61 |
| APD-97 | Arthur L. Bristol | Charleston | 19/02/44 | BU65 |
| APD-98 | Truxtun | Charleston | 09/03/44 | Taiwan *Fu Shan* (66) |
| APD-99 | Upham | Charleston | 09/03/44 | Sold 61 |
| APD-100 | Ringness | Hingham | 05/02/44 | LPR; sold 75 |
| APD-101 | Knudson | Hingham | 05/02/44 | 53-58. LPR; sold 74 |
| APD-102 | Rednour | Hingham | 12/02/44 | Mexican *Chihuahua* (69) |
| APD-103 | Tollberg | Hingham | 12/02/44 | Colombian *Almirante Padilla* (65) |
| APD-104 | William J. Pattison | Hingham | 15/02/44 | Str60 |
| APD-105 | Myers | Hingham | 15/02/44 | Sold 61 |
| APD-106 | Walter B. Cobb | Hingham | 23/02/44 | 51-57 Taiwan (66), lost 21/04/66 |
| APD-107 | Earle B. Hall | Hingham | 01/03/44 | 50-57. BU66 |
| APD-108 | Harry L. Corl | Hingham | 01/03/44 | Korean *Ah San* (66) |
| APD-109 | Belet | Hingham | 03/03/44 | Mexican *California* (63), lost 72 |
| APD-110 | Julius A. Raven | Hingham | 03/03/44 | Korean *Ung Po* (66) |
| APD-111 | Walsh | Hingham | 28/04/45 | BU68 |
| APD-112 | Hunter Marshall | Hingham | 05/05/45 | Sold 61 |
| APD-113 | Earhart | Hingham | 12/05/45 | Mexican *Papaloapan* (63) |
| APD-114 | Walter S. Gorka | Hingham | 26/05/45 | Sold 61 |
| APD-115 | Rogers Blood | Hingham | 02/06/45 | BU61 |
| APD-116 | Francovich | Hingham | 05/06/45 | BU65 |
| APD-117 | Joseph M. Auman | Dravo; Pitt | 02/05/44 | Mexican *Tehuantepec* (63) |
| APD-118 | Don O. Woods | Consolidated | 09/02/44 | Mexican *Usumacinta* (63) |

| | | | | |
|---|---|---|---|---|
| APD-119 | Beverly W. Reid | Consolidated | 04/03/44 | 67/69. LPR; sold 75 |
| APD-120 | Kline | Quincy | 27/06/44 | Taiwan Shou Shan (66) |
| APD-121 | Raymon W. Herndon | Quincy | 15/07/44 | Taiwan Heng Shan (66) |
| APD-122 | Scribner | Quincy | 01/08/44 | BU67 |
| APD-123 | Diachenko | Quincy | 15/08/44 | 44-59, 64-69. LPR; sold 75 |
| APD-124 | Horace A. Bass | Quincy | 12/09/44 | 44-59. LPR; sold 75 |
| APD-125 | Wantuck | Quincy | 25/09/44 | 44-57. Str58 |
| APD-126 | Gosselin | Defoe | 04/05/44 | 44-49. BU65 |
| APD-127 | Begor | Defoe | 25/05/44 | 45-62. LPR; Indonesia (75) |
| APD-128 | Cavallaro | Defoe | 15/06/44 | 53-59. Korean Kyung Nam (59) |
| APD-129 | Donald W. Wolf | Defoe | 22/07/44 | Taiwan Hwa Shan (65) |
| APD-130 | Cook | Defoe | 26/08/44 | 53-69. LPR; BU70 |
| APD-131 | Walter X. Young | Defoe | 30/09/44 | Target 67 |
| APD-132 | Balduck | Defoe | 27/10/44 | 53-57. LPR; Indonesia (75) |
| APD-133 | Burdo | Defoe | 25/11/44 | 45-53. BU67 |
| APD-134 | Kleinsmith | Defoe | 27/01/45 | 45-60. Taiwan Tien Shan (60) |
| APD-135 | Weiss | Defoe | 17/02/45 | 50-70. LPR; sold 75 |
| APD-136 | Carpellotti | Defoe | 10/03/45 | 45-58. BU61 |
| APD-139 | Bray | Defoe | 15/04/44 | Target 63 |

**Notes:** APD-37-86 converted from 'Buckley' class destroyer escorts 1944. APD-87-139 converted from 'Rudderow' class destroyer escorts during construction. Carried 162 troops, 4 LCVP. Ruchamkin, Beverly W. Reid, Weiss and Kirwin received FRAM refit. Reclassified LPR 1955.

Below:
**The high speed transport Cook (APD-130) in 1961.**

# MINE VESSELS

## MINELAYERS

**Details:** 5,120 tons, 8,650f/l; 454 (oa)×60'2×20; two
   shafts, steam turbines, SHP 11,000=20kt; 4×5in/38
   guns, 800 mines; 400 crew

CM-5 _____ _Terror_ _____ Philadelphia _____ 06/06/41 ___ Str70

**Notes:** In reserve 1947.

---

**Details:** 910 tons, 1,315f/l; 168'8 (pp), 189 (oa)×37×12; two
   shafts, diesel, SHP 1,200=12kt; 100 crew

ACM-11 _____ _Camanche_ _____ Marietta _____ 31/10/42 ___ Merchant _Pilgrim_ (62)
ACM-12 _____ _Canonicus_ _____ Marietta _____ 07/09/42 ___ Merchant _Ocean Star_ (62)
ACM-13 _____ _Miantonomah_ _____ Marietta _____ 24/12/42 ___ 50-55. Merchant _Nautilus_ (62)
ACM-14 _____ _Monadnock_ _____ Marietta _____ 06/10/42 ___ Merchant _Tahiti_ (64)
ACM-15 _____ _Nausett_ _____ Marietta _____ 02/06/42 ___ Sold 61
ACM-16 _____ _Puritan_ _____ Marietta _____ 05/12/42 ___ Merchant (62)

**Notes:** Acquired from Army 1949-51. Reclassified
MMA and named 1955. Eight sister ships ACM-1-3 and
5-9 transferred to Coast Guard 1946.

## LIGHT MINELAYERS

**Details:** as 'Allen M. Sumner' class, except 2,380 tons,
   3,370f/l, carried 100 mines

DM-23 _____ _Robert H. Smith_ _____ Bath _____ 25/05/44 ___ BU73
DM-24 _____ _Thomas E. Fraser_ _____ Bath _____ 10/06/44 ___ 44-55. BU74
DM-25 _____ _Shannon_ _____ Bath _____ 24/06/44 ___ 44-55. BU73
DM-26 _____ _Harry F. Bauer_ _____ Bath _____ 09/07/44 ___ 44-56. BU74
DM-27 _____ _Adams_ _____ Bath _____ 23/07/44 ___ Str70
DM-28 _____ _Tolman_ _____ Bath _____ 13/08/44 ___ Str70. Target
DM-29 _____ _Henry A. Wiley_ _____ Staten Is _____ 21/04/44 ___ Str70
DM-30 _____ _Shea_ _____ Staten Is _____ 20/05/44 ___ 44-58. BU74
DM-32 _____ _Lindsey_ _____ Beth; S Pedro _____ 05/03/44 ___ Str70
DM-33 _____ _Gwin_ _____ Beth; S Pedro _____ 09/04/44 ___ 52-58. Turkish _Muavenet_ (71)

**Notes:** Reclassified MMD 1970

## MINE WARFARE COMMAND & SUPPORT SHIPS

MCS-1-5, see Landing Ships, Vehicle. MCS-6 was the
   former LST-1069 _Orleans Parish_, stricken 1966, and
   MCS-7 was _Epping Forest_ ex-LSD-4, stricken 1969, see
   page 96.

Above:
**The converted mine countermeasures ship *Orleans Parish* (MCS-6), formerly LST-1069, in 1969.**

Below:
**Ozark (MCS-2), a mine countermeasures and support ship.**

# HIGH SPEED MINESWEEPERS

**Details:** as 'Benson-Livermore' class (page 61) except only 3×5in guns

| | | | | |
|---|---|---|---|---|
| DMS-19 | Ellyson | Federal | 25/07/41 | 41-54. Japanese *Asakaze* (54) |
| DMS-20 | Hambleton | Federal | 26/09/41 | 41-55. Str71 |
| DMS-21 | Rodman | Federal | 26/09/41 | 41-55. Taiwan *Hsuen Yang* (55) |
| DMS-23 | Macomb | Bath | 23/09/41 | 42-54. Japanese *Hatakaze* (54), Taiwan *Hsien Yang* (70) |
| DMS-25 | Fitch | Boston | 14/06/41 | 42-56. Str71 |
| DMS-26 | Hobson | Charleston | 08/09/41 | 42-52. Lost 26/04/52 |
| DMS-27 | Jeffers | Federal | 16/08/42 | 42-55. BU72 |
| DMS-30 | Gherardi | Philadelphia | 12/02/42 | 42-55. Str71 |
| DMS-31 | Mervine | Federal | 03/05/42 | 42-49. BU69 |
| DMS-32 | Quick | Federal | 03/05/42 | 42-49. BU73 |

| | | | | |
|---|---|---|---|---|
| DMS-33 | Carmick | Seattle | 08/03/42 | 42-54. BU72 |
| DMS-34 | Doyle | Seattle | 17/03/42 | 42-55. BU73 |
| DMS-35 | Endicott | Seattle | 05/04/42 | 43-54. Str69 |
| DMS-36 | McCook | Seattle | 30/04/42 | 43-49. BU73 |
| DMS-37 | Davison | Federal | 19/07/42 | 42-49. BU73 |
| DMS-38 | Thompson | Seattle | 10/08/42 | 42-54. BU72 |
| DMS-39 | Cowie | Boston | 27/09/41 | Str 70 |
| DMS-40 | Knight | Boston | 27/09/41 | Target 66 |
| DMS-41 | Doran | Boston | 10/12/41 | BU73 |
| DMS-42 | Earle | Boston | 10/12/41 | Str69 |

**Notes:** Remaining vessels were reclassified Destroyers with original DD numbers 1955.

*Below:*
**The fast minesweeper *Fitch* (DMS-25), seen in July 1953, was a former destroyer with its aft 5in gun replaced by sweeping gear.** *Marius Bar*

# MINESWEEPERS

## 'Raven'/'Auk' Classes

**Displacement:** 890 tons, 1,250f/l; 55: 810 tons
**Dimensions:** 215 (wl), 220'6 (oa)×32'2×13'5
**Machinery:** Two shafts, diesel-electric, SHP 3,500=18kt

**Armament:** 1×3in/50 gun
**Complement:** 105

| | | | | |
|---|---|---|---|---|
| AM-55 | Raven | Norfolk | 24/08/40 | Target 68 |
| AM-57 | Auk | Norfolk | 26/08/41 | Str59 |
| AM-58 | Broadbill | Defoe | 21/05/42 | 52-54. BU73 |
| AM-59 | Chickadee | Defoe | 20/07/42 | Uruguayan *Cdte Pedro Campbell* (66) |
| AM-60 | Nuthatch | Defoe | 16/09/42 | Target 67 |
| AM-61 | Pheasant | Defoe | 24/10/42 | Target 67 |
| AM-62 | Sheldrake | General | 12/02/42 | 52-68. AGS-19 (52), sold 71 |
| AM-64 | Starling | General | 11/04/42 | Mexican *Valentin Gomez Farias* (73) |
| AM-100 | Heed | General | 19/06/42 | 52-54, Sold 69 |
| AM-101 | Herald | General | 04/07/42 | 52-55. Mexican *Mariano Matamoros* (73) |
| AM-102 | Motive | General | 17/08/42 | Target 67 |
| AM-103 | Oracle | General | 30/09/42 | Target 67 |
| AM-104 | Pilot | Penn | 05/07/42 | 52-54. Mexican *Juan Aldama* (73) |

| | | | | | |
|---|---|---|---|---|---|
| AM-105 | _Pioneer_ | Penn | 26/07/42 | Mexican _Leandro Valle_ (73) |
| AM-107 | _Prevail_ | Penn | 13/09/42 | 52-64. AGS-20 (52), BU66 |
| AM-108 | _Pursuit_ | Commercial | 12/06/42 | 50-60. AGS-17 (51). Str60 |
| AM-109 | _Requisite_ | Commercial | 25/07/42 | 50-63. AGS-18 (51). BU65 |
| AM-110 | _Revenge_ | Commercial | 07/11/42 | 51-55. BU67 |
| AM-111 | _Sage_ | Commercial | 21/11/42 | 51-55. Mexican _Hermenegildo Galeana_ (73) |
| AM-112 | _Seer_ | American; Lorain | 23/05/42 | 50-55. Norwegian _Uller_ (62) |
| AM-114 | _Staff_ | American; Lorain | 17/06/42 | 52-55. BU67 |
| AM-116 | _Speed_ | American; Clev | 18/04/42 | Korean _Sunchonke_ (67) |
| AM-117 | _Strive_ | American; Clev | 16/05/42 | 52-55. Norwegian _Gor_ (59) |
| AM-118 | _Steady_ | American; Clev | 06/06/42 | Taiwan _Ping Ching_ (67) |
| AM-119 | _Sustain_ | American; Clev | 23/06/42 | 52-55. Norwegian _Tyr_ (59) |
| AM-120 | _Sway_ | Mathis | 29/09/42 | Mexican _Ignacio Altamirano_ (73) |
| AM-122 | _Swift_ | Mathis | 05/12/42 | 51-55. Sold 74 |
| AM-123 | _Symbol_ | Savannah | 02/07/42 | 50-56. Mexican _Guillermo Prieto_ (73) |
| AM-124 | _Threat_ | Savannah | 15/08/42 | Mexican _Francisco Zarco_ (73) |
| AM-126 | _Token_ | Gulf; Madison | 28/03/42 | 51-54. BU67 |
| AM-127 | _Tumult_ | Gulf; Madison | 19/04/42 | 43-54. BU69 |
| AM-128 | _Velocity_ | Gulf; Madison | 19/04/42 | Mexican _Ignacio Vallarta_ (73) |
| AM-131 | _Zeal_ | Gulf; Madison | 15/09/42 | 51-56. Target 67 |
| AM-314 | _Champion_ | General | 12/12/42 | Mexican _Mariano Escobedo_ (72) |
| AM-315 | _Chief_ | General | 05/01/43 | 52-55. Mexican _Jesus Gonzalez Ortega_ (72) |
| AM-316 | _Competent_ | General | 30/01/43 | 52-55. Mexican _Ponciano Arriaga_ (72) |
| AM-317 | _Defense_ | General | 18/02/43 | 52-55. Mexican _Manuel Doblado_ (72) |
| AM-318 | _Devastator_ | General | 19/04/43 | 52-55. Mexican _Sebastian Lerdo de Tejada_ (72) |
| AM-319 | _Gladiator_ | General | 07/05/43 | 52-55. Mexican _Santos Degollado_ (72) |
| AM-320 | _Impeccable_ | General | 21/05/43 | 52-55. BU74 |
| AM-322 | _Spear_ | Associated | 25/02/43 | Mexican _Ignacio de La Llave_ (72) |
| AM-323 | _Triumph_ | Associated | 25/02/43 | 52-55. Norwegian _Brage_ (61) |
| AM-324 | _Vigilance_ | Associated | 05/04/43 | Philippine _Quezon_ (67) |
| AM-340 | _Ardent_ | General | 22/06/43 | Mexican _Juan N. Alvarez_ (72) |
| AM-341 | _Dextrous_ | Gulf; Madison | 17/01/43 | 50-56. Korean _Koje Ho_ (67) |
| AM-372 | _Murrelet_ | Savannah | 29/12/44 | 50-57. Philippine _Rizal_ (65) |
| AM-373 | _Peregrine_ | Savannah | 17/02/45 | 45-69. AG-176 (64). BU70 |
| AM-374 | _Pigeon_ | Savannah | 28/03/54 | 50-55. BU67 |
| AM-375 | _Pochard_ | Savannah | 11/06/44 | 52-55. BU67 |
| AM-376 | _Ptarmigan_ | Savannah | 15/07/44 | 50-57. Korean _Shin Song_ (63) |
| AM-377 | _Quail_ | Savannah | 20/08/44 | BU67 |
| AM-378 | _Redstart_ | Savannah | 18/10/44 | 50-57. Taiwan _Wu Sheng_ (65) |
| AM-379 | _Roselle_ | Gulf; Madison | 29/08/44 | Mexican _Melchior Ocampo_ (73) |
| AM-380 | _Ruddy_ | Gulf; Madison | 29/10/44 | 52-56. Peruvian _Galvez_ (60) |
| AM-381 | _Scoter_ | Gulf; Madison | 26/09/44 | Mexican _Manuel Gutierrez Zamora_ (72) |
| AM-382 | _Shoveler_ | Gulf; Madison | 10/12/44 | 51-56. Peruvian _Diez Canseco_ (60) |
| AM-383 | _Surfbird_ | American; Lorain | 31/08/44 | 52-70. ADG-383 (57). BU75 |
| AM-384 | _Sprig_ | American; Lorain | 15/09/44 | 45-54. BU73 |
| AM-385 | _Tanager_ | American; Lorain | 09/12/44 | 45-54. USCG (63) |
| AM-386 | _Tercel_ | American; Lorain | 16/12/44 | 45-54. Str72 |
| AM-387 | _Toucan_ | American; Clev | 15/09/44 | 50-57. Taiwan _Chien Men_ (64), lost 06/08/65 |
| AM-388 | _Towhee_ | American; Clev | 06/01/45 | 45-54, 64-69. AGS-28 (64). BU70 |
| AM-389 | _Waxwing_ | American; Clev | 10/03/45 | 52-57. Taiwan _Chu Yung_ (65) |
| AM-390 | _Wheatear_ | American; Clev | 21/04/45 | 45-54. BU73 |

**Notes:** Reclassified MSF 1955.

*Above:*
**The 'Auk' class minesweeper *Pochard* (AM-375),
showing the appearance of the class in 1953.**
*Marius Bar*

# 'Admirable' Class

**Displacement:** 650 tons, 945f/l
**Dimensions:** 180 (wl), 184'6 (oa)×33×10
**Machinery:** Two shafts, diesel, SHP 1,710=15kt

**Armament:** 1×3in/50 gun
**Complement:** 104

| AM-159 | Change | Willamette | 15/12/42 | Str60 |
|---|---|---|---|---|
| AM-160 | Clamour | Willamette | 24/12/42 | Str59 |
| AM-161 | Climax | Willamette | 09/01/43 | Str59 |
| AM-162 | Compel | Willamette | 16/01/43 | Sold 60 |
| AM-163 | Concise | Willamette | 06/02/43 | Str59 |
| AM-164 | Control | Willamette | 28/01/43 | Sold 59 |
| AM-165 | Counsel | Willamette | 17/02/43 | Sold 73 |
| AM-214 | Crag | Tampa | 21/03/43 | Mexican *DM-15* (62) |
| AM-215 | Cruise | Tampa | 21/03/43 | Sold 73 |
| AM-218 | Density | Tampa | 06/02/44 | Str60 |
| AM-219 | Design | Tampa | 06/02/44 | Str60 |
| AM-220 | Device | Tampa | 21/05/44 | 50-54. Mexican *DM-11* (62) |
| AM-221 | Diploma | Tampa | 21/05/44 | Mexican *DM-17* (62) |
| AM-223 | Dour | American; Lorain | 25/03/44 | Mexican *DM 16* (62) |
| AM-224 | Eager | American; Lorain | 10/06/44 | Mexican *DM-06* (62) |
| AM-232 | Execute | PS Bridge | 22/06/44 | Mexican *DM-03* (62) |
| AM-233 | Facility | PS Bridge | 22/06/44 | Mexican *DM-04* (62) |
| AM-238 | Garland | Commercial | 20/02/44 | Sold 60 |
| AM-239 | Gayety | Commercial | 19/03/44 | 51-54. Vietnam *Chi Lang II* (62), Philippine *Magat Salamat* (75) |
| AM-240 | Hazard | Commercial | 21/05/44 | Sold 68 |
| AM-241 | Hilarity | Commercial | 30/07/44 | Mexican *DM-02* (62) |
| AM-242 | Inaugural | Commercial | 01/10/44 | Str67 |
| AM-249 | Incredible | Savannah | 21/11/43 | 47-54. BU60 |

| AM-252 | Instill | Savannah | 05/03/44 | 51-54. Mexican DM-10 (62) |
| AM-253 | Intrigue | Savannah | 08/04/44 | Mexican DM-19 (62) |
| AM-254 | Invade | Savannah | 02/06/44 | Mexican DM-18 (62) |
| AM-255 | Jubilant | American; Lorain | 20/02/43 | 51-54. Mexican DM-01 (62) |
| AM-256 | Knave | American; Lorain | 13/03/43 | Mexican DM-13 (62) |
| AM-261 | Mainstay | American; Lorain | 31/07/43 | 44-54. BU60 |
| AM-269 | Opponent | Gulf; Madison | 12/06/43 | Sold 61 |
| AM-275 | Pirate | Gulf; Madison | 16/12/43 | 44-50. Lost 12/10/50 |
| AM-277 | Pledge | Gulf; Madison | 23/12/43 | 47-50. Lost 12/10/50 |
| AM-280 | Prowess | Gulf; Madison | 17/02/44 | 62-70. IX-305 (66), Vietnam Ha Hoi (70) |

*Above:*
**The 'Admirable' class minesweeper Prowess (AM-280). Only a few of this class were in active service after World War 2.**

| AM-283 | Ransom | General | 18/09/43 | 51-53. Mexican DM-12 (62) |
| AM-284 | Rebel | General | 28/10/43 | Mexican DM-14 (62) |
| AM-285 | Recruit | General | 11/12/43 | Mexican DM-07 (62) |
| AM-288 | Reign | General | 29/05/44 | Str59 |
| AM-289 | Report | General | 08/07/44 | Korean Kojin (67) |
| AM-296 | Scout | Commercial | 02/05/43 | 51-54. Mexican DM-09 (62) |
| AM-297 | Scrimmage | Commercial | 16/05/43 | Merchant Giant II (62) |
| AM-298 | Scuffle | Commercial | 08/08/43 | Mexican DM-05 (62) |
| AM-299 | Sentry | Commercial | 15/08/43 | Vietnam Ky Hoa (62) |
| AM-300 | Serene | Commercial | 31/10/43 | Vietnam Nhut Tao (64), lost 20/01/74 |
| AM-301 | Shelter | Commercial | 14/11/43 | Vietnam Chi Linh (64) |
| AM-302 | Signet | Associated | 16/08/43 | Dominican Separacion (65) |
| AM-303 | Skirmish | Associated | 16/08/43 | Dominican Tortugero (65) |
| AM-304 | Scurry | Associated | 01/10/43 | Str67 |
| AM-306 | Specter | Associated | 15/02/44 | Mexican DM-04 (62) |
| AM-307 | Staunch | Associated | 15/02/44 | BU69 |
| AM-308 | Strategy | Associated | 28/03/44 | BU69 |
| AM-309 | Strength | Associated | 28/03/44 | Str67 |
| AM-310 | Success | Associated | 11/05/44 | Mexican DM-08 (62) |
| AM-311 | Superior | Associated | 11/05/44 | Str72 |
| AM-356 | Creddock | Willamette | 22/07/44 | Burmese Yan Gyi Aung (67) |

| AM-357 | Dipper | Willamette | 26/07/44 | Merchant Mermaid II (61) |
|---|---|---|---|---|
| AM-362 | Gadwall | PS Bridge | 15/07/43 | Sold 68 |
| AM-364 | Graylag | PS Bridge | 04/12/43 | Sold 69 |
| AM-365 | Harlequin | PS Bridge | 03/06/44 | Mexican DM-20 (62) |
| AM-366 | Harrier | PS Bridge | 07/06/44 | Merchant Sea Scope (63) |

**Notes:** Reclassified MSF 1955. *Reign* and *Report* never commissioned. *Scurry* used as salvage training hulk.

# 'Agile' Class (1951-53)

**Displacement:** 665 tons, 750f/l; 508-11: 720 tons, 780f/l
**Dimensions:** 165 (wl) 172 (oa)×36×14
**Machinery:** two shafts, diesels, SHP 2,280=15.5kt; 428-31: SHP 1,520

**Endurance:** 3,300/10
**Armament:** 1×40mm gun
**Complement:** 75

| MSO-421 | Agile | Luders | 19/11/55 | 56-72. Str77 |
|---|---|---|---|---|
| MSO-422 | Aggressive | Luders | 04/10/52 | 53-71. Str75 |
| MSO-423 | Avenge | Luders | 15/03/53 | 54-69. Str70 |
| MSO-424 | Bold | Norfolk | 14/03/53 | 53-71. Taiwan (75) |
| MSO-425 | Bulwark | Norfolk | 14/03/53 | 53-71. Taiwan (75) |
| MSO-426 | Conflict | Fulton | 16/12/52 | 54-72. Sold 73 |
| MSO-427 | Constant | Fulton | 14/02/53 | 54- |
| MSO-428 | Dash | Astoria | 20/09/52 | 53-82. Str82 |
| MSO-429 | Detector | Astoria | 05/12/52 | 54-82. Str82 |
| MSO-430 | Direct | Hiltebrant | 27/05/53 | 54-82. Str82 |
| MSO-431 | Dominant | Hiltebrant | 05/11/53 | 54-82. Str82 |
| MSO-432 | Dynamic | Colberg | 17/12/52 | 53-71. Spanish Guadalete (71) |
| MSO-433 | Engage ex-Elusive | Colberg | 18/06/53 | 54- |
| MSO-434 | Embattle | Colberg | 27/08/53 | 54-72. Str76 |
| MSO-435 | Endurance | Martinac | 09/08/52 | 54-72. Sold 73 |
| MSO-436 | Energy | Martinac | 13/02/53 | 54-72. Philippine Davao Del Sur (72) |
| MSO-437 | Enhance | Martinolich | 11/10/52 | 55- |
| MSO-438 | Esteem | Martinolich | 20/12/52 | 55- |
| MSO-439 | Excel | Higgins | 25/09/53 | 55- |
| MSO-440 | Exploit | Higgins | 10/04/53 | 54- |
| MSO-441 | Exultant | Higgins | 06/06/53 | 54- |
| MSO-442 | Fearless | Higgins | 17/07/53 | 54- |
| MSO-443 | Fidelity | Higgins | 21/08/53 | 55- |
| MSO-444 | Firm | Martinac | 15/04/53 | 54-72. Philippine Davao Del Norte (72) |
| MSO-445 | Force | Martinac | 26/06/53 | 55-73. Lost 24/04/73 |
| MSO-446 | Fortify | Seattle | 14/02/53 | 54- |
| MSO-447 | Guide | Seattle | 17/04/54 | 55-72. Sold 73 |
| MSO-448 | Illusive | Martinolich | 12/07/52 | 53-70, 72- |
| MSO-449 | Impervious | Martinolich | 29/08/52 | 54- |
| MSO-455 | Implicit | Wilmington | 01/08/53 | 54- |
| MSO-456 | Inflict | Wilmington | 16/10/53 | 54- |
| MSO-457 | Loyalty | Wilmington | 22/11/53 | 54-71. Sold 73 |
| MSO-458 | Lucid | Higgins | 14/11/53 | 54-70. Str76 |
| MSO-459 | Nimble | Higgins | 06/08/54 | 55-70. Str76 |
| MSO-460 | Notable | Higgins | 15/10/54 | 55-70. Sold 71 |
| MSO-461 | Observer | Higgins | 19/10/54 | 55-72. Str77 |
| MSO-462 | Pinnacle | Higgins | 03/01/55 | 55-70. Str77 |

*Above:*
***Loyalty** (MSO-457), a wooden-hulled minesweeper of the 'Agile' class.*

| | | | |
|---|---|---|---|
| MSO-463 | *Pivot* | Wilmington | 09/01/54 | 54-71. Spanish *Guadalmedina* (71) |
| MSO-464 | *Pluck* | Wilmington | 06/02/54 | 54- |
| MSO-465 | *Prestige* | Wilmington | 30/04/54 | 54-58, Lost 23/08/58 |
| MSO-466 | *Prime* | Wilmington | 27/05/54 | 54-70. Thai (75) |
| MSO-467 | *Reaper* | Wilmington | 25/06/54 | 54-72. Thai (75) |
| MSO-468 | *Rival* | Luders | 15/08/53 | 54-70. Sold 71 |
| MSO-469 | *Sagacity* | Luders | 20/02/54 | 55-70. Str70 |
| MSO-470 | *Salute* | Luders | 14/08/54 | 55-70. BU73 |
| MSO-471 | *Skill* | Luders | 03/04/55 | 55-70. Str77 |
| MSO-472 | *Valour* | Burger | 13/05/53 | 54-70. Sold 71 |
| MSO-473 | *Vigor* | Burger | 24/06/53 | 54-72. Spanish *Guadiana* (72) |
| MSO-474 | *Vital* | Burger | 12/08/53 | 55-72. Str77 |
| MSO-488 | *Conquest* | Martinac | 20/05/54 | 55- |
| MSO-489 | *Gallant* | Martinac | 04/06/54 | 55- |
| MSO-490 | *Leader* | Martinac | 15/09/54 | 55-70, 72- |
| MSO-491 | *Persistent* | Martinac | 23/04/55 | 56-71. Spanish *Guadalquivir* (71) |
| MSO-492 | *Pledge* | Martinac | 20/07/55 | 56- |
| MSO-493 | *Stalwart* | Broward | 03/12/55 | 57-66. Lost 25/06/66 |
| MSO-494 | *Sturdy* | Broward | 28/01/56 | 57-70. Str77 |
| MSO-495 | *Swerve* | Broward | 01/11/55 | 57-71. Str77 |
| MSO-496 | *Venture* | Broward | 27/11/56 | 58-71. Str77 |
| | | | | |
| MSO-508 | *Acme* | Sample | 23/06/55 | 56-70. Str76 |
| MSO-509 | *Adroit* | Sample | 20/08/55 | 57- |
| MSO-510 | *Advance* | Sample | 12/07/56 | 58-70. Str76 |
| MSO-511 | *Affray* | Sample | 18/12/56 | 58- |

**Note:** Originally classified AM. Wood hulls, non-magnetic equipment. All were to be modernised in 1960s, but only 19 were started. *Avenge* damaged by fire while under refit. Modernisation programme cancelled and minesweeping switched to helicopters.

35 additional units built for Belgium, France, Italy, Netherlands, Norway and Portugal. MSO-508-511 constitute a separate class, fitted as flagships.

# 'Ability' Class (1955)

**Displacement:** 801 tons, 950f/l
**Dimensions:** 189 (oa)×36×12
**Machinery:** two shafts, diesel, SHP 2,700=15kt

**Armament:** 1×40mm gun
**Complement:** 82

MSO-519 —— *Ability* —————————— Peterson —————— 29/12/56 —— 57-70. Str71
MSO-520 —— *Alacrity* ————————— Peterson —————— 08/06/57 —— 58-76. AG-520 (73), Str77
MSO-521 —— *Assurance* ——————— Peterson —————— 31/08/57 —— 58-76. AG-521 (73), Str77

**Notes:** Non-magnetic wood hulls, tripod masts.
520-521 converted to test equipment as sonar test ships;
minesweeping gear removed 1973.

*Below:*
***Ability* (MSO-519), an 'Ability' class minesweeper.**

# MINE COUNTERMEASURES SHIPS

**Displacement:** 1,040 tons f/l
**Dimensions:** 210 (oa)×44'4×10'6
**Machinery:** two shafts, diesel, BHP 6,800=14kt

**Armament:** 2 MG
**Complement:** 62

MCM-1 —————— *Avenger* ————————— Peterson —————— 15/06/85
MCM-2 —————— *Defender* ———————— Marinette —————— 27/04/85
MCM-3 —————— *Sentry* ———————————— Peterson —————— 19/05/86
MCM-4 —————— *Champion* ————————— Marinette ————————— Building
MCM-5 —————— *Guardian* ————————— Peterson —————— Building

**Notes:** 14 units planned. Wood and fibreglass
construction. Non-magnetic machinery. Change in type
of engines has caused construction delay.

# MINESWEEPER HUNTERS

**Details:** 450 tons f/l; 150 (oa); two shaft diesels, BHP 1,200

MSH-1 —————— *Cardinal* ————————— Bell Aerospace ——— Building

**Notes:** 17 units planned. Surface effect ship with glass
reinforced plastic hull, designed to clear US ports in wartime.

# COASTAL MINESWEEPERS

AMC-204 _____ *Minah* _____ 44-59. MHC-14 (55),Str59

---

**Details:** 270 tons, 350 f/l; 136 (oa)×24'6×8; two screws,
diesel, SHP 1,000=15kt; 1×40mm gun; complement
50

| | | | |
|---|---|---|---|
| AMS-1 _____ | *Albatross* _____ | 80 _____ | 43-58. Sold 58 |
| AMS-2 _____ | *Bobolink* _____ | 164 _____ | 43-60. MHC-44 (55), sold 61 |
| AMS-3 _____ | *Bunting* _____ | 170 _____ | 43-59. MHC-45 (55), Str60 |
| AMS-4 _____ | *Cardinal* _____ | 179 _____ | 43-56. Brazilian *Javari* (60) |
| AMS-5 _____ | *Condor* _____ | 192 _____ | 50-55. Japanese *Ujishima*(55) |
| AMS-6 _____ | *Courser* _____ | 201 _____ | 50-50. Sold 60 |
| AMS-7 _____ | *Crow* _____ | 215 _____ | 50-50. Str59 |
| AMS-8 _____ | *Curlew* _____ | 218 _____ | 43-56. Korean *Kum Hwa* (56) |
| AMS-9 _____ | *Flicker* _____ | 219 _____ | 43-50. Sold 61 |
| AMS-10 _____ | *Firecrest* _____ | 231 _____ | -55. Japanese *Etajima* (55) |
| AMS-11 _____ | *Flamingo* _____ | 238 _____ | -50. Str59 |
| AMS-12 _____ | *Goldfinch* _____ | 306 _____ | 44-54. Sold 60 |
| AMS-13 _____ | *Grackle* _____ | 312 _____ | 43-57. Brazilian *Juruena* (63) |
| AMS-14 _____ | *Grosbeak* _____ | 317 _____ | 43-55. Str59 |
| AMS-15 _____ | *Grouse* _____ | 321 _____ | 43-63. Lost 21/09/63 |
| AMS-16 _____ | *Gull* _____ | 324 _____ | 44-58. Str59 |
| AMS-17 _____ | *Hawk* _____ | 362 _____ | 43-57. Sold 58 |
| AMS-18 _____ | *Heron* _____ | 369 _____ | 49-55. Japanese *Nuwajima* (55) |
| AMS-19 _____ | *Hornbill* _____ | 371 _____ | 44-57. Sold 60 |
| AMS-20 _____ | *Hummer* _____ | 372 _____ | 50-53. Japanese *Ninoshima* (59) |
| AMS-21 _____ | *Jackdaw* _____ | 373 _____ | Brazilian *Jurua* (63) |
| AMS-22 _____ | *Kite* _____ | 374 _____ | 49-56. Korean *Kimpo* (56) |
| AMS-23 _____ | *Lark* _____ | 376 _____ | 50-53. Japanese *Moroshima* (59) |
| AMS-24 _____ | *Linnet* _____ | 395 _____ | 43-68. Sold 69 |
| AMS-25 _____ | *Magpie* _____ | 400 _____ | 43-50. Lost 07/10/50 |
| AMS-26 _____ | *Merganser* _____ | 417 _____ | 44-58. MHC-47 (55), sold 60 |
| AMS-27 _____ | *Mockingbird* _____ | 419 _____ | 44-56. Korean *Kochang* (56) |
| AMS-28 _____ | *Osprey* _____ | 422 _____ | 44-55. Japanese *Yakushima* (55) |
| AMS-29 _____ | *Ostrich* _____ | 430 _____ | 44-57. Sold 60 |
| AMS-30 _____ | *Parrakeet* _____ | 434 _____ | 44-47. Sold 47 |
| AMS-31 _____ | *Partridge* _____ | 437 _____ | 45-51. Lost 02/02/51 |
| AMS-32 _____ | *Pelican* _____ | 441 _____ | 45-55. Japanese *Ogishima* (55) |

*Left:*
**The coastal minesweeper
*Egret* (AMS-46), originally of a
large class classified 'motor
minesweepers' (YMS).**
*Martin E. Holbrook collection*

| | | | | |
|---|---|---|---|---|
| AMS-33 | Plover | 442 | 44-68. Sold 69 |
| AMS-34 | Redhead | 443 | 44-57. MHC-48 (55), Str59 |
| AMS-35 | Sanderling | 446 | 44-55. MHC-49 (55), Str59 |
| AMS-36 | Swallow | 461 | 44-55. Japanese *Yugejima* (55) |
| AMS-37 | Swan | 470 | 50-55. Sold 60 |
| AMS-38 | Verdin | 471 | 44-55. Str59 |
| AMS-39 | Waxbill | 479 | 49-58. MHC-50 (55), Str59 |
| AMS-40 | Chatterer | 415 | Japanese *Yurishima* (55) |
| AMS-41 | Barbet | 46 | Str59 |
| AMS-42 | Brambling | 109 | Sold 61 |
| AMS-43 | Brant | 113 | Str59 |
| AMS-44 | Courlan | 114 | Str59 |
| AMS-45 | Crossbill | 120 | Str59 |
| AMS-46 | Egret | 136 | Brazilian *Jutai* (60) |
| AMS-47 | Fulmar | 193 | Str68 |
| AMS-48 | Lapwing | 268 | 43-57. Sold 60 |
| AMS-49 | Lorikeet | 271 | 43-68. Sold 69 |
| AMS-50 | Nightingale | 290 | 43-59. Str59 |
| AMS-51 | Reedbird | 291 | 43-68. Sold 69 |
| AMS-52 | Rhea | 299 | 43-59. Sold 60 |
| AMS-53 | Robin | 311 | 43-61. Sold 61 |
| AMS-54 | Ruff | 327 | 43-69. Sold 70 |
| AMS-55 | Seagull | 402 | 43-57. Sold 60 |
| AMS-56 | Turkey | 444 | 44-68. Str68 |
| AMS-57 | Redpoll | 294 | 43-59. Sold 60 |
| AMS-58 | Siskin | 425 | 44-60. BU69 |
| AMS-59 | na | 451 | Not converted |

**Notes:** Survivors of 481 vessels built in 1942-43. Named and reclassified AMS in 1947. Reclassified MSCO in 1955. Six converted to minehunters (MHC) 1955.

# 'Falcon' Class

**Details:** 320 tons, 370 f/l; 144'3 (oa)×27'2×12; two shafts, diesels, SHP 1,200=14kt; complement 39

| | | | | |
|---|---|---|---|---|
| MSC-121 | Bluebird | Mare Is | 11/05/53 | 53-70. Thai (75) |
| MSC-122 | Cormorant | Mare Is | 08/06/53 | 55-71. BU74 |
| MSC-190 | Falcon | Quincy Adams | 21/09/53 | 54-71. Indonesian *Pulau Aru* (71) |
| MSC-191 | Frigate Bird | Quincy Adams | 24/10/53 | 55-71. Indonesian *Pulau Antung* (71) |
| MSC-192 | Hummingbird | Quincy Adams | 25/12/53 | 55-71. Indonesian *Pulau Alor* (71) |
| MSC-193 | Jacana | Quincy Adams | 25/02/55 | 55-71. Indonesian *Pulau Aruan* (71) |
| MSC-194 | Kingbird | Quincy Adams | 21/05/55 | 55-71. Sold 73 |
| MSC-195 | Limpkin | Broward | 21/05/54 | 55-71. Indonesian *Pulau Anjer* (71) |
| MSC-196 | Meadowlark | Broward | 28/08/54 | 55-71. Indonesian *Pulau Ampalasa* (71) |
| MSC-197 | Parrot | Broward | 27/11/54 | 55-68. Str73 |
| MSC-198 | Peacock | Harbor | 19/06/54 | 55-75. BU75 |
| MSC-199 | Phoebe | Harbor | 21/08/54 | 55-75. BU75 |
| MSC-200 | Redwing | Tampa Marine | 29/04/54 | 55-59. Spanish *Sil* (59) |
| MSC-201 | Shrike | Tampa Marine | 21/07/54 | 55-75. BU75 |
| MSC-202 | Spoonbill | Tampa Marine | 03/08/54 | 55-59. Spanish *Duero* (59) |
| MSC-203 | Thrasher | Tampa Marine | 06/10/54 | 55-75. Singapore *Mercury* (75) |

| | | | | |
|---|---|---|---|---|
| MSC-204 | _Thrush_ | Tampa Marine | 05/01/55 | 55-76. Str75 |
| MSC-205 | _Vireo_ | Bellingham | 30/04/54 | 55-75. Fijian _Kula_ (75) |
| MSC-206 | _Warbler_ | Bellingham | 18/06/54 | 55-70. Fijian _Kiro_ (76) |
| MSC-207 | _Whippoorwill_ | Bellingham | 13/08/54 | 55-75. Singapore _Jupiter_ (75) |
| MSC-208 | _Widgeon_ | Bellingham | 15/10/54 | 55-73. Sold 74 |
| MSC-209 | _Woodpecker_ | Bellingham | 07/01/55 | 56-75. Fijian _Kikau_ (75) |

**Note:** Originally ordered as AMS, reclassified MSC 1955. Wood hull. Many built for foreign countries.

*Right:*
**Thrasher (MSC-203), a 'Falcon' class coastal minesweeper.**

# 'Albatross' Class (1958)

**Details:** 378 tons; 145 (oa)×28×13; two shafts, diesels, SHP 1,000=13kt; complement 45

| | | | | |
|---|---|---|---|---|
| MSC-289 | _Albatross_ | Tacoma Boat | 26/03/60 | 61-70. Str70 |
| MSC-290 | _Gannet_ | Tacoma Boat | 26/05/60 | 61-70. Str70 |

# COASTAL MINEHUNTERS

**Formerly Coastal Minesweepers (Underwater Locator)**

| | | |
|---|---|---|
| AMCU-1 | to AMCU-6 | ex-LCT |
| AMCU-7 | to AMCU-11 | ex-LCI |
| AMCU-12 | to AMCU-13 | ex-AGSc (ex-YMS) |
| AMCU-14 | na | ex-PCS |
| MHC-15 | to MHC-42 | ex-LSIL· |
| MHC-44 | to MHC-50 | ex-MSCO (ex-YMS) |

**Notes:** AMCU reclassified MHC-1955. These vessels were named.

**Details:** 300 tons, 350 f/l; 144 (oa)×28×8; two shafts, diesel, SHP 1,200=14kt; 1×40mm gun; 45 crew

| | | | | |
|---|---|---|---|---|
| MHC-43 | _Bittern_ | Consol; NY | 04/03/57 | 57-66. BU72 |

**Notes:** Prototype minehunter. Wood hull. Three ships planned originally.

*Above:*
**Bittern (MHC-43), a prototype coastal minehunter, in 1958.** *Official US Navy*

# PATROL VESSELS

## PATROL FRIGATES (Old Designation)

**Displacement:** 1,430 tons
**Dimensions:** 285'6 (wl), 303'11 (oa)×37'6×12
**Machinery:** Two shafts, VTE, SHP 5,500=18kt

**Armament:** 3×3in/50 guns
**Complement:** 180

| | | | | |
|---|---|---|---|---|
| PF-3 | Tacoma | Kaiser | 07/07/43 | 50-51. Korean *Taedong* (51) |
| PF-4 | Sausalito | Kaiser | 20/07/43 | 50-52. Korean *Imchin* (52) |
| PF-5 | Hoquiam | Kaiser | 31/07/43 | Korean *Naktong* (51) |
| PF-6 | Pasco | Kaiser | 17/08/43 | Japanese *Kashi* (53) |
| PF-7 | Albuquerque | Kaiser | 14/09/43 | 50-53. Japanese *Tochi* (53) |
| PF-8 | Everett | Kaiser | 29/09/43 | 50-53. Japanese *Kiri* (53) |
| PF-21 | Bayonne | American; Clev | 11/09/43 | 50-53. Japanese *Buna* (53) |
| PF-22 | Gloucester | Butler | 12/07/43 | 50-52. Japanese *Tsuga* (53) |
| PF-25 | Charlottesville | Butler | 30/07/43 | Japanese *Maki* (53) |
| PF-26 | Poughkeepsie | Butler | 12/08/43 | Japanese *Momi* (53) |
| PF-27 | Newport | Butler | 15/08/43 | 50-53. Japanese *Kaede* (53) |
| PF-34 | Long Beach | Consolidated | 05/05/43 | Japanese *Shii* (53) |
| PF-36 | Glendale | Consolidated | 28/05/43 | 50-51. Thai *Tachin* (51) |
| PF-37 | San Pedro | Consolidated | 11/06/43 | Japanese *Kaya* (53) |
| PF-38 | Coronado | Consolidated | 17/06/43 | Japanese *Sugi* (53) |

*Below:*
**The patrol frigate *Glendale* (PF-36) in 1951. Loaned to and returned by the Soviet Union, it was recommissioned for service in Korea.**
*Official US Navy/Ernest Arroyo collection*

| | | | | |
|---|---|---|---|---|
| PF-39 | Ogden | Consolidated | 23/06/43 | Japanese Kusu (53) |
| PF-46 | Bisbee | Consolidated | 07/09/43 | 50-52. Colombian Capitan Tono (52) |
| PF-47 | Gallup | Consolidated | 17/09/43 | 50-51. Thai Prasae (51) |
| PF-48 | Rockford | Consolidated | 27/09/43 | Korean Apnok (50) |
| PF-49 | Muskogee | Consolidated | 18/10/43 | Korean Duman (50) |
| PF-50 | Carson City | Consolidated | 13/11/43 | Japanese Sakura (53) |
| PF-51 | Burlington | Consolidated | 07/12/43 | 51-52. Colombian Almirante Brion (53) |
| PF-52 | Allentown | Froemming | 03/07/43 | Japanese Ume (53) |
| PF-53 | Machias | Froemming | 22/08/43 | Japanese Nara (53) |
| PF-54 | Sandusky | Froemming | 05/10/43 | Japanese Nire (53) |
| PF-55 | Bath | Froemming | 14/11/43 | Japanese Matsu (53) |
| PF-70 | Evansville | LD Smith | 27/11/43 | 50-53. Japanese Kayaki (53) |

**Notes:** All loaned to USSR in 1945 and returned in 1949. Another vessel, *Belfast* (PF-35), was lost in Russian service.

# GUNBOATS

## 'Asheville' Class (1963-66)

**Displacement:** 225 tons, 245f/l
**Dimensions:** 164'6 (oa)×23'8×9'6
**Machinery:** Two shafts, CODAG and diesel, SHP 1,750=16kt; gas turbine, HP 13,300=40kt+

**Endurance:** 1,900/16
**Armament:** 1×3in/50, 1×40mm gun
**Complement:** 27

| | | | | |
|---|---|---|---|---|
| PG-84 | Asheville | Tacoma | 01/05/65 | 66/77. Str77 |
| PG-85 | Gallup | Tacoma | 15/06/65 | 66-77. Str77 |
| PG-86 | Antelope | Tacoma | 18/06/66 | 67-77. Str77 |
| PG-87 | Ready | Tacoma | 12/05/67 | 68-77. Str77 |
| PG-88 | Crockett | Tacoma | 04/06/66 | 67-77. Str77 |
| PG-89 | Marathon | Tacoma | 22/04/67 | 68-77. Str77 |
| PG-90 | Canon | Tacoma | 22/07/67 | 68-77. Str77 |
| PG-91 | na | Tacoma | na | Destroyed on stocks |
| PG-92 | Tacoma | Tacoma | 13/04/68 | 69-81. Colombian Quito Suena (83) |
| PG-93 | Welch | Petersen | 25/07/68 | 67-81. Colombian Albuquerque (83) |
| PG-94 | Chehalis | Tacoma | 06/08/68 | 69-75. Small boat Athena (76) |
| PG-95 | Defiance | Petersen | 24/08/68 | 69-73. Turkish Yildirim (73) |
| PG-96 | Benicia | Tacoma | 20/12/69 | 70-71. Korean Paekku 51 (71) |
| PG-97 | Surprise | Petersen | 07/12/68 | 69-73. Turkish Bora (73) |
| PG-98 | Grand Rapids | Tacoma | 10/01/70 | 70-77. Small boat Athena II (77) |
| PG-99 | Beacon | Petersen | 17/05/69 | 69-77 |
| PG-100 | Douglas | Tacoma | 19/06/70 | 71-77. Small boat Athena III (7) |

**Notes:** Small, fast coastal gunboats. 24 units planned. Aluminium hulls and aluminium-glass fibre superstructure. Could accelerate from full stop to 40kt in one minute, but cavitation caused propeller damage. Built for coastal patrol and blockading in response to Cuban situation of 1960s. Extensively used in Vietnam. *Antelope, Ready, Grand Rapids* and *Douglas* armed with two Standard/ARM SSM launchers 1972, after being tested on *Benicia*.

# HYDROFOIL SUBMARINE CHASER (1960)

**Details:** 120 tons; 115×31×6/17; four or two shafts, CODAG, SHP 6,200=48kt; 4×12.75in TT (removed); crew 20

*Above:*
**Antelope (PG-86) was a coastal patrol gunboat built in response to the Cuban situation in the early 1960s.** *Official US Navy*

*Below:*
**The hydrofoil submarine chaser *High Point* (PCH-1) firing Harpoon anti-ship missile during tests in 1974.** *Official US Navy*

PCH-1 _____ *High Point* _____ Martinac _____ 17/08/62 \_\_\_ 63-

**Notes:** Served as experimental craft, built of aluminium except for foils and struts. Converted to test Harpoon 1971-73. Loaned to Coast Guard during 1975.

# HYDROFOIL GUNBOATS

**Details:** 57 tons; 74'4×22×4'2; one shaft, gas turbine, SHP 3,000=52kt; 13 crew

PGH-1 _____ *Flagstaff* _____ Grumman _____ 09/01/68 \_\_\_ 68-    . USCG, WPBH-1 (76)

*Left:*
**Flagstaff** (PGH-1), a hydrofoil gunboat, seen foil-borne at speed. The vessel was one of two competitive vessels built to test the hydrofoil concept.

*Below:*
The hydrofoil gunboat **Tucumcari** (PGH-2). The second of two competitive designs, was photographed during six months active service in Vietnam.

*Bottom*
The hydrofoil missile boat **Taurus** (PHM-3) underway in 1981. Notice the single Harpoon canisters aft, since replaced by two quadruple canisters.   *Official US Navy*

**Details:** 58 tons; 71'8×19'6×4'5; one shaft, gas turbine, SHP 3,000=52kt; 1×40mm gun; 13 crew

PGH-2 _____ *Tucumcari* _____ Boeing _____ 15/07/67 ___ 68-72. Str73

**Notes:** Competitive designs, aluminium construction, differing in propulsion. *Tucumcari* was severely damaged when it ran aground off Puerto Rico 16/11/72. Served six months off Vietnam, 1970.

# HYDROFOIL MISSILE BOATS

## 'Pegasus' Class (1973-76)

**Displacement:** 198 tons, 240f/l
**Dimensions:** 147'2 (oa)×28'3×6'3/23'3
**Machinery:** Diesel engines, BHP 1,600=12kt; gas turbine, SHP 16,700=48kt+

**Endurance:** 1,225/38
**Armament:** Two quad Harpoon SSM launchers, 1×76mm gun
**Complement:** 21

PHM-1 _____ *Pegasus* _____ Boeing _____ 09/11/74 ___ 77-
           ex-*Delphinus*
PHM-2 _____ *Hercules* _____ Boeing _____ 13/04/82 ___ 83-
PHM-3 _____ *Taurus* _____ Boeing _____ 08/05/81    81-
PHM-4 _____ *Aquila* _____ Boeing _____ 16/09/81 ___ 81-
PHM-5 _____ *Aries* _____ Boeing _____ 05/11/81 ___ 82-
PHM-6 _____ *Gemini* _____ Boeing _____ 17/02/82 ___ 82-

**Notes:** Original PHM-2-6 cancelled 06/04/77, re-ordered 20/10/77. Original *Hercules* laid down 1974, cancelled when 41% complete.
   *Pegasus* was lead ship of planned 30-unit class.

Originally designed with four single Harpoon launchers, replaced with quad launcher. Far superior to previous hydrofoils.

# SUBMARINE CHASERS

**Details:** 295 tons, 450f/l; 170 (wl), 173'8 (oa)×23×10'9; two shafts, geared diesels, SHP 2,880=20kt; 1×3in/50, 1×40mm guns; 80 crew

PC-461 _____ *Bluffton* _____ Str58
PC-463 _____ na _____ Expended in tests 53
PC-465 _____ *Paragould* _____ Venezuelan *Pulpo* (61)
PC-466 _____ *Carmi* _____ Str60
PC-470 _____ *Antigo* _____ Str60
PC-483 _____ *Rolla* _____ Venezuelan *Damaron* (61)
PC-484 _____ *Cooperstown* _____ Venezuelan *Togogo* (61)
PC-485 _____ na _____ Korean *Han Rasan* (52), lost 01/62
PC-486 _____ *Jasper* _____ 42-59. Str59
PC-487 _____ *Larchmont* _____ Venezuelan *Mejillon* (61)
PC-553 _____ *Malone* _____ BU58
PC-560 _____ *Oberlin* _____ Str57
PC-564 _____ *Chadron* _____ 42-59. Korean *Sol Ak* (64)
PC-565 _____ *Gilmer* _____ Venezuelan *Alcatraz* (62)
PC-566 _____ *Honesdale* _____ Venezuelan *Calamar* (61
PC-567 _____ *Riverhead* _____ US Air Force (63)

PC-568 ____ Altus _____ Philippine *Nueva Viscaya* (68)
PC-569 ____ Petoskey _____ Str60
PC-570 ____ na _____ Thai *Longlom* (52)
PC-571 ____ Anoka _____ Str59
PC-572 ____ Tooele _____ 42-59. Sold 61
PC-579 ____ Wapakoneta _____ 42-55. Sold 61
PC-580 ____ Malvern _____ 42-58. Indonesian *Hui* (60)
PC-581 ____ Manville _____ 42-59. Indonesian *Torani* (60)
PC-582 ____ Lenoir _____ 42-50, 52-55. Venezuelan *Albatros* (62)
PC-586 ____ Patchogue _____ 42-50. Str59
PC-588 ____ Houghton _____ Str59
PC-589 ____ Metropolis _____ Str59
PC-592 ____ Towanda _____ Str59
PC-597 ____ Kerrville _____ Str57
PC-600 ____ na _____ Korean *Myo Hyang San* (50)
PC-601 ____ Arcata _____ Str60
PC-602 ____ Alturas _____ Str60
PC-603 ____ Solvay _____ 42 49. Str60
PC-606 ____ Andrews _____ Str57
PC-616 ____ na _____ Thai *Tongpliu* (52)
PC-617 ____ Beeville _____ Str57
PC-618 ____ Weatherford _____ 42-65. Target 68
PC-619 ____ Dalhart _____ Venezuelan *Gaviota* (61)
PC-620 ____ Bethany _____ Str57
PC-776 ____ Pikeville _____ Str59
PC-777 ____ Waynesburg _____ 43-50. Str59
PC-778 ____ Gallipolis _____ 43-49. Str59
PC-779 ____ Mechanicsburg _____ Str59
PC-780 ____ Maynard _____ 43-49. Str59
PC-781 ____ Metuchen _____ 43-49. Str59
PC-782 ____ Glenolden _____ 43-49. Str59
PC-785 ____ Frostburg _____ Str59
PC-786 ____ na _____ Taiwan *Hsiang Kiang* (54)
PC-808 ____ Ripley _____ 43-49. Str59
PC-817 ____ Welch _____ 43-50. Str59
PC-822 ____ Asheboro _____ Str59
PC-1077 ____ Edenton _____ Venezuelan *Caracol* (61)
PC-1078 ____ na _____ Taiwan *Tzu Chiang* (54)
PC-1079 ____ Ludington _____ Str60
PC-1081 ____ Cadiz _____ Str60
PC-1086 ____ na _____ French *Flamberge* (51), Cambodian *E-311* (56-75)
PC-1087 ____ Placerville _____ Taiwan *Tung Kiang* (57)
PC-1119 ____ Greencastle _____ Str57
PC-1120 ____ Carlinville _____ Str59
PC-1125 ____ Cordele _____ Str59
PC-1130 ____ na _____ French *L'Intrepide* (51), Vietnam *Van Kiep* (54)
PC-1135 ____ Canastota _____ Str59
PC-1136 ____ Galena _____ Str59
PC-1137 ____ Worthington _____ Sold 61
PC-1138 ____ Lapeer _____ Sold 61
PC-1139 ____ na _____ French *L'Impetueux* (51), Cambodia (54-56)
PC-1140 ____ Glenwood _____ Str60
PC-1141 ____ Pierre _____ 43-58. Indonesian *Tjakalang* (58)

PC-1142 ____ Hanford _____ Taiwan *Pei Kiang* (57)

PC-1143 ____ na _____ French *Glaive* (51), Vietnam *Tay Ket* (56)

PC-1144 ____ na _____ French *Mousquet* (51), Vietnam *Chi Lang* (55)

PC-1145 ____ Winnemucca _____ 44-55. Korean *Otaesan* (60)

PC-1146 ____ na _____ French *Trident* (51), Vietnam *Tuy Dong* (56)

PC-1149 ____ Susanville _____ Taiwan *Hsi Kiang* (57)

PC-1167 ____ na _____ French *L'Ardent* (51), Vietnam *Dong Da* (56)

PC-1169 ____ Escondido _____ Taiwan *Liu Kiang* (57)

PC-1170 ____ Kelso _____ 44-55. Str60

PC-1171 ____ na _____ French *L'Inconstant* (51), Cambodian *E-312* (56), Philippine *Negros Oriental* (76)

PC-1172 ____ Olney _____ 43-55. Sold 61

PC-1173 ____ Andalusia _____ Str60

PC-1174 ____ Fredonia _____ Str57

PC-1175 ____ Vandalia _____ Taiwan *Han Kiang* (57)

PC-1176 ____ Minden _____ Venezuelan *Petrel* (62)

PC-1177 ____ Guymon _____ Str60

PC-1178 ____ Kewaunee _____ Str59

PC-1179 ____ Morris _____ Str60

PC-1180 ____ Woodstock _____ Str60

PC-1181 ____ Wildwood _____ Str59

PC-1182 ____ na _____ Taiwan *Yuan Kiang* (54)

PC-1186 ____ Ipswich _____ Str59

PC-1191 ____ Bel Air _____ Str59

PC-1193 ____ Ridgway _____ 44-50. Str59

PC-1196 ____ Mayfield _____ 43-49. Str59

PC-1198 ____ Westerly _____ 43-50. Str59

PC-1201 ____ Kittery _____ 43-50. Str59

PC-1208 ____ na _____ Taiwan *Li Kiang* (54)

PC-1209 ____ Medina _____ 44-50. Str59

PC-1212 ____ Laurinburg _____ 43-50. Str59

PC-1213 ____ Louden _____ 43-59. Str59

PC-1216 ____ Elkins _____ Str59

PC-1225 ____ Waverly _____ Str57

PC-1228 ____ Munising _____ BU58

PC-1229 ____ Wauseon _____ Str57

PC-1230 ____ Grinnell _____ Str59

PC-1231 ____ Tipton _____ Str60

PC-1232 ____ na _____ Taiwan *Chang Kiang* (54), lost 06/08/65

PC-1233 ____ na _____ Taiwan *Kung Kiang* (54)

PC-1237 ____ Abingdon _____ Str59

PC-1240 ____ Culpeper _____ Str59

PC-1242 ____ Port Clinton _____ Str59

PC-1244 ____ Martinez _____ 43-50. Str60

PC-1246 ____ Canandaigua _____ Str57

PC-1251 ____ Ukiah _____ Str60

PC-1252 ____ Tarrytown _____ Str60

PC-1253 ____ na _____ Thai *Liulom* (52)

PC-1254 ____ na _____ Taiwan *Po Kiang* (54)

PC-1260 ____ Durango _____ Str59

PC-1262 ____ na _____ Taiwan *Chung Kiang* (54)

PC-1263 ____ Milledgeville _____ 43-59. Taiwan *To Kiang* (59)

PC-1546 ____ Grosse-Pointe _____ 44-55. Korean *Kum Chong San* (60)

PC-1547 —— *Corinth* —————————— Str58
PC-1569 —— *Anacortes* —————————— Vietnam *Van Don* (60)
PC-1590 —— *na* —————————— 46-54. Str54

**Notes:** Named 1956.

---

**Details:** 640 tons, 903f/l; 180 (wl), 184'6 (oa)×33'1×9'5;
two shafts, diesel, SHP 1,800=16kt; 1×3in, 6×40mm
(PCER none)

PCE-842 —— *Marfa* —————————— 44-55. Korean *Tang Po* (61), lost 19/01/67
PCE-843 —— *Skowhegan* —————————— 44-55. Str60
PCE-845 —— *Worland* —————————— 44-64. Str64
PCE-846 —— *Eunice* —————————— -58. Ecuadorian *Esmeraldas* (60)
PCER-849 —— *Somersworth* —————————— 44-65. Str66
PCER-850 —— *Fairview* —————————— 44-58. Str68
PCER-851 —— *Rockville* —————————— 44-68. Colombian *San Andres* (69)
PCER-852 —— *Brattleboro* —————————— 44-59. Vietnam *Ngoc Hoi* (66), Philippine *Miguel Malvar* (75)
PCER-853 —— *Amherst* —————————— -58, 65-70. Vietnam *Van Kiep II* (70), Philippine *Datu Marikudo* (76)
PCER-855 —— *Rexburg* —————————— 44-70. BU70
PCER-856 —— *Whitehall* —————————— 44-70 PCE (62), Str70
PCER-857 —— *Marysville* —————————— 45-70. Str70

PCE-870 —— *Dania* —————————— Korean *Pyok Pa* (61)
PCE-873 —— *na* —————————— Korean *Hansan* (56)
PCE-874 —— *Pascagoula* —————————— 43-59. Ecudorian *Manabi* (60)
PCE-877 —— *Havre* —————————— 44-58, 65-70. Str70

*Below:*
**Marysville (PCER-857), a rescue version of an
escort chaser, with extended forecastle.**

PCE-880 _____ *Ely* _____ 44-58, 65-70. Str70
PCE-882 _____ *na* _____ Korean *Ro Ryang* (55)
PCE-886 _____ *Banning* _____ Str61
PCE-892 _____ *Somerset* _____ 43-55. Korean *Ryul Ro* (61)
PCE-894 _____ *Farmington* _____ -58. Burmese *Yan Taing Aung* (65)
PCE-895 _____ *Crestview* _____ -58. Vietnam *Dong Da II* (61), Philippine *Sultan Kudarat* (75)
PCE-896 _____ *na* _____ Korean *Myong Ryang* (55)
PCE-898 _____ *na* _____ Korean *Okpo* (56)
PCE-899 _____ *Lamar* _____ 45-49, 50-64. USCG (64)
PCE-900 _____ *Groton* _____ 44-55. Str60
PCE-902 _____ *Portage* _____ 45-58, 65-70. Str70
PCE-903 _____ *Batesburg* _____ Korean *Sa Chon* (61)
PCE-904 _____ *Gettysburg* _____ 45-55. Str60

**Notes:** Similar hulls to 'Admirable' class
minesweepers. Surviving vessels named 02/56. *Rexburg*
used as research ship. Rescue escorts (PCER) had longer
forecastle, were unnamed.

**Details:**
251 tons, 338f/l; 130 (wl), 136 (oa)×24'6×8'7; two shafts,
    diesel, BHP 1,000=14kt; 2×3in/50 guns; complement
    50

PCS-1376 _____ *Winder* _____ 43-50. Str58
PCS-1378 _____ *Provincetown* _____ 52-54. Str57
PCS-1380 _____ *Rushville* _____ 44-54. Str57
PCS-1383 _____ *Attica* _____ Str57
PCS-1384 _____ *Eufaula* _____ Str57
PCS-1385 _____ *Hollidaysburg* _____ 44-70. Str70
PCS-1386 _____ *Hampton* _____ 44-59. Str59
PCS-1387 _____ *Beaufort* _____ -58, 65-67. Target 68
PCS-1392 _____ *Deming* _____ Str57
PCS-1400 _____ *Coquille* _____ Str56
PCS-1401 _____ *McMinnville* _____ 45-62. Str62
PCS-1413 _____ *Elsmere* _____ 45-60. Str60
PCS-1423 _____ *Prescott* _____ 43-61. Str62
PCS-1426 _____ *na* _____ Korean *Su Seong* (52)
PCS-1431 _____ *Grafton* _____ 44-65. Str65
PCS-1444 _____ *Conneaut* _____ Str57
PCS-1445 _____ *na* _____ Korean *Kum Seong* (52)
PCS-1446 _____ *na* _____ Korean *Mok Seong* (52)
PCS-1448 _____ *na* _____ Korean *Hwa Seong* (52)

**Notes:** Wood hulls, similar to YMS type
minesweepers.

# FAST PATROL CRAFT

**Details:** 58 tons; 98'6 (oa)×26×7; four shafts, 42kt

PT-809 to PT-812

**Notes:** Aluminium hulls. PT-810-811 became PTF-1-2,
stricken 1955. PT-613, 616, 619 and 620 were retained

after World War 2. PT-809 later renamed *Guardian* when used by Secret Service; in 1975 renamed *Retriever* (DR-1) as recovery vessel for aerial drones.

*Above:*
**PTF-10, a 'Nasty' class fast patrol boat built in Norway.** *Martin E. Holbrook collection*

**Details:** 85 tons f/l; 80'5×24'7×6'7; two shafts, diesels, HP 6,200=45kt; 1×81mm mortar, 1×40mm gun; crew 19

PTF-3 to PTF-22

**Notes:** 'Nasty' class, PTF-3-16 built in Norway 1963-65, PTF-17-22 built by Trumpy 1967-68. PTF-4, 8, 9, 14, 15 and 16 sunk in Vietnam.

**Details:** 105 tons f/l; 94'8×23'2×7; two shafts, diesels; 1×81mm mortar, 1×40mm gun, crew 19.

PTF-23 to PTF-26

**Notes:** 'Osprey' class, built in 1967-68 by Stewart Seacraft. Not considered a successful design.

# AUXILIARIES

## DESTROYER TENDERS

**Details:** 9,450 tons, 17,176f/l; 520 (wl) 530'6
(oa)×73'4×25'6; two shafts, steam turbines,
SHP 12,000=19.6kt; 4×5in/38, 8×40mm guns; 1,262
crew

AD-14 _____ *Dixie* _____ NY Sbdg _____ 27/05/39 ___ 40-82. Str82
AD-15 _____ *Prairie* _____ NY Sbdg _____ 09/12/39 ___ 40-
AD-17 _____ *Piedmont* _____ Tampa _____ 07/12/42 ___ 44-82. Turkish *Derya* (82)
AD-18 _____ *Sierra* _____ Tampa _____ 23/02/43 ___ 44-
AD-19 _____ *Yosemite* _____ Tampa _____ 16/05/43 ___ 44-

**Notes:** All guns removed in 1970s. All had FRAM refit.
Helicopter deck added aft.

---

**Details:** 10,820 tons, 16,650f/l; 464 (wl), 492
(oa)×69'6×27'3; one shaft, steam turbines,
SHP 8,500=18.4kt; 2×5in/38, 6×40mm guns; 860
crew

AD-16 _____ *Cascade* _____ Western Pipe _____ 06/07/42 ___ 51-74. BU75

---

**Details:** 8,560 (20), 7,919 (21) tons; 465 (wl), 492
(oa)×69'6×27'3; one shaft, steam turbines,
3HP 8,500=18.4kt; 1×5in/38, 4×3in/50, 4×40mm
guns; 857 crew

AD-20 _____ *Hamul* _____ Federal _____ 06/04/40 ___ 41-62. BU76
AD-21 _____ *Markab* _____ Ingalls _____ 21/12/40 ___ 52-55, 60-69. AR-23 (60), Str76

---

**Details:** 8,165 tons, 16,635f/l; 465 (wl), 492
(oa)×69'6×27'3; one shaft, steam turbines,
SHP 8,500=18.4kt; 1×5in/38, 4×40mm guns (22-25,
also 4×3in/50 guns; 826 crew

AD-22 _____ *Klondike* _____ Todd; S Pedro _____ 12/08/44 ___ 45-70. AR-22 (60), BU75
AD-23 _____ *Arcadia* _____ Todd; S Pedro _____ 19/11/44 ___ 51-69. Str73
AD-24 _____ *Everglades* _____ Todd; S Pedro _____ 28/01/45 ___ 51-70. Str85
AD-25 _____ *Frontier* _____ Todd; S Pedro _____ 25/03/45 ___ 51-68. BU75
AD-26 _____ *Shenandoah* _____ Todd; Tacoma _____ 29/03/45 ___ 45-80. Str80
AD-27 _____ *Yellowstone* _____ Todd; Seattle _____ 12/04/45 ___ 46-74. BU75
AD-28 _____ *Grand Canyon* _____ Todd; Tacoma _____ 27/04/45 ___ 46-78. AR-28 (71), Str78
AD-29 _____ *Isle Royale* _____ Todd; Seattle _____ 19/09/45 ___ 62-72. Str76
AD-31 _____ *Tidewater* _____ Charleston _____ 30/06/45 ___ 51-71. Indonesian *Dumai* (71)
AD-36 _____ *Bryce Canyon* _____ Charleston _____ 07/03/46 ___ 50-81. Str81

**Notes:** Although completed in 1946, *Everglades* and
*Isle Royale* were first commissioned in 1951 and 1962
respectively. *Shenandoah* and *Bryce Canyon* had FRAM
refit.

**Details:** 13,600 tons, 22,260f/l; 643 (oa)×85×22'6; one
shaft, steam turbine, SHP 20,000=20kt; 1×5in/38,
4×20mm guns (41-44: 2×40mm guns); 1,314 crew

| | | | | |
|---|---|---|---|---|
| AD-37 | *Samuel Gompers* | Puget Sound | 14/05/66 | 67- |
| AD-38 | *Puget Sound* | Puget Sound | 16/09/66 | 68- |
| AD-41 | *Yellowstone* | National | 27/01/79 | 80- |
| AD-42 | *Acadia* | National | 28/07/79 | 81- |
| AD-43 | *Cape Cod* | National | 02/08/80 | 82- |
| AD-44 | *Shenandoah* | National | 06/02/82 | 83- |

**Notes:** FY64-65 (37-38), 1975-79 (41-44). Construction
of AD-39 and 40 was cancelled in 1969 and 1974. AD-45
proposed. Installation of Sea Sparrow SAM cancelled.

# SUBMARINE TENDERS

*Holland* (AS-3) remained on the list until 1952.

**Details:** 10,100 tons, 16,500f/l (19, 1960: 10,234 tons);
520 (wl), 529'6 (oa)×73'4×25'6 (19, 1960: 574'6 oa);
two shafts, diesel-electric, SHP 11,800=18kt (15-19:
SHP 11,200); 4×5in/38, 10×40mm; 1,639 crew

| | | | | |
|---|---|---|---|---|
| AS-11 | *Fulton* | Mare Is | 27/12/40 | 51- |
| AS-12 | *Sperry* | Mare Is | 17/12/41 | 42-82. Str82 |
| AS-15 | *Bushnell* | Mare Is | 14/09/42 | 52-70. Str80 |
| AS-16 | *Howard W. Gilmore* | Mare Is | 16/09/43 | 44-80. Str80 |
| AS-17 | *Nereus* | Mare Is | 12/02/45 | 45-71 |
| AS-18 | *Orion* | Moore | 14/10/42 | 43- |
| AS-19 | *Proteus* | Moore | 12/11/42 | 44- |

**Notes:** Similar to 'Dixie' class destroyer tenders.
*Proteus* lengthened and converted to support Polaris
FBM submarines, 1959-60. Guns removed 1975. All
received FRAM II refit to handle nuclear submarines.

**Details:** 7,150 tons, 16,500f/l (13-14: 8,600 tons; 22:
8,282 tons; 465 (wl), 492 (oa)×69'6×23; one shaft,
steam turbines, SHP 8,500=18.5kt (13-14: diesel,
SHP 8,900=16.5kt); 1×5in/38, 4×3in/50 guns; 1,460
crew

| | | | | |
|---|---|---|---|---|
| AS-13 | *Griffin* | Sun | 10/11/39 | BU73 |
| AS-14 | *Pelias* | Sun | 14/11/39 | BU71 |
| AS-22 | *Euryale* | Federal | 12/04/41 | BU72 |
| AS-23 | *Aegir* | Ingalls | 15/09/43 | BU72 |
| AS-24 | *Anthedon* | Ingalls | 15/10/43 | Str61; Turkish *Donatan* (69) |
| AS-25 | *Apollo* | Ingalls | 06/11/43 | Str63 |
| AS-26 | *Clytie* | Ingalls | 26/11/43 | BU70 |

**Notes:** AS-13-14 acquired 1940, AS-22 1943. AS-23-26
built for the Navy.

**Details:** 10,500 tons, 18,300f/l; 599 (oa)×83×27; one
shaft, diesel-electric, SHP 15,000=19kt; 4×3in/50 guns
(removed); 1,501 crew

Above:
**The submarine tender *Proteus* (AS-19) after modernisation and lengthening.**
*Ernest Arroyo collection*

*Below:*
**The *Simon Lake* (AS-33) a submarine tender built to support ballistic missile submarines.** *Our Navy*

AS-31 _____ *Hunley* _____ Newport News _____ 29/09/61 ___ 62-
AS-32 _____ *Holland* _____ Ingalls _____ 19/01/63 ___ 63-

**Notes:** FY60-62. Designed to support FBM submarines. Modified from Polaris to Poseidon support 1973-75.

**Details:** 20,500 tons f/l; 643′9 (oa)×85×24′6; one shaft, steam turbines, SHP 20,000=20kt; 4×3in/50 guns; 1,387 crew

AS-33 _____ *Simon Lake* _____ Puget Sound _____ 08/02/64 ___ 64-
AS-34 _____ *Canopus* _____ Ingalls _____ 12/02/65 ___ 65-

**Notes:** FY63-64. Construction of AS-35 cancelled 1965. Designed to support FBM submarines. *Simon Lake* modified to support Trident missiles. Guns removed.

**Details:** 13,840 tons, 23,500f/l (36-37: 12,770 tons); 645′8 (oa)×85×28′6; one shaft, steam turbine, SHP 20,000=20kt; 2×5in/38 (36-37), 2×40mm guns; 1,158 crew

| AS-36 | LY Spear | Quincy | 07/09/67 | 70- |
| AS-37 | Dixon | Quincy | 20/06/70 | 71- |
| AS-39 | Emory S. Land | Lockheed | 04/05/77 | 79- |
| AS-40 | Frank Cable | Lockheed | 14/01/78 | 80- |
| AS-41 | McKee | Lockheed | 16/02/80 | 81 |

**Notes:** FY65-77. Construction of AS-38 cancelled 1969. AS-39-41 fitted specifically to support 'Los Angeles' class nuclear submarines. 5in guns removed. Similar to 'Samuel Gompers' class destroyer tenders.

*Below:*
**The submarine tender *Emory S. Land* (AS-39).**
*Martin E. Holbrook*

# REPAIR SHIPS

**Details:** 9,140 tons, 16,200f/l; 520 (wl), 529'4 (oa)×73'4×23'4; two shafts, steam turbines, SHP 11,000=19.2kt; 4×5in/38, 8×40mm guns; 1,297 crew

| AR-5 | Vulcan | NY Sbdg | 14/12/40 | 41- | |
| AR-6 | Ajax | Todd; LA | 22/08/42 | 43- | |
| AR-7 | Hector | Todd; LA | 11/11/42 | 44- | |
| | | | | | |
| ARH-1 | Jason | Todd; LA | 03/04/43 | 41- | . AR-8 (57) |

**Notes:** *Jason* completed as heavy-hull repair ship. 5in guns removed 1970s.

**Details:** 8,975 tons, 14,500f/l; 465 (wl), 490'6 (oa)×69'6×24'3; one shaft, steam turbines, SHP 8,500=17kt; 1×5in/38, 4×3in/50, 4×40mm guns; 903 crew

| AR-9 | Delta | Newport News | 02/04/41 | 51-55, 59-70. Str77 |
| AR-12 | Briareus | Newport News | 14/02/41 | 51-55. Str77 |

**Notes:** Acquired 1941 and 1943.

*Above:*
**The repair ship *Jason* (AR-8) at Sasebo, Japan, in 1960.** *Official US Navy/Ernest Arroyo collection*

*Below:*
**The *Luzon* (ARG-2) was a Liberty ship converted during World War 2 into a repair ship for internal combustion engines.**
*Our Navy/Martin E. Holbrook collection*

**Details:** 7,826 tons, 16,900f/l; 465 (wl), 492 (oa)×69'6×27'6; one shaft, steam turbines, SHP 8,500−17kt; 2×5in/38, 8×40mm guns; 921 crew

| | | | | |
|---|---|---|---|---|
| AR-13 | Amphion | Tampa | 15/05/45 | 46-71. Iranian *Chahbahar* (71) |
| AR-14 | Cadmus | Tampa | 05/08/45 | 46-71. Taiwan *Tu Tai* (74) |

**Details:** 5,801 tons (ARG-2-9: 4,621 tons; 10-11: 5,159; 12-13: 5,371; 14-15: 6,225); 416 (wl), 441'6 (oa)×56'11×23; one shaft, VTE, SHP 2,500=12.5kt; 1×5in/38, 3×3in/50, 4×40mm guns; 921 crew

| | | | | |
|---|---|---|---|---|
| AR-19 | Xanthus | Fairfield | 31/07/44 | Str62 |
| AR-20 | Laertes | Fairfield | 13/09/44 | 51-54. BU72 |
| AR-21 | Dionysus | Fairfield | 10/10/44 | 52-55. Str61 |
| | | | | |
| ARG-2 | Luzon | Fairfield | 14/05/43 | 50-60. Str61 |
| ARG-3 | Mindanao | Fairfield | 13/05/43 | Str62 |
| ARG-4 | Tutuila | Fairfield | 12/09/43 | 51-52. Taiwan *Tien Tai* (72) |
| ARG-5 | Oahu | Fairfield | 09/09/43 | BU79 |
| ARG-6 | Cebu | Fairfield | 18/10/43 | Str62 |

*Above:*
**The repair ship *Markab* (AR-23), formerly a destroyer tender.** *Official US Navy*

| | | | | |
|---|---|---|---|---|
| ARG-7 | *Culebra Island* | Fairfield | 13/11/43 | Str62 |
| ARG-8 | *Maui* | Fairfield | 18/02/44 | Str62 |
| ARG-9 | *Mona Island* | Fairfield | 11/05/44 | Str62 |
| ARG-10 | *Palawan* | Fairfield | 12/08/44 | Str63 |
| ARG-11 | *Samar* | Fairfield | 19/10/44 | Str62 |
| ARG-16 | *Kermit Roosevelt* | Fairfield | 05/10/44 | 45-59. BU60 |
| ARG-17 | *Hooper Island* | Fairfield | 18/10/44 | 52-59. BU70 |
| | | | | |
| ARV-1 | *Chourre* | Fairfield | 22/05/44 | 52-55. BU71 |
| ARV-2 | *Webster* | Fairfield | 05/08/44 | Target 75 |

**Notes:** Converted Liberty Ships.

**Reclassified vessels:**

| | | | |
|---|---|---|---|
| AR-22 | *Klondike* | ex-AD-22 | 60-70 |
| AR-23 | *Markab* | ex-AD-21 | 60-69 |
| AR-28 | *Grand Canyon* | ex-AD-28 | 71-78 |
| ARVH-1 | *Corpus Christie Bay* | ex-AV-5 | 57-73. BU75 |

# CONVERTED TANK LANDING SHIPS

*ex-LST*

| | | | |
|---|---|---|---|
| ARB-1 | *Aristaeus* | 329 | Sold 62 |
| ARB-2 | *Oceanus* | 328 | Sold 62 |
| ARB-3 | *Phaon* | 15 | Sold 62 |
| ARB-4 | *Zeus* | 132 | Sold 74 |
| ARB-5 | *Midas* | 514 | Str76 |
| ARB-7 | *Sarpedon* | 956 | Str76 |
| ARB-8 | *Telamon* | 976 | Sold 73 |
| ARB-9 | *Ulysses* | 967 | W German *Wotan* (71) |

| | | | |
|---|---|---|---|
| ARB-10 | Demeter | 1121 | Merchant Motonave (61) |
| ARB-11 | Diomedes | 1119 | W German Odin (71) |
| ARB-12 | Helios | 1127 | Brazilian Belmonte (62) |
| | | | |
| ARL-1 | Achelous | 10 | Sold 73 |
| ARL-2 | Amycus | 489 | Sold 71 |
| ARL-3 | Agenor | 490 | French Vulcain (51); Taiwan Shung Shan (57) |
| ARL-4 | Adonis | 83 | Sold 60 |
| ARL-7 | Atlas | 231 | 51-55. Sold 73 |
| ARL-8 | Egeria | 136 | Str77 |
| ARL-9 | Endymion | 513 | Sold 73 |
| ARL-10 | Coronis | 1003 | Merchant Trailer Princess (65) |
| ARL-11 | Creon | 1036 | Sold 61 |
| ARL-12 | Poseidon | 1037 | Sold 61 |
| ARL-13 | Menelaus | 971 | 50-55. Merchant Maryland Clipper (62) |
| ARL-14 | Minos | 644 | 50-55. Sold 60 |
| ARL-15 | Minotaur | 645 | 51-55. Korean Duk Su (55) |
| ARL-16 | Myrmidon | 948 | Sold 60 |
| ARL-17 | Numitor | 954 | Sold 60 |
| ARL-18 | Pandemus | 650 | 51-68. Target 69 |
| ARL-19 | Patroclus | 955 | Turkish Basaran (52) |
| ARL-20 | Pentheus | 1115 | Sold 60 |
| ARL-21 | Proserpine | 1116 | 50-56. Sold 60 |
| ARL-22 | Romulus | 962 | 52-56. Philippine Aklan (61) |
| ARL-23 | Satyr | 852 | 50-56, 68-71. Vietnam Vinh Dong (71), Philippine Yakal (77) |
| ARL-24 | Sphinx | 963 | 50-56, 67-71, 85- |
| ARL-26 | Stentor | 858 | Sold 61 |
| ARL-28 | Typhon | 1118 | Sold 61 |
| ARL-29 | Amphitrite | 1124 | Sold 62 |
| ARL-30 | Askari | 1131 | 45-56, 66-71. Indonesian Jaya Wijaya (72) |
| ARL-31 | Bellerophon | 1132 | Str77 |
| ARL-33 | Chimaera | 1137 | Merchant Santa Teresa (68) |
| ARL-35 | Daedalus | 1143 | Merchant Virginia Clipper (63) |
| ARL-36 | Gordius | 1145 | 45-55. Iranian Sohrab (61) |
| ARL-37 | Indra | 1147 | 67-70. Str77 |
| ARL-38 | Krishna | 1149 | 45-71. Philippine Narra (71) |
| ARL-39 | Quirinus | 1151 | Venezuelan Guyana (62) |
| | | | |
| ARST-1 | Laysan Island | 1098 | Str73 |
| ARST-3 | Palmyra | 1100 | Sold 74 |
| ARVE-3 | Aventinus | 1092 | 50-52. Chilean Aguila (63), lost 17/05/80 |
| ARVE-4 | Chloris | 1094 | 51-55. Sold 74 |
| ARVA-5 | Fabius | 1093 | 50-52. Sold 73 |
| ARVA-6 | Megara | 1095 | 51-55. Mexican Gen Vicente Guerrero (73) |

*ex-LSM*

| | | | |
|---|---|---|---|
| ARSD-1 | Gypsy | 549 | 51-55. Str73 |
| ARSD-2 | Mender | 550 | 51-55. Str73 |
| ARSD-3 | Salvager | 551 | 46-71. YMLC-3 (67), BU73 |
| ARSD-4 | Windlass | 552 | 46-71. YMLC-4 (67), BU73 |

**Notes:** Former medium landing ships (LSM-549-552) converted in 1944-45.

*Above:*
**Chloris (ARVE-4), an aviation repair ship for
aircraft engines.** *Marius Bar*

# SEAPLANE TENDERS

**Details:** 9,090 tons, 13,630f/l; 508 (wl)
527'4 (oa)×69'3×21'4; two shafts, steam turbines,
SHP 12,000=19kt; 4×5in/38, 2×3in/50 guns; 1,195
crew

| | | | | |
|---|---|---|---|---|
| AV-4 | *Curtiss* | NY Sbdg | 20/04/40 | 40-57. Str63 |
| AV-5 | *Albemarle* | NY Sbdg | 13/07/40 | 40-50, 57-60. *Corpus Christie Bay* (ARVH-1) (65), BU75 |

**Notes:** *Albemarle* converted to service cancelled
Seamaster jet seaplane, stricken 1962 and re-acquired
1965 for conversion to helicopter repair ship. Support
ship for Army helicopters in Vietnam. Conversion of
*Curtiss* as ARVH-2 cancelled.

**Details:** 9,030 tons, 15,170f/l; 520 (w/l)
540'5 (oa)×72×26; two shafts, steam turbines,
SHP 12,000=19.2kt; 4×5in/38, 20×40mm guns; 1,247
crew

| | | | | |
|---|---|---|---|---|
| AV-7 | *Currituck* | Philadelphia | 11/09/43 | 51-67. Str71 |
| AV-11 | *Norton Island* | Los Angeles | 28/11/43 | 45-. AVM-1 (51) |
| AV-12 | *Pine Island* | Los Angeles | 26/02/44 | 45-67. Sold 72 |
| AV-13 | *Salisbury Sound* | Los Angeles | 18/06/44 | 45-67. BU72 |

**Notes:** *Norton Sound* used as rocket testing vessel.
Seved as test ship for Loon, Viking, Regulus I, Terrier,
Tartar, Sea Sparrow and Standard SAM; for Typhon air
defence system (cancelled) 1962; and for AEGIS system
1974.

**Details:** 8,973 tons (10: 8,949 tons, 14,200f/l); 465 (wl)
492 (oa)×69'6×24'9 (10:23'9); one shaft, steam
turbines, SHP 8,500=16.5kt; 4×5in/38 guns (10:
1×5in/38, 4×3in/50, 8×40mm); 857 crew

| | | | | |
|---|---|---|---|---|
| AV-8 | *Tangier* | Moore | 15/09/39 | Merchant *Detroit* (63) |

*Above:*
**The seaplane tender *Salisbury Sound* (AV-13) in 1961. Notice the 5in guns in mounts, two forward and one next to the funnel.** *Official US Navy*

| | | | | |
|---|---|---|---|---|
| AV-9 | *Pocomoke* | Ingalls | 08/06/40 | BU61 |
| AV-10 | *Chandeleur* | Western Pipe | 29/11/41 | BU71 |

**Notes:** Acquired 1940-41.

**Details:** 8,510 tons, 14,000f/l; 465 (w/l)
492 (oa)×69'6×26; one shaft, steam turbines,
SHP 8,500=18kt; 2×5in/38, 12×40mm guns; 662 crew

| | | | | |
|---|---|---|---|---|
| AV-14 | *Kenneth Whiting* | Todd; Tacoma | 15/12/43 | 51-58. BU62 |
| AV-15 | *Hamlin* | Todd; Tacoma | 11/01/44 | Str63 |
| AV-16 | *St George* | Todd; Tacoma | 14/02/44 | Italian *Andrea Bafile* (67) |
| AV-17 | *Cumberland Sound* | Todd; Tacoma | 23/02/44 | Sold 62 |

**Notes:** Conversion of *Hamlin* and *St George* to
ARVH-3-4 cancelled

**Details:** 1,830 tons, 2,800f/l; 300 (w/l) 310'9
(oa)×41'1×14; two shafts, diesel-electric,
SHP 6,080=18kt; 1×5in/38, 8×40mm guns; 215 crew

| | | | | |
|---|---|---|---|---|
| AVP-10 | *Barnegat* | Puget Sound | 23/05/41 | Merchant *Kentavros* (62) |
| AVP-28 | *Oyster Bay* | Lake Washington | 07/09/41 | AGP-6 (43), AVP-28 (49) Italian *Pietro Cavazzale* (57) |
| AVP-30 | *San Pablo* | Associated | 31/03/42 | 48-69. AGS-30 (49), BU71 |
| AVP-37 | *Corson* | Associated | 16/07/44 | 51-56. Target 67 |
| AVP-38 | *Duxbury Bay* | Associated | 02/10/44 | 44-66. Str66 |
| AVP-39 | *Gardiners Bay* | Associated | 02/12/44 | 45-58. Norwegian *Haakon VII* (58) |
| AVP-40 | *Floyds Bay* | Associated | 28/01/45 | 45-60. Sold 61 |
| AVP-41 | *Greenwich Bay* | Associated | 18/03/45 | 45-66. BU67 |
| AVP-48 | *Onslow* | Associated | 20/09/42 | 51-60. Merchant *Pres. Quezon* (61) |
| AVP-49 | *Orca* | Associated | 04/10/42 | 51-60. Ethiopian *Ethiopia* (62) |
| AVP-50 | *Rehoboth* | Associated | 08/11/42 | 44-70. AGS-50 (48), Str70 |
| AVP-51 | *San Carlos* | Associated | 20/12/42 | 58-71. *Josiah Willard Gibbs* (AGOR-1) (58), Greek *Hephaistos* (71) |
| AVP-52 | *Shelikof* | Associated | 31/01/43 | Merchant *Kypros* (61) |
| AVP-53 | *Suisun* | Associated | 14/03/43 | 44-55. Target 66 |

*Above:*
**Valcour (AGF-1), a seaplane tender converted to a flagship for service in the Middle East: it was painted white to reflect heat.**

AVP-54 _____ *Timbalier* _____ Associated _____ 18/04/43 ___ 46-54. Merchant *Rodos* (61)
AVP-55 _____ *Valcour* _____ Associated _____ 05/6/43 ____ 46-73. AGF-1 (65), sold 77

**Notes:** Three of this class were transferred to Coast Guard 1946 and 15 others loaned in 1948. *San Pablo* and *Rehoboth* converted to surveying vessels 1949. *Mobjack* was transferred to Coast and Geodetic Survey 1946 (see later pages).

## AVIATION SUPPORT SHIPS

AVB-1 was *Alameda County* (ex-LST-32), converted 57.
AVB-2 was *Tallahatchie County* (ex-LST-1154), converted 1961.

Converted to provide support for land-based patrol aircraft and seaplanes (AVB-1) in Mediterranean.

**Details:** 23,872 tons f/l; 602 (oa)×90×29'9; one shaft, steam turbine, SHP 30,000=22.3kt; crew 41

AVB-3 _____ *Wright* _____ Ingalls _____ 29/07/69
                  ex-*Young America*
AVB-4 _____ *Curtiss* _____ Ingalls _____ 28/12/68
                  ex-*Great Republic*

**Notes:** Converted by Todd-Galveston to service Marine Corps aircraft in forward areas, 1985-86.

## AMMUNITION SHIPS

**Details:** 6,350 tons, 14,230f/l (8, 9, 13: 5,220 tons, 13,800f/l); 435 (wl), 459 (oa)×63×26'5; one shaft, diesel, SHP 6,000=15.3kt; 4×3in/50, 4×40mm guns; 280 crew

AE-3 _____ *Lassen* _____ Tampa _____ 10/01/40 ___ Str61
AE-4 _____ *Mount Baker* _____ Tampa _____ 06/08/40 ___ 51-69. Str69
AE-5 _____ *Rainier* _____ Tampa _____ 01/03/41 ___ 51-70. Str70
AE-6 _____ *Shasta* _____ Tampa _____ 09/07/41 ___ 53-67. BU70
AE-8 _____ *Mauna Loa* _____ Tampa _____ 14/04/43 ___ 55-58, 61-71. Str76

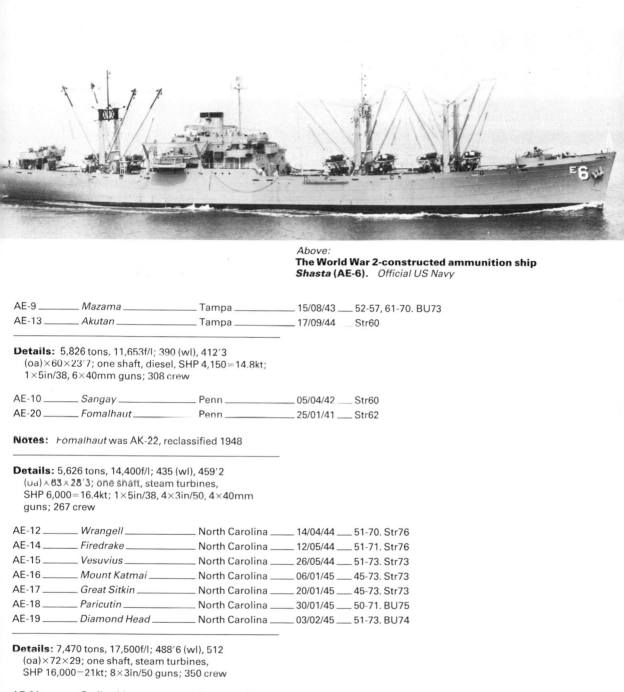

*Above:*
**The World War 2-constructed ammunition ship**
**Shasta (AE-6).** *Official US Navy*

| AE-9 | Mazama | Tampa | 15/08/43 | 52-57, 61-70. BU73 |
| AE-13 | Akutan | Tampa | 17/09/44 | Str60 |

**Details:** 5,826 tons, 11,653f/l; 390 (wl), 412'3
(oa)×60×23'7; one shaft, diesel, SHP 4,150=14.8kt;
1×5in/38, 6×40mm guns; 308 crew

| AE-10 | Sangay | Penn | 05/04/42 | Str60 |
| AE-20 | Fomalhaut | Penn | 25/01/41 | Str62 |

**Notes:** Fomalhaut was AK-22, reclassified 1948

**Details:** 5,626 tons, 14,400f/l; 435 (wl), 459'2
(oa)×63×28'3; one shaft, steam turbines,
SHP 6,000=16.4kt; 1×5in/38, 4×3in/50, 4×40mm
guns; 267 crew

| AE-12 | Wrangell | North Carolina | 14/04/44 | 51-70. Str76 |
| AE-14 | Firedrake | North Carolina | 12/05/44 | 51-71. Str76 |
| AE-15 | Vesuvius | North Carolina | 26/05/44 | 51-73. Str73 |
| AE-16 | Mount Katmai | North Carolina | 06/01/45 | 45-73. Str73 |
| AE-17 | Great Sitkin | North Carolina | 20/01/45 | 45-73. Str73 |
| AE-18 | Paricutin | North Carolina | 30/01/45 | 50-71. BU75 |
| AE-19 | Diamond Head | North Carolina | 03/02/45 | 51-73. BU74 |

**Details:** 7,470 tons, 17,500f/l; 488'6 (wl), 512
(oa)×72×29; one shaft, steam turbines,
SHP 16,000—21kt; 8×3in/50 guns; 350 crew

| AE-21 | Suribachi | Sparrows Pt | 02/11/55 | 56- |
| AE-22 | Mauna Kea | Sparrows Pt | 03/05/56 | 57- |
| AE-23 | Nitro | Sparrows Pt | 25/06/58 | 59- |
| AE-24 | Pyro | Sparrows Pt | 23/07/58 | 59- |
| AE-25 | Haleakala | Sparrows Pt | 17/02/59 | 59- |

**Notes:** FY1954-57. Modernised in 1960s, aft 4×3in
removed, fitted to carry guided missiles, helicopter deck
added, FAST

**Details:** 13,688 tons, 20,500f/l; 564 (oa)×81×25′9; one shaft, steam turbine, SHP 22,000=21kt; 8×3in/50 guns; 411 crew

*Above:*

**The ammunition ship *Butte* (AE-27). Notice the 3in guns forward and helicopter landing deck aft.**

| | | | | |
|---|---|---|---|---|
| AE-26 | *Kilauea* | Quincy | 09/08/67 | 68- |
| AE-27 | *Butte* | Quincy | 09/08/67 | 68- |
| AE-28 | *Santa Barbara* | Sparrows Pt | 23/01/68 | 70- |
| AE-29 | *Mount Hood* | Sparrows Pt | 17/07/68 | 71- |
| AE-32 | *Flint* | Ingalls | 09/11/70 | 71- |
| AE-33 | *Shasta* | Ingalls | 03/04/71 | 72- |
| AE-34 | *Mount Baker* | Ingalls | 23/10/71 | 72- |
| AE-35 | *Kiska* | Ingalls | 11/03/72 | 72- |

**Notes:** FY65-68. Helicopter landing deck aft, FAST. 4×3in removed 1970s. AE-36-40 planned.

**Reclassified vessels:**

| | | | | |
|---|---|---|---|---|
| AE-30 | *Virgo* | see AKA-20 | 66-71. | Str71 |
| AE-31 | *Chara* | see AKA-58 | 65-72. | Str72 |

# STORE SHIPS

**Details:** 6,051 tons, 12,500f/l; 435 (wl), 459′3 (oa)×63×25′10; one shaft, steam turbine, SHP 6,000=16.4kt; 1×5in/38, 4×3in/50 guns

| | | | | |
|---|---|---|---|---|
| AF-10 | *Aldebaran* | Newport News | 21/06/39 | 41-68. Str73 |

**Notes:** Acquired 1940

**Details:** 6,350 tons; 435 (wl), 459 (oa)×63×26′5; one shaft, diesel, SHP 6,000=15.3kt

| | | | | |
|---|---|---|---|---|
| AF-11 | *Polaris* | Sun | 22/04/39 | 48-57. Str57 |

**Notes:** Acquired 1941.

**Details:** 6,313 tons, 13,900f/l; 445 (wl), 468′8 (oa)×63×28; one shaft, steam turbines, SHP 6,000=15.5kt; 1×5in/38, 4×3in/50 guns; 319 crew

| | | | | |
|---|---|---|---|---|
| AF-28 | Hyades | Gulf | 12/06/43 | 44-69. Str76 |
| AF-29 | Graffias | Gulf | 12/12/43 | 44-69. Str69 |

**Details:** 3,139 tons, 7,435f/l; 320 (wl), 338'6
(oa)×50×21'1; one shaft, diesel, SHP 1,700=11.5kt;
1×3in/50 gun; 85 crew

| | | | | |
|---|---|---|---|---|
| AF-30 | Adria | Penn | 16/04/44 | 44-54. Str60 |
| AF-31 | Arequipa | Penn | 04/05/44 | 45-55. Str61 |
| AF-32 | Corduba | Penn | 11/06/44 | 45-55. Str60 |
| AF-33 | Karin | Penn | 22/06/44 | 45-58. Merchant *Typhoon* (69) |
| AF-34 | Kerstin | Penn | 16/07/44 | 45-50. Str50 |
| AF-35 | Latona | Penn | 10/08/44 | Merchant *Reefer Star* (73) |
| AF-36 | Lioba | Penn | 27/08/44 | 45-55. BU73 |
| AF-37 | Malabar | Penn | 17/09/44 | 45-55. Str60 |
| AF-38 | Merapi | Penn | 04/10/44 | 45-59. BU66 |
| AF-42 | Bondia | Penn | 09/11/44 | 51-73. BU73 |
| AF-44 | Laurentia | Penn | 12/12/44 | 50-70. BU73 |
| AF-47 | Valentine | Penn | 03/02/45 | 50-59. Str59. Merchant *Northgate* (67) |
| AF-53 | Grommet Reefer | Butler | 29/07/44 | 50-52. Lost 15/12/52 |

**Notes:** *Bondia*, *Laurentia* and *Valentine* were stricken
1946 and re-acquired 1950-51.

**Details:** 7,300 tons, 14,150f/l; 435 (wl), 459'2
(oa)×63×28; one shaft, steam turbines,
SHP 6,000=16kt; 290 crew

| | | | | |
|---|---|---|---|---|
| AF-48 | Alstede | Moore | 28/11/44 | 46-69. BU70 |
| AF-49 | Zelima | Moore | 02/03/45 | 46-69. BU81 |
| AF-50 | Bald Eagle | Moore | 07/05/42 | 50-70. BU73 |
| AF-51 | Blue Jacket | Moore | 14/02/42 | 50-70. BU73 |
| AF-52 | Golden Eagle | Moore | 15/03/42 | 50-72. *Arcturus* (61), Str76 |
| AF-54 | Pictor | Moore | 04/06/42 | 50-69. BU81 |
| AF-55 | Aludra | Moore | 14/10/44 | 52-69. Merchant *Aleutian Monarch* (78) |
| AF-60 | Sirius | Moore | 11/04/42 | 57-65. BU71 |
| AF-61 | Procyon | Moore | 01/07/42 | 61-70. BU81 |
| AF-62 | Bellatrix | Moore | 04/12/44 | 61-68. BU69 |

**Notes:** *Golden Eagle* transferred from MSTS to
commissioned status 1961.

*Below:*
**Corduba (AF-32), a store ship, c1952.**

**Details:** 6,700 tons; 436'6 (wl), 455'3 (oa)×62×28'6;
one shaft, steam turbines, SHP 8,500=17kt; 8×3in/50
guns; 225 crew

| | | | | |
|---|---|---|---|---|
| AF-56 | _Denebola_ | Oregon | 10/06/44 | 54-76. Str76 |
| AF-57 | _Regulus_ | Oregon | 07/06/44 | 54-71. Lost 16/08/71 |
| AF-63 | _Asterion_ | Calship | 27/07/44 | 62-72. BU73 |
| AF-64 | _Perseus_ | Oregon | 11/05/45 | 62-72. BU73 |

**Details:** 7,950 tons, 15,540f/l; 475 (wl), 502 (oa)×72×29;
one shaft, steam turbines, SHP 16,000=21kt; 8×3in/50
guns; 115 crew

| | | | | |
|---|---|---|---|---|
| AF-58 | _Rigel_ | Ingalls | 15/03/55 | 55- |
| AF-59 | _Vega_ | Ingalls | 26/04/55 | 55-77. Str77 |

**Notes:** FY53.

# COMBAT STORE SHIPS

**Details:** 9,200 tons, 16,500f/l; 530 (pp), 581
(oa)×79×24; one shaft, steam turbines,
SHP 22,000=21kt; 8×3in/50 guns; 403 crew

| | | | | |
|---|---|---|---|---|
| AFS-1 | _Mars_ | National | 15/06/63 | 63- |
| AFS-2 | _Sylvania_ | National | 25/08/63 | 64- |
| AFS-3 | _Niagara Falls_ | National | 26/03/66 | 67- |
| AFS-4 | _White Plains_ | National | 23/07/66 | 68- |
| AFS-5 | _Concord_ | National | 17/12/66 | 68- |
| AFS-6 | _San Diego_ | National | 13/04/68 | 69- |
| AFS-7 | _San Jose_ | National | 13/12/69 | 70- |

**Notes:** FY61-67. Designed to combine capability of AF,
AKS and AVS. Helicopter hangar and landing deck aft.
4×3in removed 1970s.

_Below:_
**The combat store ship _Sylvania_ (AFS-2).**

**Details:** 9,010 tons, 16,792f/l; 524 (oa)×72×22; one
shaft, diesel, SHP 11,520=18kt; 151 crew

| | | | | |
|---|---|---|---|---|
| AFS-8 | _Sirius_ | Swan Hunter | 07/04/66 | 81- |
| | ex-_Lyness_ | | | |

AFS-9 _____ Spica _____ Swan Hunter _____ 22/02/67 ___ 81-
                ex-*Tarbatness*
AFS-10 _____ Saturn _____ Swan Hunter _____ 16/09/66 ___ 84-
                ex-*Stromnes*

**Notes:** Built for Royal Navy and acquired 1981 and
1983 (AFS-10), to relieve shortage of underway
replenishment ships. First two originally acquired on
time charter.

# CARGO SHIPS

**Details:** 1,677 tons, 5,202f/l; 255 (wl), 269'10
(oa)×42'6×20'9; one shaft, diesels,
SHP 1,300=10.2kt

AK-87 _____ Sagitta _____ Penn-Jersey _____ 09/07/44 ___ 52-60. Str61
AK-89 _____ Vela _____ Penn-Jersey _____ 15/01/45 ___ 52-58. BU71

**Notes:** Re-acquired from Army in 1952.

---

**Details:** 2,382 tons, 7,410f/l; 321 (wl), 338'8
(oa)×50×21'1; one shaft, diesel, SHP 1,700=11.5kt;
1×3in/50 gun

AK-157 _____ Alcona _____ Kaiser; Rich _____ 09/05/44 ___ 44-55. BU60
AK-162 _____ Beltrami _____ Kaiser; Rich _____ 26/09/44 ___ 45-55. BU60
AK-170 _____ Chicot _____ Froemming _____ 16/07/44 ___ 47-51. Merchant (51)
AK-179 _____ Faribault _____ Froemming _____ 24/02/45 ___ 47-56. Str60
AK-180 _____ Fentress _____ Froemming _____ 10/03/45 ___ 50-73. Str73
AK-184 _____ Grainger _____ Butler _____ 07/05/44 ___ 47-56. Str60
AK-187 _____ Hennepin _____ Butler _____ 27/06/44 ___ 50-58. BU60
AK-188 _____ Herkimer _____ Butler _____ 02/07/44 ___ 50-73. Str73
AK-198 _____ Muskingum _____ Globe _____ 30/06/44 ___ 50-73. Str73
AK-200 _____ Pembina _____ Globe _____ 14/10/44 ___ 51-57. Merchant *Resolute* (68)
AK-213 _____ Sussex _____ LD Smith _____ 03/02/45 ___ 47-59. Str60
AK-245 _____ Capt Arlo L. Olsen _____ Jones _____ 08/05/45 ___ 50-58. BU71
AK-246 _____ Col William J. O'Brien __ Consolidated _____ 13/02/45 ___ 50-73. Str73
AK-247 _____ Pvt John F. Thorson ____ Southeastern _____ 26/02/45 ___ 50-54. BU60
AK-248 _____ Sgt George Peterson ___ LD Smith _____ 13/05/45 ___ 50-59. BU72
AK-249 _____ Short Splice _____ Consolidated _____ 03/03/45 ___ 50-73. BU73
AK-250 _____ Pvt Frank J. Petrarca ___ Consolidated _____ 07/06/45 ___ 50-59, 60-73. Str73

**Notes:** *Faribault, Fentress, Hennepin* and *Herkimer*
re-acquired 1947-51. AK-245-250 acquired 1950.

---

**Details:** 6,700 tons, 12,450f/l; 436 (wl), 455'3
(oa)×62×28'6; one shaft, steam turbines,
SHP 8,500=17kt

AK-237 _____ Greenville Victory _____ Calship _____ 24/05/44 ___ 50-81. Str81
AK-238 _____ Haiti Victory _____ Permanente _____ 20/07/44 ___ 50-70. *Longview* (AGM-3) (60), Str74
AK-239 _____ Kingsport Victory _____ Calship _____ 29/05/44 ___ 50-64. *Kingsport* (AG-164) (61)
AK-240 _____ Pvt John R. Towle _____ Oregon _____ 19/01/45 ___ 50-80. Str
AK-241 _____ Pvt Francis X. McGraw __ Calship _____ 09/06/45 ___ 50-73. Str74
AK-242 _____ Sgt Andrew Miller _____ Permanente _____ 04/04/45 ___ 50-81. Str81

AK-243 ——— *Sgt Archer T. Gammon* — Permanente ——— 31/01/45 —— 50-73. BU73

AK-244 ——— *Sgt Morris E. Crain* —— Permanente ——— 28/03/45 —— 50-74. BU75

AK-251 ——— *Lt George W. G. Boyce* — Fairfield ————— 19/09/45 —— 50-73. Str73

AK-252 ——— *Lt Robert Craig* ———— Calship ———— 28/08/45 —— 50-73. Str73

AK-253 ——— *Pvt Joe E. Mann* ——— Permanente ——— 21/07/45 —— 50-68. *Richfield* (AGM-4) (60). Str70

AK-254 ——— *Sgt Truman Kimbro* —— Permanente ——— 30/11/44 —— 50-81. Str81

AK-256 ——— *Dalton Victory* ———— Calship ———— 06/06/44 —— 50-  . *Sunnyvale* (AGM-5) (60). Str74

AKV-3 ——— *Lt James E. Robinson* — Oregon ————— 20/01/44 —— 50-81. AK-274 (59), AG-170 (62), AK-274 (64). Str81

AKV-4 ——— *Pvt Joseph F. Merrell* — Calship ———— 17/07/44 —— 50-73. AK-275 (59), lost 29/12/73

AKV-5 ——— *Sgt Jack J. Pendleton* — Oregon ————— 26/05/44 —— 50-73. AK-276 (59), lost 25/09/73

**Notes:** Acquired 1950. AK-238, 239, 253 and 256 converted and commissioned.

**Details:** As above

AK-257 ——— *Altair* ————————— Oregon ————— 30/05/44 —— 52-69. AKS-32 (52) Str73
                  ex-*Aberdeen Victory*

AK-258 ——— *Antares* ——————— Oregon ————— 19/05/44 —— 52-65. AKS-33 (59). Str65
                  ex-*Nampa Victory*

AK-259 ——— *Alcor* ————————— Oregon ————— 29/04/44 —— 52-68. BU70
                  ex-*Rockland Victory*

AK-260 ——— *Betelgeuse* ————— Calship ———— 10/04/44 —— 52-71. BU76
                  ex-*Colombia Victory*

AK-279 ——— *Norwalk* ——————— Oregon ————— 10/07/45 —— 63-79. Str79
                  ex-*Norwalk Victory*

AK-280 ——— *Furman* ———————— Oregon ————— 06/03/45 —— 64-
                  ex-*Furman Victory*

AK-281 ——— *Victoria* ————————— Permanente ——— 20/04/44 —— 65-83
                  ex-*Ethiopia Victory*

AK-282 ——— *Marshfield* ————— Oregon ————— 15/05/44 —— 70-
                  ex-*Marshfield Victory*

**Notes:** AK-279-282 are ballistic missile submarine supply ships.

**Details:** 11,400 tons, 22,000f/l; 552'10 (oa)×71'8×30; one shaft, steam turbines, SHP 9,000=17kt

AK-255 ——— *Pvt Leonard F. Brostrom* Sun ————— 10/05/43 —— 50-79. Str

AK-267 ——— *Marine Fiddler* ———— Sun ————— 15/05/45 —— 52-73

**Notes:** Acquired 1950 and 1952. Heavy-lift ships with 150-ton cranes.

**Notes:** AK-261-266 acquired for loan to Korea, 1951-60.

**Details:** 7,605 tons, 18,150f/l; 447'9 (wl), 499 (oa)×78×28'9; two shafts, steam turbines, SHP 13,200=18kt; 73 crew

AK-269 ——— *Comet* ———————— Sun ————— 31/07/57 —— 58-85. LSV-7 (63), AKR-7 (69)

**Notes:** Roll-on, roll-off ship.

*Above:*
**Mizar (T-AGOR-11). This oceanographic research ship, seen in 1965, was formerly a cargo ship for polar navigation.** *Official US Navy*

**Details:** 1,850 tons, 3,800f/l; 247'9 (wl) 266 (oa)×51'6×19; two shafts, diesel-electric, SHP 2,700=13kt

| | | | | |
|---|---|---|---|---|
| AK-270 | Eltanin | Avondale | 16/01/57 | 57 72. AGOR-8 (62), Argentine *Islas Orcadas* (74-79) |
| AK-271 | Miɪɪak | Avondale | 05/08/57 | 57-79 |
| AK-272 | Mizar | Avondale | 07/10/57 | 58- . AGOR-11 (64) |

**Notes:** Ice-strengthened hulls for Arctic supply. *Eltanin* and *Mizar* converted to oceanographic research ships

**Details:** 6,000 tons; 454 (wl), 457'9 (oa)×72'2×18; two shafts, steam turbines, SHP 3,450=15.4kt; 70 crew

| | | | | |
|---|---|---|---|---|
| AK-273 | Taurus<br>ex-*TMT Carib Queen* | Gulf | 08/46 | 59-68. LSV-8 (63), AKR-8 (68), merchant *Douglas Carver* (72) |

**Notes:** Originally laid down as *Fort Snelling* (LSD-23) and completed as merchant vessel, acquired 1959.

**Details:** 5,394 tons, 15,910f/l; 450'10 (wl), 478'2 (oa)×70×26; one shaft, steam turbines, SHP 13,750=18.5kt

| | | | | |
|---|---|---|---|---|
| AK-277 | Schuyler Otis Bland | Ingalls | 30/01/51 | 61-79. Str79 |

**Notes:** Acquired 1961.

**Details:** 16,940 tons, 21,700f/l; 499'6 (wl), 540 (oa)×83×29; two shafts, steam turbines, SHP 19,400=20kt; 47 crew

| | | | | |
|---|---|---|---|---|
| AK-278 | Sea Lift | PS Bridge | 18/04/65 | 67-85. LSV-9 (63), AKR-9 (68), *Meteor* (75) |

**Notes:** Modified *Comet* with stern and side ramps for vehicles.

*Above:*
**Schuyler Otis Bland (T-AK-277), a cargo ship.**

*Below:*
**The *Northern Light* (T-AK-284) was acquired in 1980 as a pre-positioning ship for service in the Indian Ocean.** *Martin E. Holbrook*

**Details:** 16,400 tons f/l; 483'4 (oa)×68×31; one shaft, steam turbine, SHP 12,100=18kt; 67 crew

| | | | | |
|---|---|---|---|---|
| AK-284 | *Northern Light* | Sun | 29/06/61 | 80-84 |
| | ex-*Cove*, | | | |
| | ex-*Mormacove* | | | |
| AK-285 | *Southern Cross* | Sun | 23/01/62 | 80-84, 85- |
| | ex-*Trade*, | | | |
| | ex-*Mormactrade* | | | |
| AK-286 | *Vega* | Sun | 12/05/60 | 83- |
| | ex-*Bay*, | | | |
| | ex-*Mormacbay* | | | |

**Notes:** Acquired 1980-81 as prepositioning ships in the Indian Ocean. *Northern Light* has modified bow. *Vega* is FBM supply ship, to replace *Victoria*.

---

**Details:** 41,127 gross tons, 51,815f/l; 946'3 (oa)×106×34'9; two shafts, steam turbines, SHP 120,000=33kt; 42 crew

| | | | | |
|---|---|---|---|---|
| AKR-287 | *Algol* | Rotterdam | 22/09/72 | 84- |
| | ex-*Sea-Land Exchange* | | | |
| AKR-288 | *Bellatrix* | Rheinstahl | 30/09/72 | 84- |
| | ex-*Sea-Land Trade* | | | |

*Above:*
**The cargo ship *Algol* (T-AKR-287) was acquired for rapid response to critical situations abroad. Its conversion was completed in 1984.**
*Martin E. Holbrook*

| | | | | | |
|---|---|---|---|---|---|
| AKR-289 | *Denebola* | Rotterdam | 10/05/73 | 85- |
| | ex-*Sea-Land Resource* | | | |
| AKR-290 | *Pollux* | Weser | 18/05/75 | 85- |
| | ex-*Sea-Land Market* | | | |
| AKR-291 | *Altair* | Rheinstahl | 28/04/73 | 85- |
| | ex-*Sea-Land Finance* | | | |
| AKR-292 | *Regulus* | Weser | 18/12/72 | 85- |
| | ex-*Sea-Land Commerce* | | | |
| AKR-293 | *Capella* | Rotterdam | 09/09/71 | 84- |
| | ex-*Sea-Land McLean* | | | |
| AKR-294 | *Antares* | Weser | 13/05/72 | 84- |
| | ex-*Sea-Land Galloway* | | | |

**Notes:** Acquired 1981-82. Helicopter deck and hangar aft added during conversion 1982-86. Extensive roll-on/roll-off capacity. Rapid response ships, ready for rapid loading of military equipment and sailing to crisis area.

---

**Reclassified vessel:**

AK-283 _____ *Wyandot* _____ see AKA-92

# VEHICLE CARGO SHIPS

AKR-7-9, see AK-269, 273 and 278

---

**Details:** 13,156 gross tons; 685 (oa)×102×52; one shaft, steam turbines, SHP 37,000=23kt; 42 crew

| | | | | | |
|---|---|---|---|---|---|
| AKR-10 | *Mercury* | Bath | 21/12/76 | 80- |
| | ex-*Illinois* | | | |
| AKR-11 | *Jupiter* | Bath | 01/11/75 | 80- |
| | ex-*Lipscomb Lykes* | | | |

**Notes:** Acquired 1980. Designed to carry vehicles.

# MARITIME PREPOSITIONING SHIPS

*(1st Group)*
**Details:** 40,850 tons f/l; 654'6 (oa)×105'6×29'6; one
shaft, diesel, 18kt; 38 crew

| | | |
|---|---|---|
| *2nd Lt John P. Bobo* | Quincy | 13/10/84 |
| *PFC Dewayne T. Williams* | Quincy | 16/02/85 |
| *1st Lt Baldomero Lopez* | Quincy | 29/06/85 |
| *1st Lt Jack Lummus* | Quincy | 23/11/85 |
| *Sgt William R. Button* | Quincy | na |

*(2nd Group)*
**Details:** 46,552 tons f/l; 755'6 (oa)×90×32'11; one
shaft, diesel, 17.5kt; 50 crew

| | | |
|---|---|---|
| *Cpl Louis J. Hague Jr* <br> ex-*Estelle Maersk* | Odense | 03/08/79 |
| *PFC William B. Baugh Jr* <br> ex-*Eleo Maersk* | Odense | 10/12/78 |
| *PFC James Anderson Jr* <br> ex-*Emma Maersk* | Odense | /03/79 |
| *1st Lt Alexander Bonnyman Jr* <br> ex-*Emilie Maersk* | Odense | 03/08/79 |
| *Pvt Harry Fisher* <br> ex-*Evelyn Maersk* | Odense | 12/10/79 |

*(3rd Group)*
**Details:** 48,754 tons f/l; 821 (oa)×105'6×32'3; one
shaft, steam turbine, 20kt; 37 crew

| | | |
|---|---|---|
| *Sgt Matej Kocak* <br> ex-*John B. Waterman* | Sun | 14/03/81 |
| *PFC Eugene A. Obregon* <br> ex-*Thomas Heyward* | Penn | 15/05/82 |
| *Maj Stephen W. Pless* <br> ex-*Charles Carroll* | Quincy | 24/10/82 |

**Notes:** These ships are under charter and are not
assigned hull numbers. Civilian manned. In service
1984-86. First group built for the Navy; others acquired
in 1984.

Second and 3rd groups converted by adding 157'6
and 126' mid-sections respectively.
These ships are capable of carrying military supplies
for 46,000 troops (three Marine Brigades) for 30 days.

# LIGHT CARGO SHIPS

**Details:** 465 tons, 935f/l; 165 (wl), 177 (oa)×32'9×14'3;
two shafts, diesel, SHP 1,000=12kt; 27 crew

| | | ex-FS | |
|---|---|---|---|
| AKL-1 | Camano | 256 | 47-51. Dept of Interior (52) |
| AKL-2 | Deal | 263 | 47-55. Merchant *Don Carlos* (62) |
| AKL-3 | Elba | 267 | 47-52. Dept of Interior (52) |
| AKL-4 | Errol | 274 | 47-51. Dept of Interior (52) |
| AKL-5 | Estero | 275 | 47-60. Merchant *Pres. Quirino* (62) |
| AKL-6 | Jekyl | 282 | 47-50. Merchant *Betty K. IV* (60) |

| | | | | |
|---|---|---|---|---|
| AKL-7 | Metomkin | 316 | 47-51. Dept of Interior (51) |
| AKL-8 | Roque | 347 | 47-51. Dept of Interior (51) |
| AKL-9 | Ryer | 361 | 47-55. Merchant *Ahti* (62) |
| AKL-10 | Sharps | 385 | 47-56. Korean *Kun San* (56) |
| AKL-11 | Torry | 394 | 47-51. Dept of Interior (52) |
| AKL-12 | Mark | 214 | 47-71. Taiwan *Yung Kang* (71) |
| AKL-13 | Tingles | 266 | 47-49. Merchant *Ran-Annim* (59) |
| AKL-14 | Hewell | 391 | 48-55. Merchant *Betty K* (60) |
| AKL-15 | na | 230 | 50-54. Merchant *Mereghan II* (59) |
| AKL-16 | na | 233 | 50-54. Merchant *Martha Anne* (59). Sold 59 |
| AKL-17 | New Bedford | 289 | 50- . IX 308 (69) |
| AKL-18 | na | 174 | 50-54. Merchant *Aries* (60) |
| AKL-19 | na | 175 | 50-59. Merchant *Pres. Laurel* (60) |
| AKL-20 | na | 193 | 50-54. Merchant *Star 50* (62) |
| AKL-21 | na | 259 | 50-54. Merchant *Kirk Star* (60) |
| AKL-22 | na | 276 | 50-54. Merchant (62) |
| AKL-23 | na | 288 | 50-54. Merchant (60) |
| AKL-24 | na | 309 | 50-59. Merchant *Pres. Osmena* (60) |
| AKL-25 | Banner | 345 | 50-69. AGER-1 (67). Str69 |
| AKL-26 | na | 368 | 50-54. Merchant *New Providence* (61) |
| AKL-27 | na | 369 | 50-54. Str66 |
| AKL-28 | Brule | 370 | 50-71. Korean *Ul San* (71) |
| AKL-29 | na | 371 | 50-59. Merchant *Menara Mas* (61) |
| AKL-30 | na | 400 | 50-54. US F&WS *George B. Kelez* (61) |
| AKL-31 | na | 407 | 50-70. Dept of Interior (70) |
| AKL-32 | na | 548 | 50-54. Merchant *Carlos Miguel* (62) |
| AKL-33 | na | 238 | 50-54. Merchant *Jamene* (59) |
| AKL-34 | na | 343 | 50-54. Merchant (59) |
| AKL-35 | na | 383 | 50-54. Korean *Masan* (56) |
| AKL-36 | na | 398 | 50-54. Merchant *Bertha Ann* (60) |
| AKL-37 | Alcyone | 195 | Korea (60) |
| AKL-38 | Alhena | 257 | Korea (60) |
| AKL-39 | Almaack | 283 | Korea (60) |
| AKL-40 | Deimos | 390 | Korea (60) |
| AKL-41 | Pamina | 528 | Korea (60) |
| AKL-42 | Renate | 547 | Korea (60) |
| AKL-43 | na | 219 | 62-63. Merchant *Santa Maria* (64) |
| AKL-44 | Pueblo | 344 | 67-68. AGER-2 (67), lost 23/01/68 |
| AKL-45 | Palm Beach | 217 | 67-69. AGER-3 (67). Str69 |

**Notes:** AKL-1-14 acquired from the Army as AG-130-145, 1947. AKL-33 was a smaller vessel. *Banner*, *Pueblo* and *Palm Beach* converted to ELINT vessels 1967.

*Trillium* and *Redbud* AKL-398 were loaned from Coast Guard (qv)

# DOCK CARGO SHIP

**Details:** 5,562 tons, 14,000f/l; 475 (wl), 492 (oa)×78×28; two shafts, steam turbines, SHP 12,000=18kt; 66 crew

| | | | | |
|---|---|---|---|---|
| AKD-1 | Point Barrow | Maryland | 25/05/57 | 58- . *Point Loma* (AGDS-2) (74) |

**Notes:** Built to carry supplies and vehicles to Arctic radar warning installations. Used to carry Saturn rockets from California to Cape Canaveral, 1965-70. Converted to Deep Submergence Vehicle Support Ship 1974-76.

*Above:*
**Point Barrow (T-AKD-1), a dock cargo ship converted to carry Saturn rockets, seen in 1965.**
*Martin E. Holbrook*

# GENERAL STORES ISSUE SHIPS

**Details:** 6,365 tons, 13,500f/l; 435 (wl), 459'3
(oa)×63×25'10; one shaft, steam turbines,
SHP 6,000=16.4kt; 1×5in/38, 4×3in/50 guns

| | | | | |
|---|---|---|---|---|
| AKS-1 | Castor | Federal | 20/05/39 | 50-68. BU69 |
| AKS-4 | Pollux | Federal | 23/03/42 | 50-68. BU69 |
| AKS-20 | Mercury | Federal | 15/07/39 | 42-59. BU75 |
| AKS-8 | Jupiter | Federal | 30/09/39 | 50-65. BU71 |

**Notes:** Acquired 1940, 1942 and 1939 (last two).
*Jupiter* was Aviation Supply Ship.

**Reclassified vessels:**

AKS-21 to AKS-31, see AG-73-78, 146-150
AKS-32 *Altair*, see AK-257
AVS-33 *Antares*, see AK-258

*Below:*
**The general stores issue ship *Pollux* (AKS-4) in 1959.** *Official US Navy*

# CARGO SHIPS & AIRCRAFT FERRIES

**Details:** 5,700 tons; 422 (wl), 441'6 (oa)×56'11×23; one
shaft, VTE, SHP 2,500=11kt

AKV-6 _____ *Albert M. Boe* _____ New England _____ 26/09/45 ___ 50-53. Sold 64
AKV-7 _____ *Cardinal O'Connell* _____ New England _____ 31/08/45 ___ 50-54. Str54

**Notes:** Acquired 1950. AKV-3-5 see AK-274-276.

AKV-8-43, see Escort Carriers.

# OILERS

**Details:** 7,256 tons, 25,425f/l; 525 (wl)
553 (oa)×75×31'7 (1966: 51, 98, 99: 644 oa); two
shafts, steam turbines, SHP 13,500=18.3kt; 4×5in/38
guns

AO-22 _____ *Cimarron* _____ Sun _____ 07/01/39 ___ 39-68. BU69
AO-24 _____ *Platte* _____ Sparrows Pt _____ 08/07/39 ___ 39-70. BU71
AO-25 _____ *Sabine* _____ Sparrows Pt _____ 27/04/40 ___ 40-55, 56-57, 61-69. Str69
AO-26 _____ *Salamonie* _____ Newport News _____ 18/09/40 ___ 41-68. BU71
AO-27 _____ *Kaskaskia* _____ Newport News _____ 29/09/39 ___ 41-55, 57-57, 61-69. BU70
AO-30 _____ *Chemung* _____ Sparrows Pt _____ 09/09/39 ___ 41-70. BU71
AO-32 _____ *Guadalupe* _____ Newport News _____ 26/01/40 ___ 41-74. BU75
AO-51 _____ *Ashtabula* _____ Sparrows Pt _____ 22/05/43 ___ 43-82
AO-52 _____ *Cacapon* _____ Sparrows Pt _____ 12/06/43 ___ 43-73. Str73
AO-53 _____ *Caliente* _____ Sparrows Pt _____ 25/08/43 ___ 43-73. Str73
AO-54 _____ *Chikaskia* _____ Sparrows Pt _____ 02/10/43 ___ 43-55, 56-58, 61-69. Str77
AO-55 _____ *Elokomin* _____ Sparrows Pt _____ 19/10/43 ___ 43-70. Str70
AO-56 _____ *Aucilla* _____ Sparrows Pt _____ 20/11/43 ___ 43-70. Str76
AO-57 _____ *Marias* _____ Sparrows Pt _____ 12/12/43 ___ 44-82
AO-58 _____ *Manatee* _____ Sparrows Pt _____ 18/02/44 ___ 44-73. Str73
AO-60 _____ *Nantahala* _____ Sparrows Pt _____ 29/04/44 ___ 44-50, 50-73. BU75
AO-61 _____ *Severn* _____ Sparrows Pt _____ 31/05/44 ___ 44-74. BU75
AO-62 _____ *Taluga* _____ Sparrows Pt _____ 10/07/44 ___ 44-83
AO-63 _____ *Chipola* _____ Sparrows Pt _____ 21/10/44 ___ 44-55, 56-57, 60-73. Str73
AO-64 _____ *Tolovana* _____ Sparrows Pt _____ 06/01/45 ___ 45-75. BU75
AO-97 _____ *Allagash* _____ Sparrows Pt _____ 14/04/45 ___ 45-70. Str73
AO-98 _____ *Caloosahatchee* _____ Sparrows Pt _____ 02/06/45 ___ 45-
AO-99 _____ *Canisteo* _____ Sparrows Pt _____ 06/07/45 ___ 45-
AO-100 _____ *Chukawan* _____ Sparrows Pt _____ 28/08/45 ___ 46-72. BU73

**Notes:** *Ashtabula, Caloosahatchee* and *Canisteo*
lengthened in 1960s, 34,750 tons f/l, 2×5in guns
removed.

**Details:** 5,958 tons, 21,580f/l; 488'5 (wl)
501'5 (oa)×68×30'2; one shaft, steam turbines,
SHP 12,000=16.7kt; 1×4in/50, 2×3in/50 guns; 214
crew

AO-36 _____ *Kennebec* _____ Sparrows Pt _____ 19/04/41 ___ 42-50, 51-57, 61-70. Str73
AO-37 _____ *Merrimack* _____ Sparrows Pt _____ 01/07/41 ___ 42-50, 50-54. Str59
AO-39 _____ *Kankakee* _____ Sparrows Pt _____ 24/01/42 ___ 42-55, 56-57, 61-69. BU77

Above:
**The fleet oiler *Caloosahatchie* (AO-98) after lengthening.**

**Details:** 5,882 tons; 500 (wl) 526 (oa)×68×30'10; one shaft, steam turbines, SHP 12,000=17.5kt

| AO-41 | Mattaponi | Sun | 17/01/42 | 42-49, 50-54, 56-57, 62-70. BU72 |
|---|---|---|---|---|
| AO-42 | Monongahela | Sun | 30/05/42 | 42-50, 51-55, 56-57. Str59 |
| AO-43 | Tappahannock | Sun | 18/04/42 | 42-50, 51-55, 56-57, 66-70. Taiwan (78) |
| AO-47 | Neches | Sun | 11/10/41 | 42-50, 51-55, 61-70. BU72 |

**Details:** 5,370 tons, 22,380f/l; 503 (wl) 523'6 (oa)×68×29'11; one shaft, turbo-electric, SHP 7,240=14.5kt

| AO-49 | Suamico | Sun | 30/05/42 | 48-74. BU75 |
|---|---|---|---|---|
| AO-50 | Tallulah | Sun | 25/06/42 | 48-75. AOT |
| AO-65 | Pecos | Sun | 17/08/42 | 50-74. BU75 |
| AO-67 | Cache | Sun | 07/09/42 | 48-72. AOT, Str72 |
| AO-73 | Millicoma | Sun | 21/01/43 | 48-75. AOT |
| AO-75 | Saugatuck | Sun | 07/12/42 | 48-74. AOT |
| AO-76 | Schuylkill | Sun | 16/02/43 | 48-75. AOT |
| AO-77 | Cossatot | Sun | 28/02/43 | 48-74. BU75 |
| AO-78 | Chepachet | Sun | 10/03/43 | 50-72. AOT, Str72 |
| AO-79 | Cowanesque | Sun | 11/03/43 | 48-72. Lost 23/04/72 |
| AO-138 | Cedar Creek | Sun | 15/12/43 | 48-54, 56-57. Str57 |
| AO-139 | Muir Woods | Swan Island | 09/03/45 | 48-59. BU76 |
| AO-140 | Pioneer Valley | Swan Island | 06/09/44 | 48-60, 61-72. BU73 |
| AO-141 | Sappa Creek | Alabama | 15/09/43 | 48-59. BU75 |
| AO-142 | Shawnee Trail | Swan Island | 31/05/44 | 48-57, 65-72. BU73 |
| AO-153 | Cumberland | Sun | 09/05/44 | 56-57. BU72 |
| AO-154 | Lynchburg | Swan Island | 20/05/44 | 56-57. Merchant *Marine Duval* (69) |
| AO-155 | Roanoke | Sun | 30/06/44 | 56-57. Str57 |
| AO-156 | Bull Run | Sun | 29/06/43 | 56-57. Str57 |
| AO-157 | Paoli | Sun | 31/10/44 | 56-57. Merchant *Marine Floridian* (66) |
| AO-158 | Abiqua | Alabama | 22/09/43 | 56-57. Merchant (68) |
| AO-159 | French Creek | Sun | 08/12/44 | 56-57. BU71 |
| AO-160 | Logan's Port | Sun | 30/03/45 | 56-57. BU72 |
| AO-161 | Lone Jack | Sun | 21/10/44 | 56-57. BU71 |
| AO-162 | Memphis | Sun | 17/06/44 | 56-57. BU71 |
| AO-163 | Parkersburg | Sun | 12/04/44 | 56-57. Merchant *Marine Eagle* (68) |
| AO-164 | Petrolite | Sun | 13/01/44 | 56-57. Str57 |

**Notes:** AO-49-79 str46, re-acquired 1948. *Saranac* (AO-74) was converted to a floating powerplant (YFP-9), sold 1957.

**Details:** 5,708 tons, 22,030f/l; 487'6 (wl)
501'8 (oa)×68×30'8; one shaft, steam turbines,
SHP 7,700=15.3kt

AO-69 ———— *Enoree* ———————— Sparrows Pt ———— 29/08/42 —— 50-54, 56-57. Str59
AO-72 ———— *Niobrara* ——————— Sparrows Pt ———— 28/11/42 —— 51-54, 56-57. Str

---

**Details:** 5,730 tons; 503 (wl) 523'6 (oa)×68×30'10; one
shaft, turbine electric, SHP 10,000=16.2kt

AO-80 ———— *Escambia* —————— Marinship ———— 25/04/43 —— 48-57. BU74
AO-81 ———— *Kennebago* ————— Marinship ———— 09/05/43 —— 49-57, 58-59. Str59
AO-82 ———— *Cahaba* ————————— Marinship ———— 19/05/43 —— 48-58. Str58
AO-83 ———— *Mascoma* ————————— Marinship ———— 31/05/43 —— 48-59. Merchant *Seatrain Oregon* (66)
AO-84 ———— *Ocklawaha* ———————— Marinship ———— 09/06/43 —— 48-59. BU75
AO-85 ———— *Pamanset* ———————— Marinship ———— 25/06/43 —— 48-57. Merchant *Seatrain Florida* (66)
AO-87 ———— *Sebec* ———————————— Marinship ———— 29/07/43 —— 50-55, 56-57. BU74
AO-88 ———— *Tomahawk* ———————— Marinship ———— 10/08/43 —— 48-61. Merchant *Maine* (66)
AO-93 ———— *Soubarissen* ————— Marinship ———— 12/08/44 —— 48-55, 56-58. Str61
AO-94 ———— *Anacostia* ————————— Marinship ———— 24/09/44 —— 48-57. Merchant (67)
AO-95 ———— *Caney* ———————————— Marinship ———— 08/10/44 —— 48-59. BU74
AO-96 ———— *Tamalpais* ————————— Marinship ———— 29/10/44 —— 48-57. BU74
AO-101 ——— *Cohocton* ————————— Marinship ———— 28/06/45 —— 48-58. Merchant *Transoneida* (67)

(M.=*Mission*)

AO-111 ———— *M. Buenaventura* ———— Marinship ———— 28/05/44 —— 47-60, 61-72. Str73
AO-112 ———— *M. Capistrano* ————— Marinship ———— 07/05/44 —— 47-55, 56-70. AG-162 (61), Str71
AO-113 ———— *M. Carmel* —————————— Marinship ———— 28/03/44 —— 47-57. Merchant *Houston* (67)
AO-114 ———— *M. De Pala* ————————— Marinship ———— 28/02/44 —— 47-54, 56-58. Str58, *Redstone* (AGM-20) (65)
AO-115 ———— *M. Dolores* ————————— Marinship ———— 26/04/44 —— 47-55, 56-57. Merchant *Enrico Isom* (59)
AO-116 ———— *M. Loreto* —————————— Marinship ———— 28/06/44 —— 47-55, 56-59. BU75
AO-117 ———— *M. Los Angeles* ———— Marinship ———— 10/08/45 —— 47-57. BU76
AO-118 ———— *M. Purisima* ————————— Marinship ———— 25/08/43 —— 47-55, 56-57. Str57
AO-119 ———— *M. San Antonio* ———— Marinship ———— 08/04/44 —— 47-54, 56-59, 60-65. Merchant
*Transarctic* (65)

*Below:*
**The tanker *Mission Buenaventura* (T-AO-11), seen
empty and riding high in the water.**

| | | | | |
|---|---|---|---|---|
| AO-120 | *M. San Carlos* | Marinship | 12/02/44 | 47-57. Merchant *Seatrain Maryland* (66) |
| AO-121 | *M. San Diego* | Marinship | 14/03/44 | 47-55, 56-57. Merchant *Seatrain Washington* (66) |
| AO-122 | *M. San Fernando* | Marinship | 25/11/43 | 47-55, 56-57. Str57, *Vanguard* (AGM-19) (65) |
| AO-123 | *M. San Francisco* | Marinship | 18/09/45 | 47-54, 56-57. Lost 07/03/57 |
| AO-124 | *M. San Gabriel* | Marinship | 17/04/44 | 47-49, 50-54, 56-57. Merchant *Delaware* (66) |
| AO-125 | *M. San Jose* | Marinship | 07/10/43 | 47-57. Merchant *Ohio* (66) |
| AO-126 | *M. San Juan* | Marinship | 14/10/43 | 47-58. Str58, *Mercury* (AGM-21) (65) |
| AO-127 | *M. San Luis Obispo* | Marinship | 18/06/44 | 47-55, 56-57. Merchant *Seatrain Puerto Rico* (66) |
| AO-128 | *M. San Luis Rey* | Marinship | 29/01/44 | 47-55, 56-57. BU73 |
| AO-129 | *M. San Miguel* | Marinship | 31/10/43 | 47-54, 56-57. Lost 08/10/57 |
| AO-130 | *M. San Rafael* | Marinship | 31/12/43 | 47-55, 56-59. BU71 |
| AO-131 | *M. Santa Barbara* | Marinship | 08/06/44 | 47-54, 56-57. Merchant *Seatrain Carolina* (66) |
| AO-132 | *M. Santa Clara* | Marinship | 18/05/44 | 47-59. Pakistani *Dacca* (63) |
| AO 133 | *M. Santa Cruz* | Marinship | 08/09/43 | 47-54, 56-59, 60-70. BU71 |
| AO-134 | *M. Santa Ynez* | Marinship | 19/12/43 | 47-83. AOT |
| AO-135 | *M. Solano* | Marinship | 14/01/44 | 47-57. Merchant *Jacksonville* (67) |
| AO-136 | *M. Soledad* | Marinship | 24/09/43 | 47-57. Merchant *Seatrain California* (66) |
| AO-137 | *M. Santa Ana* | Marinship | 25/07/45 | 48-50, 56-58. BU76 |
| AW-3 | *Pasig* | Marinship | 15/07/44 | 51-55. BU76 |
| AW-4 | *Abatan* | Marinship | 06/08/44 | Str70 |

**Notes:** 'Mission' class acquired 1947. AO-114, 122 and 126 converted to missile range instrumentation ships 1965. AO-112 used for acoustic tests.

**Details:** 7,423 tons, 25,440f/l (*1966*: 11,000 tons, 34,750f/l); 525 (wl) 553 (oa)×75×32'4 (*1966*: 646 oa); two shafts, steam turbines, SHP 13,500=18.3kt; 1×5in/38, 4×3in/50, 12×40mm guns; crew 110

| | | | | |
|---|---|---|---|---|
| AO-105 | *Mispillion* | Sun | 10/08/45 | 45- |
| AO-106 | *Navasota* | Sun | 30/08/45 | 46- |
| AO-107 | *Passumpsic* | Sun | 31/10/45 | 46- |
| AO-108 | *Pawcatuck* | Sun | 19/02/46 | 46- |
| AO-109 | *Waccamaw* | Sun | 30/03/46 | 46- |

**Notes:** Lengthened in 1963-64. Transferred to MTC 1974-75, guns removed.

**Details:** 5,730 tons; 584 (oa ×72×30'6; two shafts, steam turbines, SHP 22,000=20kt; 4×40mm guns

| | | | | |
|---|---|---|---|---|
| AO-110 | *Conecuh* ex-*Dithmarschen* | Schichau | 12/06/37 | 53-56. AOR-110 (52), BU60 |

**Notes:** Former German replenishment tanker acquired 1946.

**Details:** 11,600 tons, 38,000f/l; 640 (wl) 655 (oa)×86×35; two shafts, steam turbines, SHP 28,000=20kt; 2×5in/38, 12×3in/50, 6×20mm guns; 324 crew

*Above:*
**The fleet replenishment tanker *Conecuh*
(AOR-110), photographed in 1954, was acquired as
a war prize in 1946.** *Marius Bar*

*Below:*
**Hassayampa (AO-145), a fleet oiler.**
*Official US Navy*

| | | | | |
|---|---|---|---|---|
| AO-143 | *Neosho* | Quincy | 10/11/53 | 54- |
| AO-144 | *Mississinewa* | NY Sbdg | 12/06/54 | 55- |
| AO-145 | *Hassayampa* | NY Sbdg | 12/09/54 | 55- |
| AO-146 | *Kawishiwi* | NY Sbdg | 11/12/54 | 55- |
| AO-147 | *Truckee* | NY Sbdg | 10/03/55 | 55- |
| AO-148 | *Ponchatoula* | NY Sbdg | 09/07/55 | 55- |

**Notes:** Transferred to MSC 1976-80. Armament first
reduced and eventually removed. Helicopter platform
added to AO-143, 144 and 147.

**Details:** 7,950 tons, 32,950f/l; 591 (wl)
620 (oa)×83'6×32; one shaft, steam turbines,
SHP 20,400=18kt

| | | | | |
|---|---|---|---|---|
| AO-149 | *Maumee* | Ingalls | 16/02/56 | 56-85. AOT |
| AO-150 | *Potomac* | Sun | 08/10/56 | 57-61. Lost 26/09/61 |
| AO-151 | *Shoshone* | Sun | 17/01/57 | 57-84. AOT |
| AO-152 | *Yukon* | Ingalls | 16/03/56 | 57-85. AOT |

**Notes:** *Potomac*, a constructive total loss with stern
and machinery intact, was rebuilt as a merchant
vessel, later re-acquired as AO 181.

*Above:*
**The transport oiler *Yukon* (T-AO-152).**

*Below:*
**The fleet oiler *Platte* (AO-186) on trials in 1982.**
*Official US Navy*

**Details:** 8,400 tons, 31,300f/l; 615 (oa)×80×32; one
shaft, steam turbines, SHP 22,000=20kt; 57 crew

AO-165 _____ *American Explorer* _____ Ingalls _____ 11/04/58 ___ 59-84. AOT

**Notes:** AO-166-167 were to be 'jumbo-ised' 'Mission'
class tankers, cancelled 1965.

**Details:** 32,000 tons f/l; 587 (oa)×84×34'4; one shaft,
turbo-diesel, SHP 14,000=16kt; complement 30

AO-168 _____ *Sealift Pacific* _____ Todd; S Pedro _____ 13/10/73 ___ 74-
AO-169 _____ *Sealift Arabian Sea* _____ Todd; S Pedro _____ 26/01/74 ___ 75-
AO-170 _____ *Sealift China Sea* _____ Todd; S Pedro _____ 20/04/74 ___ 75-
AO-171 _____ *Sealift Indian Ocean* _____ Todd; S Pedro _____ 27/07/74 ___ 75-
AO-172 _____ *Sealift Atlantic* _____ Bath _____ 26/01/74 ___ 74
AO-173 _____ *Sealift Mediterranean* __ Bath _____ 09/03/74 ___ 74

| | | | | |
|---|---|---|---|---|
| AO-174 | *Sealift Caribbean* | Bath | 08/06/74 | 75- |
| AO-175 | *Sealift Arctic* | Bath | 31/08/74 | 75- |
| AO-176 | *Sealift Antarctic* | Bath | 26/10/74 | 75- |

**Notes:** Reclassified AOT 1978.

---

**Details:** 8,210 tons, 27,500f/l; 591 (oa)×88×35; one shaft, steam turbines, SHP 24,000=20kt; 2×20mm Phalanx CIWS; 198 crew

| | | | | |
|---|---|---|---|---|
| AO-177 | *Cimarron* | Avondale | 28/04/79 | 81- |
| AO-178 | *Monongahela* | Avondale | 04/08/79 | 81- |
| AO-179 | *Merrimack* | Avondale | 17/05/80 | 81- |
| AO-180 | *Willamette* | Avondale | 18/07/81 | 82- |
| AO-186 | *Platte* | Avondale | 30/01/82 | 83- |

**Notes:** Will be lengthened 1987-90.

---

**Details:** 7,333 tons, 34,800f/l; 620 (oa)×83'6×34; one shaft, steam turbines, SHP 20,460=18kt

| | | | | |
|---|---|---|---|---|
| AO-181 | *Potomac* | Sun | 08/10/56 | 76 83 |
| | ex-*Shenandoah* | | | |

**Notes:** Acquired 1976, reclassified AOT, 1978. Originally built as *Potomac* of 'Maumee' class; stern joined to new bow and midship sections.

---

**Details:** 8,730 tons, 45,877f/l; 672 (oa)×89×36; one shaft, diesels, SHP 15,000=16.5kt; 23 crew

| | | | | |
|---|---|---|---|---|
| AO-182 | *Columbia* | Ingalls | 12/09/70 | 76- |
| | ex-*Falcon Lady* | | | |
| AO-183 | *Neches* | Ingalls | 30/01/71 | 76-83 |
| | ex-*Falcon Duchess* | | | |
| AO-184 | *Hudson* | Ingalls | 08/01/71 | 76-84 |
| | ex-*Falcon Princess* | | | |
| AO-185 | *Susquehanna* | Ingalls | 02/10/71 | 76- |
| | ex-*Falcon Countess* | | | |

**Notes:** Acquired 1976, reclassified AOT, 1978.

---

**Details:** 39,400 tons f/l; 677'10 (oa)×97'6×35; two shafts, diesel, SHP 32,000=20kt; crew 116

| | | | | |
|---|---|---|---|---|
| AO-187 | *Henry J. Kaiser* | Avondale | 05/10/85 | n/a |
| AO-188 | *Joshua Humphreys* | Avondale | 22/02/86 | n/a |
| AO-189 | *John Lenthall* | Avondale | Building | n/a |
| AO-190 | *Andrew J. Higgins* | Avondale | Building | n/a |
| AO-191 | *n/a* | Penn | Ordered | n/a |
| AO-192 | *n/a* | Penn | Ordered | n/a |
| AO-193 | *n/a* | Avondale | Ordered | n/a |
| AO-194 | *n/a* | Penn | Ordered | n/a |
| AO-195 | *n/a* | Avondale | Ordered | n/a |

**Notes:** 21 projected.

# GASOLINE TANKERS

**Details:** 1,850 tons, 4,335f/l; 293 (wl)
310'9 (oa)×48'6×15'8; two shafts, diesel-electric,
SHP 3,100=14kt; 4×3in/50 guns; 124 crew

AOG-1 _____ *Patapsco* _____ Todd; Tacoma _____ 18/08/42 ___ 50-55, 66-69. Str74
AOG-2 _____ *Kern* _____ Todd; Tacoma _____ 07/09/42 ___ 50-56, 57-57. BU75
AOG-3 _____ *Rio Grande* _____ Todd; Tacoma _____ 23/09/42 ___ 50-56. BU72
AOG-4 _____ *Wabash* _____ Todd; Tacoma _____ 28/10/42 ___ 50-57. Str58
AOG-5 _____ *Susquehanna* _____ Todd; Tacoma _____ 23/11/42 ___ 50-59. BU73
AOG-6 _____ *Agawam* _____ Cargill _____ 06/05/43 ___ 46-57. BU75
AOG-7 _____ *Elkhorn* _____ Cargill _____ 15/05/43 ___ 44-72. Taiwan *Hsing Lung* (72)
AOG-8 _____ *Genesee* _____ Cargill _____ 23/09/43 ___ 44-49, 50-72. Chilean *Beagle* (72)
AOG-9 _____ *Kishwaukee* _____ Cargill _____ 24/07/43 ___ 44-58, 66-70. Str74
AOG-10 _____ *Nemasket* _____ Cargill _____ 20/10/43 ___ 44-59. BU61
AOG-11 _____ *Tombigbee* _____ Cargill _____ 18/11/43 ___ 44-49, 50-72. Greek *Ariadni* (72)
AOG-48 _____ *Chehalis* _____ Cargill _____ 15/04/44 ___ 44-49. Lost 07/10/49
AOG-49 _____ *Chestatee* _____ Cargill _____ 29/04/44 ___ 48-54, 56-57. BU76
AOG-50 _____ *Chewaucan* _____ Cargill _____ 22/07/44 ___ 45-75. Colombian *Tumaco* (75)
AOG-51 _____ *Maquoketa* _____ Cargill _____ 12/08/44 ___ 52-56, 57-57. BU76
AOG-52 _____ *Mattabessett* _____ Cargill _____ 11/11/44 ___ 45-68.BU69
AOG-53 _____ *Namakagon* _____ Cargill _____ 04/11/44 ___ 45-57. New Zealand *Endeavour* (62),
                                                                          Taiwan *Lung Chuan* (71)
AOG-54 _____ *Natchaug* _____ Cargill _____ 06/12/44 ___ 45-59. Greek *Arethousa* (59)
AOG-55 _____ *Nespelen* _____ Cargill _____ 10/04/45 ___ 45-75. Str75
AOG-56 _____ *Noxubee* _____ Cargill _____ 03/04/45 ___ 45-59, 66-75. Str75
AOG-57 _____ *Pecatonica* _____ Cargill _____ 17/03/45 ___ 48-61. Taiwan *Chang Pei* (61)
AOG-58 _____ *Pinnebog* _____ Cargill _____ 12/05/45 ___ 52-57
AOG-59 _____ *Wacissa* _____ Cargill _____ 16/06/45 ___ 52-54, 56-56. BU65

**Notes:** AOG-1, 3, 49, 51, 68 stricken 1946, re-acquired 1948.

---

**Details:** 845 tons, 2,900f/l; 213 (wl) 220 (oa)×37×12'10;
one shaft, diesels, SHP 800=10kt; crew 62

*Below:*
**Nespelen (AOG-55), a gasoline tanker.**

AOG-36 _____ *Ontonagon* _____ East Coast _____ 30/06/44 ___ 50-54, 56-56. BU65

**Notes:** Re-acquired from the Army 1950.

**Details:** 1,840 ton, 6,047f/l; 309 (wl)
325'4 (oa)×48'2×19; one shaft, diesel,
SHP 1,700=11kt; crew 36

AOG-68 _____ *Peconic* _____ St Johns R _____ 14/05/45 ___ 48-57. Str57
AOG-76 _____ *Tonti* _____ Todd-Houston _____ 23/08/45 ___ 49-65. Colombian *Mamonal* (65)
AOG-77 _____ *Rincon* _____ Todd-Houston _____ 05/06/45 ___ 50-68. Korea (82)
AOG-78 _____ *Nodaway* _____ Todd-Houston _____ 15/05/45 ___ 50-61, 65-84
AOG-79 _____ *Petaluma* _____ Todd-Houston _____ 09/08/45 ___ 50-82. Korea (82)
AOG-80 _____ *Piscataqua* _____ Todd-Houston _____ 10/09/45 ___ 50-74. BU75

**Notes:** Acquired 1950. *Peconic* re-acquired 1948.

**Details:** 3,459 tons, 5,700f/l; 285'6 (wl)
302 (oa)×60'11×19; two shafts, diesel-electric,
SHP 3,400=18kt

AOG-81 _____ *Alatna* _____ Staten Is _____ 16/09/56 ___ 57-72, 79-85
AOG-82 _____ *Chattahoochee* _____ Staten Is _____ 04/12/56 ___ 57-72, 79-85

**Notes:** Ice-strengthened bows. Modernised,
re-engined 1981.

# FAST COMBAT SUPPORT SHIPS

**Details:** 19,200 tons, 53,600f/l; 792'9 (oa)×107×30'4; Endurance 10,000/17; 0×3in/50 guns (1979. 4×3in/50,
two shafts, steam turbines, SHP 100,000=26kt; one Sea Sparrow launcher); 574 crew

AOE-1 _____ *Sacramento* _____ Puget Sound _____ 14/09/63 ___ 64-
AOE-2 _____ *Camden* _____ NY Sbdg _____ 29/05/65 ___ 67-
AOE-3 _____ *Seattle* _____ Puget Sound _____ 02/03/68 ___ 69-
AOE-4 _____ *Detroit* _____ Puget Sound _____ 21/06/69 ___ 70-

**Notes:** FY61-66. Construction of AOE-5 cancelled 1969. have turbines built for cancelled battleship *Kentucky*.
Designed to supply a carrier battle group with fuel, Helicopter deck and hangar aft. Two Phalanx CIWS
munitions and provisions. *Sacramento* and *Camden* replaced remaining 3in guns 1985

# REPLENISHMENT FLEET OILERS

**Details:** 12,500 tons, 38,100f/l; 659 (wl), 675 SHP 32,000=20kt; 8×3in/50 guns (1981: replaced with
(oa)×96×35; two shafts, steam turbines, Sea Sparrow launcher); 345 crew

AOR-1 _____ *Wichita* _____ Quincy _____ 18/03/68 ___ 69-
AOR-2 _____ *Milwaukee* _____ Quincy _____ 17/01/69 ___ 69-
AOR-3 _____ *Kansas City* _____ Quincy _____ 28/06/69 ___ 70-
AOR-4 _____ *Savannah* _____ Quincy _____ 25/04/70 ___ 70-
AOR-5 _____ *Wabash* _____ Quincy _____ 06/02/71 ___ 71-
AOR-6 _____ *Kalamazoo* _____ Quincy _____ 11/11/72 ___ 73-
AOR-7 _____ *Roanoke* _____ National _____ 07/12/74 ___ 76-

**Notes:** FY65-72. *Roanoke* built with helicopter hangar,
others so modified 1980.

# TRANSPORTS

**Details:** 22,800 tons; 667'6 (wl), 705 (oa)×86×30; two
shafts, steam turbines, SHP 34,500=21.5kt; 3×5in/38,
12×40mm guns

AP-21 _____ *Wakefield* _____ NY Sbdg _____ 05/12/31 ___ Str57

**Notes:** The former passenger liner *Manhattan*
acquired 1941.

---

**Details:** 12,225 tons; 547'8 (wl), 572'8 (oa)×72'2×26'4;
two shafts, steam turbines, SHP 13,500=17.5kt;
1×5in/38, 4×3in/50, 8×40mm guns.

AP-74 _____ *Le Jeune* _____ Blohm & Voss _____ 15/10/36 ___ Str57

**Notes:** The former German passenger liner *Windhuk*
acquired 1942.

---

**Details:** 11,828 tons, 20,175f/l; 573 (wl), 622'7
(oa)×75'6×25'6; two shafts, steam turbines,
SHP 18,700=20.6kt; 4×5in/38, 8×40mm guns.

| | | | | |
|---|---|---|---|---|
| AP-110 | *Gen John Pope* | Federal | 21/03/43 | 50-58, 65-70 |
| AP-111 | *Gen A. E. Anderson* | Federal | 02/05/43 | 43-58. Str58 |
| AP-112 | *Gen W. A. Mann* | Federal | 18/07/43 | 43-66. Str66 |
| AP-113 | *Gen H. W. Butner* | Federal | 19/09/43 | 44-60. Str60 |
| AP-114 | *Gen William Mitchell* | Federal | 31/10/43 | 44-66. Str66 |
| AP-115 | *Gen G. M. Randall* | Federal | 30/01/44 | 44-61. Str62 |
| AP-116 | *Gen M. C. Meigs* | Federal | 12/03/44 | 50-55. Lost 72 |
| AP-117 | *Gen W. H. Gordon* | Federal | 07/05/44 | 51-56, 61-61 |
| AP-119 | *Gen William Weigel* | Federal | 03/09/44 | 50-58, 65-67 |
| AP-176 | *Gen J. C. Breckinridge* | Federal | 18/03/45 | 45-66. Str66 |

**Notes:** AP-117 and 119 operated by Army 1946-50.
AP-110 and 116 re-acquired 1950.

*Above:*
**The transport *General William Weigel* (T-AP-119).**

**Details:** 9,676 tons, 20,120f/l; 573 (wl), 608'11
(oa)×75'6×20; two shafts, turbine-electric,
SHP 20,500 – 19kt

AP-120 ——— Gen Daniel I. Sultan ——— Alameda ——————— 28/11/43 ——— 50-69
               ex-Adm W. S. Benson
AP-121 ——— Gen Hugh J. Gaffey ——— Alameda ——————— 20/02/44 ——— 50-69. IX-507 (78)
               ex-Adm W. L. Capps
AP-122 ——— Gen Alexander M. Patch  Alameda ——————— 22/04/44 ——— 50-70
               ex-Adm R. E. Coontz
AP-123 ——— Gen Simon B. Buckner ——  Alameda ——————— 14/06/44 ——— 50-70
               ex-Adm E. W. Eberle
AP-124 ——— Gen Edwin L. Patrick ——— Alameda ——————— 27/08/44 ——— 50-66
               ex-Adm C. F. Hughes
AP-125 ——— Gen Nelson M. Walker ——  Alameda ——————— 26/11/44 ——— 50-70. Str81
               ex-Adm H. T. Mayo
AP-126 ——— Gen Maurice Rose ——— Alameda ——————— 25/02/45 ——— 50-67
               ex-Adm Hugh Rodman
AP-127 ——— Gen William O. Darby —— Alameda ——————— 04/06/45 ——— 50-67. IX-510 (83)
               ex-Adm W. S. Sims

**Notes:** Navy transports transferred to the Army and
renamed 1946; re-acquired 1950. *Gaffey* used as
accommodation ship at Bremerton from 1979 and *Darby*
at Newport News 1982.

**Details:** 9,943 tons, 16,600f/l; 496'7 (wl), 522'10
(oa)×71'6×26'6; one shaft, steam turbines,
SHP 9,000=17kt; 356 crew.

AP-134 ——— Gen R. L. Howze ——————— Richmond ——————— 23/05/43 ——— 50-57. Merchant *Guam Bear* (68)
AP-135 ——— Gen W. L. Black ——————— Richmond ——————— 23/07/43 ——— 50-55. Merchant *Green Forest* (67)
AP-137 ——— Gen S. D. Sturgis ——————— Richmond ——————— 12/11/43 ——— 50-55. Merchant *Green Port* (67)
AP-138 ——— Gen C. G. Morton ——————— Richmond ——————— 15/03/44 ——— Merchant *Green Wave* (67)
AP-139 ——— Gen R. E. Callan ——————— Richmond ——————— 23/05/44 ——— 50-58. USAF *Gen H. H. Arnold* (63),
                                                          AGM-9 (64)

AP-140 _____ Gen M. B. Stewart _____ Richmond _____ 15/10/44 __ 50-55. Merchant *Albany* (67)
AP-141 _____ Gen A. W. Greely _____ Richmond _____ 05/11/44 __ 50-55. Merchant *Hawaii Bear* (68)
AP-142 _____ Gen C. H. Muir _____ Richmond _____ 24/11/44 __ 50-55. Merchant *Chicago* (69)
AP-143 _____ Gen H. B. Freeman _____ Richmond _____ 11/12/44 __ 50-58. Merchant *Newark* (68)
AP-144 _____ Gen H. F. Hodges _____ Richmond _____ 03/01/45 __ 50-58. Merchant *James* (67)
AP-145 _____ Gen Harry Taylor _____ Richmond _____ 10/10/43 __ 50-57. USAF *Gen Hoyt S. Vandenberg* (63). AGM-10 (64)
AP-146 _____ Gen W. F. Hase _____ Richmond _____ 15/12/43 __ 50-54. Merchant *Transidaho* (69)
AP-147 _____ Gen E. T. Collins _____ Richmond _____ 22/01/44 __ 50-54. Merchant *New Orleans* (69)
AP-148 _____ Gen M. L. Hersey _____ Richmond _____ 01/04/44 __ 50-54. Merchant *St Louis* (68)
AP-149 _____ Gen J. H. McRae _____ Richmond _____ 26/04/44 __ 50-54. Merchant *Transhawaii* (70)
AP-150 _____ Gen M. M. Patrick _____ Richmond _____ 21/06/44 __ 50-58. Merchant *Boston* (68)
AP-151 _____ Gen W. C. Langfitt _____ Richmond _____ 17/07/44 __ 50-57. Merchant *Transindiana* (69)
AP-153 _____ Gen R. M. Blatchford __ Richmond _____ 27/08/44 __ 50-67. Merchant *Stonewall Jackson* (70)
AP-154 _____ Gen Leroy Eltinge _____ Richmond _____ 30/09/44 __ 50-67. Merchant *Robert E. Lee* (70)
AP-155 _____ Gen A. W. Brewster ____ Richmond _____ 21/01/45 __ 50-54. Merchant *Philadelphia* (68)
AP-156 _____ Gen D. E. Aultman _____ Richmond _____ 21/02/45 __ 50-58. Merchant *Portland* (68)
AP-157 _____ Gen C. C. Ballou _____ Richmond _____ 07/03/45 __ 50-54. Merchant *Brooklyn* (68)
AP-158 _____ Gen W. G. Haan _____ Richmond _____ 20/03/45 __ 50-57. Merchant *Transoregon* (69)
AP-159 _____ Gen Stuart Heintzelman Richmond _____ 21/04/45 __ 50-54. Merchant *Mobile* (68)
AP-193 _____ Marine Adder _____ Richmond _____ 16/05/45 __ 50-57. Merchant *Transcolorado* (67)
AP-194 _____ Marine Lynx _____ Kaiser _____ 17/07/45 __ 50-56. Merchant *Transcolumbia* (67)
AP-195 _____ Marine Phoenix _____ Kaiser _____ 09/08/45 __ 50-58. Merchant (67)
AP-199 _____ Marine Carp _____ Kaiser _____ 05/07/45 __ 52-58. Merchant *Green Springs* (67)
AP-202 _____ Marine Serpent _____ Kaiser _____ 12/06/45 __ 52-55. Merchant *Galveston* (68)

**Notes:** AP-134-159 re-acquired from Army in 1950. Carried 3,400 troops. AP-139 and 145 transferred to Air Force as Missile Range Instrumentation Ships and re-acquired 1964.

**Details:** 11,200 tons, 15,500f/l; 465'3 (wl), 492 (oa)×59'6×26'6; one shaft, steam turbines, SHP 9,350=18.6kt

AP-178 _____ Frederick Funston _____ Tacoma _____ 27/09/41 __ 50-60. BU69
AP-179 _____ James O'Hara _____ Tacoma _____ 30/12/41 __ 50-60. BU68

**Notes:** Served as APA-89-90 during World War 2, re-acquired from Army in 1950. Carried 1,100 troops.

**Details:** 10,500 tons, 15,400f/l; 465 (wl), 489 (oa)×69'6×26'9; one shaft, steam turbines, SHP 9,350=16.5kt

AP-180 _____ David C. Shanks _____ Ingalls _____ 21/10/42 __ 50-58. Str61
AP-181 _____ Fred C. Ainsworth _____ Ingalls _____ 20/11/42 __ 50-59. Str61
AP-182 _____ George W. Goethals __ Ingalls _____ 23/01/42 __ 50-59. BU71
AP-183 _____ Henry Gibbins _____ Ingalls _____ 11/09/42 __ 50-59. Merchant *Empire State IV* (60)

**Notes:** Acquired from Army in 1950. Carried 1,250 troops.

**Details:** 7,100 tons; 427 (wl), 450'2 (oa)×62×25'9; one shaft, steam turbines, SHP 9,350=18.2kt

176

*Above:*
**The transport *Marine Lynx* (T-AP-194), built in 1945.**

*Below:*
**The *Pvt Elden H. Johnson* (T-AP-184), a transport originally built as the evacuation transport *Pinkney*.**

| AP-184 | Pvt Elden H. Johnson | Moore | 04/12/41 | 50-57. BU69 |
|---|---|---|---|---|
| | ex-*Pinkney*  (APH-2) | | | |
| AP-185 | Pvt William H. Thomas | Moore | 30/12/41 | 50-57. BU71 |
| | ex-*Rixey* (APH 3) | | | |
| AP-186 | Sgt Charles E. Mower | Moore | 21/10/41 | 50-57. BU71 |
| | ex-*Tryon* (APH-1) | | | |

**Notes:**  Navy evacuation transports re-acquired from Army in 1950.

**Details:**  10,680 tons f/l; 436'6 (wl), 455'3 (oa)×62×28'6; one shaft, steam turbines, SHP 6,600=17kt

| AP-187 | Pvt Joe F. Martinez | Fairfield | 29/05/45 | 50-52. BU71 |
|---|---|---|---|---|
| AP-188 | Aiken Victory | Fairfield | 30/11/44 | 50-52. BU71 |
| AP-189 | Lt Raymond O. Beaudoin | Fairfield | 21/05/45 | 50-52. BU72 |
| AP-190 | Pvt Sadao S. Munemori | Fairfield | 06/07/45 | 50-52. Str52 |
| AP-191 | Sgt Howard E. Woodford | Fairfield | 02/06/45 | 50-52. BU72 |
| AP-192 | Sgt Sylvester Antolak | Fairfield | 16/06/45 | 50-52. BU72 |

**Notes:**  Acquired from Army in 1950.

**Details:** 11,200 tons, 19,600f/l; 499'6 (wl), 533'9
(oa)×73×27; one shaft, steam turbines,
SHP 13,500=19kt

| AP-196 | Barrett | NY Sbdg | 27/06/50 | 51-73. Empire State V (73) |
|---|---|---|---|---|
| | ex-President Jackson | | | |
| AP-197 | Geiger | NY Sbdg | 09/10/50 | 52-73. Bay State (80) |
| | ex-President Adams | | | |
| AP-198 | Upshur | NY Sbdg | 19/01/51 | 52-73. State of Maine (73) |
| | ex-President Hayes | | | |

**Notes:** Laid down as American President Line liners,
taken over during construction. Loaned to State
Maritime Academies 1973-80.

---

**Details:** 2,460 tons; 321 (wl), 338'8 (oa)×50×21; one
shaft, diesels, SHP 1,700=11.5kt

| APC-116 | Sgt Jonah E. Kelley | Southeastern | 17/03/45 | 50-69. Str70 |
|---|---|---|---|---|
| APC-117 | Sgt George D. Keathley | Butler | 07/12/44 | 50-57, 76-72. AGS-35 (67), Taiwan Chiu Hua (72) |
| APC-118 | Sgt Joseph E. Muller | Southeastern | 17/02/45 | 50-57, 63-69. AG-171 (62). Str70 |
| APC-119 | Pvt Jose F. Valdez | Butler | 27/10/44 | 50-59, 61-71. AG-169 (62). Str76 |

**Notes:** Acquired from Army in 1950.

# MISCELLANEOUS AUXILIARIES

**Details:** 100 tons; 104 (oa)×19×4'5; two shafts, diesels,
SHP 400=12kt

| AG-23 | Sequoia | Mathis | 1925 | 33-77. Str77 |
|---|---|---|---|---|

**Notes:** Presidential Yacht, acquired 1931.

---

**Details:** 5,766 tons; 416 (wl), 441'6 (oa)×56'11×23; one
shaft, VTE, SHP 2,500=12.5kt; 1×5in/38, 4×40mm guns

| AG-73 | Belle Isle | New England | 03/11/44 | AKS-21. Str60 |
|---|---|---|---|---|
| AG-74 | Coasters Harbor | New England | 17/11/44 | AKS-22. BU61 |
| AG-75 | Cuttyhunk Island | New England | 26/11/44 | AKS-23. BU60 |
| AG-76 | Avery Island | New England | 13/12/44 | AKS-24. BU61 |
| AG-77 | Indian Island | New England | 19/12/44 | AKS-25. BU60 |
| AG-78 | Kent Island | New England | 09/01/45 | AKS-26. BU60 |

**Notes:** Electronic Repair Ships. Converted Liberty Ships.

---

**Details:** 1,850 tons; 372 (wl), 381 (oa)×36'11×10'4; two
shafts, steam turbines, SHP 50,000=37kt; AG-127:
4×5in, 4×40mm guns

| AG-126 | McDougal | NY Sbdg | 17/07/36 | 36-49. BU49 |
|---|---|---|---|---|
| AG-127 | Winslow | NY Sbdg | 21/09/36 | 37-50. BU59 |

**Notes:** Ex-DD-358-359. Winslow was radar picket and
ordnance testing and trials ship. McDougal not used
after 1947.

*Above:*
**The former battleship *Mississippi* (AG-128) was used as a gunnery training and testing ship. Notice the various gun mounts situated forward and the two missile launchers aft.**
*Martin E. Holbrook collection*

**Details:** 32,000 tons; 600 (wl), 624 (oa)×97'5×30; four shafts, steam turbines, SHP 40,000=21kt; 3×14in/50 guns and others

AG-128 _____ *Mississippi* _____ Newport News _____ 25/01/17 __ 46-56. BU56

**Notes:** Ex-BB-41. Gunnery training and testing ship.

**Details:** 9,050 tons, 17,000f/l; 529'6 (wl), 564 (oa)×76'3×29; one shaft, steam turbines, SHP 19,250=20kt

EAG-153 _____ *Compass Island* _____ NY Sbdg _____ 12/03/53 __ 56-80. AG (68). Str81
 ex-*Garden Mariner*
EAG-154 _____ *Observation Island* _____ NY Sbdg _____ 15/08/53 __ 58-72, 79-  . AG (68). AGM-23 (79)
 ex-*Empire State Mariner*

**Notes:** Acquired 1956. *Compass Island* was experimental navigational ship for development of ballistic missiles. *Observation Island* used as ballistic missile test firing ship. In 1979 converted to monitor Soviet SLBM tests in North Pacific.

**Reclassified Vessels:**

AG-129 _____ *Whitewood* _____ ex-AN-63 _____ Arctic supply ship
AG-130 to AG-140 _____ to AKL-1-11 _____ na
AG-141 _____ *Whidbey* _____ ex-FS-395 _____ 47-54. Floating clinic, merchant *Sea Search* (61)
AG-142 _____ *Nashawena* _____ na _____ 47-53. Cable ship
 ex-*Col William A. Glassford*
AG-143 to AG-145 _____ to AKL-12-14 _____ na
AG-151 _____ *Richard E. Kraus* _____ ex-DD-849 _____ ASW test ship
AG-152 _____ *Timmerman* _____ ex-DD-828 _____ na
AG-157 _____ *King County* _____ ex-LST-857 _____ Missile test ship
AG-159 _____ *Oxford* _____ to AGTR-1 _____ na
AG-160 _____ *Range Tracker* _____ to AGM-1 _____ na
AG-161 _____ *Range Recoverer* _____ to AGM-2 _____ na
AG-162 _____ *Mission Capistrano* _____ ex-AO-112 _____ Sound-testing ship

*Above:*
**King County (AG-157). This former LST was used as a test ship for the Regulus II missile.**
Official US Navy

*Below:*
**Mission Capistrano (T-AG-162), the former tanker converted to a sound testing ship.**

| | | | |
|---|---|---|---|
| AG-163 | na | to AGDE-1 | na |
| AG-165 | Georgetown | to AGTR-2 | na |
| AG-166 | Jamestown | to AGTR-3 | na |
| AG-167 | Belmont | to AGTR-4 | na |
| AG-168 | Liberty | to AGTR-5 | na |
| AG-169 | Pvt Jose F. Valdez | ex-APC-119 | na |
| AG-170 | Lt James E. Robinson | ex-AK-274 | na |
| AG-171 | Sgt Joseph E. Muller | ex-APC-118 | Research support ship |
| AG-176 | Peregrine | ex-MSF-373 | na |
| AG-191 | Spokane | ex-CL-120 | Sonar test ship |
| AG-192 | S. P. Lee | ex-AGS-31 | Hydrographic research |
| AG-194 | Vanguard | ex-AGM-19 | Navigation research ship |

**Notes:** Conversion of *Spokane* cancelled 1968. For details see under classification listed. *Whitewood* damaged by ice and run aground 06/12/48 and stricken.

### Reclassified LSTs:
Former LSTs converted to electronic parts repair ships (reclassified AKS-27-31, 1951):

| | | | |
|---|---|---|---|
| AG-146 | Electron | ex-LST-1070 | 50-56. Str60 |
| AG-147 | Proton | ex-LST-1078 | 51-58. Str59 |
| AG-148 | Colington | ex-LST-1085 | Str60 |

AG-149 _____ *League Island* _____ ex-LST-1097 _____ 51-56. Str60
AG-150 _____ *Chimon* _____ ex-LST-1102 _____ 50-58. Str59

---

**Details:** 7,190 tons, 10,680f/l; 436 (wl), 455 (oa)×62×24;
  one shaft, steam turbines, SHP 8,500=17kt

AG-164 _____ *Kingsport* _____ Calship _____ 29/05/44 ___ 62-83. Str84
                  ex-*Kingsport Victory*
AG-172 _____ *Phoenix* _____ Oregon _____ 10/04/45 ___ 63-73. Str73
                  ex-*Arizona*
AG-173 _____ *Provo* _____ Oregon _____ 17/06/45 ___ 63-73. Str73
                  ex-*Utah*
AG-174 _____ *Cheyenne* _____ Oregon _____ 26/06/45 ___ 62-73. Str73
                  ex-*Wyoming*

**Notes:** *Kingsport*, formerly AK-239, Satellite
Communications Ship, converted to Hydrographic
Research Ship 1966. AG-172-174, Forward Depot Ships.
Acquisition of 12 additional vessels (AG-179-190)
cancelled.

---

**Details:** 2,460 tons; 321 (wl), 338'8 (oa)×50×21; one
  shaft, diesel, SHP 1,700=11.5kt

AG-176 _____ *Sgt Curtis F. Shoup* _____ Kaiser _____ 25/05/45 ___ 63-70. BU73

**Notes:** Survey Support Ship, acquired 1963, used as
helicopter freighter

---

**Details:** 465 tons; 177 (oa), 165 (wl)×32'9×14'3; two
  shafts, diesel, SHP 1,000=12kt

AG-177 _____ *Shearwater* _____ Hickinbotham _____ --/--/45 _____ 64-69. Str69
                  ex-*F3-411*

**Notes:** Survey Support Ship, acquired 1964.

---

**Details:** 7,360 tons; 435 (wl), 459'2 (oa)×63×28; one
  shaft, steam turbines, SHP 6,000=17kt

AG-178 _____ *Flyer* _____ Moore _____ 20/12/44 ___ 65-75. BU76
                  ex-*American Flyer*

**Notes:** Hydrographic Research Ship, acquired 1965.

---

**Details:** 63,300 tons f/l; 618'9 (oa)×115'8×46'8; two
  shafts, diesel-electric drive, SHP 13,200=10.8kt; 178
  crew

AG-193 _____ *Glomar Explorer* _____ Sun _____ 14/11/72 ___ Str77

**Notes:** Built as *Hughes Glomar Explorer*, officially
acquired 1976. Built by the Central Intelligence Agency
to raise wreck of a Soviet 'Golf' class ballistic missile
submarine which sank in mid-Pacific in 1968. During the
operation in 1974 the forward section of the submarine
was recovered from a depth of three miles. Laid up since
1980.

*Above:*
**The *Glomar Explorer* (AG-193), a large specialised vessel built by the CIA, was briefly registered on the Navy list.** *Martin E. Holbrook*

# ICEBREAKERS

**Details:** 3,500 tons, 6,500f/l; 250 (wl), 269
(oa)×63′6×25′9; three shafts, diesel-electric,
SHP 13,300=16kt; 1×5in/38, 4×40mm guns; 234 crew

| | | | | | |
|---|---|---|---|---|---|
| AGB-1 | *Burton Island* | Western Pipe | 30/04/46 | 46-67. USCG (W-283) (67) |
| AGB-2 | *Edisto* | Western Pipe | 29/05/46 | 46-65. USCG (W-284) (65) |
| AGB-3 | *Atka* | Western Pipe | 07/03/43 | 50-66. USCG *Southwind* (W-280) (66) |
| AGB-5 | *Staten Island* | Western Pipe | 28/12/42 | 52-66. USCG (W-278) (66) |
| AGB-6 | *Westwind* | Western Pipe | 31/03/43 | 52-66. USCG (W-281) (66) |

**Notes:** 1 and 2 built as AG-88-89, reclassified 1949. Others built for the Coast Guard and loaned to Soviet Union 1944. They were returned in 1949 and commissioned in USN. All turned over to Coast Guard in 1965-67.

---

**Details:** 5,100 tons, 8,775f/l; 310 (oa)×74×29; two
shafts, diesel-electric, SHP 21,000=16kt; 2×5in/38,
6×3in/50, 6×20mm guns; 339 crew

| | | | | | |
|---|---|---|---|---|---|
| AGB-4 | *Glacier* | Ingalls | 27/08/54 | 55-66. USCG (W-4) (66) |

**Notes:** Transferred to Coast Guard 1966. Guns removed.

# DEEP SUBMERGENCE SUPPORT SHIPS

AGDS-2 *Point Loma*. See AKD-1, converted 1974 to carry, launch and service *Trieste II*. Modified 1980-82 to support deep submergence vehicles and Trident missile test launches.

AGDS-1 was floating drydock *White Sands* (ex-ARD-20).

# HYDROFOIL RESEARCH SHIP

**Details:** 310 tons f/l; 212 (oa)×40′3×10/26; two shafts,
gas turbines, SHP 30,000=40kt+, diesels,
SHP 1,200=12kt

*Above:*
**The icebreaker *Atka* (AGB-3), returned to the Coast Guard in 1966 after service with the Soviet Union and the US Navy.** *John O'Leary*

*Right:*
**The icebreaker *Glacier* (AGB-4), seen in 1955, was later transferred to the Coast Guard. Much of its armament and radar were removed, but the forward 5in turret and 3in guns aft were retained.** *Official US Navy, Ernest Arroyo collection*

*Below:*
**Plainview (AGEH-1), with foils retracted, in 1972. She was the largest military hydrofoil in the world.** *Official US Navy*

AGEH-1 _____ *Plainview* _____ Lockheed _____ 28/06/55 ___ 68-    . Str78

**Notes:** FY62. Largest military hydrofoil in the world. Aluminium hull and three retractable foils. Completion delayed four years by engineering problems.

# ENVIRONMENTAL RESEARCH SHIPS

AGER-1 _____ *Banner* _____ ex-AKL-25 _____ na _____ na
AGER-2 _____ *Pueblo* _____ ex-AKL-45 _____ na _____ na
AGER-3 _____ *Palm Beach* _____ ex-AKL-45 _____ na _____ na

**Notes:** Converted small cargo ship for ELINT operations. *Pueblo* seized by North Korean ship, 1968, remains on Navy List. For details, see page 163. Conversion of 30 vessels was planned.

*Below:*
**Palm Beach (AGER-3), a small cargo ship converted to an electronics intelligence ship. *Pueblo* of this type was seized by North Korean forces in 1968.**

# MISSILE RANGE INSTRUMENTATION SHIPS

|  |  | Displacement/Built |  |
|---|---|---|---|
| AGM-1 | *Range Tracker* ex-AG-160 | 7,190/45 | 61-69. BU70 |
| AGM-2 | *Range Recoverer* ex-AG-161, ex-FS-278 | 550/44 | 60-72. YFRT-524 (72). Str74 |
| AGM-3 | *Longview* ex-AK-238 *Haiti Victory* | 7,190/44 | 60-70. Str74 |
| AGM-4 | *Richfield* ex-AK-253 *Pvt Joe E. Mann* | 7,190/45 | 60-70, 60-68. Str70 |
| AGM-5 | *Sunnyvale* ex-AK-256 *Dalton Victory* | 7,190/44 | 60-74. BU75 |

| | | | | |
|---|---|---|---|---|
| AGM-6 | Watertown | 7,190/44 | 61-72. BU74 |
| | ex-Niantic Victory | | |
| AGM-7 | Huntsville | 7,190/45 | 61-74. BU75 |
| | ex-Knox Victory | | |
| AGM-8 | Wheeling | 7,910/45 | 64-79. Target 80 |
| | ex-Seton Hall Victory | | |
| AGM-9 | Gen H. H. Arnold | 14,300/43 | 64- |
| | ex-AP-138 Gen R. E. Callan | | |
| AGM-10 | Gen Hoyt S. Vandenberg | 14,300/43 | 64- |
| | ex-AP-145 Gen Harry Taylor | | |
| AGM-11 | Twin Falls | 7,190/44 | 64-70. Str70 |
| | ex-Twin Falls Victory | | |
| AGM-12 | American Mariner | 5,080/41 | 64-66. Target 66 |
| AGM-13 | Sword Knot | 3,000/45 | 64-71. BU73 |
| AGM-14 | Rose Knot | 3,000/45 | 64-69. Str68 |
| AGM-15 | Coastal Sentry | 3,000/45 | 64-68. Str71 |
| AGM-16 | Coastal Crusader | 3,000/45 | 64- |
| AGM-17 | Timber Hitch | 3,000/44 | 64- |
| AGM-18 | Sampan Hitch | 3,000/45 | 64-68. BU73 |
| AGM-19 | Vanguard | na/43 | 66- . AG-194 (80) |
| | ex Muscle Shoals, ex-AO-122 | | |

*Above:*

**General Hoyt S. Vandenberg (T-AGM-10), a missile range instrumentation ship. The vessel was converted from a 'General' class transport by the Air Force, from which it was transferred in 1964.**

*Below:*

**The missile range instrumentation ship Redstone (T-AGM-20), formerly the tanker Mission De Pala. The 'golf balls' protect the radars.**

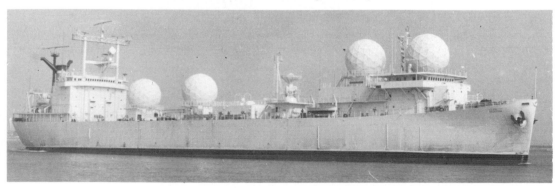

```
AGM-20 _____ Redstone _____ na/43 _____ 66-
                ex-Johnstown,
                ex-AO-114
AGM-21 _____ Mercury _____ na/43 _____ 66-69. Str70
                ex-Flagstaff,
                ex-AO-126
AGM-22 _____ Range Sentinel _____ na/44 _____ 71-
                ex-APA-205 Sherburne
AGM-23 _____ Observation Island _____ 13,060/53 _____ 79-
                ex-AG-153
```

**Notes:** These vessels conduct telemetry and recover missiles; support manned space flights. AGM-9-10 converted to support Air Force IBM tests, to USN 1964. AGM-11-18 manned by Air Force until 1964. AGM-19-21 former oilers converted 1965 to missile tracking ships, lengthened by 72'. AGM-19 converted 1979-80 to Navigation Research Ship, amidships radars removed. Conversion of AGM-11 and 16 to surveying vessels AGS-37 and 36 cancelled.

# MAJOR COMMUNICATIONS RELAY SHIPS

```
AGMR-1 _____ Annapolis _____ see CVE-107 _____ 64-69. Str77
AGMR-2 _____ Arlington _____ see CVL-48 _____ 68-70. Str75
```

**Notes:** Aircraft carriers converted to provide communications relay equipment for commands afloat. Annapolis was the former escort carrier Gilbert Islands converted 1962-64. Conversion of Vella Gulf cancelled; replaced by light carrier Saipan, 1964-66. Armament 8×3in/50 guns.

*Right:*
**The major communications relay ship Annapolis (AGMR-1) was formerly the escort carrier Gilbert Islands.**
*Our Navy/Ernest Arroyo collection*

# OCEANOGRAPHIC RESEARCH SHIPS

AGOR-1 *Josiah Willard Gibbs* was former seaplane tender *San Carlos* (AVP-51), converted 1958. AGOR-2 OSP for Norway.

**Details:** 1,200 tons; 191'6 (wl), 208'10 (oa)×37'10×15'2; two shafts, diesel-electric, SHP 10,000=13kt; 38 crew

AGOR-3 —— *Robert D. Conrad* —— Gibbs —————— 26/05/62 — 62-
AGOR-4 —— *James M. Gilliss* —— Christy ————— 19/05/62 — 62-81. Mexican *Altair* (83)
AGOR-5 —— *Charles H. Davis* —— Christy ————— 30/06/62 — 63-70. New Zealand *Tui* (70)
AGOR-6 —— *Sands* ————————— Marietta ————— 14/09/63 — 64-74. Brazilian *Almirante Camara* (74)
AGOR-7 —— *Lynch* ————————— Marietta ————— 17/03/64 — 65-
AGOR-9 —— *Thomas G. Thompson* Marinette ———— 18/07/64 — 65-
            ex-*Silas Bent*
AGOR-10 — *Thomas Washington* — Marinette ———— 01/08/64 — 65-
AGOR-12 — *De Steiguer* ————— Northwest ———— 21/03/66 — 69-
AGOR-13 — *Bartlett* ——————— Northwest ———— 24/05/66 — 69-

**Notes:** FY60-65. Ships vary in detail. Most under operational control of various civilian research organisations.

---

**Notes:** AGOR-8 and 11 converted cargo ships 1961 and 1965. Differ in appearance.

---

**Details:** 1,520 tons; 244'9 (oa)×46'3×15; two shafts, diesel, SHP 2,500 = 12.5kt; 50 crew

AGOR-14 — *Melville* ——————— Defoe ————— 10/07/68 — 69-
AGOR-15 — *Knorr* ——————————— Defoe ————— 21/08/68 — 70-

**Notes:** FY66. Single diesel engine drives two cycloidal (vertical) propellers. Bow observation dome. AGOR-19-20 cancelled 1969.

---

**Details:** 2,329 tons; 220 (wl), 246'6 (oa)×75×18'9; two shafts, steam diesels, BHP 5,400 = 13kt; 74 crew

AGOR-16 — *Hayes* ——————— Todd; Seattle ——— 02/07/70 — 71-

**Notes:** FY67. Catamaran hull; beam of each hull 24ft. Largest AGOR, nine were projected, but hull design was not considered a success. Conversion to acoustic research vessel authorised 1986, to replace IX-309 (Monob I).

*Below:*
**Hayes (T-AGOR-16), an oceanographic research ship with a catamaran hull. The design was not repeated.**

**Details:** 950 tons f/l; 176 (oa)×36×14'6; two shafts,
diesels, BHP 1,700=12kt; 34 crew

| | | | | |
|---|---|---|---|---|
| AGOR-21 | Gyre | Halter | 07/06/73 | 73- |
| AGOR-22 | Moana Wave | Halter | 23/06/73 | 74- |

**Notes:** FY71. Designed for use by research
organisations. No numbers painted on.

# OCEAN SURVEILLANCE SHIPS

**Details:** 2,285 tons f/l; 224×43×15'6; two shafts,
diesels, BHP 3,200=11kt; 30 crew

| | | | | |
|---|---|---|---|---|
| AGOS-1 | Stalwart | Tacoma Boat | 11/07/83 | 84- |
| AGOS-2 | Contender | Tacoma Boat | 20/12/83 | 84- |
| AGOS-3 | Vindicator | Tacoma Boat | 01/06/84 | 84- |
| AGOS-4 | Triumph | Tacoma Boat | 07/09/84 | 85- |
| AGOS-5 | Assurance | Tacoma Boat | 20/12/84 | 85- |
| AGOS-6 | Persistent | Tacoma Boat | 06/04/85 | 85- |
| AGOS-7 | Indomitable | Tacoma Boat | 16/07/85 | 85- |
| AGOS-8 | Prevail | Tacoma Boat | 17/12/85 | na |
| AGOS-9 | Assertive | Tacoma Boat | Building | na |
| AGOS-10 | Invincible | Tacoma Boat | Building | na |
| AGOS-11 | Audacious ex-Dauntless | Tacoma Boat | Building | na |
| AGOS-12 | Bold ex-Vigorous | Tacoma Boat | Building | na |
| AGOS-13 | Adventurous | Halter | Building | na |
| AGOS-14 | Worthy | Halter | Ordered | na |
| AGOS-15 | na | na | Ordered | na |
| AGOS-16 | na | na | Ordered | na |

**Notes:** Designed to supplement SOSUS, fixed acoustic
devices on the ocean floor, with towed SURTASS array.
Unarmed. Later units will have small waterplane area
twin hull design to operate better in bad weather.

# PATROL CRAFT TENDERS

Garrett County (AGP-786), Harnett County (AGP-821),
Hunterdon County (AGP-838) and Graham County
(AGP-1176) were converted LSTs (see page ???).

# RADAR PICKET SHIPS

**Details:** 3,600 tons; 417 (wl), 441'6 (oa)×57×23; one
shaft, VTE, SHP 2,500=12.5kt; 2×3in/50 guns; 151
crew

| | | ex- | |
|---|---|---|---|
| AGR-1 | Guardian | James G. Squires | 55-65. BU70 |
| AGR-2 | Lookout | Claude Kitchin | 55-65. BU70 |
| AGR-3 | Skywatcher | Rafael R. Rivera | 55-65. BU71 |
| AGR-4 | Searcher | James W. Wheeler | 55-65. BU70 |

*Above:*
**The radar picket ship *Interdictor* (AGR-13) c1959.**
*Official US Navy*

| | | | |
|---|---|---|---|
| AGR-5 | *Scanner* | Edwin D. Howard | 56-65. BU74 |
| AGR-6 | *Locator* | Frank O. Peterson | 56-65. BU74 |
| AGR-7 | *Picket* | James F. Harrell | 56-65. Str65 |
| AGR-8 | *Interceptor* | Edward W. Burton | 56-65. Str65 |
| AGR-9 | *Investigator* | Charles A. Draper | 57-65. BU71 |
| AGR-10 | *Outpost* | Francis I. O'Gara | 57-65. BU70 |
| AGR-11 | *Protector* | Warren P. Marks | 57-65. Str65 |
| AGR-12 | *Vigil* | Reymond Van Brogan | 57-65. BU70 |
| AGR-13 | *Interdictor* | Edwin H. Duff | 58-65. Str65 |
| AGR-14 | *Interpreter* | Dudley H. Thomas | 58-65. BU74 |
| AGR-15 | *Interrupter* | William J. Riddle | 58-65. *Tracer* (59). Str65 |
| AGR-16 | *Watchman* | Vernon S. Hood | 58-65. BU74 |

**Notes:** Converted Liberty Ships, built 1945. Provided
radar coverage of seaward approaches. Classified
YAGR-1-16 until 1958.

## SURVEYING SHIPS

| | | | |
|---|---|---|---|
| AGSC-7 | *Littlehales* | ex-PCS-1388 | 43-49, sold 50 |
| AGSC-8 | *Dutton* | ex-PCS-1396 | 44-49, sold 50 |
| AGSC-10 | *John Blish* | ex-PCS-1457 | 44-49. BU50 |
| AGSC-12 | *Harkness* | ex-YMS-242 | 43-58, AMCU-12 (51), MHC-12 (55). Str59 |
| AGSC-13 | *James M. Gilliss* | ex-YMS-262 | 43-58, AMCU-13 (51), MHC-13 (55). Str60 |
| AGSC-14 | *Simon Newcomb* | ex-YMS-263 | 43-49, lost 09/08/49 |

**Notes:** Coastal surveying vessels, converted 1944.

**Details:** 4,100 tons; 400 (wl), 426 (oa)×58×15′6; two
shafts, turbine-electric, SHP 6,000=16.5′.t

| | | | | |
|---|---|---|---|---|
| AGS-15 ____ *Tanner* _____ | Walsh-Kaiser ____ | 05/01/45 ___ | 46-69. Str69 |
| AGS-16 ____ *Maury* _____ | Walsh-Kaiser ____ | 31/01/45 ___ | 46-69. BU63 |

**Notes:** Former attack cargo ships *Pamina* and *Renate* (AKA-34 and 36), converted 1946

---

**Reclassified Vessels:**

AGS-17 ____ *Pursuit* _____ see AM-108

AGS-18 ____ *Requisite* _____ see AM-109

AGS-19 ____ *Sheldrake* _____ see AM-62

AGS-20 ____ *Prevail* _____ see AM-107

AGS-24 ____ *Serrano* _____ see ATF-112

AGS-28 ____ *Towhee* _____ see MSF-388

AGS-30 ____ *San Pablo* _____ see AVP-30

AGS-35 ____ *Sgt George D. Keathley* see APC-117

AGS-36 ____ *Coastal Crusader* _____ see AGM-16 (not converted)

AGS-37 ____ *Twin Falls* _____ see AGM-11 (not converted)

AGS-50 ____ *Rehoboth* _____ see AVP-50

---

**Details:** 7,190 tons, 13,050f/l; 436 (wl), 455'3
(oa)×62×28'6; one shaft, steam turbines,
SHP 8,500=17kt; 104 crew

| | | | |
|---|---|---|---|
| AGS-21 ____ *Bowditch* _____ | Oregon _____ | 30/06/45 ___ | 58- |
| ex-*South Bend Victory* | | | |
| AGS-22 ____ *Dutton* _____ | Oregon _____ | 08/05/45 ___ | 58- |
| ex-*Tuskegee Victory* | | | |
| AGS-23 ____ *Michelson* _____ | Oregon _____ | 14/06/44 ___ | 58-75. Str75 |
| ex-*Joliet Victory* | | | |

**Notes:** Victory ships acquired and converted 1958.

---

**Details:** 1,200 tons; 191'6 (wl), 209 (oa)×39×15; one
shaft, diesel-electric, SHP 1,200=15kt; 41 crew

| | | | |
|---|---|---|---|
| AGS-25 ____ *Kellar* _____ | Marietta _____ | 30/07/64 ___ | 69-72. Portuguese *Almeida Carvalho* (72) |
| AGS-31 ____ *S. P. Lee* _____ | Defoe _____ | 19/10/67 ___ | 68-73. AG-192 (70) |

**Notes:** Prior to completion *Kellar* sunk in hurricane at
New Orleans, 09/09/65 and completed by Boland
Machine and Mfg Co 1969. *S. P. Lee* loaned to US
Geological Survey 1974.

*Below:*
**S. P. Lee (T-AGS-31), a surveying ship, seen in
1970.** *A. & J. Pavia*

**Details:** 1,935 tons, 2,540f/l; 261'4 (wl), 285'3
(oa)×48×15; one shaft, diesel-electric,
SHP 3,600=15kt; 79 crew

| AGS-26 | Silas Bent | American; Lorain | 16/05/64 | 66- |
|---|---|---|---|---|
| AGS-27 | Kane | Christy | 20/11/65 | 66- |
| AGS-33 | Wilkes | Defoe | 31/07/69 | 71- |
| AGS-34 | Wyman | Defoe | 30/10/69 | 71- |

**Notes:** FY63-67. Differ in detail.

---

**Details:** 2,640 tons, 4,200f/l; 393'3 (oa)×54×16; one
shaft, diesels, SHP 3,600=15kt; 175 crew

| AGS-29 | Chauvenet | Upper Clyde | 13/05/68 | 70- |
|---|---|---|---|---|
| AGS-32 | Harkness | Upper Clyde | 12/06/68 | 71- |

**Notes:** FY65-66. Helicopter hangar and deck.

---

**Details:** 3,127 tons, 17,874f/l; 564 (oa)×76×32'9; one
shaft, steam turbine, SHP 19,250=20kt; 110 crew

| AGS-38 | H. H. Hess | National | 30/05/64 | 76- |
|---|---|---|---|---|
| | ex-Canada Mail | | | |

**Notes:** Acquired 1975 to replace Michelson.

# TECHNICAL RESEARCH SHIPS

| AGTR-1 | Oxford | na | 7,330/45 | 61-69, BU70 |
|---|---|---|---|---|
| | ex-Samuel R. Aitkin | | | |
| AGTR-2 | Georgetown | na | 7,330/45 | 63-69. Str69 |
| | ex-Robert W. Hart | | | |
| AGTR-3 | Jamestown | na | 7,330/45 | 63-69. Str69 |
| | ex-J. Howland Gardner | | | |
| AGTR-4 | Belmont | na | na/44 | 64-70. BU70 |
| | ex-Iran Victory | | | |
| AGTR-5 | Liberty | na | na/45 | 64-68. BU70 |
| | ex-Simmons Victory | | | |

**Notes:** ELINT ships. 'Liberty' and 'Victory' ships
acquired as AG-159, 165-168, reclassified 1964. Liberty
damaged by Israeli torpedo boats and air attack,
08/06/67.

# HOSPITAL SHIPS

**Details:** 11,400 tons, 15,400f/l; 496 (wl), 529
(oa)×71'6×24; one shaft, steam turbines,
SHP 9,000=18.3kt; 570 crew

| AH-12 | Haven | Sun | 24/06/44 | 50-67. Merchant Alaskan (69) |
|---|---|---|---|---|
| AH-13 | Benevolence | Sun | 10/07/44 | 45-50. Lost 25/08/50 |
| AH-14 | Tranquillity | Sun | 25/07/44 | Str61 |

*Above:* **The hospital ship *Sanctuary* (AH-17).**

| | | | | |
|---|---|---|---|---|
| AH-15 | *Consolation* | Sun | 01/08/44 | 45-55. Merchant *Hope* (60) |
| AH-16 | *Repose* | Sun | 08/08/44 | 45-49, 50-54, 65-70. BU74 |
| AH-17 | *Sanctuary* | Sun | 15/08/44 | 66-74 |

**Notes:** Carry 800 patients. *Sanctuary* converted to dependent support ship 1972.

---

**Details:** 106,600 tons f/l; 894 (oa)×105'9×49'3; one shaft, steam turbines, SHP 24,500=17.5kt; 597 crew

| | | | | |
|---|---|---|---|---|
| AH-19 | *Mercy* | National | 00/08/75 | na |
| | ex-*Worth* | | | |
| AH-20 | *Comfort* | National | 12/02/76 | na |
| | ex-*Rose City* | | | |

**Notes:** Tankers being converted by National Steel, 1985-86. Will provide support for RDF, to be held in readiness at US ports with skeleton crews.

# DEGAUSSING VESSELS

| | | | |
|---|---|---|---|
| ADG-8 | *Lodestone* | ex-PCE-876 | Str75 |
| ADG-9 | *Magnet* | ex-PCE-879 | Str75 |
| ADG-10 | *Deperm* | ex-PCE-883 | Str75 |
| ADG-11 | *Ampere* | ex-AM-359 | -58. Sold 61 |
| ADG-383 | *Surfbird* | ex-MSF-383 | 57-70. BU75 |

**Notes:** YDG-8-11 reclassified ADG-8-11, 1947, had been converted while building 1944-45. *Surfbird* converted 1957.

*Below:*
**Originally a minesweeper of the 'Auk' class, the *Surfbird* (ADG-383) was converted to a degaussing vessel.**

# NET LAYING SHIPS

**Details:** 560 tons, 760f/l; 146 (wl) 163'2 (oa)×30'6×13;
one shaft, diesel-electric, SHP 1,000=13kt; 1×3in/50
gun; complement 48

| | | | | |
|---|---|---|---|---|
| AN-6 | *Aloe* | Lake Washington | 11/01/41 | Str62 |
| AN-7 | *Ash* | Lake Washington | 15/02/41 | Str62 |
| AN-8 | *Boxwood* | Lake Washington | 08/03/41 | Str62 |
| AN-9 | *Butternut* | Lake Washington | 10/05/41 | 41-58. ANL-9 (69), YAG-60 (69), Str71 |
| AN-10 | *Catalpa* | Commercial | 22/02/41 | 50-55. Str62 |
| AN-11 | *Chestnut* | Commercial | 15/03/41 | Str62 |
| AN-12 | *Cinchona* | Commercial | 02/07/41 | Str62 |
| AN-13 | *Buckeye* | Commercial | 26/07/41 | Str63 |
| AN-14 | *Buckthorn* | General | 27/03/41 | Str63 |
| AN-15 | *Ebony* | General | 04/06/41 | Str62 |
| AN-16 | *Eucalyptus* | General | 03/07/41 | Str62 |
| AN-19 | *Holly* | Marietta | 17/04/41 | Str62 |
| AN-20 | *Elder* | Marietta | 19/06/41 | 41-59. Str62 |
| AN-22 | *Locust* | American; Lorain | 01/02/41 | French *Locuste* (66) |
| AN-24 | *Mango* | American; Cleve | 22/02/41 | Str62 |
| AN-26 | *Mimosa* | American; Cleve | 15/03/41 | Str62 |
| AN-27 | *Mulberry* | American; Cleve | 26/03/41 | 42-60. Ecuadorian *Orion* (65) |
| AN-28 | *Palm* | American; Lorain | 08/02/41 | Str62 |
| AN-29 | *Hazel* | American; Lorain | 15/02/41 | 42-58. Str62 |
| AN-30 | *Redwood* | American; Lorain | 22/02/41 | Str62 |
| AN-31 | *Rosewood* | American; Lorain | 01/03/41 | French *Libellule* (69) |
| AN-32 | *Sandalwood* | American; Lorain | 16/03/41 | French *Luciole* (67) |
| AN-33 | *Nutmeg* | American; Lorain | 13/03/41 | Str62 |
| AN-34 | *Teaberry* | Mathis | 24/05/41 | 52-61. Merchant *Pacific Salvor* (62) |
| AN-35 | *Teak* | Mathis | 26/07/41 | Str62 |

*Above:*
**The net-laying ship *Cohoes* (ANL-78).**

**Details:** 680 tons, 850f/l; 146 (wl) 168'6 (oa)×33'10×12;
one shaft, diesel-electric, SHP 1,500=12kt; 1×3in/50
gun; 46 crew

| | | | | |
|---|---|---|---|---|
| AN-78 | *Cohoes* | Commercial | 29/11/44 | 68-72. ANL-78 (69), sold 73 |
| AN-79 | *Etlah* | Commercial | 16/12/44 | 51-60, Dominican *Cambiaso* (76) |

| AN-80 | Suncock | Commercial | 16/02/45 | Merchant *Grass Valley* (62) |
|---|---|---|---|---|
| AN-81 | Manayunk | Commercial | 30/03/45 | Merchant *Heron* (73) |
| AN-82 | Marietta | Commercial | 27/04/45 | 52-59, Venezuelan *Puerto Santo* (62) |
| AN-83 | Nahant | Commercial | 30/06/45 | 52-68, Uruguayan *Huracan* (68) |
| AN-84 | Naubuc | Marine Iron | 15/04/44 | YRST-4 (68) Str75 |
| AN-85 | Oneota | Marine Iron | 27/05/44 | Str63 |
| AN-86 | Passaconaway | Marine Iron | 30/06/44 | Dominican *Separacion* (76) |
| AN-87 | Passaic | LD Smith | 29/06/44 | Dominican *Calderas* (76) |
| AN-88 | Shackamaxon | LD Smith | 09/09/44 | Merchant *Hafa Adai* (68) |
| AN-89 | Tonawanda | LD Smith | 14/11/44 | 52-59. Haitian *Dessalines* (60) |
| AN-90 | Tunxis | Zenith | 18/08/44 | 53-55. Venezuelan *Puerto De Nutrias* (63) |
| AN-91 | Waxsaw | Zenith | 15/09/44 | 45-60. Venezuelan *Puerto Miranda* (63) |
| AN-92 | Yazoo | Zenith | 18/10/44 | 45-62. Str63 |

# BARRACKS SHIPS

| APB-35 | Benewah | 51-56, 67-71. IX-311 (71), Str73 |
|---|---|---|
| APB-36 | Colleton | 67-69. Str73 |
| APB-37 | Echols | 76- . IX-504 (75) |
| APB-38 | Marlboro | BU65 |
| APB-39 | Mercer | 45-56, 68-69, 75- . IX-502 (75) |
| APB-40 | Nueces | 45-55, 68-71, 75- . IX-503 (75) |

*ex-LST*

| APB-41 | Wythe | 575 | Str59 |
|---|---|---|---|
| APB-42 | Yavapai | 676 | Str59 |
| APB-43 | Yolo | 677 | Str59 |
| APB-44 | Presque Isle | 678 | Str59 |
| APB-45 | Blackford | 1111 | Str60 |
| APB-46 | Dorchester | 1112 | Str73 |
| APB-47 | Kingman | 1113 | Str77 |
| APB-48 | Vanderburgh | 1114 | Str72 |
| APB-49 | Accomac | 710 | Str59 |
| APB-50 | Cameron | 928 | Str59 |
| APB-51 | Dupage | na | Str59 |

ex-*John W. Weeks*

**Notes:** APB-35-40 built 1945 to LST design. APB 41-50 were converted LSTs. 51 was a converted Liberty Ship, acquired 1951.

# CABLE REPAIR SHIPS

**Details:** 4,410 tons, 7,400f/l; 322 (wl) 370 (oa)×47×18 (6: 362oa); two shafts, VTE, IHP 4,800=14kt (1980: diesel-electric, SHP 4,000=14kt).

| ARC-2 | Neptune | Pusey & Jones | 22/08/45 | 53- |
|---|---|---|---|---|
| | ex-*William H. G. Bullard* | | | |
| ARC-6 | Albert J. Myer | Pusey & Jones | 07/11/45 | 63- |

**Notes:** *Neptune* acquired 1953, *Myer* transferred from Army 1963. FRAM refit 1978-80 and 1980-82: reconstructed and re-engined.

*Above:*
**Thor (ARC-4)**, a cable-laying and repair ship.

*Right:*
**Zeus (T-ARC-7)**, the Navy's newest cable repair ship, on trials in October 1983. The funnels are side-by-side.
*Official US Navy*

**Details:** 4,087 tons, 7,040f/l; 400 (wl) 438 (oa)×58×19′3; two shafts, turbo-electric, SHP 6,000=17kt

| | | | | |
|---|---|---|---|---|
| ARC-3 | *Aeolus* | Walsh-Kaiser | 20/05/45 | 55-85. Str85 |
| ARC-4 | *Thor* | Walsh-Kaiser | 08/06/45 | 55-74, Str78 |

**Notes:** Former Attack Cargo Ships *Turandot* (AKA-47) and *Vanadis* (AKA-49) reacquired 1955.

**Reclassified Vessels:**

| | | | |
|---|---|---|---|
| ARC-1 | *Portunus* | 52-59 | ex-LSM-275 (51), Portuguese *Medusa* (59) |
| ARC-5 | *Yamacraw* | 59-65 | ex-USCG, ex-ACM 9 |

**Details:** 8,370 tons, 14,157f/l; 502 (oa)×75×25; two shafts, diesel electric, SHP 10,200=15kt; 119 crew

| | | | |
|---|---|---|---|
| ARC-7 | *Zeus* | National | 30/10/82 | 84- |

# SALVAGE SHIPS

*Viking* (ARS-1) remained on the Navy list until 1953

**Details:** 1,530 tons, 1,950f/l; 200'6 (wl) 213'6
(oa)×39×14'8; two shafts, diesel-electric, SHP
2,400=14kt; 4×40mm guns; 120 crew

| | | | | |
|---|---|---|---|---|
| ARS-5 | *Diver* | Basalt | 19/12/42 | Merchant *Rescue* (49) |
| ARS-6 | *Escape* | Basalt | 22/11/42 | 51-78. USCG (80) |
| ARS-7 | *Grapple* | Basalt | 31/12/42 | 51-77. Taiwan *Tai Hu* (77) |
| ARS-8 | *Preserver* | Basalt | 01/04/43 | 50- |
| ARS-19 | *Cable* | Basalt | 01/04/43 | Target 77 |
| ARS-20 | *Chain* | Basalt | 03/06/43 | AGOR-17 (67), Str77 |
| ARS-21 | *Curb* | Basalt | 24/04/43 | Str81 |
| ARS-22 | *Current* | Basalt | 25/09/43 | 51-72. Str73 |
| ARS-23 | *Deliver* | Basalt | 25/09/43 | 44-79. Korean *Gumi* (79) |
| ARS-24 | *Grasp* | Basalt | 31/07/43 | 50-78. Korean *Chang Won* (78) |
| ARS-25 | *Safeguard* | Basalt | 10/11/43 | 52-79. Turkish *Isin* (79) |
| ARS-27 | *Snatch* | Basalt | 08/04/44 | AGOR-18 (67), Str70 |
| ARS-33 | *Clamp* | Basalt | 24/10/42 | Str63 |
| ARS-34 | *Gear* | Basalt | 24/10/42 | Str81 |
| ARS-38 | *Bolster* | Basalt | 23/12/44 | 45- |
| ARS-39 | *Conserver* | Basalt | 27/01/45 | 45- |
| ARS-40 | *Hoist* | Basalt | 31/03/45 | 45- |
| ARS-41 | *Opportune* | Basalt | 31/03/45 | 45- |
| ARS-42 | *Reclaimer* | Basalt | 25/06/45 | 45- |
| ARS-43 | *Recovery* | Basalt | 04/08/45 | 46- |

**Notes:** 19 and 21 loaned to Maritime Commission
1947, 34 and 27 in 1953 and 1960. *Clamp* Str63,
re-acquired 1973.

*Below:*
**The salvage vessel *Conserver* (ARS-39) entering
Pearl Harbor in July 1960.** *Official US Navy*

**Details:** 2,880 tonsf/l; 255×50×15; two shafts, diesel;
   BHP 4,200=14kt; 2×20mm guns; 87 crew

| | | | | |
|---|---|---|---|---|
| ARS-50 | *Safeguard* | Peterson | 12/11/83 | 85- |
| ARS-51 | *Grasp* | Peterson | 21/04/84 | 85- |
| ARS-52 | *Salvor* | Peterson | 28/07/84 | na |
| ARS-53 | *Grapple* | Peterson | 08/12/84 | na |

# SUBMARINE RESCUE SHIPS

**Details:** 1,780 tons, 2,140f/l; 240 (wl) 251'4
   (oa)×44×14'10; one shaft, diesel-electric, SHP
   3,000=14.9kt; 2×3in/50, 2×40mm guns; 102 crew

| | | | | |
|---|---|---|---|---|
| ASR-7 | *Chanticleer* | Moore | 29/05/42 | 42-70. Str73 |
| ASR-8 | *Coucal* | Moore | 29/05/42 | 43-77. Target 77 |
| ASR-9 | *Florikan* | Moore | 14/06/42 | 43- |
| ASR-10 | *Greenlet* | Moore | 12/07/42 | 43-70. Turkish *Akin* (70) |
| ASR-13 | *Kittiwake* | Savannah | 10/07/45 | 46- |
| ASR-14 | *Petrel* | Savannah | 26/09/45 | 46- |
| ASR-15 | *Sunbird* | Savannah | 03/04/46 | 50- |
| ASR-16 | *Tringa* | Savannah | 25/06/46 | 47-77. Str77 |

**Notes:** Large tug type vessels.

*Right:*
**Kittiwake (ASR-13), a
submarine rescue vessel, in
1961.** *Marius Bar*

**Details:** 1,235 tons; 195 (wl) 205 (oa)×38'6×15'4; one
   shaft, diesel-electric, SHP 3,000=17kt; 1×3in/50,
   4×40mm guns

| | | | | |
|---|---|---|---|---|
| ASR-12 | *Penguin* | Charleston Sb | 20/07/43 | 52-69. Merchant *Percheron* (74) |
| ASR-19 | *Bluebird* | Charleston Sb | 15/02/46 | 46-50. Turkish *Kurtaran* (50) |
| ASR-20 | *Skylark* | Charleston Sb | 19/03/46 | 51-73. Brazilian *Gastao Moutinho* (73) |

**Notes:** Former fleet tugs converted while under
construction.

---

**Details:** 2,725 tons, 4,200f/l; 251 (oa)×86×21'6; two
   shafts, diesel, SHP 6,000=15kt; 2×3in/50 guns; 181
   crew

| | | | | |
|---|---|---|---|---|
| ASR-21 | *Pigeon* | Alabama | 13/08/69 | 73- |

197

ASR-22 _____ *Ortolan* _____ Alabama _____ 10/09/70 ____ 73-

**Notes:** FY67-68. Largest catamaran ships, beam of
each hull 26ft. Built to carry DSRV. Armament removed.

*Left:*
**The submarine rescue vessel**
***Ortolan* (ASR-22), with a**
**catamaran hull.**
*Martin E. Holbrook*

# FLEET TUGS

**Details:** 1,235 tons, 1,675f/l; 195 (wl) 205
(oa)×38'6×15'4; one shaft, diesel-electric, SHP
3,000=17kt; 1×3in/50, 4×40mm guns; 85 crew

| | | | | |
|---|---|---|---|---|
| ATF-67 | *Apache* | Charleston SB | 06/05/42 | 51-74. Taiwan *Ta Wan* (74) |
| ATF-68 | *Arapaho* | Charleston SB | 22/06/42 | Argentine *Cdte General Zapiola* (61) |
| ATF-69 | *Chippewa* | Charleston SB | 25/07/42 | Str69 |
| ATF-70 | *Choctaw* | Charleston SB | 18/10/42 | Colombian *Pedro De Heredia* (60) |
| ATF-71 | *Hopi* | Charleston SB | 07/09/42 | 43-55. Str63 |
| ATF-72 | *Kiowa* | Charleston SB | 05/11/42 | 43-72. Dominican *Macorix* (72) |
| ATF-73 | *Menominee* | United Eng | 14/02/42 | Indonesian *Rakata* (61) |
| ATF-74 | *Pawnee* | United Eng | 31/03/42 | Str62 |
| ATF-75 | *Sioux* | United Eng | 27/05/42 | 52-72. Turkish *Gazal* (72) |
| ATF-76 | *Ute* | United Eng | 25/06/42 | 51-80. USCG (80) |
| ATF-81 | *Bannock* | Charleston SB | 07/01/43 | 51-55. Merchant (62) |
| ATF-82 | *Carib* | Charleston SB | 07/02/43 | Str63; Colombian *Sebastian de Belalcazar* (79) |
| ATF-83 | *Chickasaw* | United Eng | 23/07/42 | 43-66. Taiwan *Ta Tung* (66) |
| ATF-84 | *Cree* | United Eng | 17/08/42 | 43-78. Target 78 |
| ATF-85 | *Lipan* | United Eng | 17/09/42 | 43-80. USCG (80) |
| ATF-86 | *Mataco* | United Eng | 14/10/42 | 43-77. Str77 |
| ATF-87 | *Moreno* | Cramp | 09/07/42 | Str61 |
| ATF-88 | *Narragansett* | Cramp | 08/08/42 | Str61 |
| ATF-90 | *Pinto* | Cramp | 05/01/43 | Peruvian *Rios* (60) |
| ATF-91 | *Seneca* | Cramp | 02/02/43 | 43-71 |
| ATF-92 | *Tawasa* | Commercial | 22/02/43 | 43-75. Str75 |
| ATF-93 | *Tekesta* | Commercial | 20/03/43 | 43-50, 58-60. Chilean *Yelcho* (60) |
| ATF-94 | *Yuma* | Commercial | 17/07/43 | 43-55, 58-59. Pakistani *Madadgar* (59) |
| ATF-96 | *Abnaki* | Charleston SB | 22/04/43 | 43-78. Mexican *Yaqui* (78) |
| ATF-97 | *Alsea* | Charleston SB | 22/05/43 | 43-55. Str62 |
| ATF-98 | *Arikara* | Charleston SB | 22/06/43 | 44-71. Chilean *Sergente Aldea* (71) |

ATF-100 ____ Chowanoc _____ Charleston SB ____ 20/08/43 ___ 44-77. Ecuadorian *Chimborazo* (77)
ATF-101 ____ Cocopa _____ Charleston SB ____ 05/10/43 ___ 44-78. Mexican *Seri* (78)
ATF-102 ____ Hidatsa _____ Charleston SB ____ 29/12/43 ___ 44-48. Colombian *Rodrigo De Bastidas* (79)
ATF-103 ____ Hitchiti _____ Charleston SB ____ 29/01/44 ___ 51-78. Mexican *Cora* (78)
ATF-104 ____ Jicarilla _____ Charleston SB ____ 25/02/44 ___ 44-50. Colombia (79)
ATF-105 ____ Moctobi _____ Charleston SB ____ 25/03/44 ___ 50-85
ATF-106 ____ Molala _____ United Eng _____ 12/12/42 ___ 43-78. Mexican *Otomi* (78)
ATF-107 ____ Munsee _____ United Eng _____ 21/01/43 ___ 43-69. Merchant *Oceanic* (70)
ATF-108 ____ Pakana _____ United Eng _____ 03/03/43 ___ 43-48. Merchant *Virginia City* (66)
ATF-109 ____ Potawatomi _____ United Eng _____ 03/04/43 ___ 43-48. Chilean *Janequeo* (63), lost 15/08/65
ATF-110 ____ Quapaw _____ United Eng _____ 15/05/43 ___ 44-48, 50-85
ATF-111 ____ Sarsi _____ United Eng _____ 12/06/43 ___ 44-52. Lost 27/08/52
ATF-112 ____ Serrano _____ United Eng _____ 24/07/43 ___ 44-50, 60-70. AGS-24 (60) BU72
ATF-113 ____ Takelma _____ United Eng _____ 18/09/43 ___ 44-83
ATF-114 ____ Tawakoni _____ United Eng _____ 29/10/43 ___ 44-78. Taiwan *Ta Han* (78)
ATF-115 ____ Tenino _____ United Eng _____ 10/01/44 ___ Str62
ATF-116 ____ Tolowa _____ United Eng _____ 17/05/44 ___ Venezuelan *Felipe Larrazabal* (62),
                                                                                    lost 08/70
ATF-118 ____ Wenatchee _____ United Eng _____ 07/09/44 ___ Str62
ATF-148 ____ Achomawi _____ Charleston SB ____ 14/06/44 ___ Str62
ATF-149 ____ Atakapa _____ Charleston SB ____ 11/07/44 ___ 51-81
ATF-150 ____ Avoyel _____ Charleston SB ____ 09/08/44 ___ USCG (56)
ATF-151 ____ Chawasha _____ Charleston SB ____ 15/09/44 ___ Str63
ATF-152 ____ Cahuilla _____ Charleston SB ____ 02/11/44 ___ Argentine *Cdte Gen Irigoyen* (61)
ATF-154 ____ Chimariko _____ Charleston SB ____ 30/12/44 ___ Str63
ATF-155 ____ Cusabo _____ Charleston SB ____ 26/02/45 ___ Ecuadorian *Los Rios* (60)
ATF-156 ____ Luiseno _____ Charleston SB ____ 17/03/45 ___ 45-75. Argentine *Francisco de Churruca*
                                                                                    (75)
ATF-157 ____ Nipmuc _____ Charleston SB ____ 12/04/45 ___ 45-78. Venezuelan *Antonio Picardi* (78)
ATF-158 ____ Mosopelea _____ Charleston SB ____ 07/05/45 ___ 45-81
ATF-159 ____ Paiute _____ Charleston SB ____ 04/06/45 ___ 45-85
ATF-160 ____ Papago _____ Charleston SB ____ 21/06/45 ___ 45-85
ATF-161 ____ Salinan _____ Charleston SB ____ 20/07/45 ___ 46-78. Venezuelan *Miguel Rodriguez* (78)
ATF-162 ____ Shakori _____ Charleston SB ____ 09/08/45 ___ 45-80. Taiwan (80)
ATF-163 ____ Utina _____ Charleston SB ____ 31/08/45 ___ 46-71. Venezuelan *Felipe Larrazabal* (71)

**Notes:** *Serrano* converted to surveying vessel 1960.
*Cree* damaged in accidental bombing by USN aircraft
18 January 1978.

*Below:*
**The fleet tug *Utina* (ATF-163).**

**Details:** 2,200 tons f/l; 225 (oa)×42×15; two shafts,
   diesels, BHP 4,500=15kt; 21 crew

ATF-166 ____ *Powhatan* _____ Marinette _____ 06/06/78 ___ 79-
ATF-167 ____ *Narragansett* _____ Marinette _____ 28/11/78 ___ 79-
ATF-168 ____ *Catawba* _____ Marinette _____ 22/09/79 ___ 80-
ATF-169 ____ *Navajo* _____ Marinette _____ 20/12/79 ___ 80-
ATF-170 ____ *Mohawk* _____ Marinette _____ 05/04/80 ___ 80-
ATF-171 ____ *Sioux* _____ Marinette _____ 30/10/80 ___ 81-
ATF-172 ____ *Apache* _____ Marinette _____ 20/12/80 ___ 81-

**Notes:** FY75-78. Operated by MSC.

*Right:*
**Powhatan (T-ATF-169), a fleet
tug, in August 1981. Notice
the large open space aft and
side-by-side funnels.**
*Official US Navy*

# AUXILIARY OCEAN TUGS

**Details:** 610 tons, 860f/l; 134'6 (wl), 143
   (oa)×33'10×13'2; one shaft, diesel-electric,
   SHP 1,500=13kt; 1×3in/50 gun; 45 crew

ATA-121 ____ *Sotoyomo* _____ Levingston _____ 09/10/42 ___ 51-55. Mexico (63)
ATA-123 ____ *Iuka* _____ Levingston _____ 20/12/42 ___ Str 62
ATA-174 ____ *Wateree* _____ Levingston _____ 18/11/43 ___ 53-55. Peruvian *Unanue* (61)
ATA-175 ____ *Sonoma* _____ Levingston _____ 29/01/44 ___ Str62
ATA-176 ____ *Tonkawa* _____ Levingston _____ 01/03/44 ___ 44-56. Taiwan *Ta Sueh* (62)
ATA-178 ____ *Tunica* _____ Levingston _____ 15/06/44 ___ 44-62. Str62
ATA-179 ____ *Allegheny* _____ Levingston _____ 30/06/44 ___ 44-68. Merchant (69)
ATA-181 ____ *Accokeek* _____ Levingston _____ 27/07/44 ___ 44-72
ATA-182 ____ *Unadilla* _____ Levingston _____ 05/08/44 ___ 51-55. Str61
ATA-183 ____ *Nottoway* _____ Levingston _____ 16/08/44 ___ Str62
ATA-184 ____ *Kalmia* _____ Levingston _____ 29/08/44 ___ 52-71. Colombian *Bahia Utria* (71)
ATA-185 ____ *Koka* _____ Levingston _____ 11/09/44 ___ 44-71. Samoan *Talatiga* (71)
ATA-186 ____ *Cahokia* _____ Levingston _____ 18/09/44 ___ 44-71. Taiwan *Ta Teng* (72)
ATA-187 ____ *Salish* _____ Levingston _____ 29/09/44 ___ 44-72. Argentine *Comodoro Somellera* (72)
ATA-188 ____ *Penobscot* _____ Levingston _____ 12/10/44 ___ 44-71. Str75
ATA-189 ____ *Reindeer* _____ Levingston _____ 19/10/44 ___ Str62

Above: **Penobscot (ATA-188), an auxiliary ocean tug.**

| | | | | |
|---|---|---|---|---|
| ATA-190 | Samoset | Levingston | 26/10/44 | 45-69. Haitian *Henri Christophe* (71) |
| ATA-192 | Tillamook | Levingston | 15/11/44 | 45-71. Korean *Ian Yang* (71) |
| ATA-193 | Stallion | Levingston | 24/11/44 | 49-69. Dominican *Enriquillo* (80) |
| ATA-194 | Bagaduce | Levingston | 04/12/44 | 45-59. USCG *Modoc* (59) |
| ATA-195 | Tatnuck | Levingston | 14/12/44 | 45-71. Str71 |
| ATA-196 | Mahopac | Levingston | 21/12/44 | 45-71. Taiwan *Ta Peng* (71) |
| ATA-197 | Sunnadin | Levingston | 06/01/45 | 45-69. Merchant *Kahuna* (71) |
| ATA-198 | Keosanqua | Levingston | 17/01/45 | 45-56. Korean *Yong Mun* (62) |
| ATA-199 | Undaunted | Gulfport | 22/08/44 | Str62 |
| ATA-201 | Challenge | Gulfport | 23/09/44 | Str62 |
| ATA-202 | Wampanoag | Gulfport | 23/09/44 | USCG *Comanche* (59) |
| ATA-203 | Navigator | Gulfport | 26/10/44 | 45-60. Str62 |
| ATA-204 | Wandank | Gulfport | 09/11/44 | 52-71. Merchant (71) |
| ATA-205 | Sciota | Gulfport | 26/11/44 | Str62 |
| ATA-206 | Pinola | Gulfport | 14/12/44 | 49-56. Korean *Do Bong* (62) |
| ATA-207 | Geronimo | Gulfport | 04/01/45 | 62-69. Taiwan *Chiu Lien* (69) |
| ATA-208 | Sagamore | Gulfport | 19/01/45 | 45-72. Dominican *Caomabo* (72) |
| ATA-209 | Umpqua | Gulfport | 02/02/45 | 45-71. Colombian *Bahia Hondo* (71). Lost 13/02/75 |
| ATA-210 | Catawba | Gulfport | 15/02/45 | 45-72. Argentine *Alferez Sobral* (72) |
| ATA-211 | Navajo | Gulfport | 03/03/45 | 45-62. Merchant (68) |
| ATA-212 | Algorma | Gulfport | 20/03/45 | 45-50. Str62 |
| ATA-213 | Kewaydin | Gulfport | 09/04/45 | 45-70. Haiti (81) |

**Notes:** Named 1955. ATA-239-244 were un-numbered vessels acquired from the Army in 1950 and stricken in 1971 (ATA-244 in 1959).

# SALVAGE & RESCUE SHIPS

**Details:** 3,117 tons f/l; 282'8 (oa)×50×15'2; two shafts,
diesels, BHP 6,000=16kt; 4×20mm guns; 103 crew

| | | | | |
|---|---|---|---|---|
| ATS-1 | Edenton | Brooke Marine | 15/05/68 | 71- |
| ATS-2 | Beaufort | Brooke Marine | 20/12/68 | 72- |
| ATS-3 | Brunswick | Brooke Marine | 14/10/69 | 72- |

**Notes:** FY66-67. ATS-4-5 not built.

# AUXILIARY CRANE SHIPS

| | | | | |
|---|---|---|---|---|
| ACS-1 | Keystone State | National | 02/10/65 | 84- |
| | ex-President Harrison | | | |
| ACS-2 | Gem State | National | 22/03/65 | 86- |
| | ex-President Monroe | | | |
| ACS-3 | Grand Canyon State | National | 23/01/65 | na |
| | ex-President Polk | | | |

**Notes:** Cargo ships converted 1984-86. Conversion of
ACS-4-6 authorised 1986. These are Merchant Marine
ships and not Navy-owned.

# UNCLASSIFIED VESSELS

| | | |
|---|---|---|
| IX-13 | Hartford | 1858 frigate. Str57 |
| IX-15 | Prairie State | Former battleship *Illinois*. BU56 |
| IX-20 | Constellation | 1798 frigate. Str55 |
| IX-21 | Constitution | 1797 frigate. Number withdrawn 75 |
| IX-25 | Reina Mercedes | Spanish cruiser. BU57 |
| IX-40 | Olympia | 1895 cruiser. Str57 |
| IX-43 | Freedom | Yacht. Str68 |
| IX-47 | Vamarie | Yacht. Str55 |

*Above:*
**The former 'Cleveland' class light cruiser *Atlanta* (IX-304) operating in its role as an explosives test ship. The superstructure and masts are replicas of structures on new destroyer construction.**
*Ernest Arroyo collection*

*Below:*
**NR-1, the nuclear submersible research craft, under tow. Only 136ft long, her small size can be gauged by the crewman on the bridge.**
*Official US Navy*

| IX-48 | Highland Light | Yacht. Str65 |
|---|---|---|
| IX-49 | Spindrift | Cutter. Str52 |
| IX-87 | Saluda | Yacht, YAG-87 (68). Str74 |
| IX-205 | Callao | Captured 44. BU51 |
| IX-235 | Royono | Yacht, sold 68 |
| IX-300 | Prinz Eugen | German cruiser, sunk at Bikini 1946 |
| IX-301 | Dithmarschen | to AO-110 |
| IX-302 | na | not used |
| IX-303 | na | not used |
| IX-304 | Atlanta | ex-CL-104, explosives test vessel |
| IX-305 | Prowess | ex-M5F-280 |
| IX-306 | na | ex-FS-221, torpedo testing ship |
| IX-307 | Brier | ex-WLI-299, explosive test instrumentation vessel. Str82 |
| IX-308 | New Bedford | ex-AKL-17, torpedo testing ship |
| IX-309 | (Monob I) | Mobile listening barge, acoustic research |
| IX-310 | na | Barge |
| IX-311 | Benewah | ex-APB-38 |
| IX-501 | Elk River | ex-LSMR-501, deep sea diving and salvage test and training ship |
| IX-502 | Mercer | ex-APB-39 |
| IX-503 | Nueces | ex-APB-40 |
| IX-504 | Echols | ex-APB-37 |
| IX-505 | na | ex-YTM-759. Str77 |
| IX-506 | na | ex-YFU-82, trials tender |
| IX-507 | Gen H. J. Gaffey | ex-AP-121, barracks |
| IX-508 | na | ex-LCU-1618, satellite navigation systems trials |
| IX-509 | na | Damage control barge |
| IX-510 | Gen Wm. O. Darby | ex-AP-127, barracks |
| IX-511 | na | ex-LST-399, missile range support ship |
| | | |
| NR-1 | Groton | 25/01/69 |

**Notes:** Nuclear Submersible Research Vehicle. Equipped with lights, television cameras, and wheels for driving on the ocean floor. Able to remain on the ocean floor up to 30 days.

# US COAST GUARD

The United States Coast Guard operated in peacetime under the Treasury Department until 1967 and since then under the Department of Transportation.

All Coast Guard vessels are referred to as 'cutters', and bear numbers similar to Navy designations prefixed with the letter 'W'. Cutters less than 100ft in length are designated by five digit numbers of which the first two digits represent the vessel's length.

Since 1967 all vessels are painted with a red and blue diagonal stripe on the bow.

## HIGH ENDURANCE CUTTERS
## (Formerly Gunboats)

### 'Champlain' Class

**Displacement:** 1,979 tons
**Dimensions:** 256 (oa)×42×16
**Machinery:** Two shafts, turbine-electric, SHP 3,220=16kt

**Armament:** 1×3in/50, 2×40mm guns
**Complement:** ???

| WPG-163 | Mocoma | Staten Is | 08/10/31 | Sold 55 |
|---|---|---|---|---|
| | ex-HMS *Totland* | | | |
| | ex-USCGC *Cayuga* | | | |
| WPG-164 | Tampa | General Eng | 12/04/30 | Sold 59 |
| | ex-HMS *Banff* | | | |
| | ex-USCGC *Saranac* | | | |
| WPG-319 | Champlain | Quincy | 11/10/28 | Sold 48 |
| | ex-HMS *Sennen* | | | |
| | ex-USCGC *Champlain* | | | |
| WPG-321 | Itasca | Quincy | 16/11/29 | BU51 |
| | ex-HMS *Gorleston* | | | |
| | ex-USCGC *Itasca* | | | |

**Notes:** Survivors of 10 vessels loaned to UK in 1941.

### 'Treasury' Class

**Displacement:** 2,216 tons, 2,656f/l
**Dimensions:** 308 (wl), 327 (oa)×41×12'6
**Machinery:** Two shafts, steam turbines, SHP 6,200=20kt

**Armament:** 1×5in/38, 2×40mm guns (1980)
**Complement:** 128

| WPG-31 | Bibb | Charleston | 14/01/37 | Str85 |
|---|---|---|---|---|
| WPG-32 | Campbell | Philadelphia | 03/06/36 | Str83 |
| WPG-33 | Duane | Philadelphia | 03/06/36 | Str85 |
| WPG-35 | Ingham | Philadelphia | 03/06/36 | na |
| WPG-36 | Spencer | New York | 06/01/37 | Sold 81 |
| WPG-37 | Taney | Philadelphia | 03/06/36 | na |

**Notes:** Highly successful vessels. *Spencer* decommissioned 1974, used as stationary training ship. All reclassified WHEC 1966.

### 'Owasco' Class

**Displacement:** 1,563 tons, 1,913f/l
**Dimensions:** 255 (oa)×43×17
**Machinery:** One shaft, turbo-electric, SHP 4,000=18.4kt

**Endurance:** 12,000/10
**Armament:** 2×5in/38, 4×40mm AA guns (1×5in removed)
**Complement:** 140

| WPG-39 | Owasco | Western Pipe | 18/06/44 | Sold 74 |
|--------|--------|--------------|----------|---------|
| WPG-40 | Winnebago | Western Pipe | 02/07/44 | Sold 74 |
| WPG-41 | Chautauqua | Western Pipe | 14/05/44 | na |
| WPG-42 | Sebago | Western Pipe | 28/05/44 | Sold 72 |
| WPG-43 | Iroquois | Western Pipe | 22/10/44 | Sold 65 |
| WPG-44 | Wachusett | Western Pipe | 05/11/44 | Sold 74 |
| WPG-64 | Escanaba | Western Pipe | 23/03/45 | Sold 74 |
| WPG-65 | Winona | Western Pipe | 22/04/45 | na |
| WPG-66 | Klamath | Western Pipe | 02/09/45 | Sold |
| WPG-67 | Minnetonka | Western Pipe | 21/11/45 | na |
| WPG-68 | Androscoggin | Western Pipe | 16/09/45 | Sold 74 |
| WPG-69 | Mendota | Curtis Bay | 29/02/44 | na |
| WPG-70 | Pontchartrain | Curtis Bay | 29/02/44 | na |

**Notes:** Reclassified WHEC 1966.

*Above:*
**The 'Treasury' class cutter
Bibb (WPG-31), later
(WHEC-31), c1960.**

*Right:*
**Minnetonka (WPG-67), an
'Owasco' class cutter, in
1959.** *Danske Filmmuseum*

## 'Hamilton' Class

**Displacement:** 2,716 tons, 3,050f/l
**Dimensions:** 350 (wl), 378'3 (oa)×42'10×20
**Machinery:** Two shafts, diesel or gas turbine (CODOG), SHP 28,000=29kt

**Endurance:** 14,000/11
**Armament:** 1×5in/38, 2×71mm mortars; 6×12.75in ASW TT added
**Complement:** 155

| | | | | |
|---|---|---|---|---|
| WHEC-715 | Hamilton | Avondale | 18/12/65 | na |
| WHEC-716 | Dallas | Avondale | 01/10/66 | na |
| WHEC-717 | Mellon | Avondale | 11/02/67 | na |
| WHEC-718 | Chase | Avondale | 20/05/67 | na |
| WHEC-719 | Boutwell | Avondale | 17/06/67 | na |
| WHEC-720 | Sherman | Avondale | 23/09/67 | na |
| WHEC-721 | Gallatin | Avondale | 18/11/67 | na |
| WHEC-722 | Morgenthau | Avondale | 10/02/68 | na |
| WHEC-723 | Rush | Avondale | 16/11/68 | na |
| WHEC-724 | Munro | Avondale | 05/12/70 | na |
| WHEC-725 | Jarvis | Avondale | 24/04/71 | na |
| WHEC-726 | Midgett | Avondale | 04/09/71 | na |

**Notes:** 36 units were originally planned. Superstructure of aluminium, helicopter hangar and flight deck aft of twin stacks. *Jarvis* struck a reef in Iliuliuk Bay, Alaska and was badly damaged 15/11/72. 5in gun replaced by 76mm Oto Melara gun from 1985. FRAM programme for these ships will commence in 1985.

*Below::*

**The 'Hamilton' class high endurance cutter *Chase* (WHEC-718), wearing the new paint scheme introduced in 1967. Notice the helicopter flight deck aft and the twin stacks built into the superstructure.**

# MEDIUM ENDURANCE CUTTERS

**Displacement:** 220 tons
**Dimensions:** 125 (oa)×23'6×9
**Machinery:** Two shafts, diesel, BHP 800=11kt

**Armament:** 1×3in/50 gun
**Complement:** 38

| | | | | |
|---|---|---|---|---|
| WPC-125 | Active | NY Sbdg | 30/11/26 | Sold 62 |
| WPC-126 | Agassiz* | NY Sbdg | 30/11/26 | Str69 |
| WPC-127 | Alert* | NY Sbdg | 30/11/26 | Sold 69 |
| WPC-129 | Bonham | NY Sbdg | 30/11/26 | Sold 59 |

*Right:*
**Marion (WMEC-145), a medium endurance cutter of the 'Active' class.**

| | | | | |
|---|---|---|---|---|
| WPC-130 | Boutwell | NY Sbdg | 27/01/27 | Sold 64 |
| WPC-131 | Cahoone* | NY Sbdg | 27/01/27 | Sold 69 |
| WPC-132 | Cartigan* | NY Sbdg | 27/01/27 | Sold 69 |
| WPC-133 | Colfax | NY Sbdg | 22/03/27 | Sold 56 |
| WPC-134 | Crawford | NY Sbdg | 27/01/27 | Sold 47 |
| WPC-135 | Diligence | NY Sbdg | 27/01/27 | Sold 63 |
| WPC-137 | Ewing* | NY Sbdg | 15/03/27 | Sold 69 |
| WPC-139 | Frederick Lee | NY Sbdg | 15/03/27 | Sold 66 |
| WPC-140 | General Greene* | NY Sbdg | 14/02/27 | Str68 |
| WPC-143 | Kimball* | NY Sbdg | 25/04/27 | Sold 70 |
| WPC-144 | Legare* | NY Sbdg | 14/02/27 | Sold 68 |
| WPC-145 | Marion | NY Sbdg | 15/03/27 | Sold 63 |
| WPC-146 | McLane* | NY Sbdg | 22/03/27 | Sold 69 |
| WPC-147 | Morris* | NY Sbdg | 04/04/27 | Str71 |
| WPC-153 | Travis | NY Sbdg | 18/04/27 | Sold 63 |
| WPC-154 | Vigilant | NY Sbdg | 25/04/27 | Sold 56 |
| WPC-156 | Yeaton* | NY Sbdg | 02/05/27 | Sold 70 |
| WPC-157 | Cuyahoga | NY Sbdg | 27/01/27 | WIX. Lost 20/10/78 |

**Notes:** *Reclassified WMEC, 1966. *Active, Cartigan, Crawford, Frederick Lee* and *Kimball* stationed on Great Lakes.

**Details:** 337 tons; 165 (oa)×25'3×9'6; two shafts, diesels, BHP 1,340=16kt; 2×3in/50, 2×20mm guns; 50 crew

| | | | | |
|---|---|---|---|---|
| WPC-100 | Argo | Mathis | 12/11/32 | Sold 55 |
| WPC-101 | Ariadne* | Lake Union | 21/07/34 | Sold 69 |
| WPC-102 | Atalanta | Lake Union | 16/06/34 | Sold 54 |
| WPC-103 | Aurora* | Bath | 28/11/31 | Sold 68 |
| WPC-104 | Calypso | Bath | 01/01/32 | Sold 55 |
| WPC-105 | Cyane | Lake Union | 30/08/34 | Sold 54 |
| WPC-106 | Daphne | Bath | 27/01/32 | Sold 54 |
| WPC-107 | Dione | Manitowoc | 30/06/34 | Sold 64 |
| WPC-109 | Hermes | Bath | 23/02/32 | Sold 58 |
| WPC-111 | Nemesis | Marietta | 07/07/34 | Sold 66 |
| WPC-112 | Nike | Marietta | 07/07/34 | Sold 66 |
| WPC-113 | Pandora | Manitowoc | 30/06/34 | Str59 |

WPC-114 ___ *Perseus* _____ Bath _____ 11/04/32 ___ Sold 59
WPC-116 ___ *Triton*\* _____ Marietta _____ 00/00/34 ___ Sold 69

**Notes:** \*Reclassified WMEC, 1966.

---

**Displacement:** 1,715 tons, 1,925f/l
**Dimensions:** 230 (oa)×43×14
**Machinery:** One shaft, diesel-electric,

SHP 1,800=13.5kt
**Armament:** 2×3in/50 guns, later 1×3in, 2×40mm guns
**Complement:** 106

WAG-38 ___ *Storis* _____ Toledo _____ 04/04/42 ___ na

**Notes:** Strengthened for ice breaking. Reclassified WAGB, 1966; WMEC, 1972.

**Former Navy vessels: all WMEC 1966**

|  |  | Navy Number | Transferred | Fate |
|---|---|---|---|---|
| WAT-167 ___ *Acushnet* | | ARS-9 | 1946 | WAGO (68-78) |
| WAT-168 ___ *Yocona* | | ARS-26 | 1946 | na |
| WAT-150 ___ *Avoyel* | | ATF-150 | 1946 | Str70 |
| WATF-153 ___ *Chilula* | | ATF-153 | 1946 | na |
| WATF-165 ___ *Cherokee* | | ATF-165 | 1946 | na |
| WATF-166 ___ *Tamaroa* | | ATF-166 | 1946 | na |
| WATF-194 ___ *Modoc* | | ATF-194 | 1959 | Str80 |
| WATF-202 ___ *Comanche* | | ATF-202 | 1959 | Str80 |
| WMEC-76 ___ *Ute* | | ATF-76 | 1980 | na |
| WMEC-85 ___ *Lipan* | | ATF-85 | 1980 | na |
| WMEC-6 ___ *Escape* | | ARS-6 | 1980 | na |

---

**Displacement:** 1,830 tons, 2,800f/l
**Dimensions:** 300 (wl), 310′9 (oa)×41′1×14
**Machinery:** Two shafts, diesel-electric, SHP 6,080=18kt

**Armament:** 1×5in/38, 8×40mm guns
**Complement:** 150

WAVP-370 ___ *Casco* _____ Puget Sound _____ 15/11/41 ___ Target 59
WAVP-371 ___ *Mackinac* _____ Puget Sound _____ 15/11/41 ___ Target 59
WAVP-372 ___ *Humboldt* _____ Boston _____ 17/03/41 ___ BU70
WAVP-373 ___ *Matagorda* _____ Boston _____ 18/03/41 ___ Target 59
WAVP-374 ___ *Absecon* _____ Lake Washington __ 08/03/42 ___ Vietnam *Tham Ngu Lao* (72)
WAVP-375 ___ *Chincoteague* _____ Lake Washington __ 15/04/42 ___ Vietnam *Ly Thoung Kiet* (72), Philippine *Andres Bonifacio* (76)
WAVP-376 ___ *Coos Bay* _____ Lake Washington __ 15/05/42 ___ Target 68
WAVP-377 ___ *Rockaway* _____ Associated _____ 14/02/42 ___ WAGO. Str73
WAVP-378 ___ *Half Moon* _____ Lake Washington __ 12/07/42 ___ BU70
WAVP-379 ___ *Unimak* _____ Associated _____ 27/05/42 ___ WTR
WAVP-380 ___ *Yakutat* _____ Associated _____ 02/07/42 ___ Vietnam *Tran Nhat Duat* (71). BU76
WAVP-381 ___ *Barataria* _____ Lake Washington __ 02/10/43 ___ Sold 70
WAVP-382 ___ *Bering Strait* _____ Lake Washington __ 15/01/44 ___ Vietnam *Tran Quan Khai* (71), Philippine *Diego Salang* (76)
WAVP-383 ___ *Castle Rock* _____ Lake Washington __ 11/03/44 ___ Vietnam *Tran Vinh Trong* (71), Philippine *Francisco Dagahoy* (76)
WAVP-384 ___ *Cook Inlet* _____ Lake Washington __ 13/05/44 ___ Vietnam *Tran Quoc Toan* (71). BU76
WAVP-385 ___ *Dexter* _____ Puget Sound _____ 23/05/41 ___ Target 68
ex-*Biscayne* AGC-18, AVP-11

WAVP-386 — *McCulloch* —————— Lake Washington — 10/07/43 — Vietnam *Ngo Quyen* (72), Philippine
ex-*Wachapreague* *Gregorio de Pilar* (76)
AGP-8, AVP-56

WAVP-387 — *Gresham* —————— Lake Washington — 21/08/43 — BU73
ex-*Willoughby* AGP-9,
AVP-57

**Notes:** 385-387 acquired 1946, others acquired 1948-49 on loan.

*Below:*
**Chincoteague (WAVP-375), a former seaplane tender on loan from the Navy. Notice the hedgehog forward of the bridge.** *Official US Coast Guard*

# DESTROYER ESCORTS

*Chambers, Durant, Falgout, Finch, Forster, Koiner, Lansing, Lowe, Newell, Ramsden, Richey* and *Vance* acquired on loan from Navy 1951-52, returned 1954. Numbers changed to 400 series with prefix WDE.

*Right:*
**The 'Edsall' class escort *Richey* (WDE-485), seen in Coast Guard paint scheme in 1958.** *Ernest Arroyo collection*

**Displacement:** 950 tons, 1,007f/l
**Dimensions:** 200 (wl), 210'6 (oa)×34×10'6
**Machinery:** Two shafts, diesel and gas turbines,

SHP 5,000 = 18kt (620-630, diesel only)
**Armament:** 1×3in/50, 2×40mm guns
**Complement:** 84

| | | | | |
|---|---|---|---|---|
| WMEC-615 _ *Reliance* | Todd; Houston | 25/05/63 | WTR (75-82) |
| WMEC-616 _ *Diligence* | Todd; Houston | 20/07/63 | na |
| WMEC-617 _ *Vigilant* | Todd; Houston | 23/12/63 | na |
| WMEC-618 _ *Active* | Christy | 31/07/65 | na |
| WMEC-619 _ *Confidence* | Curtis Bay | 08/05/65 | na |
| WMEC-620 _ *Resolute* | American; Lorain | 30/04/66 | na |
| WMEC-621 _ *Valiant* | American; Lorain | 14/01/67 | na |
| WMEC-622 _ *Courageous* | American; Lorain | 18/03/67 | na |
| WMEC-623 _ *Steadfast* | American; Lorain | 24/06/67 | na |
| WMEC-624 _ *Dauntless* | American; Lorain | 21/10/67 | na |
| WMEC-625 _ *Venturous* | Curtis Bay | 11/11/67 | na |
| WMEC-626 _ *Dependable* | American; Lorain | 10/06/67 | na |
| WMEC-627 _ *Vigorous* | American; Lorain | 04/05/68 | na |
| WMEC-628 _ *Durable* | Curtis Bay | 29/04/67 | na |
| WMEC-629 _ *Decisive* | Curtis Bay | 14/12/67 | na |
| WMEC-630 _ *Alert* | American; Lorain | 19/10/68 | na |

**Notes:** Helicopter deck, no funnel.

*Left:*
**Vigilant (WMEC-617), a 'Reliance' class cutter, with a helicopter landing on deck aft.** *Official US Coast Guard*

# 'Bear' Class

**Displacement:** 1,820 tons f/l
**Dimensions:** 255 (wl), 270 (oa)×38×13′6
**Machinery:** Two shafts, diesels, SHP 7,000=19.5kt
**Endurance:** 6,370/15
**Armament:** 1×76mm/62 gun
**Complement:** 98

| | | | |
|---|---|---|---|
| WMEC-901 _ *Bear* | Tacoma | 25/09/80 | na |
| WMEC-902 _ *Tampa* | Tacoma | 19/03/81 | na |
| WMEC-903 _ *Harriet Lane* | Tacoma | 06/02/82 | na |
| WMEC-904 _ *Northland* | Tacoma | 07/05/82 | na |
| WMEC-905 _ *Spencer* | Derecktor | 17/04/84 | na |
| WMEC-906 _ *Seneca* | Derecktor | 17/04/84 | na |
| WMEC-907 _ *Escanaba* | Derecktor | 06/02/85 | na |
| WMEC-908 _ *Tahoma* | Derecktor | 06/02/85 | na |
| WMEC-909 _ *Campbell* | Derecktor | Building | na |
| WMEC-810 _ *Thetis* | Derecktor | Building | na |
| WMEC-911 _ *Forward* | Derecktor | Building | na |
| WMEC-912 _ *Legare* | Derecktor | Building | na |
| WMEC-913 _ *Mohawk* | Derecktor | Building | na |

**Notes:** Officially known as 'Famous' class. For long range at low speeds. Space provided for Harpoon missiles and Phalanx.

*Right:*
**Bear (WMEC-901) was the first of a new class of cutters named after famous Coast Guard cutters of the past. She carries a 3in gun forward and a helicopter deck aft.**
*Official Fifth Coast Guard District*

# SURFACE EFFECTS SHIPS

**Details:** 100 tons; 110 (oa)×39; diesel, BHP 2,900=33kt; 14 crew

WSES-1 _____ *Dorado* _____ Bell-Halter _____ 00/12/79 ____ Returned to USN 81

**Notes:** Designed to skim across the water on great bubbles, they are neither air-cushion vehicles nor hydrofoils.

---

**Details:** 145 tons; 110 (oa)×39×8'4; two shafts, diesels, BHP 3,200=30kt ; 2×mg; 18 crew

|  |  |  | Commissioned |  |
|---|---|---|---|---|
| WSES-2 | *Sea Hawk* | Bell-Halter | 16/10/82 | na |
| WSES-3 | *Shearwater* | Bell-Halter | 16/10/82 | na |
| WSES-4 | *Petrel* | Bell-Halter | 17/06/83 | na |

**Notes:** Improved *Dorado*. Used for anti-drug patrol in the Caribbean.

---

WPBH-1 _____ *Flagstaff* _____ ex-PGH 1 (76)

**Notes:** Transferred from USN 1976.

# PATROL BOATS

**Details:** 105 tons; 95 (oa)×20×6; two shafts, diesels, BHP 2,324=20kt; 1×81mm mortar, 1×MG; 14 crew

WPB-95300 to WPB-95335

**Notes:** Large patrol craft with 'Cape' names, designed for search and rescue and port security. All built at Curtis Bay 1953-59, named 1964. Steel hulls. Two transferred to Ethiopia and new units built; one transferred to Haiti and nine to South Korea. Additional boats of this type (not included in Coast Guard list) were built for Iran (four), Thailand (four) and Saudi Arabia (one).

**Details:** 67 tons; 83 (oa)×18×6; two shafts, diesels, BHP 1,600=20kt; 1×81mm mortar, 1×MG; 8 crew

WPB-82301 to WPB-82379

**Notes:** Small patrol craft with 'Point' names, designed for search and rescue and law enforcement. Built 1960-70, named 1964. 26 boats of this class were transferred to South Vietnam 1969-70. All built at Curtis Bay. Steel hulls.

---

**Details:** 161 tons; 110 (oa)×21×7'3; two shafts, diesels, BHP 6,000=26kt; 16 crew.

WPB-1301-1316: *Farallon, Manitou, Matagorda, Maui, Monhegan, Nunivak, Ocracoke, Vashon, Aquidneck, Mustang, Naushon, Sanibel, Edisto, Sapelo, Matinicus, Nantucket.*

**Notes:** Built 1986-87 by Bollinger Machine. British design. Designed for offshore surveillance and search and rescue.

# TUGS

**Details:** 290 tons; 110'6 (oa)×24×10'6; one shaft, diesel-electric, SHP 800=12kt

| | | | | |
|---|---|---|---|---|
| WYT-86 | Calumet | Charleston | 1934 | Sold 68 |
| WYT-87 | Hudson | Portsmouth | 1934 | Str70 |
| WYT-88 | Navesink | Charleston | 1934 | Sold 70 |
| WYT-89 | Tuckahoe | Charleston | 1934 | Str69 |

**Notes:** Reclassified WYTM, 1966.

**Details:** 370 tons; 110 (oa)×26'6×10'6; one shaft, diesel-electric, SHP 1,000=12kt

| | | | | |
|---|---|---|---|---|
| WYT-60 | Manitou | Curtis Bay | 29/09/42 | na |
| WYT-61 | Kaw | Curtis Bay | 06/10/42 | Str79 |
| WYT-71 | Apalachee | Bushey | 29/04/43 | Str86 |
| WYT-72 | Yankton | Bushey | 29/04/43 | Str84 |
| WYT-73 | Mohican | Bushey | 16/06/43 | na |
| WYT-90 | Arundel | Gulfport | 24/06/39 | na |
| WYT-91 | Mahoning | Gulfport | 22/07/39 | na |
| WYT-92 | Naugatuck | Defoe | 23/03/39 | na |
| WYT-93 | Raritan | Defoe | 23/03/39 | na |
| WYT-96 | Chinook | Bushey | 16/06/43 | na |
| WYT-97 | Ojibwa | Bushey | 10/09/43 | na |
| WYT-98 | Snohomish | Bushey | 10/09/43 | Str86 |
| WYT-99 | Sauk | Bushey | 10/09/43 | na |

**Details:** 662 tons f/l; 140 (oa)×37'6×12'6; one shaft, diesel-electric, SHP 2,500=14.7kt; 17 crew

| | | | | |
|---|---|---|---|---|
| WTGB-101 | Katmai Bay | Tacoma | 08/01/79 | na |
| WTGB-102 | Bristol Bay | Tacoma | 05/04/79 | na |
| WTGB-103 | Mobile Bay | Tacoma | 06/05/79 | na |
| WTGB-104 | Biscayne Bay | Tacoma | 08/12/79 | na |
| WTGB-105 | Neah Bay | Tacoma | 18/08/80 | na |
| WTGB-106 | Morro Bay | Tacoma | 25/01/81 | na |
| WTGB-107 | Penobscot Bay | Tacoma | 00/00/84 | na |
| WTGB-108 | Thunder Bay | Tacoma | 31/07/85 | na |
| WTGB-109 | Sturgeon Bay | Tacoma | na | na |

**Notes:** Fitted for ice breaking.

# ICEBREAKERS

**Displacement:** 3,500 tons
**Dimensions:** 250 (pp), 269 (oa)×63'6×25'9
**Machinery:** Two shafts, diesel-electric,
SHP 10,000=16kt
**Armament:** Removed
**Complement:** 157

| | | | | |
|---|---|---|---|---|
| WAGB-278 | Staten Island | Western Pipe | 28/12/42 | Sold 76 |
| | ex-AGB-5, | | | |
| | ex-Severni Veter, | | | |
| | ex-Northwind | | | |
| WAGB-279 | Eastwind | Western Pipe | 06/02/43 | Sold 73 |

WAGB-280 — *Southwind* —————— Western Pipe ——— 07/03/43 — Sold 74
　　　　　　ex-*Atka* AGB-3,
　　　　　　ex-*Kapitan Belusov*
WAGB-281 — *Westwind* —————— Western Pipe ——— 31/03/43 — na
　　　　　　ex-AGB-6,
　　　　　　ex-*Severni Polius*
WAGB-282 — *Northwind* —————— Western Pipe ——— 25/02/45 — na
WAGB-283 — *Burton Island* ————— Western Pipe ——— 30/04/46 — Sold 78
　　　　　　ex-AGB-1
WAGB-284 — *Edisto* —————————— Western Pipe ——— 29/05/46 — Sold 77
　　　　　　ex-AGB-2

**Notes:** 278, 280 and 281 loaned to Soviet Union 1944 and returned to USN 1949. 281 transferred from USN 1951 and 278, 280, 283-84 in 1966. Helicopters added. Bow propellers removed. 281 and 282 re-engined 1973-74, funnels raised. *Eastwind* severely damaged in collision 20/01/49.

---

**Displacement:** 5,252 tons
**Dimensions:** 290 (oa)×75×19
**Machinery:** Three shafts, diesel-electric,
　SHP 10,000=18.7kt
**Complement:** 127

WAGB-83 — *Mackinaw* ————————— Toledo ————————— 04/03/44 — na

**Notes:** Designed for Great Lakes service, unarmed.

---

**Note:** *Glacier* (WAGB-4) transferred from USN 1966.

---

**Displacement:** 10,430 tons, 13,190f/l
**Dimensions:** 399 (oa)×83'6×33'6
**Machinery:** Three shafts, (CODOG) gas turbines,
　SHP 60,000; diesels, SHP 18,000=18kt
**Armament:** 2×40mm MG
**Complement:** 163

WAGB-10 — *Polar Star* —————— Lockheed ————— 17/11/73 — na
WAGB-11 — *Polar Sea* —————— Lockheed ————— 25/04/75 — na

**Notes:** Hangar and flight deck aft, two helicopters carried. Did not achieve designed speed of 21kt. Six planned, but no more were built.
　Two new icebreakers will be designed to enter service in 1990.

*Left:*
**The *Polar Star* (WAGB-10), seen operating with a Sea Guard helicopter off Alaska in 1976. The largest icebreaker type in service outside the Soviet Union she did not achieve her designed speed.**
*Official US Coast Guard*

# LIGHTHOUSE TENDERS

**Miscellaneous types:**

| | Displacement | Built | |
|---|---|---|---|
| WAGL-223 — *Althea* | 120 | 1930 | Sold 64 |
| WAGL-203 — *Arbutus* | 960 | 1933 | WLM. Sold 69 |
| WAGL-408 — *Aster* | 450 | 1943 | Sold 63 |
| WAGL-641 — *Azalea* | 178 | 1958 | WLI. Sold 79 |
| WAGL-294 — *Barberry* | 178 | 1942 | WLI. Sold 71 |
| WAGL-205 — *Beech* | 255 | 1928 | Sold 64 |
| WAGL-256 — *Birch* | 76 | 1939 | Sold 64 |
| WAGL-367 — *Black Rock* | na | 1924* | Haitian *Amiral Killick* (55) |
| WAGL-313 — *Bluebell* | 178 | 1944 | WLI |
| WAGL-257 — *Bluebonnet* | 184 | 1939 | WLI. Sold 66 |
| WAGL-299 — *Brier* | 178 | 1943 | WLI. USN (IX-307) (69) |
| WAGL-642 — *Buckthorn* | 178 | 1964 | na |
| WAGL-207 — *Cedar* | 1,370 | 1916 | Sold 55 |
| WAGL-258 — *Cherry* | 202 | 1932 | WLI. Surinam (65) |
| WAGL-286 — *Clematis* | 93 | 1944 | WLI. Str77 |
| WAGL-208 — *Columbine* | 323 | 1931 | WLI. Sold 67 |
| WAGL-293 — *Cosmos* | 178 | 1942 | WLI |
| WAGL-288 — *Dahlia* | 175 | 1933 | WLI. Surinam (65) |
| WAGL-259 — *Dogwood* | 230 | 1941 | WLR |
| WAGL-260 — *Elm* | 69 | 1937 | WLI. Str72 |
| WAGL-304 — *Fern* | 315 | 1942 | WLR. Str72 |
| WAGL-212 — *Fir* | 989 | 1939 | WLM |
| WAGL-63 — *Forsythia* | 230 | 1942 | WLR. Sold 77 |
| WAGL-285 — *Foxglove* | 350 | 1945 | WLR. Sold 77 |
| WAGL-213 — *Goldenrod* | 235 | 1938 | WLR. Str73 |
| WAGL-215 — *Hawthorn* | 875 | 1921 | Sold 65 |
| WAGL-217 — *Hemlock* | 960 | 1934 | Sold 61 |
| WAGL-219 — *Hickory* | 400 | 1933 | WLI. Sold 69 |
| WAGL-220 — *Hollyhock* | 989 | 1937 | WLM |
| WAGL-261 — *Jasmine* | 184 | 1935 | WLI. Sold 66 |
| WAGL-224 — *Juniper* | 794 | 1940 | WLM. Sold 75 |
| WAGL-310 — *Lantana* | 235 | 1943 | WLR |
| WAGL-227 — *Lilac* | 770 | 1933 | WLM. Str72 |
| WAGL-228 — *Linden* | 323 | 1931 | WLI. Sold 70 |
| WAGL-234 — *Maple* | 375 | 1939 | WLI. Str73 |

| WAGL-237 — Mistletoe | 1,040 | 1939 | WLM. Sold 69 |
| WAGL-263 — Myrtle | 186 | 1932 | Sold 64 |
| WAGL-238 — Narcissus | 375 | 1939 | WLI. Guyana (71) |
| WAGL-239 — Oak | 875 | 1921 | WLM. Str67 |
| WAGL-264 — Oleander | 90 | 1941 | WLR. Sold 77 |
| WAGL-265 — Palmetto | 170 | 1916 | Sold 59 |
| WAGL-266 — Poinciana | 120 | 1930 | Sold 63 |
| WAGL-241 — Poplar | 235 | 1938 | WLR. Str73 |
| WAGL-316 — Primrose | 178 | 1944 | WLI |
| WAGL-298 — Rambler | 178 | 1943 | WLI |
| WAGL-267 — Rhododendron | 114 | 1935 | Sold 59 |
| WAGL-287 — Shadbush | 93 | 1944 | WLI. Sold 76 |
| WAGL-315 — Smilax | 178 | 1944 | WLI |
| WAGL-311 — Sumac | 315 | 1944 | WLR |
| WAGL-268 — Sycamore | 230 | 1941 | Sold 77 |
| WAGL-248 — Tamarack | 400 | 1934 | Sold 71 |
| WAGL-409 — Thistle | 450 | 1943 | Sold 58 |
| WAGL-317 — Verbena | 178 | 1944 | WLI. Sold 77 |
| WAGL-250 — Violet | 1,012 | 1930 | Sold 63 |
| WAGL-251 — Wakerobin | 575 | 1927 | Str55 |
| WAGL-252 — Walnut | 989 | 1939 | WLM. Honduras (82) |
| WAGL-254 — Wisteria | 323 | 1933 | WLI. Sold 68 |
| WLM-541 — White Alder | 435 | 1943 | Lost 12/07/68 |
| WLM-542 — White Bush | 435 | 1943 | na |
| WLM-545 — White Heath | 435 | 1943 | na |
| WLM-543 — White Holly | 435 | 1943 | na |
| WLM-546 — White Lupine | 435 | 1943 | na |
| WLM-547 — White Pine | 435 | 1943 | na |
| WLM-544 — White Sage | 435 | 1943 | na |
| WLM-540 — White Sumac | 435 | 1943 | na |
| WAGL-255 — Zinnia | 375 | 1939 | WLI. Str72 |

\* Acquired 1942

**Notes:** Reclassified 1965, as indicated. 'White' class are former Navy lighters (YF).

---

**Details:** 935 tons; 180 (oa)×37×12; one shaft; diesel-electric, SHP 1,200=14kt

| WAGL-406 — Acacia | Zenith | 07/04/44 | na |

*Below:* **The lighthouse tender *Cactus* (WLB-270).**

WAGL-62 __ *Balsam* _____ Zenith _____ 1942 _____ Sold 77
WAGL-388 __ *Basswood* _____ Marine _____ 1943 _____ na
WAGL-389 __ *Bittersweet* _____ Zenith _____ 1943 _____ na
WAGL-390 __ *Blackhaw* _____ Marine _____ 18/06/43 ___ na
WAGL-391 __ *Blackthorn* _____ Marine _____ 20/07/43 ___ Lost 28/01/80
WAGL-392 __ *Bramble* _____ Zenith _____ 1943 _____ na
WAGL-306 __ *Buttonwood* _____ Marine _____ 28/11/42 ___ na
WAGL-270 __ *Cactus* _____ Marine _____ 25/11/41 ___ Lost 29/09/71
WAGL-300 __ *Citrus* _____ Marine _____ 15/08/42 ___ WMEC (79)
WAGL-292 __ *Clover* _____ Marine _____ 1942 _____ WMEC (80)
WAGL-301 __ *Conifer* _____ Marine _____ 03/10/42 ___ na
WAGL-277 __ *Cowslip* _____ Marine _____ 1942 _____ Sold 77
WAGL-295 __ *Evergreen* _____ Marine _____ 1942 _____ WAGO (73), WMEC (82)
WAGL-393 __ *Firebush* _____ Zenith _____ 1944 _____ na
WAGL-290 __ *Gentian* _____ Zenith _____ 23/05/42 ___ na
WAGL-394 __ *Hornbeam* _____ Marine _____ 15/08/43 ___ na
WAGL-395 __ *Iris* _____ Zenith _____ 10/03/44 ___ na
WAGL 297 __ *Ironwood* _____ Curtis Bay _____ 00/03/42 ___ na
WAGL-291 __ *Laurel* _____ Zenith _____ 04/08/42 ___ na
WAGL-302 __ *Madrona* _____ Zenith _____ 11/11/42 ___ na
WAGL-396 __ *Mallow* _____ Zenith _____ 1943 _____ na
WAGL-397 __ *Mariposa* _____ Zenith _____ 07/01/44 ___ na
WAGL-305 __ *Mesquite* _____ Marine _____ 14/11/42 ___ na
WAGL-308 __ *Papaw* _____ Marine _____ 1943 _____ na
WAGL-307 __ *Planetree* _____ Marine _____ 1943 _____ na
WAGL-398 __ *Redbud* _____ Marine _____ 11/09/43 ___ USN (49-70), Philippine *Kalinga* (72)
WAGL-399 __ *Sagebrush* _____ Zenith _____ 30/09/43 ___ na
WAGL-400 __ *Salvia* _____ Zenith _____ 15/09/43 ___ na
WAGL-401 __ *Sassafras* _____ Marine _____ 1943 _____ na
WAGL-402 __ *Sedge* _____ Marine _____ 1943 _____ na
WAGL-296 __ *Sorrel* _____ Zenith _____ 28/09/42 ___ na
WAGL-403 __ *Spar* _____ Marine _____ 02/11/43 ___ na
WAGL-404 __ *Sundew* _____ Marine _____ 08/02/44 ___ na
WAGL-405 __ *Sweetbriar* _____ Marine _____ 30/12/43 ___ na
WAGL-309 __ *Sweetgum* _____ Marine _____ 1943 _____ na
WAGL-303 __ *Tupelo* _____ Zenith _____ 28/11/42 ___ Sold 79
WAGL-289 __ *Woodbine* _____ Zenith _____ 1942 _____ Str72
WAGL-407 __ *Woodrush* _____ Zenith _____ 28/04/44 ___ na

**Notes:** *Sorrel* and *Gentian* modernised 1983-83. WLB, 1965.

---

**Details:** 1,240 tons; 188'6 (oa)×37×12; two shafts, VTE, SHP 1,200=13kt

WAGL-331 __ *Heather* _____ Marietta _____ 24/03/42 ___ Sold 68
            ex-*Obstructor* ACM-7,
            ex-*Sylvester*
WAGL-329 __ *Ivy* _____ Marietta _____ 18/08/42 ___ Sold 70
            ex-*Barbican* ACM-5,
            ex-*Armistead*
WAGL-330 __ *Jonquil* _____ Marietta _____ 02/12/41 ___ Sold 70
            ex-*Bastion* ACM-6,
            Ex-*Hunt*

*Above:*
**Jonquil WAGL-330, a lighthouse tender, in 1961.
Built as the Army mineplanter Col Henry J. Hunt,
she was later transferred to the Navy as Bastion.**
*Official US Coast Guard, Ernest Arroyo collection*

WAGL-328 — *Magnolia* ———————— Marietta ———————— 16/07/42 —— Sold 72
            ex-*Barricade* ACM-3,
            ex-*Story*
WAGL-332 — *Willow* ———————— Marietta ———————— 1941 ——— Sold 71
            ex-*Picket* ACM-8,
            ex-*Knox*
WAGL-333 — *Yamacraw* ———————— Marietta ———————— 15/08/42 —— Navy ARC-5 (59). BU67
            ex-*Trapper* ACM-9
            ex-*Murray*

**Notes:** Transferred from USN, 1946. Built as Army
mineplanters. *Yamacraw* served as cable vessel. WLB
1965.

**Details:** 512 tons; 157 (oa)×33×6; two shafts, diesel,
BHP 1,800=13kt

WAGL-685 — *Red Wood* ———————— Curtis Bay ———————— 04/04/64 —— na
WAGL-686 — *Red Beech* ———————— Curtis Bay ———————— 1964 ——— na
WAGL-687 — *Red Birch* ———————— Curtis Bay ———————— 1965 ——— na
WLM-688 —— *Red Cedar* ———————— Curtis Bay ———————— 1970 ——— na
WLM-689 —— *Red Oak* ———————— Curtis Bay ———————— 1971 ——— na

# CARGO SHIPS

WAK-169 —— *Nettle* ———————— na ———————— na ——— na
WAK-170 —— *Trillium* ———————— na ———————— na ——— na
WAK-185 —— *Unalga* ———————— na ———————— na ——— na
WAK-186 —— *Kukui* ———————— na ———————— na ——— na
WAK-246 —— *Spruce* ———————— na ———————— na ——— na

# TRAINING CUTTERS

**Details:** 1,816 tons f/l; 231 (wl), 295 (oa)×39′2×17; one
shaft, auxiliary diesels, HP 700=10kt, 18kt under sail;
65 crew

WIX-327 ——— *Eagle* ——————— Blohm & Voss ——— 13/06/36 —— na
               ex-*Horst Wessel*

**Notes:** Acquired as reparations from Germany 1946.
Steel hull, Barque rig. Can accommodate 195 cadets.

---

*Courier* (WAGR-410) was a former cargo ship of Navy
'Alcona' class which served as a radio relay
transmission ship for the Voice of America and later as a
training ship. Additional vessels to be named
*Messenger, Envoy, Harbinger, Interpreter* and *Ariel*.
WAGR-411-415 were projected but not acquired.

---

**Notes:** Other training cutters have included *Cuyahoga*
(WIX-157) of 'Active' class; *Unimak* (WAVP-379); former
Navy minesweeper *Tanager* (WTR-885), ex-MSF-385;
former Navy patrol escort *Lamar* (WTR-899,
ex-PCE-899).

*Right:*
**The sail training ship *Eagle*
(WIX-327) at the Bicentennial
Review at New York, in 1976.**

*Below:*
**The training ship *Tanager*
(WTR-885), formerly a Navy
minesweeper of the 'Auk'
class, was transferred in 1964.**

# NATIONAL OCEANIC & ATMOSPHERIC ADMINISTRATION

NOAA conducts ocean surveys of a non-military nature for the US Government. It is an agency of the Department of Commerce. Until 1965 the ships were operated by the US Coast & Geodetic Survey, originally organised in 1807.

| Old No | No | Name | Tons/Year | Fate |
|---|---|---|---|---|
| na | na | Hydrographer | 987/31 | Discarded 66 |
| OSS-28 | na | Explorer | 1,800/39 | BU72 |
| OSS-30 | na | Pathfinder | 1,850/42 | Stricken |
| OSS-31 | na | Pioneer | 1,695/43 | BU66 |
| | | ex-Mobjack AGP-7 | | |
| na | na | Derickson | 250/43 | Sold |
| | | ex-AGS-6 | | |
| na | na | Bowie | 250/44 | Sold |
| | | ex-PCS-1405 | | |
| na | na | Hodgson | 250/44 | Sold 67 |
| | | ex-PCS-1450 | | |
| na | na | Unward | 573/44 | Sold |
| | | ex-USCG Spruce WAK-246 | | |
| na | R-552 | John N. Cobb | 250/50 | na |
| OSS-32 | S-132 | Surveyor | 3,150/60 | na |
| OSS 1 | R 101 | Oceanographer | 3,959/64 | na |
| OSS-2 | R-102 | Discoverer | 3,959/64 | na |
| OSS-3 | R-103 | Researcher | 2,875/68 | na |
| CSS 28 | S 328 | Peirce | 700/62 | na |
| CSS-29 | S-329 | Whiting | 760/62 | na |
| CSS-30 | S-330 | McArthur | 995/65 | na |
| CSS-31 | S-331 | Davidson | 995/65 | na |
| MSS-22 | S-222 | Mount Mitchell | 1,798/66 | na |
| ASV-90 | S-590 | Rude | 214/66 | na |
| ASV-91 | S-591 | Heck | 214/66 | na |
| na | R-223 | Miller Freeman | 1,920/67 | na |
| MSS-20 | S-220 | Fairweather | 1,798/67 | na |
| MSS-21 | S-221 | Rainier | 1,798/67 | na |
| ASV-92 | S-492 | Ferrel | 363/68 | na |

**Notes:** Pioneer acquired from USN 1946.

*Right:*
**Discoverer (OSS-2), a research vessel and the largest in the service of the NOAA.**
*Martin E. Holbrook collection*

# INDEX

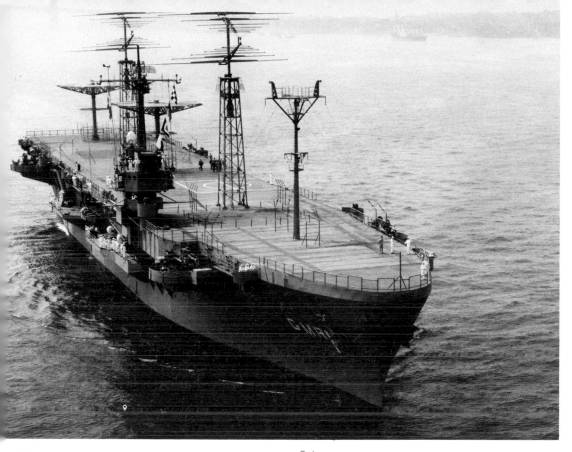

Above:
**Annapolis (AGMR-1)**, formerly CVE-107 *Gilbert Islands* until conversion to a major communications relay ship in 1963. *US Navy*

Below:
**Arbutus (W-203)**, later reclassified as WAGL-203, was used as a lighthouse tender until sold in 1969.

***Detroit* (AOE-4) a fast combat support ship entered service in 1970.** *US Navy*

Above:
**Francis Marion (APA-249)**, later reclassified as LPA-249, an amphibious transport sold to Spain in 1980. *US Navy*

Below:
**George Clymer (APA-27)**, was built in 1941 and served until being stricken in 1967. *Marius Bar*

*Above:*
**Peleliu (LHA-5), an amphibious assault ship of the 'Tarawa' class, was built in 1978.**

*Below:*
**Point Gammon (CG 82328) is seen here in Vietnam grey paint.**

236

*Above:*
**Tallahatchie County (AVB-2)** was originally
LST 1154, being converted to an aviation support
ship in 1961.   *A. & J. Pavia*

*Below:*
**Tanner (AGS-15)**, was built in 1945 and served as a
surveying ship from 1946-1969, being stricken in
that year. **Requisite (AGS-18)** is alongside.